nton Wilson's

Cinema Workshop

ACKNOWLEDGEMENTS

Over the past twelve years I have received incalculable assistance while writing these many Cinema Workshops. It would be impossible to credit the innumerable engineers, technicians and friends who have donated their expertise to these pages. In many cases I have attempted to acknowledge assistance within individual topics where appropriate, however these instances only reflect a mere fraction of the cooperation I have received from both individuals and corporations.

Special thanks must go to Herb Lightman who encouraged me to begin this series over ten years ago. During his period as editor of American Cinematographer he had to endure my eccentricities including the total inability to remember publishing deadlines. My mother also deserves a special thanks, not only for bearing me but for typing most of the original manuscripts. Much of the blame for bringing this anthology together must be borne by Charles Lipow who convinced me that he was not the only person who would enjoy such a volume. Finally credit must be given to Richard Patterson and the current staff of American Cinematographer without whose efforts this book would never have come to fruition.

Anton Wilson

Library of Congress
Catalogue Number
83-71274

1782 North Orange Drive
Hollywood, California 90078

ISBN: 0-935578-02-1

Anton Wilson's Cinema Workshop column has been one of the most popular features in American Cinematographer magazine for the past decade. His conversational style combined with his practical experience as a cameraman has enabled him to present the most complex technical subjects in a readily accessible manner. His columns have covered the basics of virtually every aspect of cinematography, and he has reworked them here into a uniquely readable reference which will be of value to the beginning student and the seasoned pro alike. It is a book to be consulted, studied and *enjoyed*.

American Cinematographer

Contents

Film 5

Raw Stock • Latitude • Granularity • Storage • Pitch and Perforations • Cores and Spools • Mechanical Properties •

Cameras 23

Variable Shutters • Panning • Reflex Viewing Systems • Reflex Viewing System Calibration • Film Registration • Lost Loops • Shutters • D.C. Servo Motors • Crystal Sync • Cold Weather Filming • Transporting Equipment • Power Cables •

Formats 57

TV Format • Wide Screen Formats • Anamorphic Wide Screen • Techniscope • Super-16 • Cinerama • 48 FPS—A New Standard? • Film vs Television Aspect Ratio •

Lenses 85

The Care of Lenses • Zoom Lenses • Image Sharpness • Optics • Lens Perspective • Lens Mounts • Arriflex 16BL and 16SR Lenses • Lens Equivalents • T-Stops Revisited •

Filters 111

Polarizing Filters • The Care of Filters • Neutral Density Filters •

Light 119

Color Temperature • Fluorescent Lighting • Flashing • Photographic Daylight • Light Meters • Calibration of Light Meters • Types of Light Meters • TTL Professional Metering Systems • The Great F-Stop Mystery • Incident Illumination •

Sound 151

Magnetic Sound Recording • Sound Recording Tape • Care of Magnetic Tape • Recorder Alignment • Sound Basics • Quality Limitations • Loudness • Level Meters • Microphones • Directivity of Microphones • Electret Condenser Microphones • Hand Microphones • Two-Track Recording • Noise Reduction • Headphones • High Frequency Bias •

Batteries 205

Batteries and Power • Battery Capacity • Charging NiCad Batteries • NiCad Battery Life • Battery Memory • Separate Power Source for Camera and VTR • Electric Current •

Underwater 235

Underwater Technique • Underwater Lenses • Underwater Cinematography •

Video 243

The 'Film Look' • Electronic Cinematography • Lighting for Television • Video vs Film • Video Lenses • The Video Camera • Video Recording • The Video Tape Recorder • The Video Signal • Inside the Video Recorder • Registration • Back Focus Instant Push • Microwave Links • Solid State Video •

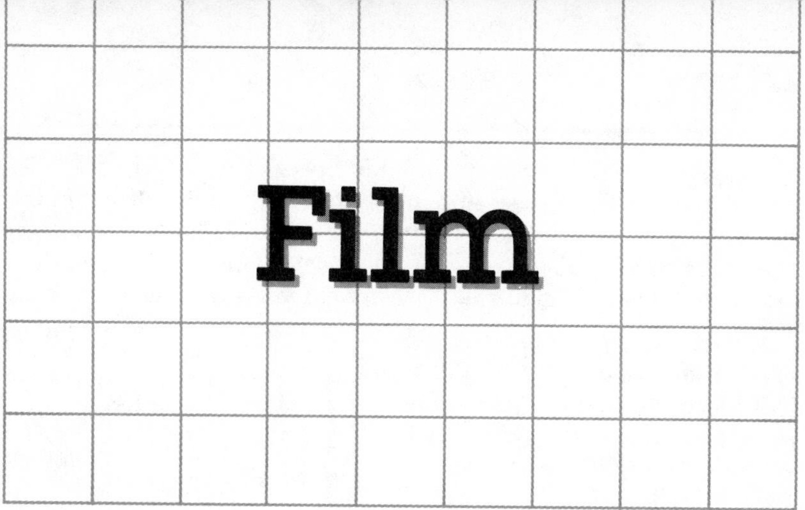

RAW STOCK

The cinematographer, like any artist, carefully selects his tools to match the particular situation. The type of camera, lens, filter, etc., will be chosen on the basis of the visual effect desired. This same care should be exercised in selecting the raw stock, and the method of printing.

Each type of film stock exhibits unique characteristics that will determine its suitability for a particular situation. A series of tests has been devised to rate each raw stock according to several different criteria. The results of these tests will reflect the 'personality' of the particular film stock. The cinematographer can then select the stock that will provide those qualities important to the specific application.

The test data most relevant to the cinematographer are the exposure index, color balance, latitude, resolving power, RMS granularity and modulation-transfer curve. Each motion picture raw stock on the market has a film data sheet on which the value of each of the mentioned criteria is listed. Proper interpretation of these values will reveal the film's visual and recording personality: contrast, sharpness, graininess, detail, etc. One can determine lighting levels, lighting contrast ratio, and effective subject contrast ratio, in addition to the proper filters to use under abnormal light sources.

It is obviously to the cinematographer's advantage to have a thorough knowledge of the terms used in the data sheets and an understanding of the relationship between the values listed and the respective visual qualities. The best approach to becoming familiar with the data sheet is to fully understand the procedure involved for determining the value of each criterion.

The modulation transfer curve is most closely associated with the image-detail characteristics of the film. Specifically, it will reveal the tendency of the film to lose efficiency in reproducing fine details of the image. This is usually due to diffusion of light within the emulsion layers or, possibly, to adjacency effects in development. The procedure for determining the modulation transfer curve is logical and direct.

The test chart consists of a series of black and white bars (FIGURE 1). Note two important facts about these bars, however. A close look will reveal that they are not sharply defined black and white areas, but rather an area of white that gradually goes through the gray scale to black and vice versa. This is actually a sinusoidal pattern; the areas change from light to dark to light, etc., sinusoidally. Moving left to right, note also that the spacing of the areas gets progressively smaller, or expressed sinusoidally, the frequency of the pattern increases progressively. This test chart is photographed on the raw stock in question. FIGURE 2 shows the photographed test chart magnified to the size of the original chart.

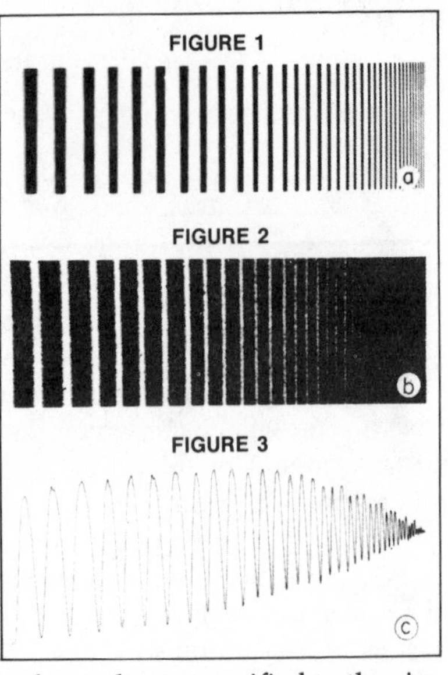

The photographed image is then scanned with a microdensitometer. The microdensitometer is essentially an ultra-ultra-narrow beam spot light meter that is used to measure light transmittance (density) through a minute area of the film. This area is extremely small, usually a circle with a diameter less than one thousandth of a millimeter, much smaller than the spacing of the photographed pattern. As the microdensitometer scans the chart from left to right, it will respond to the light and dark areas. The needle will move sinusoidally back and forth indicating the respective changes in light transmittance (density). FIGURE 3 is a chart recording of the microdensitometer as it scans the negative in FIGURE 2.

Note that, as the frequency of the pattern increases, the microdensitomer no longer records a full swing from black to white; the response begins to fall off. In other words, the film did not faithfully record these fine changes in light. Due to diffusion in the emulsion, the light and dark areas begin to blend into a gray. Looking again at FIGURE 3, the frequency will reach a point where the microdensitometer can distinguish no pattern at all, but only a middle gray (extreme right).

The results of FIGURE 3 are used to plot the Modulation Transfer Curve that is found on most film data sheets. The curve is merely a plot of the response of the microdensitometer as a function of the spatial frequency of the pattern.

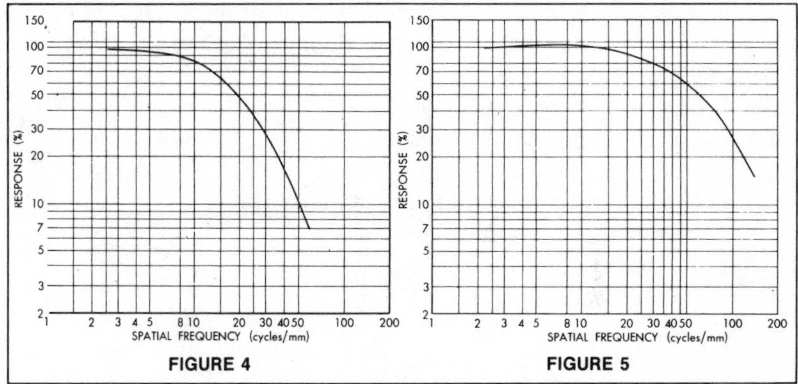

FIGURE 4 **FIGURE 5**

FIGURES 4 and 5 are the actual Modulation Transfer Function (MTF) curves from the data sheets of two different raw stocks. The curve in FIGURE 4 shows that response begins to drop out only 10 cycles/mm and dives to a response of only 10% at 50 cycles/mm. The film represented in FIGURE 5, on the other hand, shows a much smoother response with a more gradual roll-off. At 50 cycles/mm it still shows a response of 60%. One can predict that the film stock represented in FIGURE 5 will visually appear to record finer details of the image than the film represented in FIGURE 4.

Moreover, for a given printing system, the film in FIGURE 5 will maintain its superior MTF characteristics through to the release print. One can actually predict the image-detail characteristics of a print by the multiplication of ordinates of MTF curves for each film and optical system used to make the final print.

LATITUDE

Ideally there should be a direct and linear relationship between the processed density of the emulsion and the magnitude of exposure. Areas of the film receiving a greater amount of light should have proportionately greater density and vice versa. Most photographic media will exhibit this linear relationship. However, there always exists one serious limitation. The range over which this relationship exists is usually very narrow. For a particular film stock, the emulsion will only record images within a small range of exposure; that is, above a certain level the film becomes fully exposed (maximum density for a negative). Higher values of exposure cannot possibly be recorded; the film is overexposed or saturated. Likewise, values of exposure lower than a certain value will not even begin to register on the emulsion. The emulsion remains as if unexposed (minimum density on a negative). The emulsion can thus only record images when the light energy is within this particular "range."

FIGURE 6 shows the plot of the "sensitometric curve" of a typical negative material. This curve provides a clear graphic representation of this phenomenon. The horizontal axis is the magnitude of exposure. The vertical axis represents the density of the emulsion. Note that the curve is linear between points B and C. Exposure levels within this region will produce an accurate image, as the density will vary proportionately with the exposure. As exposure increases the curve enters the "shoulder" (C-D) region. The curve begins to level off, and increases in exposure will not produce a proportional increase in density. As the exposure increases above the 0.00 level, the curve virtually flattens; maximum density has been reached and no further detail can be recorded regardless of how high the exposure may go.

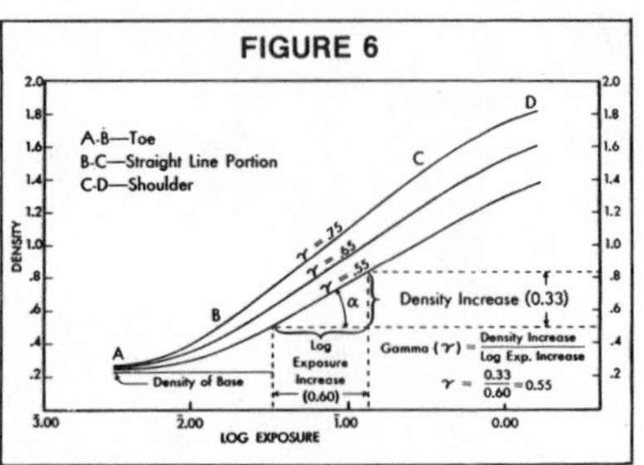

FIGURE 6

Exposure levels below B in the example, will be in the portion of the curve called "Toe" (A-B). Like the "shoulder", the curve levels off in this region and the density is no longer linearly related to the exposure level. The density approaches the actual density of the clear base material. In other words, values of exposure much below the 2.00 level will not even register on the emulsion, and the developed film in these areas will be virtually "clear" or unexposed. Thus for exposure levels below the 2.00 level, no detail can be recorded.

For a well-exposed and detailed image on the emulsion depicted in FIGURE 6, exposure levels from the various areas of the scene should be between $\bar{0}.25$ and $\bar{1}.75$ (B to C on curve). Each step of the Log Exposure Scale is approximately 3⅓ stops. This is usually expressed by saying that the film has a latitude or luminance range of five stops, (or a latitude of plus and minus 2½ stops). The emulsion will still record some detail just above and just below the linear region. In the example of FIGURE 6, the emulsion will continue to record limited detail for an additional ½ to 1 stop on both sides of the linear region. (Partially into the 'Toe' and 'Shoulder'.) Thus the total luminance range would be 6 to 7 stops.

It is imperative that the cinematographer be cognizant of the latitude of the raw stock he is using. Using the film depicted in FIGURE 6, the cinematographer must keep all important elements of the scene within a spread of five stops. For example, a scene may consist of areas that are in direct sunlight and areas in the shade. If an incident reading indicates a five-stop difference between the two areas, you can be sure that most details will be lost for light objects in the sunlight area as well as dark objects in the shade. When using films with particularly narrow latitudes, fill light must usually be employed to provide even lighting. As a rule, negative materials have a wider latitude than reversal stocks. Likewise, black and white stocks exhibit wider latitudes than most color stocks.

The curves in FIGURE 6 are all for the same film stock. Each curve represents a different "gamma" (γ). The gamma indicates the extent of development and a particular emulsion can be developed to a wide range of"gamma'. Notice that the gamma is the "slope" of the characteristic curve. That is, for a larger value of gamma there will be a greater change in density for a given change in exposure. The gamma is one of the many factors that contribute to the overall contrast of the resulting image. Higher values of gamma will produce greater changes in density over a given latitude, and will thus provide greater contrast in most cases. Every manufacturer usually recommends a specific gamma that will give best overall results (fine grain, best resolution, etc.). This is

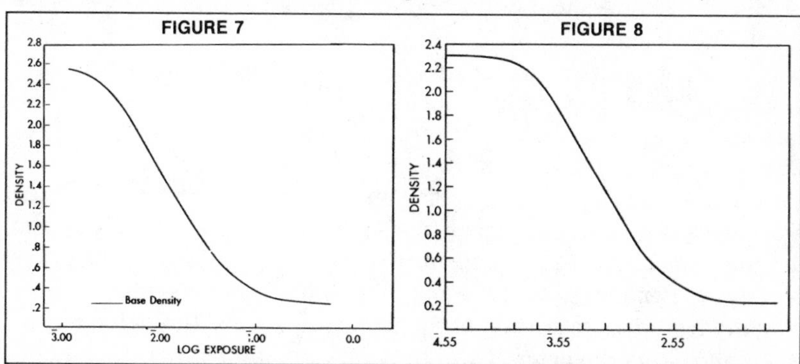

particularly true of reversal stock. The film data sheets for reversal stocks will usually display only one sensitometric curve rather than a family of curves for different gammas. This one curve represents the specific gamma that the manufacturer recommends, and one can be certain that almost all film labs will follow this recommendation strictly.

FIGURES 7 and 8 are, respectively, actual curves for TRI-X and 4-X black and white reversal film. Note first that these curves slope in the opposite direction from that in FIGURE 6. These films are reversal stocks and, therefore, density decreases as exposure increases. The sensitometric curve also indicates film "speed". This can be clearly demonstrated by comparing FIGURES 7 and 8. The linear region for Tri-X (FIGURE 7) corresponds to an exposure from $\bar{1}.40$ to $\bar{2}.5$. The linear portion of the 4-X curve corresponds to an exposure from $\bar{2}.85$ to $\bar{3}.75$. Thus, 4-X can record images with a lower exposure and is, therefore, a faster film.

GRANULARITY

The final image on the film consists of minute masses of metallic silver. Usually called "grains", these little specks are the building blocks of what appears to be a continuous deposit. Much like the fine dots that make up a picture in a newspaper, this inhomogeneity of the silver image, or granularity, becomes increasingly apparent at greater magnifications. Every type of film will exhibit different granularity characteristics. However, the granularity of the emulsion is of importance only insofar as it produces a sensation of "graininess" for the viewer. In other words, the granularity of an emulsion can reach a point where the audience will perceive the inhomogeneity of the image they are viewing. It is obviously the desire of the cinematographer to minimize the apparent "graininess" in the final image and to produce a picture that appears smooth, continuous and homogeneous. It is to the cinematographer's advantage that he understands the granularity rating of a film stock, and the many additional factors that will affect the "graininess" of his final image.

Almost every film stock will exhibit in its data sheet a number for RMS granularity. The method for obtaining this value is very straightforward. A sample of the emulsion in question is uniformly exposed and developed. The developed film appears to have a solid uniform density. However, our old friend, the microdensitometer, will prove otherwise. Remember that the microdensitometer is essentially super magnifying a minute portion of the image, as it scans through an aperture only 48μ in diameter. It will thus pick up and register the inhomogeneity of the image. That is, instead of registering a smooth continuous line indicating a uniform density, the trace will fluctuate up and down as it passes over areas where several grains are grouped tightly and then areas that are sparse.

An emulsion that has a very fine grain structure will produce a trace similar to that in FIGURE 9A. Note that the deviations are small and of high frequency. On the other hand, the emulsion represented in FIGURE 9B has a much coarser grain structure as reflected by the larger deviations. The information in these traces is converted to a number known as the root mean square (RMS) granularity. A higher RMS granularity number will indicate a coarser grained film and thus a relatively greater sensation of graininess.

When the magnitude of graininess is great enough to be visible to the audience, a difference of about 6% in the effective value of RMS granularity will correspond to a "just noticeable difference" in the visual impression of graininess.

In addition to the inherent characteristics of the emulsion, there are several other factors that affect granularity of the raw stock and the resulting print.

Processing and printing techniques can greatly affect the granularity of color stock. As development is increased (pushed) the granularity will increase proportionately. Conversely, pull-processing or reducing development time can decrease granularity, however, a reduction in contrast also results. Decreasing print density to compensate for an underexposed negative will tend to increase perceived graininess. Generally an increase in print density will result in a reduction of graininess. The contrast of the print film is also proportional to granularity. For example, if an original of RMS 5 is printed on a stock of contrast 2.0, the resulting print will have a granularity of approximately 10.

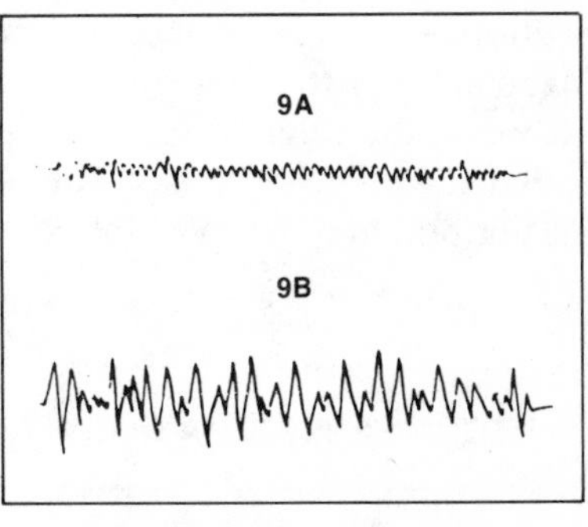

Exposure parameters can also affect the graininess of color negatives. Underexposure causes an increase in graininess due to either forced processing or the decrease in print density resulting from timing compensation. Luminance ratio can also affect graininess, for example, the blacks in a scene lit to a 100-to-1 ratio will appear more grainy than the blacks of the same scene lit to a 10-to-1 ratio, thus lower luminance ratios usually result in a reduced perception of grain. Overexposure coupled with pull processing can reduce graininess, however overexposing usually decreases highlight detail while the pull processing lowers overall contrast. Thus this technique should be used with caution.

When considering the aforementioned correlations, keep in mind that the three colored dye layers of Eastman color print films do not affect perceived graininess equally. The relative importance of the green, red and blue layers are in the proportion of 60/30/10 respectively.

Lastly, the sensation of graininess is roughly proportional to image magnification. That is, if the size of the viewing screen is double, the sensation of graininess will be approximately doubled for a given distance from the screen. Likewise, for a given screen size, the sensation of graininess will increase as the viewer sits closer to the screen. These

STORAGE

The cinematographer must properly handle his film stock, both before and after exposure, if optimum results are to be expected. All film stocks are affected by heat, moisture, age and a variety of other factors. Over a period of time, a film stock can lose some of its speed, exhibit lower contrast and develop an increased fog level. The problem is compounded with color film stocks. The aforementioned deterioration may affect each of the three color layers to a different extent, thus upsetting the color balance.

Refrigeration is the most common method for maintaining the original quality of the film stock. Storing film at reduced temperatures will maintain the original speed of the stock, as well as ensure even color balance with color stocks. The temperature of the storage area should be uniform in order to maintain constant characteristics from roll to roll.

FIGURE 10

RECOMMENDED MAXIMUM TEMPERATURES FOR FILM STORAGE

Type of Film	Maximum Storage Temperature for Periods up to 6 months
Black and White Film	
1. Negative, reversal, and sound films	55F
2. Positive Films	65F
Color Film	
1. Negative	50F
2. Reversal	65F

The maximum temperature at which films should be stored is reflected in FIGURE 10. Keep in mind that these are *maximum* values. Lower temperatures are quite acceptable. As a matter of fact, temperatures below freezing are commonly employed for long periods of storage.

Most cinematographers use a common food-type refrigerator for storing film. This provides an ideal temperature environment of approximately 40°F and will maintain film for the better part of a year or longer. If long periods of storage are anticipated (in excess of 4-6 months), the film can be kept in a freezer. Film stored at reduced temperatures must be allowed to reach ambient temperature before the can is unsealed. This is *most* important. If the can of film is opened while its temperature is still below the dew point, moisture will condense on the film and may cause spotting. FIGURE 11 lists recommended warm-up times for films in standard packages.

Film rolls should always be stored in their original *sealed* cans. The seals should not be removed until the film is ready to be loaded into the camera. Humidity in the storage area is relatively unimportant. However, values above 70% should be avoided, as rusting of the cans and molding of the containers may result.

After the film has been exposed, the same care should be exercised in handling. High temperatures and excessive humidity can actually alter the latent image. This situation is even more critical with color stocks, where each of the three dye images can be affected unevenly, thus impairing the overall color balance. The best practice is to process films as soon as possible after exposure. Cameras and magazines should be unloaded as soon as possible. If exposed film must be stored for a period of time it should be treated the same as raw stock; i.e., resealed in a low-humidity environment and then stored at a reduced temperature. Under no circumstance should film, whether in can, camera or magazine, be left in confined areas where heat may build up. The most cardinal no-no is leaving a loaded camera or film in the trunk or glove compartment of a car on a hot day.

Film must also be protected while in the camera. On hot days, and when filming in direct sunlight, a white barney on the magazine will reflect the heat and keep the film cooler. If a white barney is not available, covering the magazine with aluminum foil will be equally effective. This technique is also used in the studio or on an animation stand where the magazine is in close proximity to hot lamps. When the loaded camera is not being used, or for long periods between takes, the camera should be put in the shade or other cool spot.

I have been stressing the desirable effects of storing film at reduced temperatures. However, it is *not* desirable to *shoot* with film that is very cold. At temperatures below freezing, the film becomes very brittle. This not only increases the probability of the film breaking, but it also increases the film's "plastic memory." All film has "plastic memory," that is, it retains the shape it was formerly in. If film was on a spool, one can straighten it out, but it will curl up again when it is let go. The pressure plate and aperture plate in the camera must keep the film perfectly flat during exposure, even though the film naturally wants to curl up. At low temperatures this effect is magnified and it is possible that the curling forces in the film may cause "breathing" in the gate. In low temperature filming, it is a good idea to keep extra cans of film in pockets close to your body. Where possible, keep film indoors until the last moment.

FIGURE 11

APPROXIMATE WARM-UP TIME FOR FILM PACKAGES TO AVOID MOISTURE CONDENSATION AFTER REMOVAL FROM COLD STORAGE				
Difference between Room temperature and Refrigerator temperature	25F		100F	
Relative humidity in room	70%	90%	70%	90%
	Warm-up time (hours)			
Single 16mm role	½	1	1	1½
Single 35mm roll	1½	3	3	5
Carton of ten 35mm rolls	12	28	30	46

PITCH AND PERFORATIONS

You may think that ordering raw stock is the easiest task in making a film. Guess again. If you are not careful you can get film stock with the wrong pitch, perforation size, rows of perforations, wind or core/spool. If this seems complicated, it is. Kodak has almost 80 different specification numbers, each one designating a specific perforation, pitch, wind and spool/core combination. Add to this the 50 or more film stocks that Kodak manufactures (such as: ECO-7252, CNII 7247, etc.) and you get a staggering number of combinations. Kodak lists almost 500 catalog numbers. But do not despair or switch to video tape; armed with a few facts the film ordering process can be made very simple.

The pitch of a film stock is the distance between the center of two successive perforations. In 16mm this would also be the distance between the centers of each successive frame. Yes, Virginia, there are two different pitches for both 16mm and 35mm raw stocks, but for a good reason. When the camera original is contact printed, it is bi-packed with raw print stock and the two films, pressed together emulsion-to-emulsion, are routed around a large sprocket wheel where the actual exposure takes place. During this process the camera original is on the inside and the print stock is on the outside. With most printers, the diameter of the print sprocket is such that the print stock has about a .2% to .4% greater distance to travel because it is on the outside. If both the original and print stock were the same pitch, it should be obvious that something would have to give, and what would happen would be a constant slipping between original and print.

This would undoubtedly blur the printed image and cause a loss in sharpness and definition. To prevent this from occurring, the print stock is designed with a pitch that is approximately 0.2% longer than that of the camera original. Thus, most 16mm camera original has a pitch of .2994″ (2994 pitch), while 16mm print stocks will have a pitch of .3000″ (3000 pitch). Likewise, 35mm camera original stock is usually .1866″ while the print stock is .1870″.

Confusion arises from the unfortunate reality that most Kodak camera original stocks are available in *both* the long and short pitches (with the notable exception of Eastman Color Negative). This is due to the fact that certain high-speed cameras require the longer (printer) pitch.

Thus, when ordering film for camera original, make sure that the pitch is short (that is, .2994 for 16mm and .1866 for 35mm). The only exception is for high-speed cameras that specifically recommend the longer pitch. Very often, in 35mm, a particular stock may only be offered in one pitch.

Then there is the matter of perforations. For 16mm there is only one shape of perforation, but you can have one or two rows (single-perf or double-perf). For 35mm there are *always* two rows, but there exists a variety of shapes. When employing a 16mm camera with double-perf sprockets or twin pull-down claws, it is obvious that double-perf film must be used. For the more popular single-perf sprocket cameras with single pull-down claw and registration pin, the cameraman has the option to use either single- or double-perf film. On the film box and in the catalog sheets the rows of perforations are usually coded with the film pitch, (for example, "2R-2994" would be double-perf with a 2994″ pitch). Almost all 35mm cameras, including process cameras, employ the "BH" perforation (see FIGURE 12). The exception is certain high speed applications where the KS perforation is used. The KS perf is also used for most release printing.

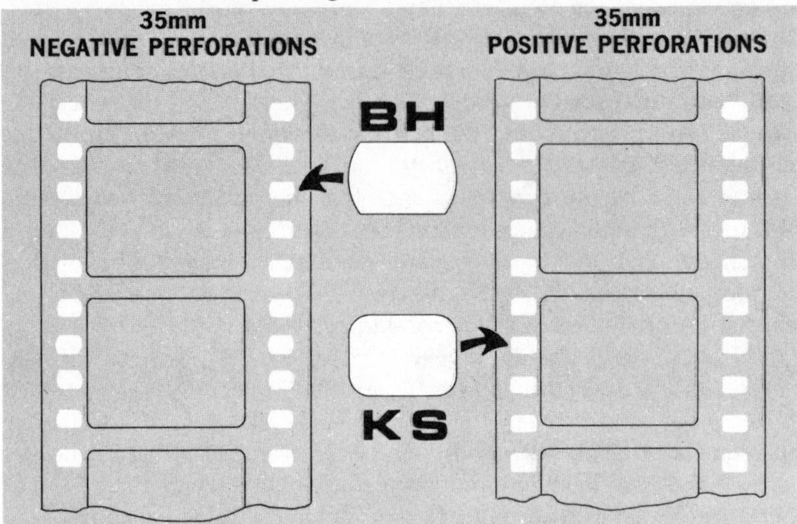

FIGURE 12

Most intermediate stocks employ the BH perforation. There is also a CS perforation which is smaller than both the BH and KS type. It is specifically designed to provide space for multiple sound tracks on Cinemascope releases. On 35mm film boxes and catalog sheets the perforation type is usually combined in code with the pitch; for example, "BH-1866" or "KS-1870", etc.

There is one more complication with 16mm single-perforated stock. These films can be supplied in either winding A or winding B (see FIGURE 13). With film wound emulsion-in and spooling off the top to the right (clockwise), winding A will have perforations towards you, while winding B will have them on the far side. Camera original and stock for optical printing should invariably be "B" winding. Winding A is used mostly for contact printing. Once you have determined the proper pitch, perforations shape, rows of perforations and winding, there is still the matter of spool or core and which type and size.

CORES AND SPOOLS

Almost all motion picture camera stocks are available on both cores and spools. In the 35mm format, film is almost always ordered on cores, as spools are usually available only in 100′ lengths. Raw stock in the 16mm format, on the other hand, comes in a wide variety of core and spool sizes.

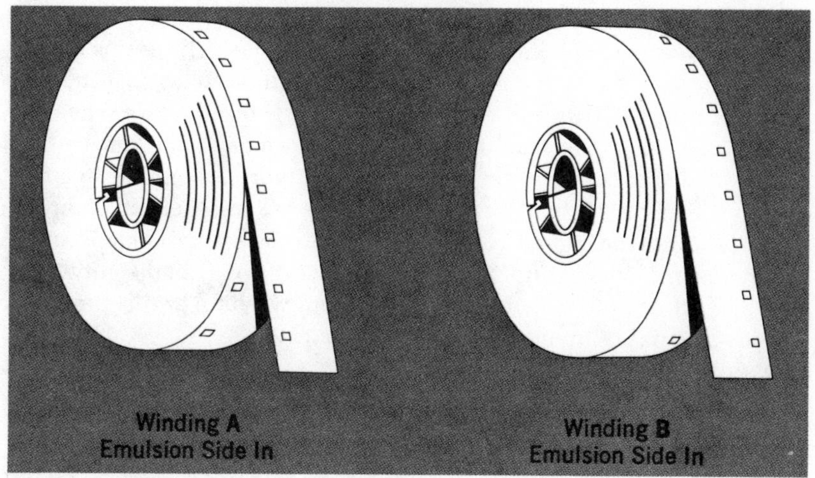

There are several points to consider before deciding on a core or spool. Most obvious is the fact that certain magazines will only accept core loads. Many Arriflex 200 ft. and 400 ft. magazines as well as Bolex Rex V 400′ magazines are "displacement" magazines (or single-compartment magazines). These magazines are more compact than the more conventional Mitchell-type magazine (double-compartment).

The displacement magazine achieves its smaller size by utilizing the center space of the magazine twice. That is, when the roll is started, the center portion of the magazine is being occupied by the large feed roll of film. As the film is used, the feed roll gets smaller and the take-up roll gets larger. By the end of the roll the center space is now occupied by the take-up roll. Thus, the distance between spindles in a displacement magazine can be almost half that of a double-compartment magazine. It should be obvious that one drawback of this system is that it is impossible to employ daylight spools; there just isn't any room. Thus, core loads must be employed with displacement magazines.

There is one exception to this rule. Daylight spools of half the rated magazine capacity may be used in most displacement magazines. Thus 200′ spools can be used in 400′ mags and 100′spools will fit the 200′ magazines.

Double-compartment magazines, such as the Mitchell type or coaxial styles, will usually accept either cores or daylight spools. Daylight spools have obvious advantages, most notably the ability to field-load without a changing bag. There are several precautions to consider however. Spools should be loaded under very subdued light. This is even more important when *unloading* spools. The film is wound onto the spools at the factory with a reciprocating motion (see FIGURE 14A), adjacent layers being butted against opposite flanges. This forms a fairly light-tight seal that prevents ambient light from seeping past the first layers of film, FIGURE 14B illustrates that this is not the case when the film is wound in the take-up spool in the camera. The film usually winds up against one flange, making the roll more susceptible to edge-fogging. For this reason, more care must be taken when unloading a spool. The camera should be unloaded in the darkest possible location and *never* outdoors in direct sunlight. Always leave a good eight-to-ten feet at both ends of a spool. This is far from wasteful and is probably the best insurance investment you can make.

Nothing is more frustrating than having that last dynamite shot on the roll flared out by edge-fog.

Use care when removing a spool from the camera. Never pull hard on the circumference of the flange, as this will spring the alignment and cause edge-fogging. Always employ the ejector on cameras that have them or the spindle release as used on the Arriflex.

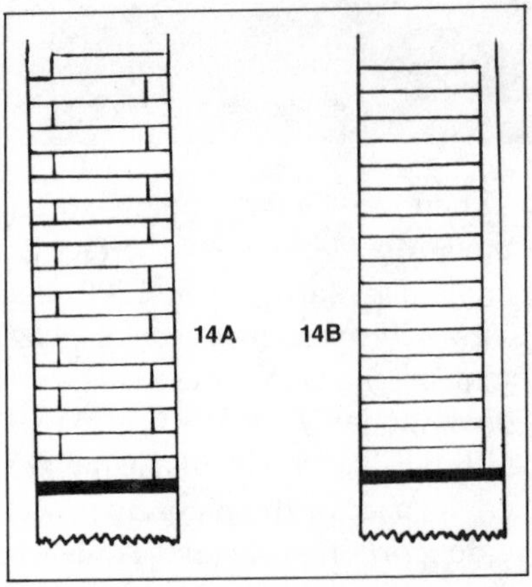

14A 14B

FIGURE 14—Film at the factory is wound with a reciprocating motion so adjacent layers are butted against opposite walls of the spool (a). However, film wound on the take-up spool in a camera usually winds up as in (b) with the film all against one side of the spool.

There are some drawbacks to the use of daylight spools. As mentioned previously, displacement magazines, such as the Arriflex, will not accept spools. Cameras that can enjoy either spools or core loads will undoubtedly run quieter with a core load. This is an important consideration when using quiet cameras, such as the Eclair NPR or ACL. If filming is to be done inside in a quiet but "live" room, the difference between a core load and a spool will most likely be audible.

Another consideration is availability. In 16mm, 200′ loads are almost always spools whereas 400′ loads are usually available on both cores and spools. To obtain 200′ cores, the film would have to be wound down from 400′ or 1200′ rolls. This is a practice that should be strictly avoided. Winding down film can cause static electricity marks, and will undoubtably get some dust particles on the film. Only labs specifically set up to wind down film should attempt to do so.

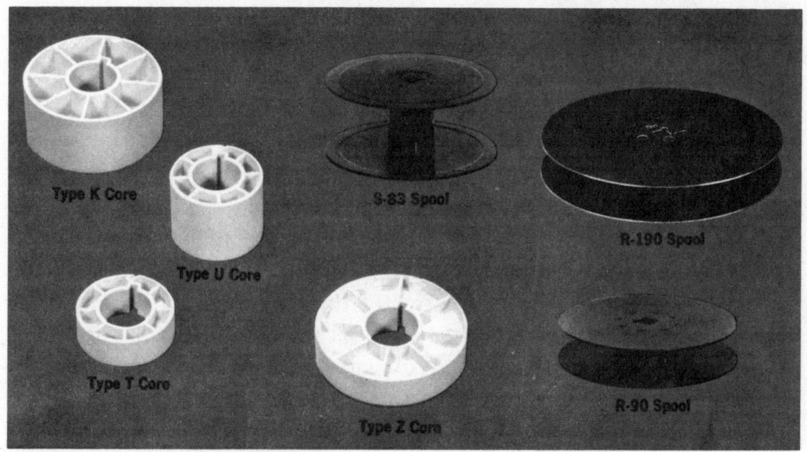

FIGURE 15—Some of the more popular core and spool types used by Kodak

FIGURE 15 illustrates some of the more popular core and spool types used by Kodak. The "T" core is 2″ in diameter with a 1″ inside hole with keyway. This core is used for 16mm stocks in lengths up to and including 400″. The "Z" core is a 3″ diameter core used for 16mm stocks in lengths over 400′. The "K" core is a 35mm core of 3″ diameter and is used mostly on rolls of 2000′ and 3000′ lengths and sometimes for 1000′ lengths.

The three spools shown are the R-90 (16mm—100′), R-190 (16mm—200′) and the S-83 (35mm—100′). Not shown is the S-153, which is a 400′ 16mm spool.

If you order spools, make sure you take the aforementioned precautions when loading and unloading. If the camera uses a displacement magazine or maximum quietness is necessary a core load is the obvious choice.

MECHANICAL PROPERTIES

We have previously discussed the various emulsion characteristics of film stocks, such as: resolution, granularity, latitude, etc. When it comes time to order film, there are several other physical characteristics to consider, including perforations, winding, pitch and base material.

The film base is the support that carries the thin emulsion layer. The base accounts for more than 90% of the total thickness of the film stock, the emulsion being only a thin coating applied to the base. A good base must be strong to resist tearing, dimensionally stable, yet remain flexible and optically transparent.

Most films use cellulose triacetate as the base material. This material fulfulls the aforementioned criteria of a good base and can be easily spliced, using a suitable solvent.

Contrary to popular conception, the solvent cement is not a "glue," but is literally a solvent, and the resulting splice can be more accurately described as a "weld." The solvent actually dissolves or "plasticizes" the triacetate base at the splice. The solvent is very volatile and evaporates rapidly allowing the material at the splice to reharden.

If the splice has been made correctly, the two pieces of film literally become one, and the splice should be as strong as the base itself. A "hot" splicer merely maintains an elevated temperature in the vicinity of the splice to promote quicker evaporation of the solvent.

I have brought up these details of the splicing process because they may explain the limited use of a newer type of film base commonly known as "ESTAR Base". The "ESTAR" material is actually polyethylene terephthalate polyester (now you know why they call it ESTAR). It is a very tough material, chemically and dimensionally stable, and very tear-resistant. Because of its increased strength, the ESTAR base is significantly thinner than triacetate base and, thus, an increased amount of footage can be accommodated on a standard size reel or core. The only serious drawback to the new product (you guessed it) is that it cannot be solvent spliced. At the present time ESTAR base film must be tape spliced or welded with a sophisticated inductive heating device which melts and fuses the film ends.

Most films incorporate some form of antihalation backing. Light passing through the emulsion is reflected by the base-emulsion interface and passes back through the emulsion again. This causes a second exposure which will reduce the sharpness of the image and cause the familiar halation around bright objects. The antihalation backing is designed to reduce these effects.

Some films incorporate a gray dye in the base or an undercoat between the emulsion and the base. A jet black coating can also be used on the back of the base. Each film stock incorporates a specific form of halation protection; it is not a variable that can be specified by the cinematographer.

Likewise, latent image numbering is another feature of certain film stocks that cannot be specified. Those film stocks that do come supplied with edge numbering employ consecutive numbers placed every 20 frames (6 inches) for 16mm stocks at every 16 frames (12 inches) for 35mm stock. Many Eastman Kodak 35mm films employ a letter code prefix printed ahead of each edge number to identify the film emulsion type. This letter prefix is not used with any 16mm films (with the exception of some color intermediates). All Eastman Kodak 16mm film stocks are latent image numbered, as are 35mm Ektachromes. The remainder of the 35mm stocks are ink footage numbered.

As we have seen, almost all currently available films use the triacetate base, employ latent image edge numbering and have some form of antihalation backing. None of the above have to be specified when ordering film.

VARIABLE SHUTTERS

The variable shutter has long been the most frequently misunderstood element of the motion picture camera. For many, the situations in which a variable shutter should or should not be used are not very well defined.

Most professional motion picture cameras employ a 180° shutter which will yield an exposure time of one half the length of a complete revolution or frame. Thus, the camera is essentially recording only half of the action and missing the other half. The closed half cycle allows the film to be advanced and registered for the next exposure or frame. Most camera manufacturers and designers feel that a full half-cycle is necessary, as registration accuracy could be jeopardized by a shorter and quicker advance stroke.

Even though the 180° shutter misses half the action, the remaining half provides sufficient information for the viewer's mind to perceive a relatively smooth flow of motion. This is accomplished by a phenomenon called blur (yes, BLUR!).

Our eyes have a tendency to sustain an image on the retina even after it no longer exists. This is known as *persistence of vision,* and is similar in effect to a characteristic of early vidicon tubes where an object would leave a momentary "after-image" subsequent to its removal from the scene. If the object is moving in a continuous path, the result of the after-images is effectively a blur; the combination of the actual image and the series of decaying after images. Our vision operates in the identical manner, and when we are confronted with a rapidly moving object, whether it be a waving arm or a pair of talking lips, it is perceived as a blur. Our minds have become so acclimated to this perceptual quirk that we cease to be consciously aware of it in most cases; yet, the fact remains.

Thus, when the motion picture camera operates with a 180° shutter or larger, it has effectively a persistence of vision similar to our eyes. Anything moving within that frame will be blurred. Upon projection, the eyes will perceive a very accurate sense of realism, as this blur is almost identical to the blur that would be perceived if one were actually viewing the scene live.

A variable shutter can reduce the amount of exposure time. However, it will also record a smaller portion of the action. For example, a 45° shutter will expose 12½% of the action and miss 87½% (see FIGURE 16). Thus, the smaller the opening, the less action is caught in the frame, and as a result the blur effect is minimized. Upon viewing a film shot with a small shutter opening, one sees a series of sharp distinct images which represent a very small sampling of the overall action. Contrary to popular belief, the effect is not a sharper picture, but rather an unnatural choppy or stroboscopic effect. Camera movements especially exaggerate this phenomenon.

It is for this reason that both the SMPTE and the ASC do not recommend the use of shutter openings much smaller than 180 degrees for almost all filming applications. The use of a small shutter opening to reduce excess light or to allow for the use of a larger aperture (to reduce depth of field) is not a recommended practice. In both of these situations, better results will be obtained by employing neutral density filters. In addition, the variable shutter in most professional cameras is not suitable for fades. It should be obvious now that the variable shutter is an extremely limited device on a production camera. There are however, several specialized situations where a variable shutter can be extremely helpful.

Those areas of cinematography requiring frame-by-frame analysis as opposed to smooth motion can benefit from a small shutter opening. Football training films are a good example of this category. Of prime importance is the ability to view every detail of a play, usually with the projector running at a very slow speed or even single-framed. In this case, one wants a sharp, distinct image on the film, and the aforementioned blur effect is unnecessary and undesirable. By employing a smaller shutter opening, the exposure time is decreased and a sharper image results. However, this also records a smaller portion of the action and it is feasible that an extremely quick and subtle move on a play may be missed by the camera.

Many cinematographers who specialize in sports analysis filming employ a higher camera speed, usually 30-36 fps. This provides a shorter exposure time (and thus sharper frames) without any loss of action. By combining these techniques, one can arrive at a camera speed and shutter opening relationship that will provide the necessary sharpness and yet capture sufficient action to maintain continuity for the specific analytical purpose.

While the variable shutter is almost superfluous on the production camera, it is an invaluable component of animation and optical printer cameras.

FIGURE 16

SHUTTER OPENING	% OF ACTION RECORDED	EXPOSURE TIME @ 24-25 fps	EXPOSURE COMPENSATION
180	50	1/50	0
135	37½	1/65	1/3
90	25	1/100	1
45	12½	1/200	2
22½	6¼	1/400	3

PANNING

A pan is merely the horizontal rotation of the camera. What could be more simple? Guess again. If a cinematographer is not careful, his "perfect pan" could turn out a horizontal horror. Most cameramen are familiar with the so-called stroboscopic effect caused by rapid panning. The cause of this skipping effect is quite complex and depends on several factors, including physiological and perceptual phenomena of vision, as well as viewing characteristics such as screen brightness and distance from the screen. These factors are obviously out of the cameraman's control and we will not discuss them.

The most important factors causing the stroboscopic effect are the camera shutter and focal length of the lens. Most motion picture cameras employ a shutter opening of 180° or less. The shutter is closed for as long as it is open and, thus, it is missing at least half the action that takes place in front of it. In FIGURE 17, for example, if a car were to pass across the screen in half a second (17A), the camera would actually record 12 semi-blurred images (frames) as in 17B. The blank spaces represent action missed while the shutter was closed. It should be obvious that the displacement of the object from one frame to the next is a function of its speed. FIGURE 17C represents a slower-moving object and 17D is extremely rapid movement. In the case of 17D action is missed over one-fourth of the screen.

In the case of 17C, the eye and mind will attempt to link the successive closely-spaced images into a continuous motion. However, as the action is sped up, a point will be reached where the visual connection of images will break down, due to the large displacement between successive frames. (17B & 17D)

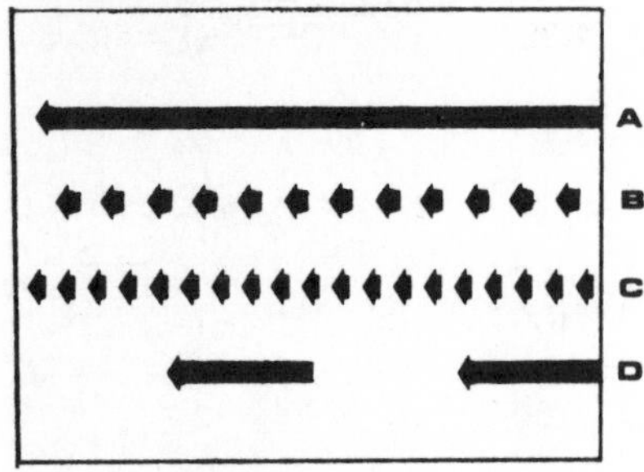

FIGURE 17—As an object moves in front of the camera (A), the camera records only half the action, due to the 180° shutter (B). If the object moves slowly, the distinct images are close together (C). A larger displacement exists between images when moving fast (D).

Now, taking the same example, assume the car is parked and the camera is panning across the static scene. The same reasoning applies. At some point the pan will be fast enough to cause the eye to see distinct displaced images as opposed to continuous motion. This effect is closely related to the focal length of the camera lens. FIGURE 18A represents an 18mm lens on a 35mm camera which takes in a horizontal view of about 62°. If the camera with this lens were panned 5° in one second, the image would only move about 8% across the screen in that second. However, in 18B the same one-second 5° pan with a 250mm lens (6° horizontal angle) would almost totally displace the entire scene. Visually the 5°-per-second pan is quite acceptable with the 18mm lens, as it will take a full 12 seconds for the scene to move across the frame. The same 5°-per-second pan is definitely not acceptable with the 250mm lens, as the scene will fly across the screen in about one second flat.

There are charts and tables of recommended pan rates for various focal length lenses and film formats. As it turns out, the scene should not pass fully across the frame in less than about 7 seconds, no matter what the focal length or format. This is an easy rule to remember and use. As the cameraman tries out a pan, he merely picks a specific object in the scene and counts the number of seconds it takes from its appearance on one side of the frame to its departure on the opposite side.

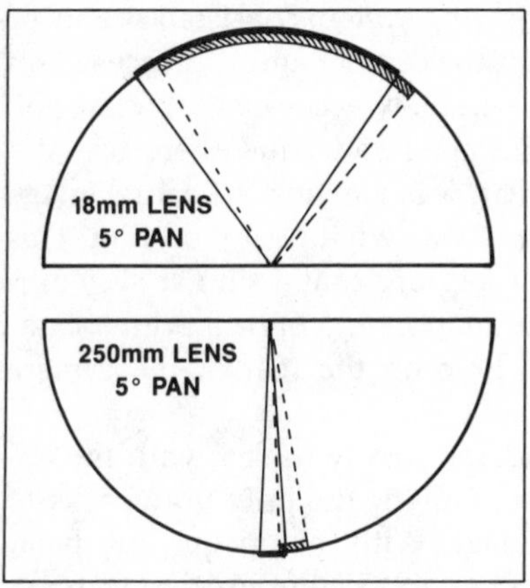

FIGURE 18—Given a 5° pan, the scene will change only 8% with an 18mm lens. Yet, the same 5° pan will cause an almost complete scene shift with a 250mm lens.

If it takes less than 7 seconds, the pan should most likely be slowed down according to ASC recommended rates. Film tests may reveal faster pans of acceptable quality. However, this seven-second rule will always yield a smooth pan. Interestingly, a pan can become so fast that the strobe effect will cease. The displacement between successive frames is so great (17D) that the visual mechanism only perceives a fast blur sensation. This is the so-called *swish* pan.

This discussion applies to pans of static scenes only. When following action, of course, any pan speed is permissible.

REFLEX VIEWING SYSTEMS

The necessity of a reflex viewing system was recognized while the motion picture industry was still in its infancy. Cinematography involves continually changing composition, distance, field, etc., and any system based on a separate viewfinder will undoubtedly impede the cameraman's accuracy, speed and creativity. The two greatest problems relating to a viewfinder are parallax and focus. Because the viewfinder and the filming lens are not on a common axis, the viewfinder is "seeing" the subject from a slightly different angle. Moreover, this angle increases as the subject moves closer. This parallax error and the inability to critically focus, have, in the past, rendered the filming of tight close-ups almost impossible.

The first reflex viewing systems were designed over 50 years ago. Probably the simplest and most accurate was the system that viewed the image right on the film itself. The pressure plate in the gate was constructed with an opening in the frame area much like an aperture plate. Thus the film was exposed to the lens system from the front, and a viewing system from the rear. The viewing system consisted simply of a lens tube that extended out the rear of the camera and was focused on the film in the gate. This system was extremely accurate and foolproof. The film itself was used as the ground glass and, thus, there was virtually no room for error. The cameraman was viewing the actual image formed on the film, so that what he saw was what he got on film. This system proved to be so accurate and foolproof that a similar system is still used today to calibrate Oxberry animation and optical printer cameras. (Note the small round plugged hole on the rear of the camera housing)

Unfortunately, this system was rendered totally useless with the advent of anti-halation backings on film. One of the only drawbacks of this system was the dimness of the image. With the opaque anti-halation backing, the image became virtually non-existent. As film technology stepped forward with this improved backing, the technology of reflex viewing was thrown backward.

Various viewing methods evolved during the twenties and thirties. The rack-over system provided reflex viewing before a shot but not during it. This was very helpful for setting up a tight close-up but it was obviously not the final answer. Beam-splitting optics were sometimes employed. However, most cinematographers were reluctant to use such a system for fear that the splitting optics would impair the filmed image. This system also reduced the light available to the film at a time when fast film did not exist and lighting was extremely difficult.

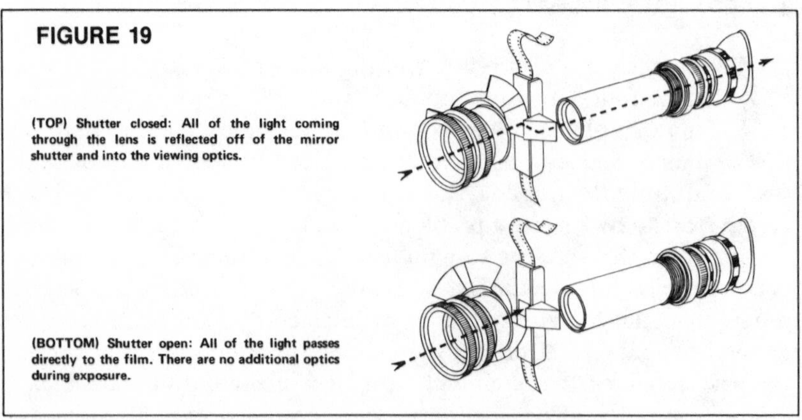

FIGURE 19

(TOP) Shutter closed: All of the light coming through the lens is reflected off of the mirror shutter and into the viewing optics.

(BOTTOM) Shutter open: All of the light passes directly to the film. There are no additional optics during exposure.

The major breakthrough in reflex viewing occurred in 1936 when Messrs. Arnold and Richter of Munich perfected the mirror-reflex shutter. Their camera was named the Arriflex; ('AR' for Arnold, 'RI' for Richter and 'Flex' for reflex). The mirror-reflex shutter system used in the first Arriflex is usually the same system used in all modern mirror-reflex shuttered cameras today.

The shutter is constructed of a piece of solid glass. The back is opaqued, and the front surface is polished and silvered to an opticaly flat mirror. Some manufacturers use magnesium or stainless steel shutters, but in each case the front surface is a polished mirror. The shutter rotates on an axis 45° to the optical axis. When the shutter is open, the light travels directly to the film, as in a conventional shutter system. However, when the shutter is closed, the light is reflected off the front surface of the shutter and into the viewfinding system. (See FIGURE 19). Thus the light through the lens is shared by both the film and the viewing system.

The advantages of this system are multiple. One hundred percent of the light is available to the film during exposure. There are no additional optics to impair image quality. All the light is available for viewing while the shutter is closed. Quantitatively, 100% of the light is available for viewing while the camera is off. Camera running, the viewfinder receives approximately 40% of the light. This figure would be exactly 50% if it were not for a narrow black strip painted onto the mirror. This black strip breaks each image to the viewfinder into two equal parts. While this reduces the actual light level an additional 10%, it effectively doubles the flicker rate and produces an overall steadier and more distinct image.

The mirror-reflex shutter under discussion has been of the rotating variety. There is another type of mirror-reflex system known as the reciprocating or "guillotine" shutter. This system operates on the same basic principle, except that the shutter oscillates either linearly or rotationally between the viewing and exposing positions. This system is usually found in less expensive cameras and does not produce quite as bright an image as the rotational shutter. (Camera running, the reciprocating system produces a viewing image of approximately 25% of the light.)

Many modern professional and semi-professional cameras employ a form of beam-splitter viewing system. This system has evolved somewhat from the earlier double-prism systems. The more expensive cameras employ a thin pellicle type beam-splitter. For all practical purposes, the image to the film remains intact. A small portion of the light is diverted to the viewfinder at all times, even while the film is being exposed. While this provides a flickerless viewing image, it does rob a certain percentage of light from the film. This loss of light must be compensated by an increased aperture which may be a drawback in low light level conditions. The brilliance of the viewing image is approximately 30% of the light with the increased aperture included.

In almost all modern reflex systems, a ground glass is used as the image-forming device. Unlike the original reflex system that viewed the image on the film itself, these modern reflex systems rely on the assumption that the ground glass is indeed in the exact same position as the film, relative to the lens system. If this is not true, the reflex system is rendered useless. There are several simple tests the cameraman can perform to ascertain that his system is operating accurately.

REFLEX VIEWING SYSTEM CALIBRATION

In 1948, Robert Flaherty was the first cinematographer in this country to use a handheld reflex camera for shooting a feature film ("LOUISIANA STORY"). Despite the fact that he had been making films for over a quarter of a century, he said that this new camera made him feel like a beginning film student again. The reflex camera opened up so many new avenues of creativity that even the seasoned cinematographer began to develop new techniques to exploit the flexibility of this new viewing system.

The great response to such a viewing system is understandable. In essence, the cameraman's eye shares the exact same optical system with the film itself. The cameraman can focus, frame and compose for his eye with the confidence that the identical image that he sees is being recorded on the film. There is a catch, however. The cameraman is actually viewing a ground glass and not the film itself. The system operates as designed only if the ground glass is in the exact same position as the film aperture, relative to the optical system (lens and shutter). If the ground glass is even slightly out of adjustment, the reflex system is rendered absolutely useless. Similarly when the image is sharp in the viewfinder, it can be totally out of focus on the film. The cameraman may be viewing a tight close-up of a pair of lips and wind up with a big nose on the film. It should be apparent that the professional cinematographer must periodically check the alignment of his reflex system in order to assure that his creative efforts will be recorded as he sees them.

There are basically two adjustments: framing and focus. Two simple film tests can quickly determine if the ground glass is correctly aligned in both of these planes.

The step chart test is used to check the focus calibration. The "step chart" is very easy to construct. It consists of three "resolution targets" affixed to a single board or chart but on three different planes. In FIGURE 20A it can be seen that the three targets, when viewed from the camera, appear directly above one another. However, a side view re-

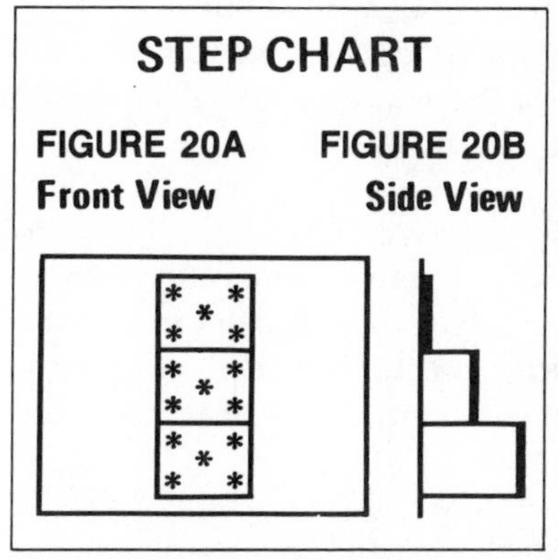
STEP CHART

FIGURE 20A Front View

FIGURE 20B Side View

veals that the top target is affixed directly to the board, the middle target is affixed to a block so that it protrudes approximately one inch forward, and the bottom target is affixed to a block that protrudes twice the distance of the middle target. To make the film test, a fixed focal length lens should be used, preferably a 50mm with 16mm cameras, and a 100mm lens with 35mm cameras. The chart should be placed as close as possible to the camera, usually about three feet, and lighted in such a way as to achieve an almost wide open iris. The lens should then be focused *very critically* on the middle target. Only several feet of film need be exposed. The processed film should be viewed under a microscope. However, a powerful magnifier can sometimes suffice.

If the ground glass is properly adjusted, the center target should be razor sharp and the upper and lower targets should be *equally* soft (slightly out of focus).

FRAMING CHART

FIGURE 21

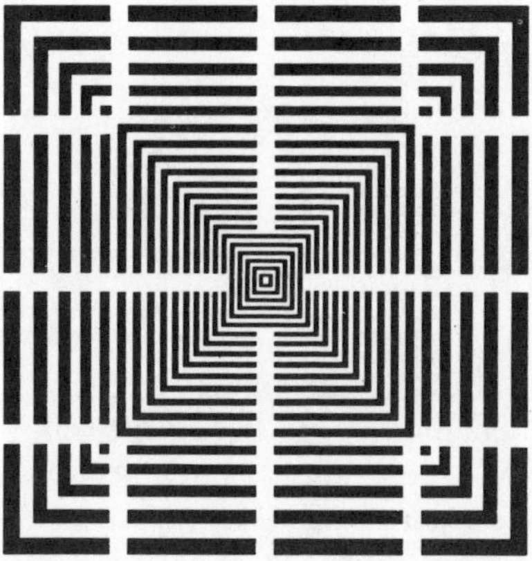

If the center target is slightly soft, and one of the outside targets is significantly softer than the other, the ground glass is out of adjustment. If one of the outside targets is actually sharper than the center target, the ground glass is way out of adjustment. It is a good idea to refocus several times during the original filming of the test to cancel out any errors introduced by the person focusing the lens.

The framing test is equally simple to perform. A framing chart consists merely of a family of concentric rectangles (FIGURE 21). The chart is placed in front of the camera at a distance that will just slightly overfill the framing area (aperture). The chart should be carefully framed so that the center of the chart is dead center with the viewfinder. Only several feet of film need be exposed. Upon viewing the processed film the rectangles should appear centered within the frame lines. That is, the four sides of the frame should appear perfectly concentric with the photographed family of rectangles. If the photographed family of lines are not perfectly centered within the frame area, the ground glass is laterally out of adjustment.

If either of these tests indicate a misalignment, the camera should be sent to an authorized repair facility for calibration. The calibration of the optical viewing system is quite a complex process and can only be accomplished by a professional repairman with the proper equipment. Under no circumstances should a cameraman attempt to readjust the mirror shutter or the ground glass himself.

If both tests indicate proper alignment, the cinematographer can be confident that the image he composes will be faithfully recorded on the film.

FILM REGISTRATION

Registration accuracy is one of the most important criteria of a professional motion picture camera. Poor registration causes the image to jump and vibrate on the screen and is particularly objectionable for multi-screen or split-screen opticals and titles. It is the camera movement that is responsible for precise image steadiness. This mechanism advances each successive frame into position and accurately registers it for exposure, which is no simple task. The film has a finite mass that must be accelerated to a fantastic velocity as it is being advanced to the next frame. It then must be stopped dead, precisely in the correct aperture position. This film advance cycle must be accomplished in less than 1/50 of a second and be repeated 24 times a second with consistent accuracy.

It is difficult attempting to relate to a piece of film being advanced inside a camera. Therefore, imagine a large Mack truck accelerating down the highway to 100 mph. Upon reaching 100 mph the driver sees an egg in the middle of the road 100 yards ahead. He applies the brakes and goes into a screeching panic stop. When the truck finally comes to a halt, its front wheel is actually just touching the egg but hasn't rolled over it. Now picture the driver going back and repeating this over and over with the same precise results. The analogy may seem a bit melodramatic; however, it does present an accurate idea of the task the camera movement is designed to perform.

In non-professional and most semi-professional cameras, the movement consists of the aperture plate, pressure plate, and a pull-down claw. The pressure plate is spring-loaded and sandwiches the film against the aperture plate. An advance stroke consists of the pull-down claw entering a perforation in the film and accelerating it to the next frame; however, it is only the friction of the pressure plate and aperture plate sandwiching the film that brings it to a halt in the next position. As you can imagine, it is difficult to position the film by relying predominantly on the plate friction for steadiness and accuracy. Surprisingly, this system functions better than its simplicity would suggest and it is quite acceptable for non-professional and even some professional applications.

Most professional cameras, however, employ some additional system for precisely registering each successive frame in exactly the identical position within the aperture. Such a system usually employs some form of pin registration. One of the earliest forms of pin registration was a system designed by A.S. Howell for the Bell & Howell 2709 studio cameras. The heart of the device was two pilot pins firmly affixed to either side of the aperture plate. One pin is dimensioned to exactly fill a film perforation, both height and width, while the other pin is dimensioned to tightly fit just the height, with some clearance in width. The film slides through a moveable guide or "shuttle" located behind the aperture plate. During an advance stroke, the shuttle swings back and a set of pull-down claws engage the film perforations and advance the film to the next position. At this point the shuttle swings forward and impales the film firmly on the two pilot pins. Because these pilot pins are part of the aperture and dimensioned to exactly the size of the perforation, the film is precisely located frame after frame. Although the 2709 camera is a thing of the past, an almost identical system is employed in the Oxberry animation and printer cameras and is considered by many to still be the most accurate method of registration. (This B & H shuttle system is capable of repeatable registration accuracy of 30 millionths of an inch.)

An equally successful system is the Mitchell Eccentric movement. In this case the film-guide channel is stationary and it is the registration pins that move. During an advance stroke, a set of claws advances the film to the next position. At this point an additional pair of pins slides into the top perforations from behind. Like the B & H pilot pins, these moveable registration pins are dimensioned to exactly the size of the film perforation and, thus, each successive frame is rigidly "nailed" to the exact same spot.

Two things should be obvious. For the system to function properly the registration pins must be dimensioned absolutely to the size of the perforation and must be alloyed to prevent wear. In addition the film manufacturer must maintain the identical tolerance on the perforations.

While this critical dimensioning on the part of both the film and camera manufacturers is practical for the 35mm format, an entirely different approach was taken for the smaller 16mm format.

A system sometimes referred to as the "loose registration pin" is employed on most professional 16mm cameras (Arriflex, Eclair NPR, etc.) and is not dependent on an exact fit between pin and perforation. The registration pin is dimensioned smaller than the film perforation and has a slight bevel on the front of the lower edge. In operation the pull-down claw advances the film to the next frame but positions the film a couple of thousandths of an inch short of the correct position. At this point the registration pin enters the perforation and the bevel on the lower edge nudges the film precisely into place. Using the analogy of the truck, imagine going into the panic stop, only purposely coming to a halt several inches short of the egg. Then the driver puts the truck into its lowest gear and slowly eases up to and stops at the egg. It should be clear that this system does not depend on a precise fit between pin and perforation, and it thus maintains accuracy regardless of wear and improper dimensioning of film (including shrinkage and warpage.)

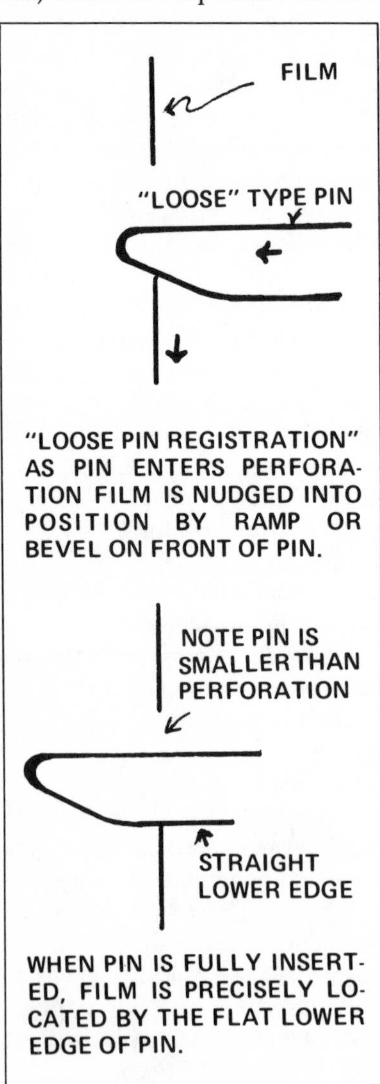

FIGURE 22

There is a third type of registration system, made popular by the Arriflex 35 and now incorporated on other cameras both 35mm and 16mm. This system uses one claw for both pull-down and registration. At the end of the pull-down stroke, the claw "dwells" for an instant before retracting. This dwell accomplishes somewhat the same thing as the loose registration pin and the results are quite good.

The camera manufacturers have designed these registration systems to provide impeccable image steadiness. It is the responsibility of the individual cinematographer to assure that these systems are always functioning properly. A very simple test can be performed to check the registration accuracy of a camera. Prepare a black piece of paper or cardboard with a series of evenly spaced thin white lines both vertical and horizontal. (A piece of black graph paper with white lines is ideal.) Place the camera on a rigid support or tripod and film the pattern so that it fills the entire frame. After several feet, cap the lens and crank the film back to the beginning. Repeat the exposure, only this time move the pattern slightly off center both vertically and horizontally. Upon projecting the film, both patterns should appear as if they were filmed in one pass. If you can perceive the slightest motion of the two patterns relative to one another, then the registration accuracy of the camera has been impaired.

LOST LOOPS

One of the more frequent complaints I have heard over the years concerns the loss of the film loop in the quick change magazine of Eclair ACL's. Unfortunately, a rumor has begun that this is a chronic problem with these cameras. Not so! There is a simple procedure that can assure against loop-loss in these cameras. I use one of these cameras and have never lost a loop even during a rock concert where I shot 43 magazines in one evening. The trick is twofold. When loading the magazine, one should favor the lower loop by one-half to one frame. That is, if there is any question as to the size of the upper and lower loop, it is better to have the lower loop slightly larger by about one-half frame, but not more than one frame.

More important, when the magazine is snapped onto the camera, the inching knob should be turned several times by hand *before* the motor is turned on for the first time. Likewise, if the magazine is removed and then refitted, or if the camera is transported, the inching knob should again receive several twists before the motor is turned on. That's all there is to it. No more lost loops or jam-ups.

There is a simple explanation for the lost loop problem and the subsequent easy solution, and I would feel remiss if I did not explain it (with at least one diagram). When the magazine is snapped onto the camera, the odds are one in a thousand that the sprocket hole will fall exactly on the spot where the pulldown claw enters the film. (FIGURE 23A) More likely the sprocket hole will fall somewhere mid-frame, as in FIGURE 23B). When the camera is turned on for the first time, the claw attempts to enter the film. The claw is spring-loaded so that when it hits the film where the sprocket hole is not present (FIGURE 23B), it will just stop at the film surface and not puncture the film (as would be the case with some misloaded cam/registration pin-movement cameras). As the downward advance motion starts, the claw will slide along the film surface until it reaches the sprocket hole, at which time, if everything goes well, it will fall into the sprocket hole engaging the film. As the claw finishes its stroke, it pulls the film into proper registration. Upon the next stroke of the claw, the sprocket holes are now all lined up and the claw will directly enter the hole before the downward motion commences. (FIGURE 23A)

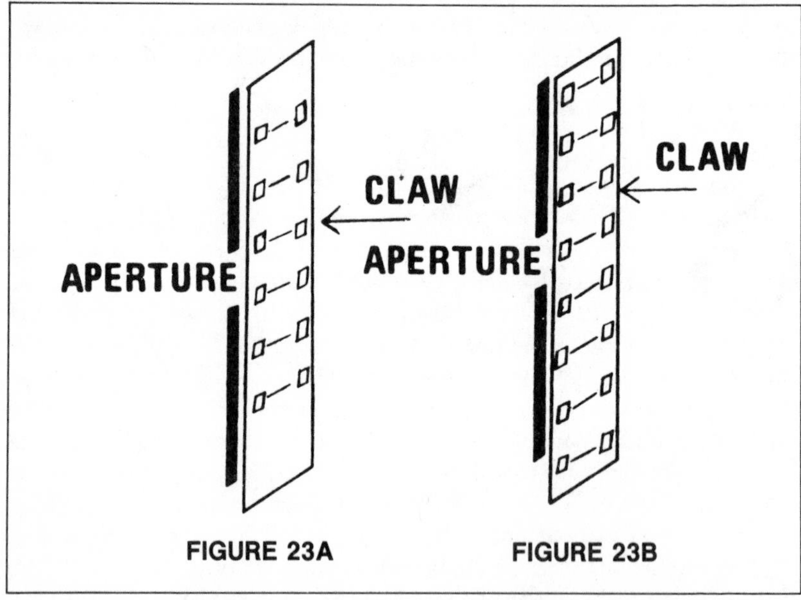

FIGURE 23A FIGURE 23B

There is one slight problem. Going back to FIGURE 23B, the claw is sliding along the film on its downward stroke. With the new high-torque crystal motors, the claw can reach maximum velocity by the time it reaches the sprocket hole halfway down its stroke. At this point it can be going so fast that it slides right over the hole, not having enough time to drop in—much like a golfer who putts too hard, causing the ball to go right over the hole. Once the claw has passed over the sprocket hole in this manner, the odds are it will do it several times before engaging. By this time it is too late. For, while the film has remained idle in the gate, the lower sprocket wheel has been turning, taking up all the slack in the lower loop.

The solution becomes obvious: by slowly turning the inching knob, the claw is assured of engaging the film on its first down stroke, thus registering the film. Now, when the motor is turned on, the claw will directly engage a sprocket hole before the pulldown.

Hopefully, this should end lost-loop problems.

SHUTTERS

Most light meters are calibrated on the basis of a motion picture camera having a shutter opening of 180 degrees. One revolution of the shutter is 360 degrees, so a 180-degree opening means that the shutter is open for exactly one-half-a-cycle and closed for the remaining one-half. This yields an exposure time of 1/48 second at 24 fps. However, not all cameras employ a 180-degree shutter.

The closed portion of the cycle allows the film to be advanced and registered precisely. The shutter can open only after the film has come to a complete halt and must close before the film begins to move to the next frame. The camera designer would theoretically like to have as large a shutter opening as possible. This would increase exposure time and be most helpful in low-light situations. There are several cameras that do employ shutter openings larger than 180 degrees. A shutter opening of 230 degrees will yield an exposure increase of ⅓-stop, while a ⅔-stop exposure increase will result from a 285-degree shutter.

There is, of course, a definite tradeoff. In the case of a 285-degree shutter, the film must be advanced and registered in the remaining 75 degrees of the cycle ($285° + 75° = 360°$). Since the more conventional 180-degree shutter provides 180 degrees of cycle for pulldown, the 285-degree camera must advance the film almost two-and-a-half times faster than the 180-degree camera. Obviously, this requires greatly increasing the velocity and acceleration of the film during pulldown, which not only places greater stress on both the camera movement and the film, but also jeopardizes a steady image. Other factors will also be adversely affected. For example, the noise level of the camera will increase. In the case of a noiseless-type camera, the designer would then be faced with employing extra noise dampening techniques in order to maintain a particular level of quietness. This would undoubtedly result in a larger and heavier camera. A quicker pulldown would most likely cause accelerated camera wear, requiring more frequent service.

After considering all these factors, most camera designers feel the drawbacks of the large shutter opening are not worth the ¼-to-½-stop exposure increase and opt for the more conventional 180-degree shutter.

As a matter of fact, many designers go one step further. A great number of cameras employ shutter openings significantly *less* than 180 degrees. Openings of 144 degrees to 170 degrees are very common, especially among 16mm cameras. The resulting exposure loss is usually under ⅓-stop and typically less than 1/5-stop. The designer feels that reduction in exposure is usually not objectionable and yet it buys him a quieter and usually steadier camera movement. The cinematographer should check his camera specifications carefully. The odds are very good that his so-called 180-degree shutter may be missing a few degrees here or there.

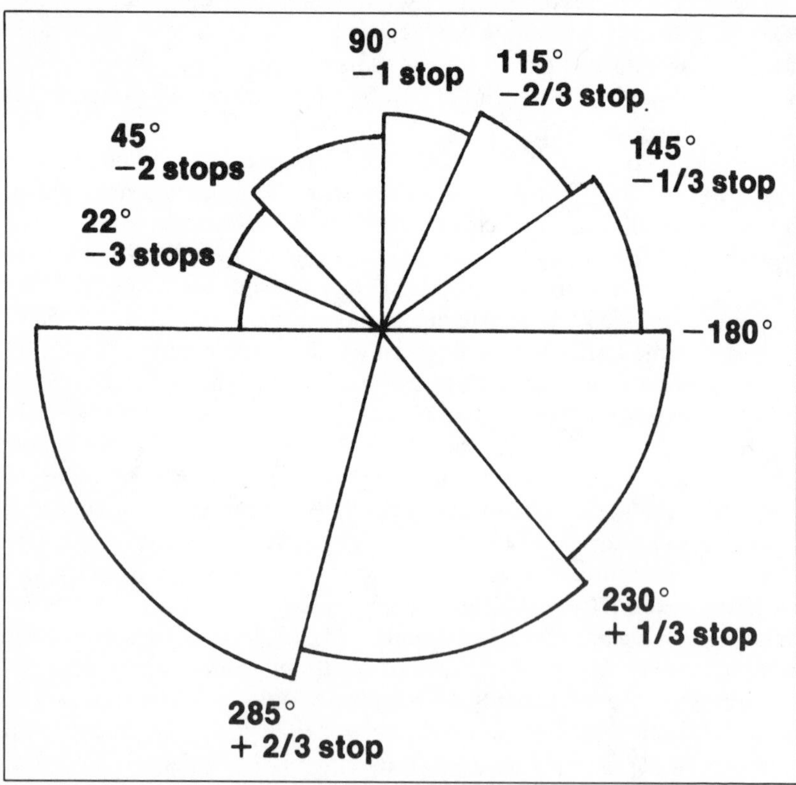

FIGURE 24—Exposure Increase or Decrease Relative to a 180° Shutter.

Shutters also come in a variety of shapes and forms. FIGURE 25 depicts the most common focal plane shutter. This type of shutter is used by Bell & Howell and Bolex, and many other manufacturers. The focal plane shutter is simple, effective and, because of its low mass, quiet. There would have been no reason to improve upon the focal

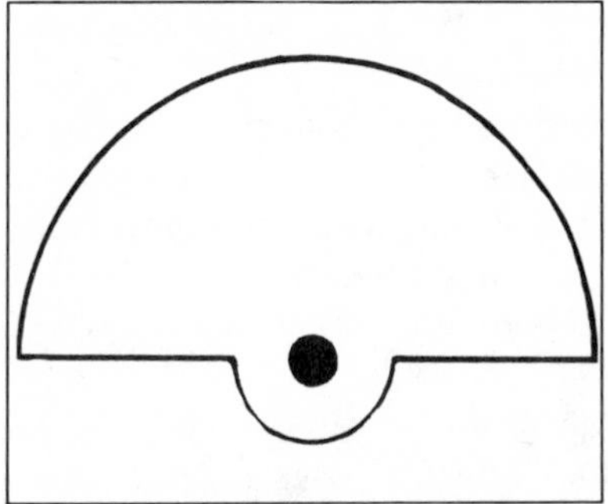

FIGURE 25—Focal plane shutter, such as that used in Bell & Howell, Bolex and many other cameras. It is simple, effective, and, because of its low mass, quiet.

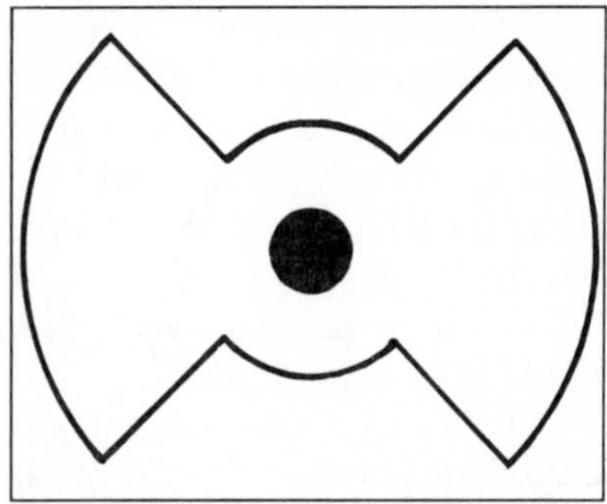

FIGURE 26—'Butterfly' type, dual-bladed mirror shutter, as used in Arriflex cameras. The two symmetrical openings keep this type of shutter perfectly balanced and vibrationless when running.

plane shutter had the need for a reflex system not arisen.

Arnold and Richter devised a reflex system based on a shutter constructed of a solid piece of glass. By coating the front surface with a mirror finish and placing the shutter axis at 45 degrees to the film plane, they created the first commercially available single lens reflex motion picture camera. FIGURE 26 depicts the Arriflex shutter design. This obviously looks different from that in FIGURE 26, but the function is the same. Remember that the focal plane shutter is made of extremely light sheet metal, whereas the Arri shutter is a hefty hunk of glass. If the Arri glass shutter were constructed as in FIGURE 25, a tremendous imbalance would result, which would cause such a horrendous vibration when the camera was turned on that the camera would undoubtedly shake itself from the cameraman's hand.

FIGURE 26 represents the simple solution. By making the shutter twin bladed with two symmetrical openings, the device is perfectly balanced and vibrationless when running. The dual bladed shutter must obviously turn at half speed, which also reduces noise. This type of shutter has remained popular with many camera designers to this day. Various materials have been employed, such as polished magnesium. However, glass construction seems to remain the most popular.

It would seem difficult to improve upon the Arri innovation. The mechanism is simple: merely one rotating element. Rotating parts are inherently quieter and less complex than mechanisms involving some form of push-pull movement. Add to the fact that the shutter rotates at half speed and you have the perfect blend of simplicity, form and function. However, the double-bladed or "butterfly" reflex shutter does have one drawback: size. Because of the dual blades and the oblique mounting angle, the shutter does require more room in the camera housing. The Eclair ACL and Beaulieu retain the advantages of the mirror reflex shutter, yet achieve extreme compactness by employing reciprocating, as opposed to rotating, mirror shutters.

Each, however, employs a totally different and unique alternative to the rotary design.

The Beaulieu employs a reciprocating mirror shutter that moves linearly up and down. It is sometimes referred to as a "guillotine" shutter because its movement resembles that infamous device. Like the Arriflex design, the Beaulieu mirror shutter performs a dual function. It blocks the light from reaching the film during pull-down and also reflects the image onto the ground glass for viewing. The Beaulieu design is very compact and is one of the very few mirror-reflex cameras that accept 'C' mount lenses. Because of the linear type mechanism, the Beaulieu is not a quiet camera. However, it makes no pretense of being a noiseless design.

The Eclair ACL takes a different approach. Because it is a noiseless type camera, the pure reciprocating or guillotine type shutter was ruled out. The Eclair engineers chose an oscillating design which is a hybrid of both the rotating and linear principles. More important, the ACL does not employ a "mirror-reflex shutter" in the true sense of the expression. The ACL employs a standard focal-plane shutter, as well as the totally separate oscillating mirror. The rotating focal-plane shutter is responsible for blocking the light from the film during the pull-down, while the mirror is responsible only for reflecting the image to the ground glass while the focal-plane shutter is closed. Like a rotary mirror shutter, the ACL mirror pivots about an axis, but it does not make a complete revolution.

FIGURE 27 is an exploded view of an Eclair ACL shutter mechanism. The mirror is indicated by an arrow at the end of part "A". The mirror arm ("A") rotates on the axis "B", but it only swings a small arc that is merely a fraction of a complete revolution. The connecting rod "C" swings the mirror assembly across the image path, where it comes to rest just to the right of the aperture. At this point in time, the focal-plane shutter "D" opens for exposure and then closes. After it closes, the mirror swings across the image path again, and this time comes to rest on the left side of the aperture at which time the focal-plane shutter opens again. Thus, while the focal-plane shutter rotates at full speed, the mirror arm swings alternately from side to side at half the cycle rate of the frame speed. When the mirror swings across the image path, the image is reflected upwards to the ground glass and reflex optics ("E").

Though this design is somewhat more complex than a simple rotating shutter, it is extremely quiet and compact. As a matter of fact, the mirror assembly requires so little depth that the ACL incorporates a behind-the-lens filter holder that is located before the mirror, as well as accepting "C" mount lenses with their short flange-to-focal plane distance.

What lies ahead in the world of shutter design? Would you believe a shutter with no moving parts? Better believe it; the solid state shutter is just around the corner. Scientists are perfecting a material that turns from transparent to opaque and back again according to an applied

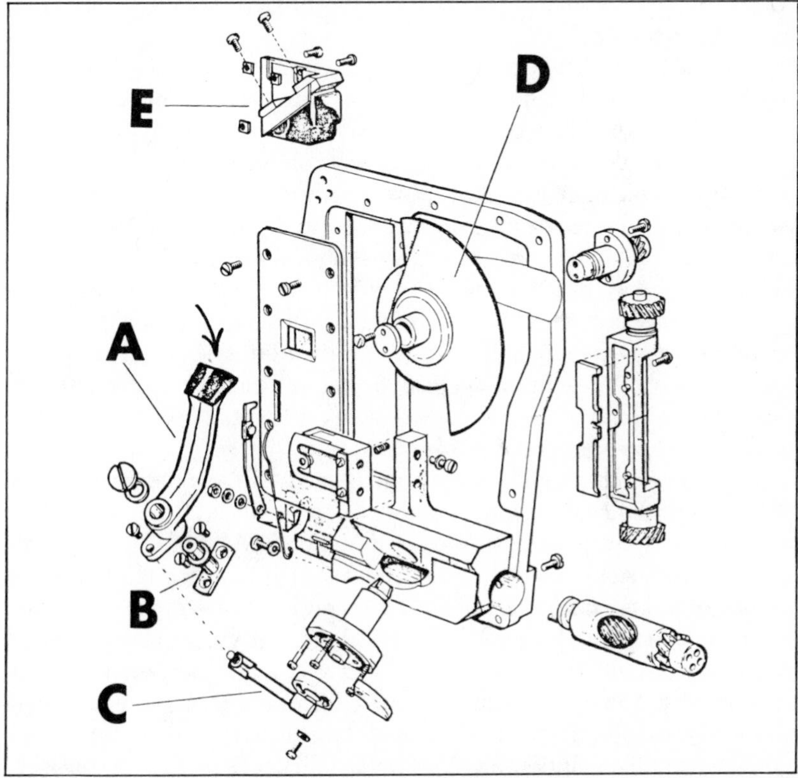

FIGURE 27—Exploded view of shutter and reflex mechanism of the Eclair ACL camera. The mirror (arrow) swings on the end of the mirror arm (A), which pivots on axis (B). Connecting rod (C) is geared to the motor and drives the mirror arm back and forth across the aperture. As the mirror passes through the light path, the image is reflected up to the ground glass/viewing assembly (E). Note that the swinging mirror is *not* a shutter, but is only used for reflecting the image for viewing. It is the rotating focal-plane shutter (D) that blocks the image from the film plane during pull-down.

voltage, if they can take that one step further—have the material turn alternately clear and then reflectively opaque—they will have a completely solid state, no moving parts, mirror reflex shutter. What will they think of next? Maybe a camera that doesn't use film and can send pictures through the air.

Before we leave the topic of shutters, I should mention what is perhaps the most frequently asked question on the subject: "How come the Arri mirror shutter has a black painted stripe in the middle of the mirror?" A reasonable question. After all, the main purpose of the mirror is to reflect the brightest image possible onto the ground glass, so why would you reduce the amount of reflecting surface by painting part of the mirror black?

When the mirror reflex shutter was first introduced, it caused quite a reaction in the film industry. Almost everyone is now familiar with the obvious attributes. However, there is one drawback that is now taken for granted, FLICKER. Cameramen were not accustomed to the image turning on and off while they were attempting to compose a frame. Arnold & Richter decided it would be wise to reduce this flicker effect to a minimum, as some cameramen were bound to find it objectionable. The obvious way to reduce flicker would be to decrease the dark or off period of the shutter. This was impractical because it would mean a smaller shutter opening and less light for the film. The less obvious way would be to reduce the perceived flicker by increasing the effective flicker rate. This cure is based on a very important phenomenon of motion pictures, the *critical flicker frequency.*

Early experimenters in motion pictures found that, due to the so called "persistence of vision", (the eye/brain holds an image for a short instant after that image is removed) motion could be perceived from a series of still pictures. They established that these pictures had to be flashed at a rate of approximately 16 a second or faster for the sensation of relatively smooth motion. However, there was still a flicker. In other words, the simulation of motion was successful, but the viewer was still aware of the flicker. The situation is identical to a mirror reflex camera where the motion in the image *is* real, but flickering.

The key to the solution was the "critical flicker frequency". This is the rate at which the eye will no longer perceive the two distinct areas. For example, consider a disc that is half white and half black and you can only see a portion of the disc through a small aperture. As the disc begins to rotate, you will see alternately white and then black in this "window". Eventually the disc can be made to spin fast enough so that the window will appear a smooth gray with no apparent flicker. That point is the critical flicker frequency.

As it relates to motion pictures, the critical flicker frequency turns out to be about 45 images per second. Thus, 16 fps projectors were designed with three shutter blades to create 48 images per second on the screen. In essence, each "frame" was projected three times in succession on the screen. To this day, all 24/fps projectors have twin-bladed shutters to create 48 images per second. One of the blades does block the image from the screen during pull-down, but the second blade merely interrupts the image to double the flicker rate. The result is no perceptible flicker.

The black painted band on the mirror shutter is exactly like the dummy blade in the projector. It breaks up the image to produce two flashes for each frame. The result is a reduction in perceived flicker with negligible loss of brightness. The flicker is only partially reduced because the stripe is extremely small compared to the large opening for exposure.

The painted black stripe on the Arriflex mirror reflex shutter was introduced as a means of reducing the perceived flicker by increasing the effective flicker rate. Due to the "persistence of vision" phenomenon, doubling the flicker rate actually makes the flicker less obvious.

With the advent of behind-the-lens exposure meters, it became imperative that the mirror shutter stop in the viewing position. Electronic controls were added to the motor to halt the shutter at the proper point, but the black stripe had to go. By breaking the mirror into two smaller areas, the stripe created "targets" too small for the electronic controls to hit accurately. The newer cameras with BTL meters have no stripe—just one large mirror segment. In addition, some camera designs (such as the CP-16R) employ shutters which are too compact for dual segments.

It appears that the intriguing black stripe may be a thing of the past.

D.C. SERVO MOTORS

The D.C. servo motor is the standard drive unit of modern motion picture cameras. Virtually every professional camera designed in the last ten years has incorporated a D.C. servo motor. In addition, after-market D.C. servo crystals are available for all professional motion picture cameras, including Arriflex (16S, M, BL and

35 II C), Eclair (NPR, CM-3), Mitchell, etc. Exactly what is a D.C. servo drive, and why have they become so popular?

The technical nomenclature for these motors is actually "closed-loop, phase-locked, pulse-width-modulated D.C. servo-controlled motor, with crystal reference". You would probably get some strange looks if you actually called one of these motors by that name. Most cameramen refer to these motors as simply "Crystal Motors" or "D.C. Servo Crystal Motors". Some cameras have D.C. servo drives that are not crystal referenced (i.e., Beaulieu). Our discussion here will deal with the crystal type, as these are used almost exclusively in professional applications.

Why crystal; why servo? First we should briefly review sync-sound requirements. The longest scene one could possibly shoot would be an entire roll of 1200′ 16mm. At 40 frames per foot, that would be 48,000 frames. If we define sync as ± ½ frame, then we would need an accuracy of one in 96,000 or approximately one part per 100,000. This is usually expressed as 10 parts per million (10 ppm) or .001% (one thousandth of one percent). Simply, then, if we wanted to shoot a 1200′ roll of film and have it in perfect sync with a recorder, using no cables or other sync devices, the motor must run the camera with an accuracy of 10 ppm or .001%.

The standard governor motor runs with an accuracy of ±1%. Thus, a motor necessary to run cordless sync would have to operate with an accuracy *1000 times greater* than that of a conventional governor motor. This is why a camera run with a governor motor needs a sync cable. The pilotone cable system records the inaccuracies of the governor motor which are later compensated in the transfer process. If, however, a motor were designed to run with an accuracy of .001%, then the sync

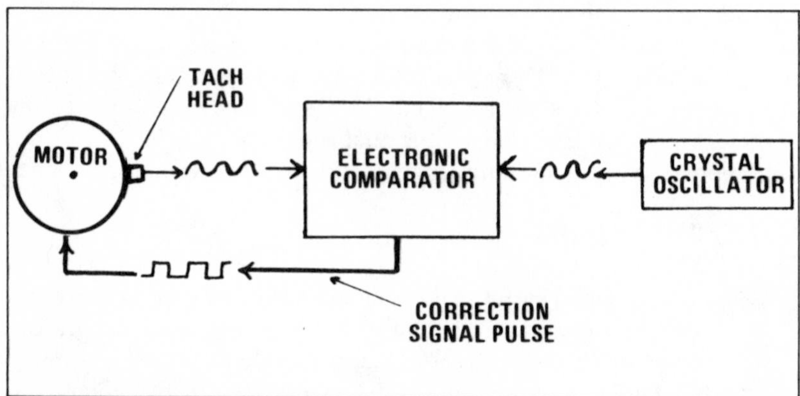

FIGURE 28—Block diagram of DC servo motor.

cable would serve no function and could be eliminated, as there would be no irregularities to record or compensate. This is precisely the function of the D.C. servo crystal motor.

A crystal is merely a source of extremely accurate high-frequency signals. The crystals employed for camera drives usually have an accuracy of 10ppm or .001%. The crystal is the reference for the required accuracy. The trick is to get the motor to run with the same precision as the crystal.

In practice, the circuitry for a crystal servo motor is as complex as the wiring of a Boeing 747, but the theory is quite simple. A "tach head" is placed on the motor. This is usually a magnetic pulser or a photoelectric device that generates a precise frequency at a specific motor speed (e.g., An Arri 16BL will put out exactly 6000 Hz. at exactly 24 fps). This tach signal (see FIGURE 28) is fed to the crystal unit, where it is compared with the signal coming from the crystal. The two signals must match exactly. If there is even a minute trace of a drift between the two signals, a correction pulse is sent up to the motor *before* it can deviate from the crystal signal. Thus the camera motor is "locked onto" the crystal signal. If the crystal has an accuracy of 10ppm, then the camera

FIGURE 29—An Arriflex camera with a crystal motor.

must be running with the same precise accuracy. Our original definition of cordless sync is, thus, satisfied.

In summary, the crystal servo motor is a precision clock, running the camera at exactly sound speed; 24fps, ±.001%. There are no speed irregularities and, thus, no necessity for any sync cable. Any number of cameras equipped with such motors will be in absolute sync with each other.

Some crystal motors provide additional functions. By unswitching the crystal reference frequency and substituting a variable frequency source, the motor can become a variable speed motor. This is somewhat more sophisticated than the conventional "wild" motor. Once a specific speed is selected, the servo circuitry will maintain that speed over a wide range of voltages and loads. Thus, it is more like a governor motor with adjustable speeds.

Some crystal motors can be "slaved" to an external source. The crystal frequency is disconnected and an external frequency can be made to control the camera speed. For example, a 60Hz signal from the mains can be fed into the servo system. The camera motor will lock onto this frequency and thus function as a synchronous motor.

CRYSTAL-SYNC

Crystal-Sync has provided the cameraman and producer with a new dimension in freedom and flexibility. By employing cameras with crystal-drives and crystal-equipped recorders, the producer can use any number of cameras or recorders to cover a particular scene. Moreover, set-up time is cut to a minimum because each camera and recorder is an autonomous unit; there are no inter-connections. Certain shots that would normally be post-synced can now be shot lip-sync, thus cutting post-production time and costs. This would include air-to-ground shots and shots from (or of) moving vehicles.

Most important to the cameraman is his liberation from the "umbilical" cord or sync cable. To many cameramen, the sound man and recorder are not unlike a ball and chain around his neck. With the absence of the sync cable, the cameraman is now a free agent with virtually no distance limitations between himself and the soundman.

The crystal-drive on the camera, as we have seen, actually drives the camera at a precise sound speed. The crystal on the recorder does something a little different. The crystal-drive on the camera can insure precise film speed because it is mechanically interlocked with the film via the sprocket holes.

On the other hand, a ¼″ tape transport does not enjoy this mechanical intimacy with the tape it drives. Driving a tape transport at a precise speed would not insure that the tape itself was moving at the same precise speed. The tape could slip in the capstan drive. Even if the tape did not slip in the capstan, sync could still be affected by capstan wear, tape slippage or capstan wear on playback, or tape stretch or shrinkage.

For these reasons, a control signal is still necessary on the tape track. In essence, the pilotone signal is still recorded, but it comes from a crystal in the recorder and not from the camera. The crystal in the recorder does not "drive" the recorder (unlike the camera), but merely puts out a precise 60-Hz signal that goes through the conventional pilotone circuitry of the recorder. The tape is resolved in the normal fashion; as a matter of fact, one need not inform the transfer house that the roll was shot crystal in lieu of a sync cable. In practice, one merely plugs a crystal into the pilotone input of the recorder and—*presto*!—perfect sync with every crystal camera in the world.

So far, everything we have discussed about crystal has provided simplicity and flexibility. It is now time to bring up the topic of slating. If you normally use clapsticks, continue to do so. If, however, you have been using the automatic slate lamps and oscillator in the recorder, you are in for a surprise. The signal to the oscillator in the recorder came down from the camera through the pilotone sync cable. With crystal there is no cable; no cable—no automatic slate. Before you start crying, there are several alternative methods to establishing a start mark with crystal sync.

The easiest method consists of a flashing light on the recorder connected to the start-mark oscillator. At the beginning or end of a take, the cameraman points the camera at the soundman and zooms in on the recorder. The soundman then momentarily pushes a button which will flash the light and activate the start-mark oscillator in the recorder. In essence, the result is the same as that with the conventional automatic slate, except that the bulb is at the recorder instead of inside the camera. This system works well with one camera or several cameras that will all start or stop at the same time. This system worked well for me at a rock concert we filmed employing multiple cameras. At the end of each number all the cameras pointed to the recorder and bulb. The soundman then hit the button and all cameras were simultaneously end-slated along with the corresponding beep on the track. There are several commercially available units on the market that perform this function. This type of device is also easy to construct for those of you who are do-it-yourselfers.

COLD WEATHER FILMING

Cold weather usually means problems for cameramen filming outdoors. Subfreezing temperatures can cause failure of the power source, breaking of the power cable, binding of the camera movement, icing of both the camera and lens mechanisms and rusting of metal parts. This may seem cause enough to stay in bed on very cold days. However, with proper understanding and precautions these problems can be minimized.

Most professional cameras (e.g., Arriflex, Eclair, etc.) are designed to function at temperatures down to approximately −4°F (−20°C), Operation of the camera above this temperature does not require any "modifications" or "winterizing". Certain precautions should be taken, however, when filming outdoors in the range between 0°F and +32°F. The biggest problem is usually the battery and power cable. Do not use a plastic (PVC) type of cable. These become very brittle at low temperatures and will crack. The best choice is a pure neoprene cable. The capacity of the NiCad battery is seriously reduced at low temperatures. This is caused by two factors. As temperatures drop, the camera mechanism becomes "tighter" due to different coefficients of expansion of mating parts, such as bearings and bushings. In addition, the viscosity of the lubricants increases. Thus, at low temperatures, the motor must supply greater torque to run the camera and will draw greater current from the battery. At reduced temperatures the battery itself loses effective capacity due to an increase in internal resistance. This reduction in capacity is compounded by the fact that the camera is drawing additional current. These three factors combine to cause a very significant loss in effective capacity at reduced temperatures (See FIGURE 30).

Keep batteries warm until the last minute. When taking them outdoors, wear them under clothing as close to the body as possible. (Brave cameramen have been known to place batteries beneath their under-

FIGURE 30

EFFECTIVE CAPACITY OF BATTERIES
As a FUNCTION OF TEMPERATURE

CAPACITY	TEMPERATURE
100%	70°F
85%	55°F
65%	40°
50%	32°
25%	20°

wear.) Always take extra batteries. Make sure all batteries are *fully* charged.

No particular preparation need be done to the camera as long as temperatures do not drop much below zero F. It might be a good idea to punch several holes around the rubber eyecup to prevent moisture or ice forming on the eyepiece lens. A camera at room temperature may be taken directly into subfreezing temperatures without creating any problems. It should *not,* however, be taken from room temperature into a snow storm. The snow and ice particles hitting the warm camera will melt and moisture will collect *inside* the camera. As the camera temperature rapidly drops, this moisture will quickly solidify, possibly causing a complete freeze-up of the camera mechanism.

When it is snowing, it is good practice to pre-freeze the camera to a temperature of approximately 30°F. Avoid keeping the camera out in extremely cold temperatures for long periods of time. A plain black barney will help somewhat in keeping the camera warm. It will absorb heat from the sun and also keep in what little heat is generated by the camera motor.

Care should be taken when bringing a camera out of subfreezing temperatures. If a camera that has been used in subfreezing conditions is to be used again in subfreezing temperatures after a short interim, the camera should remain in a subfreezing environment for that interim. If the camera is to be brought into a warm room, it must first be sealed in an airtight plastic bag until it has reached equilibrium temperature. Even if the camera is in the storage case, it must first be wrapped in the airtight plastic bag. This way, moisture will condense on the outside of the plastic bag and not on the camera. If, for some outlandish reason, a camera has been brought inside from the cold without the protective plastic bag, make sure it has plenty of time to dry out (at least several hours or overnight). If this precaution is not observed, and filming is continued in subfreezing conditions, any remaining moisture will quickly freeze, causing interference, a complete freeze-up and possibly rusting of metal parts.

When filming in temperatures much below zero°F for extended periods, a specially modified camera is called for. Arriflex, for example, has a winterizing package they install that allows the camera to be used in the −4°F to −49°F range. Once the camera has been modified for this temperature range, it is *not* suitable for use at normal temperatures. The modification includes larger bearing clearances, special viscosity lubricants, special tantalum capacitors and selected transistors for the motor.

If you plan to encounter sustained temperatures below zero, it is best to contact the camera manufacturer for specific instructions.

Cameras

TRANSPORTING EQUIPMENT

In past chapters we have covered many points on the care and maintenance of motion picture and video equipment. However, even with the best care and calibration, your equipment can arrive on location in less than optimum condition. As a matter of fact, I have seen equipment leave the studio in A-1 condition and reach its destination in a state of partial disassembly or total destruction.

The naive may ask, "How is this possible? Who would want to hurt my beloved camera?" The seasoned cameraman knows the answer—C.R.U.S.H. Contemptible and Ruthless Union of Shippers and Handlers. Yes, at this very moment this international group of airline cargo personnel, truckers, mail loaders, cargo handlers, etc., are meeting. They are carefully plotting new ways to drop, vibrate, smash, compress, distort, shock, irrigate and in other ways render useless your precious camera and recording gear.

Without going into the sordid details of their nefarious deeds, it should be apparent that the forces out to sabotage your equipment are formidable and well organized. There is nothing that can be done to stop these sadists. However, there are certain procedures that can be employed to minimize the effects.

Firstly, cameras and recorders should be shipped in shipping cases, not carrying cases. There is a big difference. Many of the popular camera cases are constructed of aluminum-covered wood with wooden fixtures and partitions inside designed to accept a specific model camera and accessories. The wooden interior is usually lined with a soft material (corduroy or velvet) to protect the camera finish. This is a carrying or storage case. It is *not* a shipping case. This type of carrying case has no provision for absorption of shock or impact. It has no provision for damping vibration or dissipating deformation of the outer shell. This type of case makes an excellent storage case or carrying case when the camera is personally hand-carried on an assignment. However, when the camera is to be shipped by common carrier, this type of case is a definite no-no! For those of you who already own this type of case, refrain from using it for shipping the camera. It is far better to ship the camera in a foam-filled cardboard container than the aforementioned type carrying cases. For example, the Arriflex cameras, for years, have been sold in form-fitted, foam-filled boxes, These make excellent shipping devices. Place the camera in the foam-filled box as it originally came. Then place that box within a larger corrugated box with ample packing material between the two boxes (crumpled newspaper or bubble plastic, etc.) This method offers far greater protection against shocks and vibration than shipping in a carrying case. If more than one item is shipped in a box, make sure the items are well isolated from each other. Quite frequently damage is caused by two items knocking together.

If you are in the market for a new camera or recorder case and you expect to be shipping your gear frequently, choose one of the foam-filled shipping cases. These cases are characterized by an outer shell of extruded aluminum or molded high impact plastic. The inside is semi-rigid foam, form-fitted to the specific camera, or VTR. The outer shell is designed to distribute any blow or impact evenly over a large area. The foam interior is an energy-absorbing medium designed to damp vibrations and absorb most jolts or impacts. There are several pointers to look for in a good case. Avoid cases with sharp corners and edges. Those cases with round corners and gradually sloping curves will stand up better when dropped. Also check the consistency of the foam interior. Some cases use a very soft foam, almost like foam rubber. This type of foam should be avoided as it allows too much movement within the case and does not absorb the majority of the impact energy. In addition, this type of foam can tear and two items within a case will then collide with each other. The foam should be fairly stiff and dense but with a slight give to the touch. It should not feel like a pillow. Make sure there is ample cross-section of foam between the camera and the outer shell as well as between each item within the case. Two inches is a minimum. Remember that the protection is only as good as the thinnest cross-section of foam. Thus if there are three inches of foam all around your camera, except the protrusion of the viewfinder, when there is only ¾″ of foam, any shock will be transmitted to the camera at that point, despite the fact that the rest of the camera has a much thicker coating of protection.

The hardware on the case is most important. Check out the strength and construction of the hinges and latches. Many cases do not have ample clamping force, and the two halves do not close tightly. A case that is water-tight is obviously preferable. In addition to floating if it falls overboard, this type of case protects against dew and moisture. In any event it is a good idea not to leave your gear outdoors (in a car or porch) overnight. That morning dew that you see covering the grass and your car will also be covering your camera lenses and accessories even if they are in what seems to be a good case. Only the most airtight cases can protect fully against moisture.

Although "C.R.U.S.H." is responsible for most shipping damages, some cameramen unwittingly join forces with this group when transporting their own gear. A camera case transported in the trunk of a car is subjected to several perils: As the car rounds corners the case will slide from one side of the trunk to the other. The resulting impacts can be greater than a ten-foot drop. The normal road vibrations could be enough to loosen every screw and lens element. This condition is further aggravated in hot weather. In a closed trunk, temperatures can easily rise above 100.° At these elevated temperatures, the cement used on the lens elements can begin to soften. In this condition even the normal road vibrations may be enough to cause the elements to shift, totally destroying the optical calibration of the lens. To protect the camera in the trunk, many cinematographers build a foam-lined trough which is mechanically fastened to the trunk floor. The camera case nestles in this trough where it is prevented from sliding around and is also somewhat isolated from vibrations. Where this is not feasible, the trunk should be completely filled with other gear or even empty cardboard boxes to restrict the movement of the camera case. Keeping the camera case inside the car on a seat is a good idea but even here precautions should be employed to keep it from sliding around.

The choice of a shipping case and the method of packing gear is most important. One of the largest professional camera corporations reports that as many as two out of ten cameras received for overhaul or repair are damaged in shipment due to improper or inadequate packing methods employed by the customer. "C.R.U.S.H." is obviously succeeding with their evil plans. Don't become their next victim. Choose a good case, pack your equipment well and pray. With a little luck your equipment may arrive in one piece.

POWER CABLES

What part of the camera system can be more simple than the power cable? It is just a piece of wire between the camera and the battery, right? Wrong! This kind of attitude can get you in a lot of trouble. The power cable is the lifeline of the camera. A faulty power cable can cause a camera to run out of sync, run slow or stop dead. Probably more jobs are ruined or delayed due to faulty power cables than any other single camera malfunction. This is why all rental houses supply every camera with at least two power cables and, in some instances, three or more. There is nothing more exasperating than to be shooting with a $15,000 camera and be held up due to a faulty $15 cable.

There are basically two things you should know about power cables. The first are physical characteristics: preferred types of insulation, areas of greatest stress, etc. Secondly, there are the electrical characteristics. A poor choice in a power cable can cause the camera to run slow or out of sync due to excessive voltage drop.

The power cable is essentially a conductor of electricity, but it is also a resistance between the camera and the power source. The amount of resistance in a power cable is proportional to its length and cross-section. A long thin cable will offer much greater resistance than a short, large-gauge cable. When the camera is turned on and current begins to flow through the cable, the battery voltage will partially "drop" across the cable.

Therefore, the voltage available to the camera is somewhat less than the battery is actually putting out. The amount of voltage drop across the cable is also directly proportional to the current drain of the particular camera. For example, an Eclair NPR and an Arriflex 16 BL each draw approximately 2 amps, as opposed to an Eclair ACL or a Bolex MST, which each draw under 1 amp. With identical power cables, the 16BL and NPR will experience over twice the voltage drop as will the ACL and Bolex MST. As a general rule, it is best to use as short a power cable as the situation will allow. In addition it is best to choose one of 16-gauge as opposed to 18-gauge wire. Be particularly wary of coiled cables. A two-foot coiled cable is actually over 12 feet of wire. If you must use a coiled cable, it is best to use the one-foot length which extends to six feet.

Voltage drop in the power cable can of course be eliminated by mounting the battery right on the camera. Virtually all video cameras come from the manufacturer with an integral Anton/Bauer Snap-On™ battery bracket mounted on the rear. The attached battery not only makes the camera a one piece unit, but it also perfectly balances the camera as well as eliminating power cable problems.

The increasing popularity of crystal and servo-controlled motors has introduced an additional problem to the selection of a power cable. These servo-controlled motors almost exclusively operate on the principle of pulse-width modulation. This means that the motor is powered by quick pulses rather than a continuous current. While the *average* current drain of these servo motors is somewhat less than conventional motors, the *instantaneous* current drain of each pulse can be three times higher. Since the voltage drop in a cable is proportional to instantaneous current, these crystal and servo motors will experience about three times the voltage drop of the same camera with a conventional motor. It is therefore particularly important to use a short cable when using a crystal or servo type motor. In these cases, a coiled cable should be avoided completely.

FIGURE 31 is designed to give the cinematographer some quantitative

FIGURE 31

Wire gauge	wire length	Bolex H-16, Beaulieu Scoopic, etc. (approx. 1 amp)	Arri 16S, Arri 16BL, Eclair NPR, etc. w/conventional motors (approx. 2 amps)	Arri 35 II C	Arri 16 BL, Eclair NPR, etc. w/crystal type motors.
18	6 feet (1 foot coiled)	1/12 V	1/6 V	1/4 V	1/4 V
	12 feet (2 feet coiled)	1/6 V	1/3 V	1/2 V	1 V
	20 feet (3 feet coiled)	1/4 V	1/2 V	3/4 V	1½ V
16	6 feet	1/20 V	1/10 V	1/6 V	1/3 V
	12 feet	1/10 V	1/5 V	1/3 V	2/3 V
	20 feet	1/6 V	1/3 V	1/2 V	1 V
20	12 feet	1/4 V	1/2 V	3/4 V	1½ V

'feel' for the voltage drops across various lengths of cable for several popular cameras. Keep in mind, also, that many cameras draw over 10 amps during start-up, which can mean more than a two-volt drop on long cables.

Being a resistance, the cable also draws power proportional to the voltage drop. Thus a cable that drops one volt from a twelve-volt battery will also rob one watt of power from every 12 watts delivered by the battery. Essentially, 1/12 of the power being delivered by the battery is being dissipated by the cable.

The adverse effects of the cable voltage drop in most cases are minimal. It does cause a slight decrease in effective battery power and will also decrease top speed of the camera for slow motion. Probably the most serious effect of the cable voltage drop occurs with cameras that employ sophisticated electronic components such as a behind-the-lens metering system. Excessive voltage drops in the cable have been known to cause these systems to malfunction completely.

Physically there are two things to look for in a power cable. The type

FIGURE 32

INSULATION ON WIRE

Property	Rubber	Neoprene	PVC	Polyethelene	Nylon	Teflon
Resistance to abrasion	E	E	F	G	E	E
Flexibility	E	E	G	F	P	F
Weatherability	P	E	E	E	E	E
Temperature Range [°C]	−40 +70	−30 +90	−20 +80	−60 +80	−40 +120	−70 +250
Resistance to Solvents:						
Alcohols	P	G	P	G	E	E
Aromatics (Gasoline-Benzene)	P	P	P	G	G	E
Chlorines (Tri-chloro-Ethylene)	P	P	F	G	E	E

E – Excellent G – Good F – Fair P – Poor

of insulation, and the effectiveness of the strain-relief on each connector. The strain-relief is usually a collar or ring around the wire as it enters the connector at each end. The strain-relief should be tight enough so that if the cable is accidentally yanked, the strain-relief will absorb the shock and not the actual electrical connections inside the plug. An ineffective or loose strain-relief accounts for most cable failures. Always carefully inspect the strain-reliefs on the power cable. If they appear loose or they are missing, do *not* repair the strain-relief. The plug should first be taken apart and the internal solder connections inspected. A loose strain-relief usually indicates that the electrical connections have already been weakened.

The choice of insulation is usually rubber, neoprene or PVC (Poly Vinyl Chloride). Neoprene is probably the best choice for general use, however. The chart in FIGURE 32 reflects most of the insulations in common use and the various properties that may help in the selection of an insulation for a particular situation.

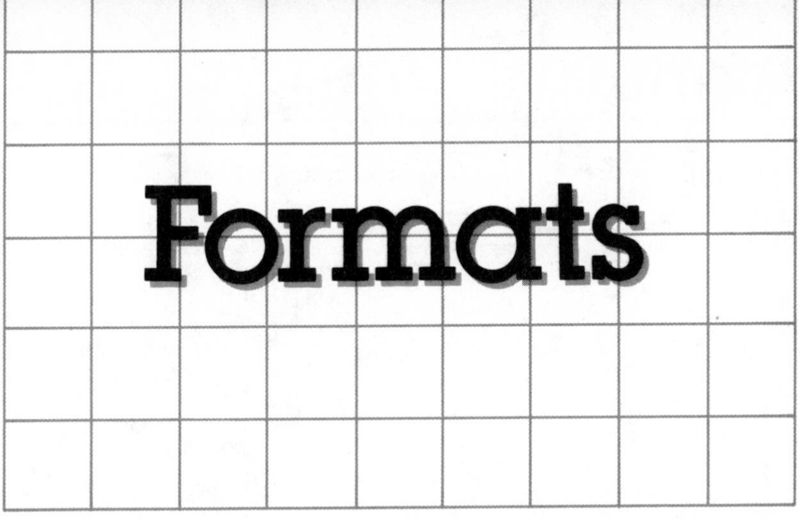

FORMATS

There are a myriad of facts to consider when comparing any two film format sizes. A film format is not merely a set of dimensions, but rather an entire complex system including available cameras, lenses, film stock, processing, editing equipment, projection areas, etc. The points to consider are almost endless and any comparison of film formats must be a comprehensive analysis of these many factors.

However, you have to start somewhere and most format discussions will undoubtedly commence with the question of image area. How big is the picture on the film? The question is basic, but as good a place as any to start.

FIGURES 33 and 34 show the aperture dimensions for Super-8 and

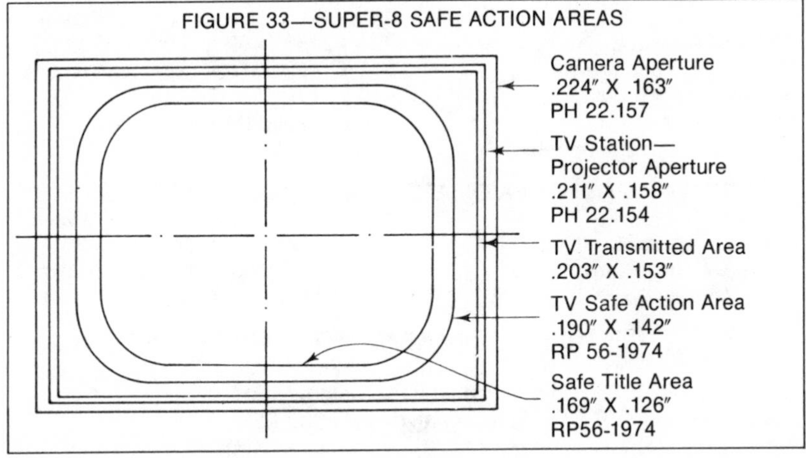

FIGURE 33—SUPER-8 SAFE ACTION AREAS

FIGURE 34—TELEVISION FILM APERTURES AND SAFE AREAS

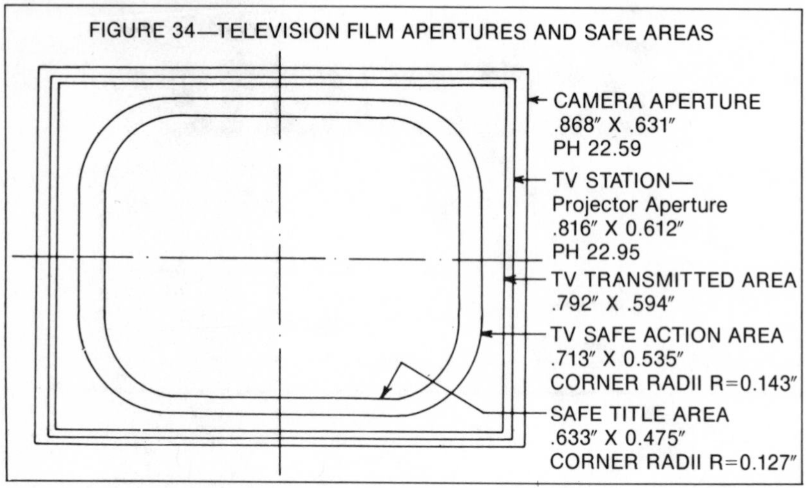

35mm formats, respectively, FIGURE 35 lists these dimensions and those for 16mm. FIGURE 36 lists the areas for the camera, projection, and safe action areas of the three formats. FIGURE 37 gives the percentages of the format areas relative to one another. In the final analysis, the 16mm image is more than three times as large as the Super-8 image, and the 35mm image is more than 14 times that of Super-8, and between four and five times that of 16mm. Of course, all these statistics are in respect to the standard 1.33:1 aspect ratio.

What do these figures mean? Taken alone, not much. The total format system must be considered before any comparisons can be made. Most

FIGURE 35—DIMENSIONS OF APERTURES FOR VARIOUS FORMATS

	Super-8	16mm	35mm
Camera Aperture	.224 x .163	.402 x .292	.868 x .631
Projection Aperture	.211 x .158	.379 x .284	.816 x .612
Safe Action Area	.190 x .142	.331 x .248	.713 x .535
Safe Title Area	.169 x .126	.294 x .221	.633 x .475

FIGURE 36—IMAGE AREA OF APERTURES FOR VARIOUS FORMATS

	Super-8	16mm	35mm
Camera Aperture	.0365	.117	.548
Projection Aperture	.0333	108	.489
Safe Action Area	.0260	.0790	.367

FIGURE 37—RELATIVE IMAGE AREAS OF THE THREE FORMATS

Super-8 relative to 16mm: 31%
Super-8 relative to 35mm: 6.8%
16mm relative to 35mm: 22%

important is the application. Production technique must also be included in the analysis. There may be applications where the Super-8 image is acceptable, yet the production would be more practical in 16mm.

Probably the greatest factor affecting image quality is the generation of the projector print. I have recently seen some large screen projection tests, and am convinced that projected Kodachrome Super-8 original is indistinguishable from (if not better than) standard third-generation 16mm. This is a prime consideration for camera-original direct projection applications, such as film-to-video and sports analysis.

The cinematographer should be familiar with the basic statistics for a reference. However, an exhaustive and comprehensive analysis of the format systems must precede a final decision on format size.

TV FORMAT

The aspect ratio of television is 1.33:1, the same as 16mm and Academy 35mm motion picture formats. This is no coincidence, the television format was obviously designed to be compatible with the existing motion picture standards. This fact may give a cameraman the impression that anything he shoots with a standard 1.33:1 ratio wil work as well for a television transmission as for a direct screen projection. Not true.

In most cases footage that was not specifically shot for television will suffer from the broadcast process. This is due to technical as well as aesthetic differences between television and large screen direct projection. The specific techniques for exploiting the dramatic capabilities of television could easily form a complete discussion in itself. We will explore that subject later; however, for the present we will look at the technical considerations.

What the cameraman sees is not what the audience gets. The viewfinder image (camera aperture) is shaved away as it passes through the film chain. By the time it reaches the home receiver, the image may be reduced to as little as ½ of its original area. While this may be a worse case figure, the received image rarely represents more than 75% of the original composition, with a figure of 65% to 75% being average. In other words, the TV audience gets to see only ½ to ¾ of what the cameraman put on the film. This is, of course, assuming the original footage was shot 1.33:1. If an anamorphic screen format was employed during the original filming, the TV image will represent an even smaller percentage of the original scene. Would you believe that the TV audience may be viewing as little as ¼ of an original scene filmed in

Cinemascope, never getting to see the other 75% of the cinematographer's composition? (See page 82)

What happens to this lost information? In the case of the wide screen formats, it should be obvious that a bulk of the image is lost by cropping the sides off the original scene to re-establish the 1.33:1 aspect ratio. However, once the 1.33:1 ratio is established, the image is further cropped as it makes its way through each process in the tele-cine chain.

The film records the full image as the cameraman sees it. This is called the camera aperture. (See FIGURE 34.) When the film is projected, a small portion of the image is cropped by the "Projection Aperture", which is specifically designed to be smaller than the camera aperture. This will insure that the frame lines and the side boundaries of the original image will not appear on the screen. The smaller projection aperture will also cover up any misalignment that may have existed between camera and projector centerlines.

Next along the line is the TV camera or scanner which picks up the projected image. The TV camera aperture crops the projector image for similar reasons: to compensate for slight component misalignment, etc.

The final and most heinous blow is struck by the home receiver. Firstly, some of the corner detail is lost due to the curved nature of the cathode ray tube (minimized in recent years by the newer rectangular tubes). Most of the loss is due to "over-scan". The home receiver is designed to spread the transmitted image larger than the actual face of the tube. The tube thus crops the image, insuring that those "ugly black areas" will not appear on the sides of the screen. While most of the cropping done at the projection and transmission stages is controlled by SMPTE standards, and held to a minimum, the loss at the home receiver due to over-scan is a function of individual set adjustment. Unfortunately the over-scan is usually quite excessive. To insure that the image will not vignette during low voltage or "brown-out" situations, (where the image usually shrinks), TV servicemen will crank in gobs of overscan. Better to have the customer lose a little image (which he probably won't even notice), than to have him complain about those black areas on the side of the screen.

FIGURE 34 tells the whole story. FIGURE 38 gives the statistics. Read them and weep. The "TV safe action area" represents the average home receiver image area. While the cameraman should consider the full camera aperture in terms of keeping unwanted details (microphones, etc.) out of the scene, he should keep all pertinent action and composition within the limits of the "safe action area".

The "safe title area" represents a worst-case situation for home receiver over-scan. The viewer may not notice a slight cropping of action,

FIGURE 38

APERTURE	DIMENSIONS (35mm)	AREA	% of CAMERA APERTURE
Camera	0.868 x 0.631	0.5477	100 %
Projection	0.816 x 0.612	0.4993	91 %
Transmission	0.792 x 0.594	0.4704	85 %
Safe Action	0.713 x 0.535	0.380	70 %
Safe Title	0.633 x 0.475	0.300	50 % — 55 %

but he will certainly spot a couple of letters missing from his favorite actor's name.

In a nutshell, action within the "safe action area" will appear on all but the most outrageously misadjusted receivers. The cinematographer must take these croppings into account when composing. A TV "safe action" ground glass would certainly be beneficial.

WIDE-SCREEN FORMATS

One of the more controversial subjects is wide-screen systems for 35mm release. Through the years there have been a myriad of special wide-screen techniques, each with its advantages and drawbacks. Only a handful of systems are still in active use, yet the arguments are still heard as to the relative merits of each.

Wide-screen 35mm release systems can be broken down into two basic categories: anamorphic and flat. Flat wide-screen systems use standard lenses on the camera, and achieve the greater horizontal dimension by cropping the height of the frame and projecting with a shorter focal-length lens. This system is inherently very simple, but it is extremely wasteful of film. In addition, projected image quality suffers, since a much larger screen area must be filled by a smaller negative area.

The unused image area of this wide-screen system is in addition to the already existing waste inherent in the standard Academy Aperture. To understand the magnitude of this waste, it is necessary to step back to the year 1932 when standards for the sound motion picture format were first established. Before this time, the full available negative area was used as in FIGURE 39. This was from frameline to frameline, and sprocket hole to sprocket hole, with obvious clearances. The actual dimensions were .735″ x .980″, which is an area of .720 sq. in. The aspect ratio or ratio of width to height was 4 to 3 or 1.33:1. With the introduction of sound, a portion of the negative area was allocated for the soundtrack as shown in FIGURE 40. Of course this soundtrack area was created at the expense of the picture area. As a result, the width of the image area was reduced to .868″ from the full .980″. But to maintain the original 1.33:1 aspect ratio, the height of the camera aperture had to be proportionately reduced from .735″ to .631″. This is what is known as the Academy Aperture, and has an actual aspect ratio of 1.37:1, and a negative area of .548 sq. inches. By this one step, the negative area was reduced by 24%. Stated conversely, the Silent or Full Aperture had over 31% more negative area than the present Academy Aperture.

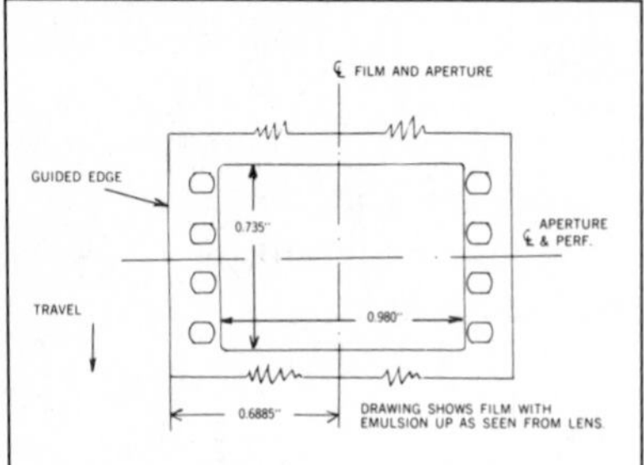

FIGURE 39—Full or silent aperture, which utilized the total available negative area.

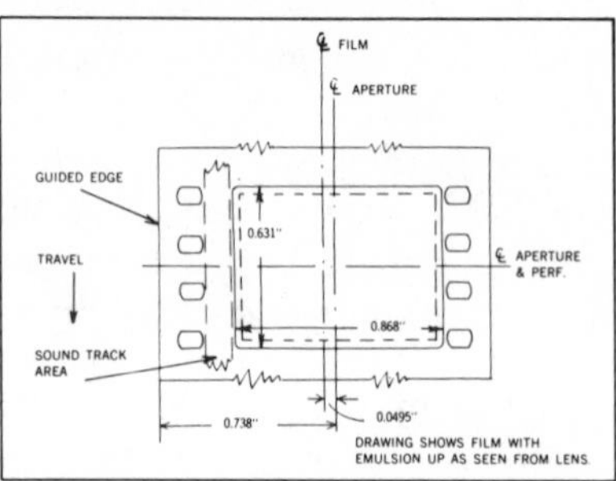

FIGURE 40—The Academy Aperture. Note the area reserved for sound track and the reduced height (.631″, as compared to .735″ in FIGURE 39.)

Not all of this difference can be considered "waste", since a portion of the unused area is reserved for the sound track. However, the reduction of frame height to maintain the 1.33:1 aspect ratio results in pure unadulterated waste. This waste takes the form of a thick black frame line in lieu of the hair-thin line associated with silent films and 16mm. This large frame line amounts to about 16% of the image area and represents about 1/7 of the total negative area. That's about 14% of the film that is wasted.

Now enter flat wide-screen. By cropping the height of the aperture and maintaining the .868″ width, the aspect ratio can be increased to any desired figure. In practice, there are three ratios that are most often employed: 1.66:1, 1.75:1, 1.85:1. The 1.66:1 ratio is most popular in Europe, while the 1.85:1 format is almost exclusively employed in the U.S.

The 1.85:1 ratio is achieved by chopping the frame height to 0.469″, which yields an effective negative area of 0.407 sq. inches.

For those keeping score, the picture looks something like this: (See FIGURE 41). The negative area of the 1.85:1 wide-screen is only 0.407 sq. in. The wasted negative area is 0.231 sq. in. or over 56% of the area actually being used for the image. Thus, over 36% of the available negative area is wasted. To see where we have progressed in 50 years, the cinematographer in 1930 was using 77% more negative area than a modern cameraman shooting 1.85:1.

FIGURE 41

WASTED AREA OF CONVENTIONAL
4-PERFORATION PULLDOWN

	APERTURE DIMENSIONS	IMAGE AREA	WASTED AREA	% OF FULL APERTURE	% OF TOTAL AREA WASTED
Full (Silent)	.735 x .980	.720	0	100	0
Academy (1.33:1)	.631 x .868	.548	.090	76%	14%
1.66:1	.523 x .868	.454	.184	63%	29%
1.75:1	.496 x .868	.430	.207	60%	33%
1.85:1	.469 x .868	.407	.231	57%	36%

THEORETICAL 3-PERFORATION PULLDOWN—25%
LESS FILM STOCK FOR ALL FORMATS

	APERTURE DIMENSIONS	IMAGE AREA	WASTED AREA	% OF TOTAL AREA WASTED
1.58:1 (minimum)	.550 x .868	.477	0	0
1.66:1	.523 x .868	.454	.023	5%
1.75:1	.496 x .868	.430	.047	10%
1.85:1	.469 x .868	.407	.070	15%

The waste of the flat wide-screen system could be dramatically reduced by the adoption of a 3-perforation pulldown system in lieu of the standard 4-perf pulldown. Immediately there is a 25% reduction in the amount of raw stock for all flat wide-screen systems. Waste figures are reduced drastically. Unused area for the 1.66 ratio is only 5%, down from 29% with the 4-perf system. Likewise, 1.75 is reduced to 10%, down from 33%, and the 1.85 ratio wastes 15%, as opposed to the former 36%. While a 3-perf pulldown would not help the image, it would certainly ease the pain by improving the budget 25% across the board for raw stock, processing the prints, not to mention storage and freight costs. Moreover, magazines would last ⅓ longer reducing the number of pauses for reloading. However, it is pretty late in the game to ever hope that the 3-perf system could become a reality.

In a nutshell, flat wide-screen systems are simple, but wasteful, and employ reduced negative area in proportion to an increased screen image, resulting in a loss of image quality.

ANAMORPHIC WIDE-SCREEN

The anamorphic process is a viable alternative. It not only eliminates the waste associated with the flat wide-screen systems, but actually reclaims the wasted negative area lost by the addition of the soundtrack back in 1932.

The basic idea for the anamorphic system can be traced back to the 1820's when Fresnel began experimenting with cylindrical lenses. In

1930 Professor Henri Chrétien developed his "Hypergonar" anamorphic lens system, which is the basis of all modern anamorphic systems. In 1952 Twentieth Century-Fox acquired the rights to the Chrétien process and contracted Bausch & Lomb to manufacture the optics in the U.S.A. The process was dubbed "CinemaScope", and the rest is history.

The anamorphic process is quite simple in concept. The lens on the camera compresses or squeezes the image in the horizontal direction by a factor of two-to-one. Vertical dimensions remain normal. The filmed image thus contains twice the normal amount of horizontal information. Compared to a regular "spherical" lens, the anamorphic lens "sees" twice as much horizontally, but *squeezes* it to fit the standard 35mm film width. The projection anamorphic lens performs the inverse function and *unsqueezes,* or spreads the image out to fill a screen twice the normal width.

While the system is simple in concept, the practical aspects are somewhat complex. Anamorphic lenses are far more sophisticated than spherical types and require great care in design and manufacture to maintain high optical quality and reduce distortions to a minimum. It is no secret that the early anamorphic systems had their problems. Close-ups were difficult, due to distortions caused by shifts in compression coefficients. Lenses were available in limited focal lengths ("THE ROBE" was shot almost entirely with one lens), and zooms did not exist for several years.

The picture has changed drastically over the last thirty years. The anamorphic system has been perfected and the cinematographer now has a complete selection of optically superb lenses. Panavision currently offers more than forty anamorphic lenses in their catalogue, including several zoom lenses with ranges up to 10:1. These optics have gained an international reputation for quality and superb image definition. The hardware is obviously there, but what does the anamorphic system really buy you? Plenty!

Would you believe 60% more image area than the 1.85:1 flat system? FIGURES 42 and 43 tell the complete story. Note that the anamorphic aperture has *no* waste at all. It actually regains the image area lost since 1932 when the Academy Aperture was established. In FIGURE 42A the Full (Silent) aperture height is 0.735. This was reduced to 0.631 in FIGURE 42B to maintain the 1.33:1 aspect ratio with the Academy Aperture. Note in FIGURE 42D that the image height of the CinemaScope format is once again 0.735, thus utilizing the total available negative area. The original CinemaScope format employed a four track magnetic sound system with an aspect ratio of 2.55:1. The specifications were later modified to include an optical soundtrack and a resulting ratio of 2.35:1.

The anamorphic system with its 100% utilization of negative area should be quite popular in these waste-conscious times, not to mention the fact that the anamorphic process undoubtedly produces the finest quality image of any 35mm wide-screen format. There are many other advantages of the anamorphic system.

At the camera end, the anamorphic lens "sees" twice as much in the horizontal plane. As a result, the focal length in the horizontal is effectively halved. A 50mm anamorphic can be compared with a 25mm spherical lens in terms of horizontal composition. As a matter of fact, the effective focal length is also slightly reduced in the vertical. The 1.85:1 ratio maintains the same effective focal lengths as the Academy aperture in the horizontal, while manifesting a slightly *longer* effective length in the vertical.

When the higher aspect ratios were first introduced, some cinematographers were concerned over the awkward composition problems that might result. There is no denying that a format with twice the horizontal dimension of Academy will require some aesthetic adaptation. However, once the cinematographer is acclimated to the 2.35:1 ratio, several advantages will become apparent. In a majority of cases composition and movement are in a horizontal plane. Because of this the cinematographer can establish more pertinent visuals in the

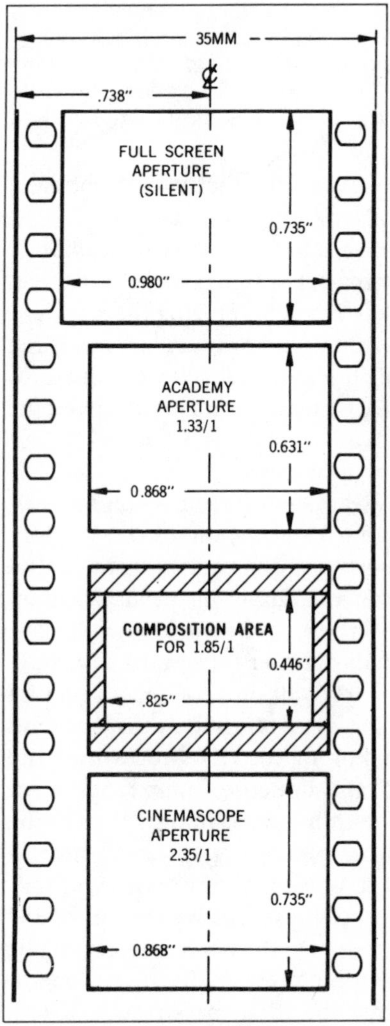

FIGURE 42—Diagram showing relative waste of the 35mm frame by various formats indicates that the CinemaScope (anamorphic) format is least wasteful.

	IMAGE AREA	WASTED AREA	% AREA RELATIVE TO CINEMASCOPE	% OF TOTAL AREA WASTED
CINEMASCOPE 2.35:1	.638	0	100%	0
ACADEMY 1.33:1	.548	.090	86%	14%
Wide Screen 1.66:1	.454	.184	71%	29%
Wide Screen 1.75:1	.430	.207	67%	33%
Wide Screen 1.85:1	.407	.231	64%	36%

FIGURE 43—Numerical comparisons not only reveal in startingly concrete terms the "efficiency" of the anamorphic frame (as represented by CinemaScope and Panavision), but the appalling amount of waste inherent in the 1.85:1 pseudo-wide-screen format which is standard in America and which manages to not show 36% of the potentially available image information area of the 35mm frame.

2.35:1 format, while excluding extraneous details that would normally appear in the vertical plane, usually above the pertinent action.

This aspect not only makes for a more aesthetically pleasing composition, but can also simplify matters for the set designer, as his sets need be only half the height of that necessary when employing the standard 1.33:1 format to cover the same horizontal composition. In the same vein, since most action is horizontal, the high aspect ratio can also simplify camera movements due to its greater horizontal coverage. These arguments obviously apply to all wide screen processes, but particularly to the 2.35:1 ratio of 'scope.

The 1.85:1 format does offer an advantage when it comes to TV compatibility. A producer can play both ends to the middle by employing cameras with full or Academy apertures. The reticles in the viewfinders are masked for 1.85:1. The cinematographer keeps all pertinent action within the confines of the 1.85 mask, yet maintains full 1.33:1 composition by excluding all objectionable elements from the full viewfinder area (mike booms, light stands, assistant director, etc.). The film can then be projected 1.85:1 in theatrical release and still be run at 1.33 in the tele-cine chain without any cropping or costly reprocessing. The anamorphic print, on the other hand, must undergo severe cropping or reprinting employing 'pan and scan' techniques. While the reprinting process can re-establish satisfactory composition in most cases, there is always the chorus line that is reduced from twenty dancers down to six.

Cinematographers are bound to argue the respective virtues of the various wide screen formats, but in terms of theatrical projection the picture is quite lucid. Here the anamorphic process offers decided advantages. The main factor is print magnification. Based on a 17-foot screen height (see FIGURE 44) the 1.85:1 frame is magnified 208 thousand times. For the same height the anamorphic frame will provide 30% *more* screen area with *lower* magnification of only 163 thousand. The reduced magnification resulting from the 60% larger print area will project a significantly superior image. Dirt and scratches will be less noticeable and apparent grain will be similarly reduced. Of equal importance is the fact that longer focal length projection lenses are employed with the anamorphic system. The 1.85:1 projector must use a short focal length (wide angle) lens in order to fill the wide screen with the small print image. As a result the back focus distance is more critical, and any "breathing" in the gate will be projected as a most annoying in/out focus syndrome. The anamorphic print requires less magnification and, thus, a longer focal length projection lens which will minimize the effects of breathing. The 'scope print will produce an all-around image that is superior to that of any other 35mm format.

The bottom line in making any format selection is the application. One can extol the virtures of the many formats—yet, the application will usually be the determining factor. If the application happens to be a low budget feature that will most likely play in small neighborhood

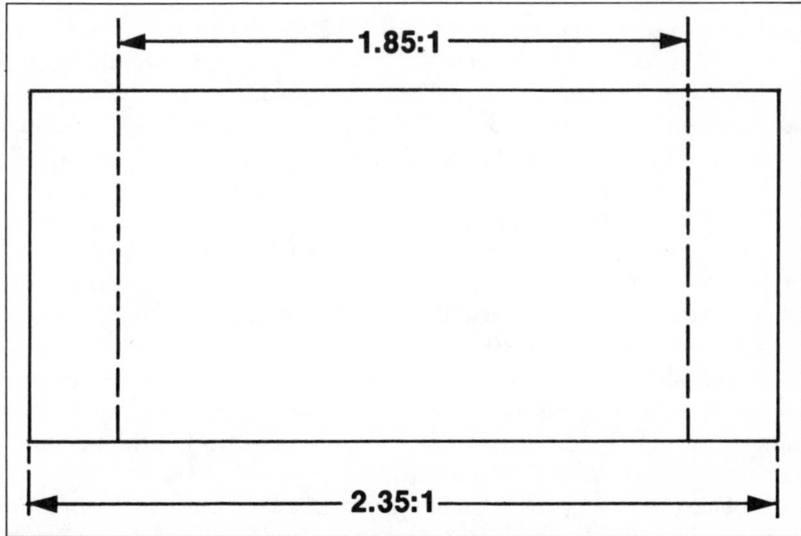

FIGURE 44—Diagram showing comparison of wide-screen (1.85:1) and anamorphic (2.35:1) aspect ratios. Based on a 17-foot screen-height, the 1.85:1 frame is magnified 208 thousand times. For the same height, the anamorphic frame will provide 30% more screen area with a lower magnification of only 163 thousand. The reduced magnification resulting from the 60% larger print area will project a significantly superior image.

theatres and the 2.35:1 ratio of 'scope is desirable, then there is an additional format that could be considered: Techniscope.

TECHNISCOPE

The basic drawback of flat wide-screen systems is the inherent waste of film stock. Almost 40% of the negative area remains unused in the 1.85:1 format. The anamorphic system reclaims this waste, utilizing 100% of the available negative area, and produces a significantly superior projected image. Higher budget productions which are usually released into large theatres with long throws benefit greatly from the large image area of the anamorphic format. However, there is another, more economical alternative to the wasteful 1.85:1 wide-screen format: Techniscope.

A quick look back at the anamorphic process will help explain the Techniscope principle. The C'scope aperture utilizes the full available image area, which is a height of .746″, representing a pulldown of four perforations, and a width of .868″, which is the maximum distance between perforations on the one side and the soundtrack on the other. These dimensions yield an aspect ratio of 1.18:1. The C'scope process, in essence, doubles the effective width of the frame with the 2:1 squeeze and, thus, also doubles the aspect ratio to 2.35:1. This same aspect ratio can also be achieved by *halving the height* as opposed to doubling the width. This is precisely what the Techniscope format does. By employing a two-perforation pull-down in lieu of the standard four, the frame height is cut in half, resulting in a dimension of .373″ height by the full .868″ width and yielding the standard C'scope aspect ratio of 2.35:1.

The Techniscope process offers some attractive features along with the obvious limitations. For openers, the system uses standard lenses. Any 35mm lens can be used with the Techniscope format. As a rule, shorter focal-length lenses will be employed with the 2-perf pull-down to achieve the same general vertical composition as Academy or standard flat wide-screen formats. This fact will yield a relatively greater depth of field. Because the pulldown is only 2 perfs in lieu of 4, film moves through the camera at only 45 feet/min instead of the standard 90 feet/min (at 24 fps). Obviously, a roll of film will go twice as far. Raw stock and processing costs are literally cut in half. Only half as much film need be carried around on location. Camera magazines will run twice as long, yielding an effective capacity double that of standard 35mm; 200′ mags can be considered 400′, 400′ as 800′, and 1000′ gets you 2000′. Production can move along quicker with magazine changes occurring with half the normal frequency, or smaller magazines can be employed with usual running times.

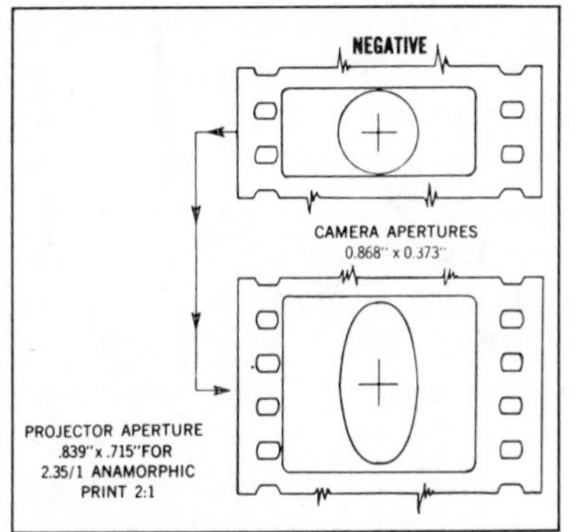

FIGURE 45—Standard printing procedure of original half-frame Techniscope to anamorphic 4-perforation 35mm release print.

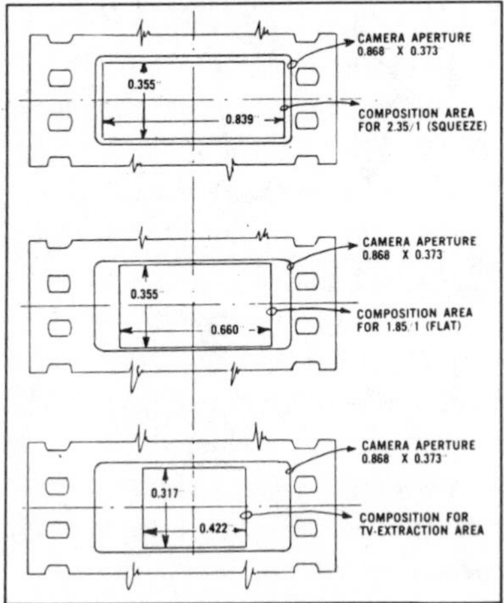

(FROM TOP) FIGURES 46A, 46B, and 46C, showing composition areas for various release formats generated from original 2-perforation Techniscope.

The camera original can be printed in a multitude of formats. Work prints are printed as standard C'scope anamorphic (FIGURE 45), and require no special editing equipment. Some manufacturers make equipment that directly accepts the 2-perf format. Release prints are normally in the standard C'scope process, according to FIGURE 45. The aspect ratios match perfectly, as can be seen in FIGURE 46A. The Techniscope original can also be released in several other formats. With very little cropping, the 2-perf frame can be printed up to flat 70mm. Referring to FIGURES 46B and 46C, the 2-perf frame can be cropped and printed for 1.85:1 flat wide-screen and standard 1.33:1 Academy for television release. Sixteen millimeter release is also possible in both C'scope (FIGURE 46A) and standard 1.33:1 (FIGURE 46C) formats.

The Techniscope process appears very attractive. Standard lenses, 50% savings in raw stock and processing, twice the capacity of magazines, standard C'scope editing and a wide choice of release methods.

There are obviously some major trade-offs. Techniscope uses exactly half the negative area of anamorphic 35mm. A film shot in 35 C'scope uses 100% more image area and need be magnified only half as much as a Techniscope original to fill the same size screen. The anamorphic original will obviously produce a far superior image.

When cropped to a 1.33:1 format, as for television, Techniscope offers little advantage over 16mm. The cropped dimensions of the 2-perf are .373" x .497", about the same as 16mm (.295 x .402), yet the Techniscope uses 170% more raw stock which is mostly waste. FIGURE 47 lists some relevant statistics. Another shortcoming is the scarcity of Techniscope cameras. The newer self-blimped cameras such as the Arri 35BL are not available in the 2-perf pulldown. Special printing techniques are necessary for both workprints and release prints, which could cause hassles.

Despite these drawbacks, the 2-perf system is attractive to the low-budget producer who wants a 2.35:1 format with the tremendous economic advantage of the 2-perf frame. From FIGURE 47, the 1.85:1 flat wide-screen system provides only 27% more image area than Techniscope, yet consumes 100% more raw stock. For some producers, two perfs may be better than four.

The full benefit of Techniscope is obviously realized when the full 2.35:1 aspect ratio is employed. Flat wide-screen 1.85:1 uses an image only 27% larger than Techniscope, yet consumes *100%* more raw stock. The 1.85:1 wastes 36% of its area, the 2-perf format wastes none.

When cropped for 1.85:1, the Techniscope format wastes about 20% of its area. Standard 4-perf 1.85:1, then, encompasses 58% more image area than the 1.85:1 cropped Techniscope, but still consumes 100% more film stock.

If a major release is planned in 1.85:1 rather than 2.36:1 and budget is a major factor, Super 16 would probably make more sense.

When cropped for 1.33:1, the Techniscope format uses only about 50% of its total area, the other half going to waste. The area being used is only 55% greater than standard 16mm, yet the 2-perf 35mm consumes *170%* more film stock.

FIGURE 47

IMAGE AREA	SQ. INCHES
Techniscope 1.85:1	.319
	.407
Techniscope Cropped 1.85:1	.257
Standard 4-perf 1.85:1	.407
Techniscope Cropped 1.33:1	.185
Standard 16mm 1.33:1	.119

SUPER-16

The Super-16 system is, no doubt, the latest of format configurations, having been introduced commercially early in 1970. The pioneers of this format can probably best explain the design concepts. In Sweden, cinematographer Rune Ericson, who was using the 35mm format almost exclusively, was confronted with a project that required traveling around the world for six months with a small documentary-type crew. The project did not seem possible in 35mm, considering the size and weight of cameras, magazines, and film stock. Yet, Ericson was wary of a 16mm blow-up, especially due to the area wasted by the cropping necessary to achieve the 1.66:1 ratio for European wide-screen 35mm projection. Ericson conceived the idea of extending the width of the 16mm frame into the area normally reserved for the soundtrack. By doing so, he established an aspect ratio of 1.66:1 which required no cropping to fill a 35mm 1.66 blow-up. The tremendous increase in usable negative area and the resulting improvement in visual quality was great enough to make Super-16 a viable alternative for shooting a low-budget or documentary-style feature for ultimate 35mm wide-screen release.

While size, weight and mobility were Ericson's main concerns, Adrian Mosser of Cineservices in Hollywood was equally concerned with the monetary advantages of shooting in 16mm. Mosser, a specialist in 16mm-to-35mm blow-ups, was well aware of the financial and aesthetic advantages of the smaller format. Yet, like Ericson, he was struck with the inherent waste of the wide-screen crop on the already miniature format. In an effort to improve the quality of his 35mm blow-ups, Mosser also envisioned a wide-aspect ratio 16mm format.

This little historical retrospective of Super-16 began by mentioning 1970 as the introduction date of the wide-ratio 16mm format. This is most significant. At that time there were several self-blimped 16mm hand-held cameras, while no such instrument was available in the 35mm format. The Panaflex and Arri 35BL were still under development. The year 1970 also marked the introduction of the new fine-grain ECO 7252, as well as the new CRI color reversal internegative. All these facts enhanced the already attractive advantages of the newly introduced "Super-16" format.

Now, down to cold facts. First off, the term "Super-16" is somewhat of a misnomer. "Super-8" provides 50% more image area than regular 8 by employing narrower sprocket holes, thereby increasing frame width. Moreover the *pitch* of the film is proportionately increased to *maintain the same aspect ratio* (1.37:1). Super-8 has fewer frames per foot and, subsequently, less running time than a given length of regular 8. The so-called Super-16 does not modify sprocket holes, nor does it change pitch, but merely increases the width of the frame to establish a wider aspect ratio. The names "Wide Ratio 16", "Hi Aspect 16", or simply "Wide Screen 16" would have been more appropriate and descriptive. However, "Super 16" is, in any case, undoubtedly more in keeping with the American vernacular.

What is important here is not the name, but the fact that Super-16 has a very limited and specific application: namely, the ultimate blow-up to a wide screen 35mm release of 1.66:1 ratio or greater. The Super-16 format offers no advantage whatsoever if the final release ratio is 1.33:1, as for television (16 or 35). As a matter of fact, a 1.33:1 release from a Super-16 original will suffer, due to the optical step necessary to crop off the additional frame-width symmetrically from each side. A standard 16 original is merely contact-printed and will not suffer any unnecessary degradation.

Now that we know what it isn't, let's take a look at what Super-16 really buys you. The standard 16mm camera aperture is .295″ x .404″, yielding an area of .119 in^2 at an aspect ratio of 1.37:1. When this is blown-up to 35mm wide screen it must be cropped, as in FIGURE 48, yielding areas of .098 in^2 (1.66) and .088 in^2 (1.85).

The Super-16 format increases the width of the frame into the sound-track area. The resulting .488″ width and the full standard height of .295″ nets an area of .144 in^2 at an aspect ratio of 1.66:1. This represents an increase of 47% more image-area over regular 16 cropped for the 1.66:1 ratio. To achieve the 1.85 ratio more popular in the U.S., the Super-16 frame height must still be cropped, but only to .263″ netting an area of .128 in^2. This represents an increase of 46% more image-area than regular 16 cropped for 1.85 wide screen.

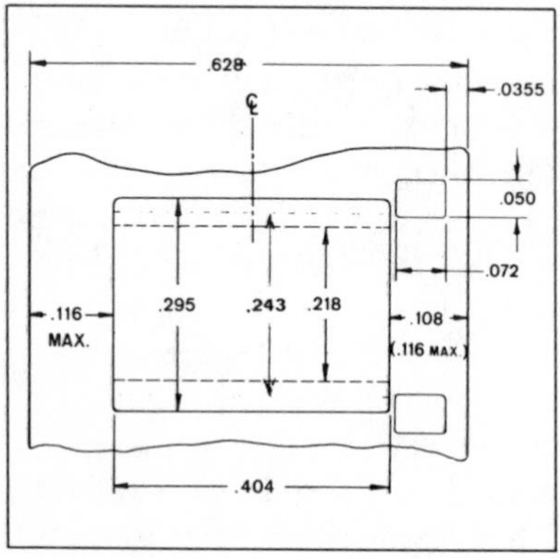

FIGURE 48—Regular 16mm. Notice that height is cropped from .295″ to .243″ for 1.66:1 and to .218″ for 1.85:1. This represents a waste of 18% and 26% respectively.

The greatest advantage of Super-16 is realized with a projection ratio of 1.66:1 where the "original-to-screen" magnification ratio will be least, resulting in the best projected image quality. Still, at the 1.85 ratio the Super-16 format offers almost 50% more image area than cropped regular 16mm. In this respect the wide-ratio 16mm format may justify its name "Super".

Super-16 is not just a camera format, but a complete system, and in addition to its assets, it does have some drawbacks.

For openers, the Super-16 conversion of a standard camera is quite an extensive operation. As an example, an Eclair NPR requires modification in no fewer than 14 different areas. Most obvious is the increased size of the aperture. The viewfinder must also be modified and, most critical, the optical axis of the lens must be shifted laterally. This lens-mount displacement makes a modified Super-16 camera unsuitable for standard 16mm. Thus, once a camera is converted for Super-16 it can no longer be used for the regular 16mm format. Moreover, only certain cameras can be modified to Super-16. The Arriflex 16BL, for instance, is not suitable for Super-16 conversion. Most often the Arriflex 16SR, Aäton or Eclair ACL/NPR cameras are chosen, although some of the Auricon-type cameras have also been successfully converted. Each magazine of an Eclair camera must also be modified. The rollers and film guides must be undercut so as not to scratch the film in the former soundtrack area.

This brings up an important point. The handling of Super-16 footage from the camera through development, editing, and printing, is a hairy matter, to say the least. The image area extends almost to the edge of the film opposite the sprocket holes. This leaves *very* little room for film handling. In the camera, care must be taken that the film does not breathe in the gate and, as mentioned above, rollers and guides must be precisely undercut to avoid damaging the film in the formerly unused

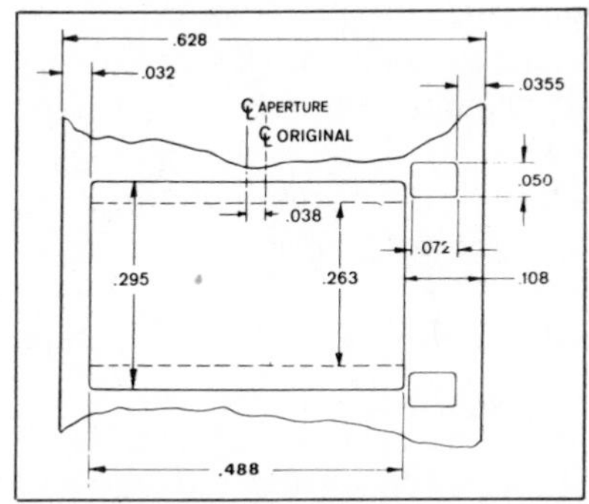

FIGURE 49—Super-16. Width of frame is increased to .488″. Note that left edge is reduced to .032″ from the standard .116″ in FIGURE I. The height must still be cropped to .263″ for the 1.85:1 format. The full frame (.488″ x .295″) yields a ratio of 1.66:1.

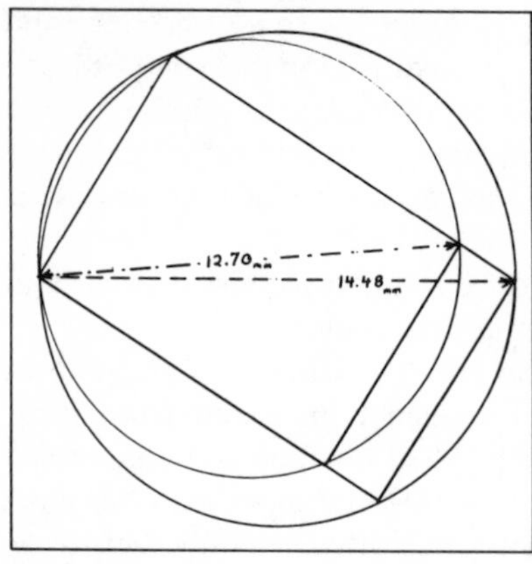

FIGURE 50—The Super-16 aperture has a diagonal of 14.48mm, which is significantly larger than the diagonal of standard 16mm (12.70mm). For this reason, standard 16mm cine zoom lenses will not cover the larger Super-16 format.

and unprotected area. This narrow edge also causes handling problems throughout the processing, editing, and printing of the film. The extended film area is very vulnerable to scratching and few labs are equipped to properly handle Super-16 footage.

To make matters worse, there are few zoom lenses suitable for Super-16 use. From FIGURE 50 it can be seen that the diagonal for the wide-screen 16mm is 14.48mm, while that for standard 16mm is only 12.70mm. As a result, most standard 16mm cine lenses will not cover the Super-16 aperture. Lenses designed for the 35mm format will obviously cover the Super-16 aperture, but the large size and weight will negate the inherent advantage of the wide-screen 16 system. The lens situation is improving. The "Zeiss Super Speeds, for example, *will* cover the Super-16 format.

On the practical level, Super-16 is not all peaches and cream; special cameras with limited application, special costly lenses from a limited selection, potential problems of scratching, and, in general, a format that is difficult to handle—and exhibiting all the problems of a non-standard format. Financially the picture is not rosy either. Because Super-16 requires special attention throughout production, lab fees usually run higher than regular 16mm. The biggest bite is the liquid-gate optical blow-up to 35mm which is no cheap endeavor. Lastly, a price tag must be put on the inevitable time, effort, and aggravation that is always encountered whenever attempting to create a 35mm image from a 16mm frame. As a result, the financial advantages of Super-16 are not clearly apparent.

Lastly, the size and weight advantages of Super-16 are now disputable since the introduction of lightweight hand-held 35mm self-blimped cameras such as the Arriflex 35BL and the Panaflex. So where does that leave Super-16 at the present time?

It appears that under normal circumstances the advantages of shooting Super-16 over 35mm are dubious at best. Once the pros and cons are balanced, the 35mm format will most likely involve less hassles and an obviously superior image. The one exception would be a documentary-style film for theatrical release involving the transport of equipment and film into remote and inaccessible locations, such as jungles or mountaintops. Here the savings in size and weight of equipment and *film* justify the inherent problems and limitations of Super-16. However, in most other situations, a careful analysis of cost and quality may suggest a 35mm production.

FIGURE 51—Regular 16 versus Super 16

Regular 16mm	Aspect Ratio	Dimensions	Area	%Waste
	1.37:1	.404 x .295	.119	0
	1.66:1	.404 x .243	0.98	18%
	1.85:1	.404 x .218	.088	26%
Super 16	**Aspect Ratio**	**Dimensions**	**Area**	**%GREATER AREA THAN REG. 16mm**
	1.66:1	.488 x .295	.144	47%
	1.85:1	.488 x .263	0.128	46%

CINERAMA

An old friend recently wrote me a letter containing a small piece of 35mm film he had found among some ancient scraps at an editing house. It was a standard piece of 35mm motion picture film, except that the color image was six perforations high instead of the more normal four perforations. What kind of format was this?

Since the 1890s there must have been over 100 different film formats. Film widths included 3mm, 8mm, 9½mm, 11mm, 13mm, 17mm, 17½mm, 18mm, 22mm, 24mm, 26mm, 28mm, 30mm, 35mm, 50mm, 62mm, 63mm and 65mm to name a few. Perforations were round, square, oblong or slots and ran on one edge, both edges, down the center or a combination thereof. The number of perforations per frame exhibited similar variety. Even before 1898, there were various formats using one, four, five and six perfs per frame, usually on both edges. By the 1920s, two and three perfs per frame were also being used, thus running the full gamut from one to six perfs per frame.

Formats

Most interesting is the lack of chronological progression in format development. Some of the earliest formats were strikingly similar to the most modern now in use. For example, in 1897 the Veriscope Co used a 63mm stock with a five-perf pull-down that is not unlike Todd-A-O or Super Panavision 70. By the early 1900s, four-perf, 35mm formats, similar to our current standard, were already being used.

·All this variety and lack of chronological development would seem to make the identification of a particular sample of film difficult. However, such is not the case. In most instances identification is quite simple. There is usually some distinctive characteristic or combination of factors that pin point a specific format. The sample I received was no exception. The giveaway was the aspect ratio, which was less than one; that is, the frame was higher than it was wide (due, of course, to the six perf pull-down). The piece of film had to be from a Cinerama release.

Of all formats employed for general release over the almost 100 years of motion picture history, Cinerama has to be one of the most unique and interesting. Cinerama employed three divergent cameras covering a horizontal viewing angle of 146 degrees. Theatrical release required three separate divergent projectors that formed a single composite image on a deeply curved screen comprised of over-lapping vertical strips. The overall aspect ratio was 2.59:1. However, the effective viewing aspect ratio for most of the audience was somewhat less, due to the deep curvature of the screen.

FIGURE 52 tells the complete technical story of Cinerama. The original Cinerama format called for a frame rate of 26 fps. Note that there is no provision for a sound track. Sound was reproduced from a separate seven-track 35mm magnetic film transport. Five of the tracks fed a five-speaker system spread out behind the screen, while the remaining two tracks fed speakers located to the left and right of the audience. Additional speakers to the rear of the theater could be cued according to action on the screen.

The three-camera shooting system for Cinerama has long been abandoned. Toward the end, some Cinerama productions were shot with a single 65mm camera and 1.25 squeeze (Ultra Panavision 70), then optically printed onto three 35mm strips for projection in Cinerama theaters. As Cinerama theaters abandoned the three projector system, the 65mm original would then be printed on a single 70mm release with integral six-track magnetic sound. The print was usually made optically, employing a special "rectifying" optic to reduce elongation of the image that would normally occur at the extremities of the deeply curved Cinerama screen. Likewise, earlier Cinerama three-camera productions could be reduced onto a single 70mm release in this same manner for

FIGURE 52
CINERAMA

27MM LENS
Angular Field Coverage — Camera Aperture

Horizontal 146° **Vertical 55½°**

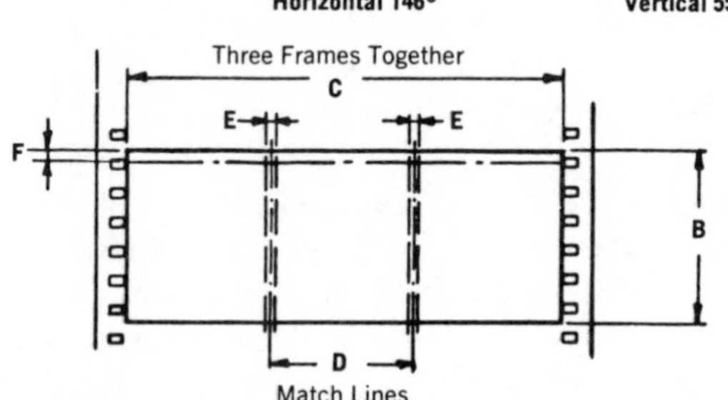

C 2.895" To Perforations
D 0.9478" Between Match Lines
E 0.051" Overlap From Perforations
F 0.062" Keep Important Composition Below This Line.

CAMERA ASPECT RATIO 2.59 to 1

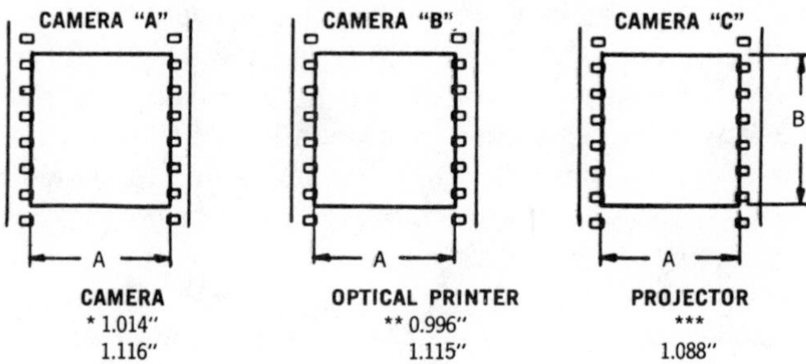

	CAMERA	OPTICAL PRINTER	PROJECTOR
A	* 1.014"	** 0.996"	***
B	1.116"	1.115"	1.088"

NOTES:
* Runs into perforations.
** Special Acme Head 0.985"
*** Because of vignetting "gigolos" projector aperture width is meaningless. There is no specification.

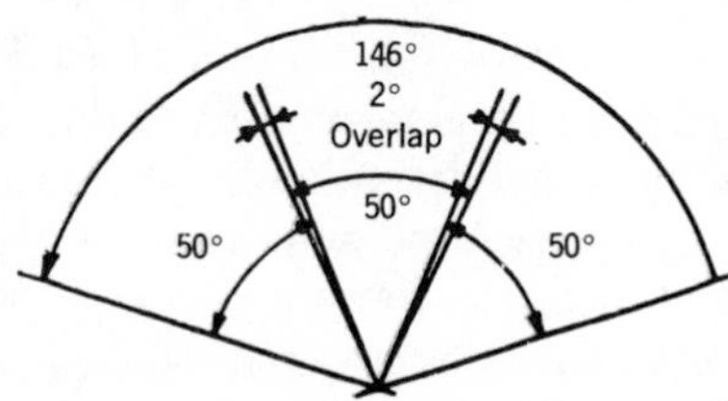

projection in theaters no longer equipped with the three divergent projectors.

To my mind there has never been a more impressive general release format. I can still recall Lowell Thomas introducing the original Cinerama, and then clutching the arms of the seat as the rollercoaster began its downward plunge.

48FPS—A NEW STANDARD?

There has recently been some new experimentation with frame rates higher than 24fps in order to achieve sharper and higher quality images. Some of the proposed alternatives are seriously attempting to challenge the long incumbent 24fps. In light of this renewed interest in higher frame rates, a discussion of the topic seems appropriate.

The physiological phenomenon of "persistence-of-vision" is largely responsible for the existence of motion pictures. The human visual mechanism retains an image for a fraction of a second, thus enabling rapidly changing successive images to blend into a continuum. It was found that the perception of continuous motion could be achieved with frame rates as low as 12fps, but the effect was not natural. At frame rates of 16 or 18fps the sensation of motion becomes more natural and at 24fps the sensation of continuous motion is, for all intents and purposes, complete. The current evidence suggests that frame rates higher than 24fps will *not* significantly improve image quality in terms of the persistence-of-vision phenomenon. However there are other factors that enter into the discussion.

While 24fps is sufficient to achieve the perception of continuous motion, it still suffers from a prominent "flicker motion". This is due to an interesting phenomenon called the "critical flicker frequency" (CFF). The CFF is the frequency at which a pulsating light source or image appears continuous. Specifically, consider a rotating disk that is half-black and half-white. The disk is covered, with the exception of a small window. As the disk spins increasingly faster, a point will eventually be reached where the eye can no longer perceive the changing tone and the window will appear a smooth continuous grey. This point is the CFF. While the CFF is dependent on brightness to a certain extent, the CFF at standard screen illumination turns out to be about 48 images per second. Thus, while 24fps is sufficient to achieve a continuity of motion, 48 images per second is necessary to remove the perception of flicker.

This last criterion is easily made with the twin-bladed projector shutter. Almost every professional projector has a double-bladed shutter;

one blade closes the projector beam as the frame is being advanced, while the second blade merely interrupts the existing frame for a similar period of time. In essence, each frame is projected twice. The image rate is 48fps, while the frame rate is 24fps. Thus, the CFF of 48fps and the persistence of vision rate of 24fps are both satisfied. What then can be achieved by increasing the frame rate?

The 24fps frame rate with a nominal 180° yields an exposure time of about 1/50 sec. As any still photographer can tell you, this is a marginally slow speed, especially if any action is involved. Moderate action usually calls for at least 1/125 or 1/250 sec., while fast sports-type action usually demands a speed of 1/500 or 1/1000 sec. to assure a sharp image. In comparison, the 1/50 sec. cine exposure seems inadequate, to say the least. Frame-by-frame analysis of even the most simple actions will reveal a blurred recording at 24fps.

A logical solution often suggested is a smaller shutter angle. A 90° shutter will provide an effective exposure of about 1/100 sec. but this solution is unacceptable. It must be realized that the nominal 180° shuttered camera records only one-half of all the action. This may seem academic, but the camera misses half of all the action taking place in front of the lens. It chops time into little pieces of 1/50 sec. and then only records every other one on the frame, skipping the intervening pieces of action. The shutter blade on the projector is much smaller, as the projector pulldown is much quicker than that of the camera. In broad relative terms, the projected image is almost "on" continuously. Thus a picture that really only captured 1/48 sec. of action is projected on the screen for almost a full 1/24 sec. and is meant to represent a full 1/24 sec. of action. While this seems to be acceptable to a greater or lesser extent, the 90° shutter situation is not. The 90° shutter only captures 25% of the action and totally misses the other 75%. It chops time into pieces of about 100th sec. duration, recording every fourth piece and skipping the other three in between. When projected, this little piece of action appears on the screen for almost a full 1/24 sec. and is made to represent a piece of time four times longer than it really is. The eye is asked to fill in the 75% missing action while given only the 25% that the image actually captured.. Clearly the eye rebels. While the images will be sharper due to the faster shutter speed the results are very jerky and strobescopic. The results become increasingly aggravated with progressively shorter shutter angles.

The 48fps proposal incorporating a nominal 180° shutter appears to be a viable solution. The 48fps rate provides a shutter speed of 1/100 sec., yet still captures 50% of the action. Each frame is much sharper, due to the increased shutter speed, yet there is no tendency to strobing that is associated with the 90° shutter. Moreover, proponents argue that despite the fact that 24fps is theoretically sufficient, the 48fps rate also provides a smooth and more natural sensation of motion.

The results speak for themselves. Almost everyone who has previewed these new systems has raved about the superior quality of the images. Yet the system has its obvious drawbacks. Film and processing costs double, film magazines become effectively half the normal capacity necessitating twice the number of magazine changes, and the effective speed of the film is essentially halved. Is the increased quality worth the price? Unfortunately, most people in the front office will probably answer in the negative.

An interesting point to ponder is the coupling of 48fps frame rate to the TECHNISCOPE format. Costs and magazine capacities would remain the same as standard 24fps. Only the effective film ASA would still be reduced. However, I would be inclined to believe that anyone attempting to achieve the increased benefits of the 48fps rate would not want to compromise the negative area of the image. Maybe this would be a good time to introduce the very practical 1:1.85 three-perf pulldown with a 48fps frame rate. This would provide the full 1:1.85 negative area the full benefit of the 48fps, yet with only a 50% increase in cost and only a 33% reduction in magazine capacity. I am not going to hold my breath.

FILM VS TELEVISION ASPECT RATIO

I refuse to watch recently released motion pictures on television. Many of my friends consider this attitude quite snobby or elitist, to say the least. However, when friends mention the fact that they have just watched the movie on television, I always ask them when will they watch the other two-thirds of the movie which they have missed. This usually produces a perplexed look, which is always followed by a request to explicate. It is then, with fiendish glee and a touch of cinematic sadism, that I begin my explanation, knowing that I will irreparably impair the listener's ability to ever again fully enjoy a movie on television.

Almost every American film shot for theatrical release uses one of the wide-screen formats; either 1.85:1, 35mm Anamorphic, 70mm, or ULTRA 70mm (1.25 squeeze). Television has an aspect ratio of 1.33:1, the so-called Academy format. It is quite obvious that the wide aspect ratio formats will have to be butchered somewhat to fit the relatively square 1.33:1 format. However, there is more whittling away of the original cut than meets the eye.

Cropping the wide screen image to fit the 1.33:1 ratio is only step one. The broadcast industry is very conservative and they want to make sure that they don't transmit the edge of the projector aperture plate, so they don't quite scan the entire projector aperture. This smaller area is called the "Television Transmitted Area" or "Scanned Area" and usually represents approximately a 6% loss in negative area.

The most cruel cut of all is inflicted in the viewer's home by the television receiver. All manufacturers incorporate a certain amount of "overscan" in their television sets. This means that the scanning circuits blow up the image as if the picture tube were larger than it really is. In reality the smaller picture tube "crops" the image much like an 8″ x 10″ frame on an 11″ x 14″ photograph. The manufacturer does this to insure that the home viewer will never have to encounter those sinister black blanking areas that surround the transmitted picture. This black area that surrounds the picture is deemed so repulsive that manufacturers add from 9% to 15% of horizontal overscan to make absolutely certain that the viewer never need be subjected to the horrible sight of blanking area even under the most adverse conditions such as "brown-outs" or low voltage mains. Assuming proportional amounts of vertical overscan yields a picture area loss of from 15% to 25% in addition to the loss due to the wide-screen format being cropped. In other words, even an old vintage movie shot in the 1.33:1 format will lose 20% to 30% of its picture area by the time it gets to the home screen. Thus, you only get to see 70% to 80% of your favorite old movie on television. If this sounds like you are getting cheated, you ain't seen nothing yet!

Meanwhile, back at the wide-screen, this 20% to 30% loss must be added to the losses suffered by cropping the wide format back to 1.33:1. The final score may be shocking. The figures in FIGURE 53 are based on the "TV Safe Action Area" and "TV Safe Title Area" convention, as standardized by the broadcasting industry. The "TV Safe Action Area" represents a horizontal overscan of approximately 11%, which is about average or a little better than average for most home receivers. The "TV Safe Title Area" figures represent a "worst case" overscan condition. Most home receivers will fall somewhere between these two figures, more likely closer to the safe action area. (A small minority of sets may even exhibit losses slightly less than the TV Safe Action Area figures.)

In actuality, if a recent movie was shot 1.85:1, the home viewer is seeing only 41% to 53% of the movie he would have seen projected in a theater. The figures are worse for Anamorphic (Panavision, CinemaScope). Here the viewer only sees 32% to 41% of the theater projected image, but the *coup de grace* is dealt to Ultra-Panavision 70, where the television screen allows the viewer only a mere peek at 28% to 35% of

FIGURE 53—Picture area losses of wide screen formats relative to "TV Safe Action Area" and "TV Safe Title Area"

	1.85:1 Wide Screen	70mm	Anamorphic CinemaScope Panavision	Ultra 70mm (1.25 squeeze)
TV Safe Action Area	47%	56%	59%	65%
TV Safe Title Area	59%	65%	68%	72%

Percentages above are *lost* area

the theatrical image, missing a good two-thirds of the film as it was projected in theaters.

In practical terms, there are many techniques that the broadcasters use to offset these losses. Major films are reprinted in special TV versions where the action is optically followed like a pan. Or a wide-screen "two shot" may be cut into alternating left and right "one shots". Moreover, many films shot with TV distribution in mind employ a full-frame camera aperture with both 1.85:1 and 1.33:1 markings in the camera viewfinder. By keeping all pertinent action within the 1.85 markings, yet keeping the 1.33 area clean of microphone booms and the like, the final print can be used for 1.85:1 theatrical distribution, as well as TV

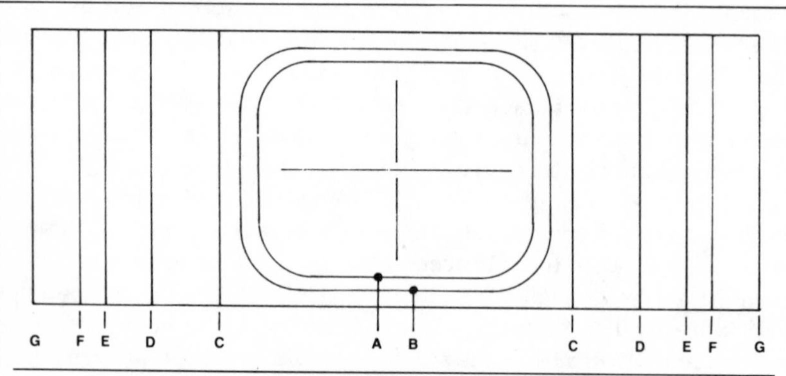

FIGURE 54—Relative Areas of TV and Theatrical Film Formats, Drawn to Scale

A—TV Safe Title Area
B—TV Safe Action Area
C—1.33:1 Projection Aperture
D—1.85:1 Projection Aperture
E—70mm Projection Aperture
F—Anamorphic (CinemaScope, Panavision) Effective Projection Aperture
G—Ultra 70mm (1.25 squeeze) Effective Projection Aperture

distribution, without any additional cropping. Most cinematographers do not like to shoot with this technique and prefer a hard 1.85 matte in the camera. The hard matte precludes composition errors that could occur if a projectionist or optical printer does not center the frame properly. In any case, all these techniques bastardize the original integrity and mood of the film and, while it may make the film easier to view on TV, the percentage of missing image remains almost the same. If 50 girls are in the chorus line of a CinemaScope picture, the home viewer is only going to see 20 to 25 of them any way you slice it.

So that's why I never watch recent movies on TV. I figure that since I will have to go to the theater to see the other two-thirds anyway, I might as well see the whole thing in the theater at once. Besides, that little box in my living room ain't nothing like the Big Wide Silver Screen. Popcorn anyone?

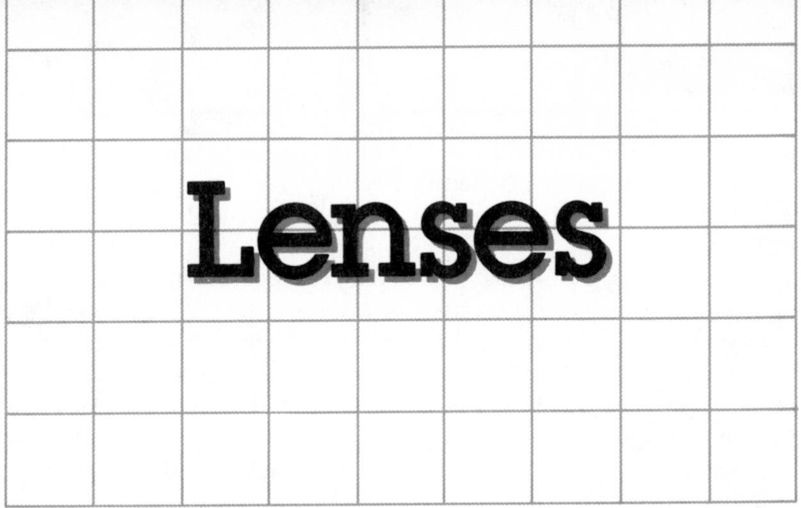

THE CARE OF LENSES

The lens is one of the most delicate components of a motion picture or video camera. By adhering to several basic rules of lens care, the cinematographer can be assured of optimum performance from his optics.

The first rule of lens care is to clean a lens as *in*frequently as possible. All professional lenses have a very thin anti-reflective coating on the front element. Repeated cleaning will eventually wear away this coating and impair the quality of the image. Therefore, precautions should be taken to preclude the necessity of cleaning a lens. A lens cap should be used whenever the lens is not in use; fingers should be kept off the front surface; etc. In most cases where a lens appears dirty, a camels hair brush can remove most particles and cleaning with a tissue is unnecessary. Dust particles on the lens do not affect image quality and the cameraman should not be overly concerned about them.

A fingerprint on the front element is one of the few cases that demands instant cleaning of the lens. The body oils in the print will tend to etch the lens coating if not removed immediately. However, before touching a lens tissue to a lens, dust particles *must* first be removed with a camels hair brush. If a tissue were applied to a lens that had not been brushed, the dust particles on the lens would adhere to the tissue, and the combination would not be unlike sandpaper.

Use a name-brand lens cleaner, as off-brands usually have a high alcohol content which tends to streak upon drying. Hold the lens perfectly upright and place one drop of cleaner in the center of the element. Immediately spread the cleaner with the tissue using circular motions. Do not allow the cleaner to drip down the element to the side of the lens. For best results the tissue should be rolled up like a cigarette and then torn in half. The frayed ends should be used for cleaning. Do not use anything but a lens tissue for cleaning; other fabrics may appear soft to the touch, but actually contain stiff fibers that can scratch the lens coating.

Lenses are very vulnerable to vibration. If a lens (either on the camera or separate) is carried in the truck of a car or other vehicle, the vibrations will soon loosen and shift the elements causing severe degradation of quality. It is best to keep lenses and cameras in foam shock-absorbing cases. When traveling by car or plane, keep your lenses (and camera if possible) with you, either on the seat or, if this is not possible, under it.

Lenses are also adversely affected by extreme heat. All lenses consist of some cemented elements. This lens cement melts at elevated temperatures and can begin to soften at temperatures above 100°F. If the cement is allowed to soften, air bubbles can form between elements, and the elements can shift relative to one another. Lenses should therefore be protected from high temperatures where possible. If a lens has been subjected to temperatures above 100°F, extreme care should be taken not to shake, jolt or vibrate the lens. While the cement is in the softened condition, the elements can be shifted out of place by the least jar or vibration.

Cleanliness is the most important word in lens care, and this applies to the lens seat as well as the optical surfaces. The focus calibration on a lens is dependent on an exact flange-to-focal-plane distance. That is, a lens must seat an exact distance from the focal plane of the camera. That part of the lens that mates with the camera and determines this distance is called the "flange." (FIGURE 55) If dirt or grit builds up in this surface, the lens will not seat properly and the flange-to-focal plane distance will be elongated. On certain lenses a change of as little as a thousandth of an inch can cause noticeable degradation of quality or soft focus. Every time a lens is placed on a camera, the flange surfaces

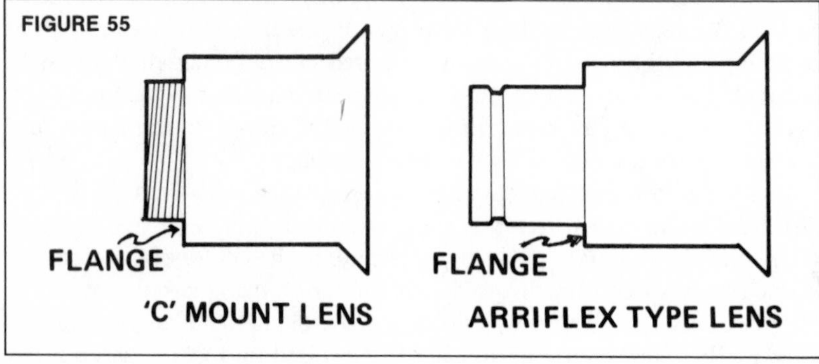

on both the lens and the camera should be cleaned with a cloth, preferably dampened with a mild solvent.

If one remembers that everything that ends up on the film must be "funneled" through the *lens* and that the image can be only as sharp as the *lens* allows, then the prime importance of proper lens care becomes glaringly evident.

ZOOM LENSES

The care and maintenance procedures for fixed focal-length lenses apply without exception to zoom lenses. The zoom lens, however, has several sets of moving elements that enable it to change focal-length over a wide range. Moreover, the lens must maintain a constant focus and relative aperture, as the focal-length is varied. The mechanical and optical components that accomplish these functions are quite complex and, thus, an additional set of rules is necessary for the proper use and maintenance of the zoom lens.

The first rule is always use "T" stops for aperture settings. "T" stops should be used for fixed focal-length lenses also, but with a zoom lens it is mandatory. Because of the complex optical arrangement, the zoom lens absorbs and reflects a significant portion of the incident light. The "F" stop does not take this into account, and would, thus, underexpose the film by as much as one stop. The "T" stop calibration is determined by altering the aperture an amount that will, preferably, compensate for the light loss within the lens, assuring accurate exposures.

To obtain consistent results from a zoom lens it *must always be focused at its longest focal-length and maximum aperture*. Failure to follow this most basic rule of the zoom lens has caused much grief for many a cinematographer and producer. Attempting to focus visually at shorter than the maximum focal-length will invariably result in a soft image at longer focal-lengths. If the scene involves panning or following a subject whose distance from the camera is changing, follow-focus techniques can be employed. However, the longer focal-lengths should be avoided if one wishes to achieve maximum sharpness.

In theory, the optical axis of a zoom lens should intersect the film plane at the dead center of the aperture. Even in the best zoom lenses, this criterion is almost impossible to realize. Thus, if an object is centered at a short focal-length, the center will invariably shift as the lens is zoomed in. For such a shot, the object should be centered at the longest focal-length before beginning the take.

The mechanism that moves the zoom elements usually consists of a cam and a follower. While the lens is being transported (whether on a camera or not) any jolt or knock could cause the follower to bang against the cam and create a dent. After this has occurred, every time the lens is zoomed there will be a visible jolt in the image as the follower passes over the dent in the cam. For this reason the zoom lever should always be placed in one of the two extreme positions whenever the lens is being transported. In this way, should a jolt occur, the resulting detent will be at the end of the zoom travel where it cannot jar the image.

The greatest difference between a zoom lens and a fixed focal-length lens lies in their respective focusing mechanisms. The focusing principle of the fixed focal-length lens is ridiculously simple; the entire lens is merely moved in or out relative to the film plane. Thus, for very close work, the lens is moved a distance away from the film plane (via focusing adjustment or extension tubes), and vice versa. It should be apparent that lens seating is not that critical, for as long as the image is focused on ground glass, the results will be sharp. (Lens seating is the relationship between lens and film plane. Focus is defined in the identical manner for a fixed focal-length lens. Thus, one factor can more or less compensate for the other.)

The focus principle for a zoom lens is entirely different and infinitely more complex. Image focusing is accomplished by moving the front lens group only. The main body of the lens and all the remaining elements do not move during the focusing process. The position of the focal plane is determined by the rear lens group, which is factory-adjusted for a specific flange-to-focal-plane distance (lens seating). Almost all of the soft focus problems associated with the zoom lenses can invariably be traced to faulty lens seating. (Improper back-focus.)

The rear element of the zoom lens focuses the image onto the film plane or video tubes. This image is in focus not only at the film plane, but for a certain distance both in front of and behind the film plane. This area of sharp focus is called depth-of-focus. (See FIGURE 56). Like depth-of-field, this distance varies with focal-length. However, it does

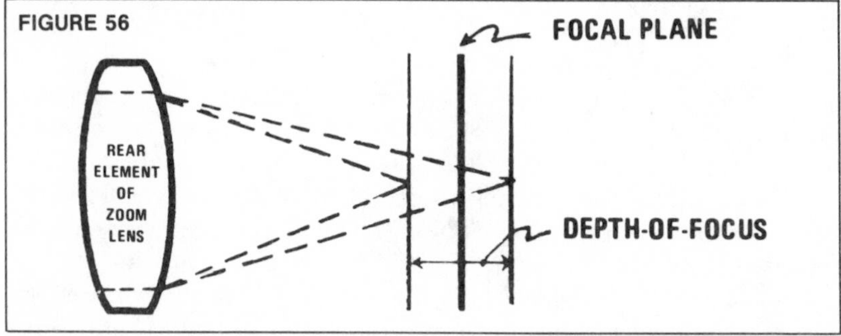

so inversely; that is, depth-of-focus is maximum for long focal-lengths and smallest for short focal-lengths.

At long focal-lengths, where the depth of focus is great, it is possible for a lens to be improperly seated and still have the film plane fall within the area of sharp focus (See FIGURE 57A) However, as the lens is zoomed to a shorter focal-length and the area of sharp focus narrows, the film plane may now fall outside this area and the image will then go soft. (See FIGURE 57B) This is why the image may appear sharp while focusing (long focal-length) and then appear soft at the shorter focal-lengths. To be specific, the depth-of-focus at short focal lengths (9.5mm–12mm) and maximum apertures is typically less than 1 mil. (.001″). Thus, *any* play between lens and camera, or any least bit of dirt on the lens or camera flanges, can impair image quality. Moreover, there is no way to compensate for this condition with the front-focus adjustment of the lens. (See "adjusting back focus" in the video chapter, page 287.)

Conventional lens mounts were never designed to hold such close tolerances (or such large and heavy lenses) and it is for this reason that most of the professional camera manufacturers (Arriflex, Eclair, Mitchell, etc.) have introduced special heavy-duty bayonet mounts specifically for zoom lenses. These mounts assure that there is absolutely

FIGURE 57

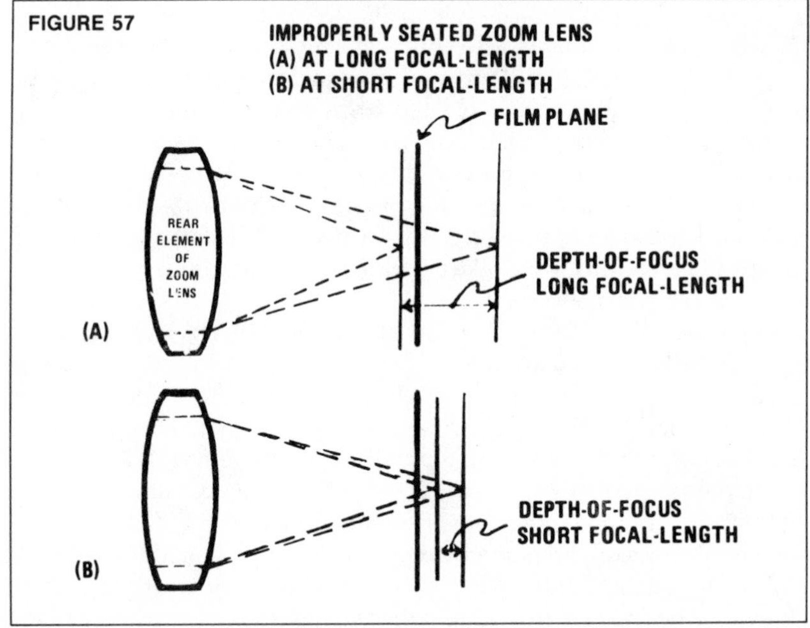

no play between camera and lens. Of course all ENG/EFP video cameras employ special heavy duty zoom lens mounts. Those cinematographers employing large zoom lenses (12mm–120mm or larger) in other than the new bayonet mounts should use some form of external support (cradle) for the lens. In addition, every effort should be made to insure that the lens is seated all the way into the camera. This is particularly important with two-part mounts, such as an Angenieux 12mm–120mm on an Auricon C-mount.

It should be obvious that extension tubes cannot be used with zoom lenses. Diopter lenses can be employed for close-up work with excellent results. They permit the full zoom range to be used and do not require any exposure compensation. (For maximum sharpness, diopters above ½ and 1 should be avoided.)

The use of behind-the-lens filters should also be avoided when employing zoom lenses of extremely short focal-length ranges. A behind-the-lens filter will slightly lengthen the back focus distance of the lens. This slight relocation could place the film plane outside the area of sharp focus at extremely short focal-lengths, thus causing a softening of the image. Cameras with built-in filter wheels have compensated for this shift.

IMAGE SHARPNESS

There are so many different parameters that must be considered when designing a lens and an equally staggering number of variables must be considered when determing the performance of a lens. When evaluating a lens, one must consider chromatic aberration, spherical aberration, astigmatism, acuteness, resolution, contrast and that all encompassing question: "Yeah, but is it sharp?"

Rather than looking at lenses from the designer's point of view (what makes a lens sharp?), we'll take a look from the cameraman's angle (so how come the image is soft?).

The problem of getting a sharp image through the lens has been aggravated by the complexity of the zoom lens. When developing a fixed-focal-length lens, the designer can optimize parameters for the particular focal length. Not so with a zoom lens. The designer of a zoom lens is constantly faced with compromises and trade-offs. It is impossible to design a zoom lens that will compensate all aberrations equally throughout the zoom range. It is true that every zoom lens will exhibit varying degrees of aberration correction as the focal length is changed.

Actually, a zoom lens will display its best compensation at only two or three specific focal lengths. At all other values during the zoom, correction will be plus or minus these optimum parameters. So, if a zoom lens appears to be sharper at certain focal lengths, one may assume it is a problem with the original lens design—right? Not quite.

Rarely can a soft image be blamed on this phenomenon of zoom lens design. Technology has reached the level where these deviations from optimum correction are kept to a minimum and only in rare and exacting circumstances will these deviations be visually apparent. In most cases a less than perfect image is the result of damage to the lens, improper lens seating or improper use of the lens.

In many cases it is within the power of the cameraman to improve the image through the lens. Every lens has an optimum aperture. This is usually between two and three stops down from wide open. For an f/1.8 lens, the optimum aperture would be about f/4. True, there will be greater depth-of-field at smaller apertures, but the image will not be sharper. As the lens is stopped down, a phenomenon known as diffraction begins to degrade the image.

Diffraction occurs around the edge of the iris blades and can best be described as a bending of the light rays. (FIGURE 58). The construction of the iris can affect the amount of diffraction. A better lens will minimize diffraction by incorporating good iris design, optimum materials and fine blade-edge finish. Although the manufacturer can attempt to minimize diffraction, it is always present. And the smaller the aperture, the greater the diffraction effect. Because these peripheral rays are bent where they should be straight, the net result is a softening of the image. The optimum aperture is, thus, a compromise point. At wider apertures, diffraction is less, but aberration correction is not as good. At smaller apertures diffraction softens the image. In general, the best aperture, as previously stated, is two to three stops down from open wide.

The rate of image degradation caused by diffraction is dependent on the focal length of the lens. The physical size of the aperture in a wide angle lens will be smaller than the aperture of a telephoto at the same "f" stop. For example, the aperture of a 10mm lens at f/2 will be ⅛ the size that of an 80mm lens at f/2. It should be obvious, then, that the problem of diffraction will be more severe at shorter focal lengths. The threshold point where diffraction will seriously degrade the image will occur sooner with a wide-angle lens. A cameraman may feel secure stopping a telephoto down to f/11–f/16. However, for a shorter focal length lens, severe diffraction will begin much sooner—at f/8 or f/5.6, depending on focal length.

This boils down to the following: for maximum sharpness, try to film at the optimum aperture. The only reason for stopping down to a smaller aperture would be to gain depth of field, but only at the expense

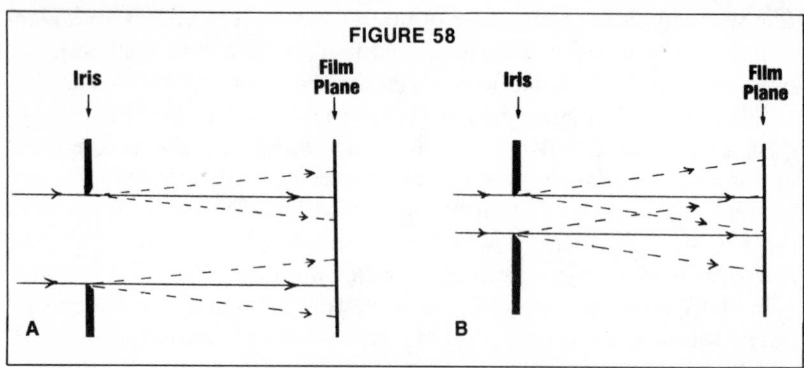

DIFFRACTION: As light passes through the edge of the iris, it begins to propagate as a new spherical wave front emanating from the iris edge. FIGURE 58A shows a bundle of parallel light and two such diffraction rays from each edge. Although diffraction is always present, in FIGURE 58A the diffraction rays are few relative to the bundle of light, but in FIGURE 58B, where the iris opening is much smaller, the diffracted rays now comprise a significant portion of the incoming light. The image will be proportionally impaired.

of overall sharpness. The visual effect of image degradation due to diffraction will be more apparent at shorter focal lengths and, thus, stopping down wide angle lenses to small apertures should be particularly avoided.

These rules hold generally true for zoom lenses, also. If going to a larger aperture aggravates this condition, the cause is more probably improper lens seating, rather than diffraction.

In terms of sharpness, it is generally better to employ neutral density filters than to stop down much past the optimum aperture. However, if not properly done, filtering can hinder, not help, the situation.

OPTICS

A lens is basically a curved piece of glass, not unlike a Coke bottle. So how come a Coke bottle is cheaper? To find the answer to this and other profound mysteries, I contacted my good friend, Paul Foote, at Angenieux Corp. Paul is a living legend in the optical field and is a virtual walking encyclopedia of optical information. He has been involved in motion picture optics longer than I've been alive and can usually shed more light on my optical problems than an f/0.95 lens.

Of course, not everyone asks the above question in so eloquent a fashion. However, the implication is always the same. Why must a lens be so complex and costly, and what is the big deal about forming a simple image? In a word: ABERRATIONS. True, a simple single-element lens, like Sherlock Holmes' famous magnifying glass, will form an image. However, the quality would be totally unacceptable for photographic purposes. The reason is aberrations. The simple single-element lens does not form a perfect image. The image is distorted and impaired by several optical phenomena inherent in a spherical lens element. The more dominant of these imperfections include spherical aberration, coma, astigmatism, field curvature, image distortion, longitudinal and lateral chromatic aberration. After considering all these problems, it's a wonder that a lens can form any image at all. This is where the science of lens design begins; to minimize or cancel these aberrations that are inherent in all optical systems. This topic should be of interest to all motion picture and video cameramen and identifying the various aberrations seems the best place to begin.

Chromatic aberration is probably the easiest to comprehend. Almost everyone has played with a simple prism and is familiar with the fact that white light is broken into all the colors of the rainbow as it passes through a piece of non-parallel glass. This phenomenon results from the fact that glass exhibits different indices of refraction for various wave lengths. Each wave length or color is bent a slightly different amount, which accounts for the color spread or rainbow effect of a prism.

Unfortunately, this same phenomenon occurs in a lens. As a lens forms an image, it affects the various wave lengths by different amounts resulting in two types of aberrations. FIGURE 59 exemplifies "longitudinal chromatic aberration." It is quite evident that the white ray entering the lens is split into color components, as the blue ray is bent to a greater

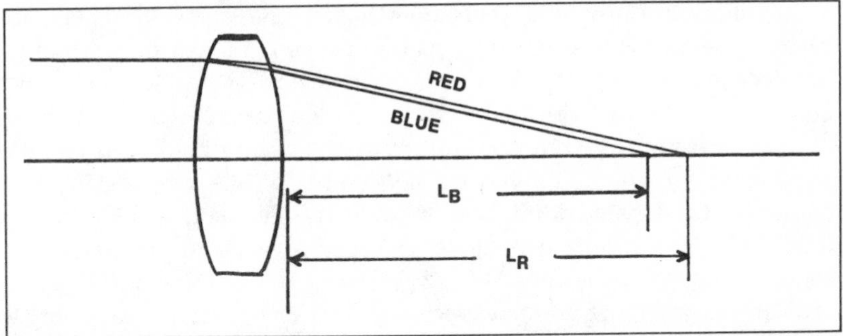

FIGURE 59—Like a prism, a lens will bend various colors by different amounts, resulting in a color spread. As a result, every color will come to focus in its own image plane. This is known as longitudinal chromatic aberration.

degree than the red. As a result, the blue and red components of the image will be focused on *different image planes.* As a matter of fact, every color will have its own image plane. (See FIGURE 60A) Obviously, the film can only be in one plane at a time, and, thus, only one specific color can be in sharp focus, while all the others must be *out of focus* to varying degrees. On color this is noticeable as color fringing, while on black and white stocks the result is generally soft or uncrisp image.

Here is where the complexity and cost of the lens begins its ascension. The lens designer can create a combination of positive and negative lens elements employing glasses of various refractive qualities that will yield a common plane of focus for two specific wave lengths (colors). Such a lens is said to be *achromatic* and is represented in FIGURE 60B. Notice that all wavelengths other than the two chosen still focus outside the film plane. However, the net result is that the maximum deviation from the actual film plane has been reduced from the uncorrected lens of FIGURE 60A.

The third type of lens is the *apochromat,* which corrects for three specific colors, as in FIGURE 60C. Wave lengths other than the chosen three are still focused outside the film plane; yet, the maximum deviation is even less than that of FIGURE 60B. While it appears that the apochromat would be the preferred design, Paul informs me that latest computer-generated achromatic designs are yielding apochromatic quality and correction. This is reflected in FIGURE 60D. The lens is still fully corrected at only two specific colors. However, the curve is much flatter. Those colors that do not fall precisely on the film plane tend to stay closer to the actual plane of focus and the maximum deviation is no more than that of the apochromat (FIGURE 60C).

Longitudinal chromatic aberration is just one problem. There are basically seven types of aberrations that prevent a lens from forming a "perfect" image. These aberrations each distort or impair the image quality in some way. The challenge for the lens designer is to minimize or eliminate such aberrations. This process is quite complex, as correcting one type of aberration may aggravate another. As each aberration is corrected, the lens grows in both complexity and cost. A high-quality, fixed-focal-length lens may have as many as a dozen lens elements arranged in various groups.

While a cameraman is not expected to be a lens designer, the ability to identify lens problems could prove quite helpful. We have looked at longitudinal chromatic aberration. Now we will consider lateral color aberration. It should be made clear that these are two distinct and very different aberrations. Although both phenomena come under the heading of "chromatic aberration," the qualification: *longitudinal* or *lateral,* should always be included.

As previously discussed, longitudinal color results from a shift in back focus distance as a function of wave length (color). This causes various colors to come into focus on different image planes. On the other hand, lateral color is caused by a shift in *focal length* as a function of wave length (color). As a result, images of different colors may lie in

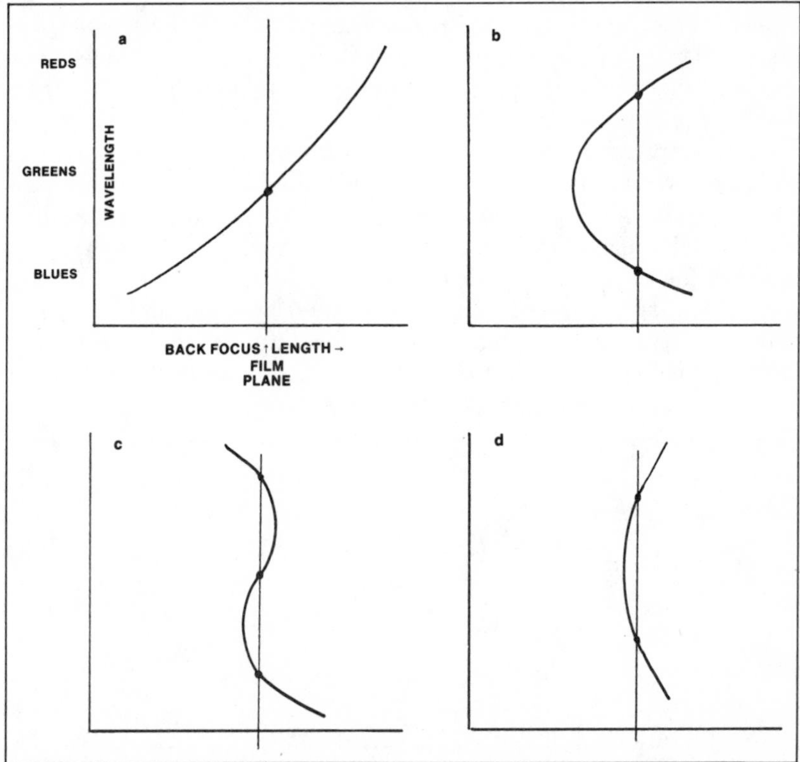

FIGURE 60—(a) A simple lens has no correction for longitudinal chromatic aberration. As a result, the short focal lengths will focus short of the film plane, while the longer wavelengths will focus beyond the image plane. Only one color will be in sharp focus. (b) An "achromatic" lens is corrected for sharp focus at two specific wavelengths. However, wavelengths other than these two will still fall outside the film plane. (c) The "apochromat" is corrected for three specific wavelengths. Even though all other wavelengths are still outside the film plane, the maximum deviation is much less than that of the achromatic lens of 2b. (d) The latest generation of achromatic lenses are still only corrected at two specific colors, as in 2b. However, the maximum deviation has been held to a minimum. As a result, the new achromatic designs exhibit correction on the same order as previous apochromats.

the same focal plane, but will have *different magnifications*. Lateral color is sometimes called *chromatic difference of magnification*, which is a more discriptive label.

FIGURE 61 tells the entire story most graphically. An image with both red and blue components is focused on the film plane. Note that both colors do focus on the same focal plane, indicating that longitudinal color has been fully corrected. However, the focal lengths of the two colors are different. Because of an optical phenomenon, the lens exhibits a longer focal length for red. In the example it is obvious that f_R' is longer than f_B'. If an oblique principal ray is analyzed, it becomes apparent that the image height for the reds (H_R') will be greater than that for the blues (H_B').

Quite simply, if an object is comprised of red and blue components, it will form two images on the same focal plane: a smaller blue image and a larger red one. This phenomenon is visible as color fringing. The effect is most noticeable off axis, as the amount of fringing is directly proportional to the distance from the center of the lens.

Even a small amount of lateral color is quite apparent and objectionable. The lens designer places far greater importance on correcting lateral color. In practice, the tolerances for lateral color are 10 times more stringent than those for longitudinal correction.

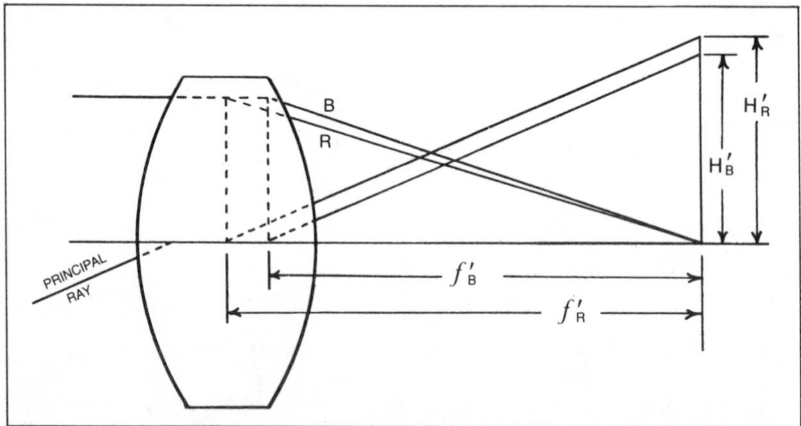

FIGURE 61—The lens appears to have a longer focal length for red than for blue. This phenomenon results in lateral chromatic aberration, which causes greater magnification of the long wave lengths (reds) and less magnification of the short ones (blue). Thus, different colors will be magnified by different amounts, resulting in color fringing off axis. In this example, note that the focal length for red fR′ is greater than that for blue fB′. An oblique principal ray will thus yield a greater image height for the red HR′ than for blue HB′, even though the two heights were obviously the same on the actual object.

These two aberrations are visibly distinguishable. An image suffering from longitudinal color will exhibit color fringing across the entire image area. Moreover, the "quality" of this fringing can be altered by slight adjustments of critical focus (not improved, but merely altered). This is most apparent in a collimator. Lateral color will also be exhibited as color fringing. However, it will be most blatant at the periphery of the frame with very little occuring in the center. It can not be altered with an adjustment of focus, and it will be more noticeable on lines perpendicular to radii.

Field Curvature—The aperture plate and pressure plate of all motion picture cameras are perfectly flat, holding the raw stock precisely in the film *plane*. In video applications the image is also focused onto a plane surface. The key word here is "plane", a flat surface.

Unfortunately, the image of a plane object formed by a simple lens should fall on a curved image surface. This is evident from FIGURE 62. Note that point B of the object is a greater distance from the lens than point A. It follows that B′, the image of B, should fall closer to the lens and have less magnification than A′, the image of A.

This problem is minimized in cheap still cameras by actually curving the film plane and using a simple lens. This was the technique em-

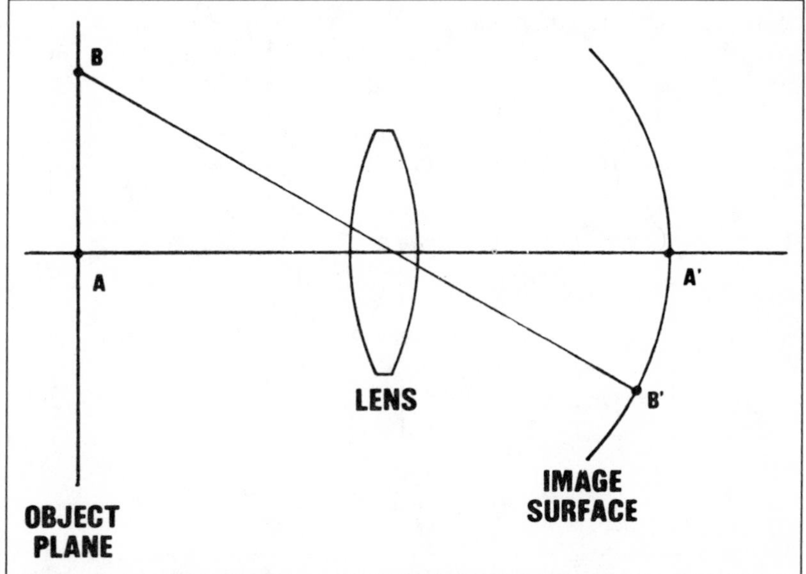

FIGURE 62—FIELD CURVATURE: A simple lens will focus a plane object onto a curved image surface. A good quality photographic lens must correct for this "field curvature," because the film is held in a flat plane.

ployed by Kodak in the design of some of the early Brownie type cameras. However, for motion picture, video and professional still applications, the image is formed on a plane surface and the lens must be specifically designed to minimize field curvature. A field curvature problem is characterized by a sharp focus in the center of the picture area with a gradual softening toward the edges, or vice versa, depending on back focus distance and focus of the lens.

Distortion—The easiest aberration for the cameraman to spot is distortion because it will be blatantly evident right in the viewfinder. Distortion, simply defined, is a change in magnification with field angle. For example, a good lens design should reproduce a square as a square, as shown in FIGURE 63A. Positive distortion will cause the image to get larger at greater field angles. Thus, a point further from the center of the lens will exhibit greater magnification. This is evident in FIGURE 63B, where point B on the square, being a greater distance from the center than point A, is exaggerated outward yielding the obviously distorted square. This is known as *pincushion* distortion. *Negative* distortion produces the exact opposite effect, as exemplified in FIGURE 63C. Point B is now undermagnified compared to point A, resulting in barrel distortion.

Distortion should be kept below 1% if it is to remain unnoticeable. However, under certain circumstances, it is impossible to keep distortion below this amount. For example, a fisheye lens that covers a full 180° field of view would require an infinitely large flat image plane. Therefore these designs must exhibit great degrees of negative distortion.

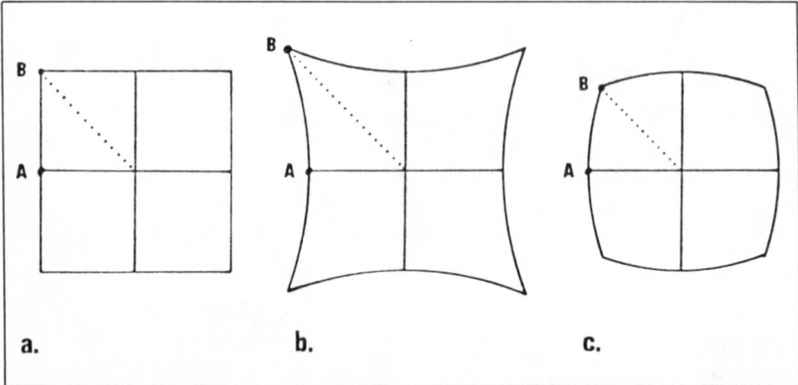

FIGURE 63—DISTORTION: A lens exhibiting no distortion would reproduce a square as in FIGURE A. FIGURE B shows an example of positive or "pincushion" distortion. FIGURE C is indicative of negative or "barrel" distortion (see text).

LENS PERSPECTIVE

When are things really in their proper perspective? In general, this question rarely has a concrete answer—except where photography is concerned. Simply stated, a photograph or projected image is being viewed in proper perspective when the viewer is at the center of perspective where all objects in the picture are in porportion to the original scene as it appeared from the position of the camera lens.

Scenes that are relatively two-dimensional with little depth can be viewed from almost any distance and look reasonably accurate. However, scenes with great depth will appear grossly out of proportion when viewed from other than the center perspective. For example, when viewed from beyond the center of perspective, foreground objects appear disproportionately large and depth is exaggerated. An object moving either toward or away from the lens will appear to be moving at a greater than normal speed, and objects aligned axially with the lens will seem elongated and distorted. When viewed from less than the center of perspective, the exact opposite occurs. Axial motion appears slower than normal, axial dimensions seem compressed and distorted and there is a general foreshortening of depth.

Most of these phenomena are familiar and sometimes referred to respectively as *wide-angle distortion* or the *telephoto effect.* However, there really is no "distortion" or "effect", per se. Actually the center of perspective is moving back and forth within the theatre, depending upon the focal length of the lens used on the camera. The theatre is usually designed to place the center of perspective approximately halfway between the screen and the rear of the theatre for a scene that was shot with a normal lens. Thus, a viewer sitting in the center of the theatre will be at the center of perspective for a scene shot with a normal lens. However, a scene that was taken with a wide-angle lens will exhibit a center of perspective that is much closer to the screen. The viewer in the middle of the theatre is now significantly behind the proper center of perspective and experiences the aforementioned elongation and exaggerated depth ("wide-angle distortion"). However, if the viewer were to get up and move closer to the screen so as to be at the center of perspective of the wide-angle scene, the picture would no longer seem distorted, but would appear perfectly natural and properly proportioned.

In the same manner, a scene shot with a long lens will cause the center of perspective to shift to the rear of the theater. Once again, the resulting telephoto effect would be neutralized by the viewer moving back in the theatre to coincide with the center of perspective. So, in reality, the center of perspective is shifting about the viewer in direct relation to the focal length of the camera lens.

The next questions are: What is a normal lens? How does the choice of lens affect perspective? The answer to the first question may surprise you. In essence, the establishment of a "normal lens" for any format is quite arbitrary. In still photography it was decided, purely by convention, that the normal lens for a given format should be a focal length equal in millimeters to the diagonal of the photographed image. Using this formula, a 35mm still frame produces an image 24mm by 36mm. The diagonal of this frame is approximately 43mm, and most 35mm fixed-lens rangefinder cameras do employ lenses of approximately this focal length. Most interchangeable SLR type cameras consider the normal lens to be the slightly longer 50mm optic.

Using the same formula for motion picture formats yields the normal focal lengths indicated in FIGURE 65. The "silent" or full 35mm motion picture format has a diagonal of 31mm and the more prevalent Academy aperture yields a diagonal of 27mm. The 16mm camera aperture has a diagonal of 12.7mm.

At first glance this should seem very strange. These figures are about half of what is usually considered a normal lens focal length for the

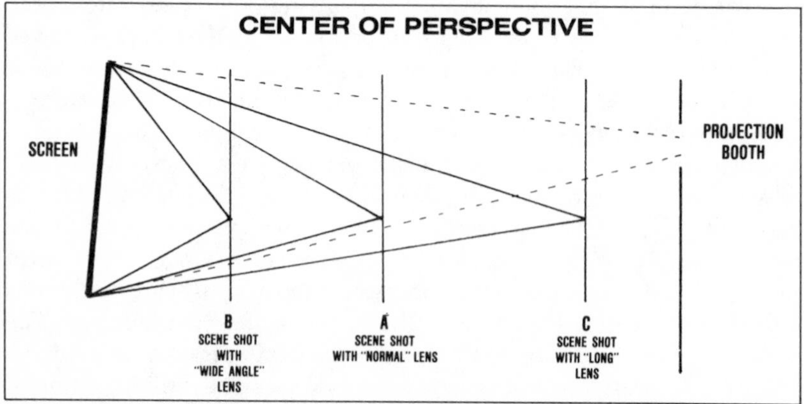

FIGURE 64—Originally, motion picture theatres were designed to provide proper perspective for a viewer sitting approximately halfway between the screen and the rear of the theatre. This is assuming that the scene on the screen was shot with a "normal" lens. This is represented by point A in the figure. If, however, the scene was shot with a "wide angle" lens, the center of perspective will be closer to the screen, (point B). The viewer seated in the center at point A is now signifcantly behind the center of perspective (see text). Likewise, the viewer at A will be foward of the center of perspective for a scene shot with a telephoto lens (point C).

respective formats. To shed some light on this paradox, I contacted my old friend Paul Foote. It seems that some time way back in the 1920's, a group of the SMPTE got together to make recommendations for lens focal lengths. They were obviously aware of the aforementioned rule-of-thumb concerning the calculation of a "normal" lens for a still camera. However, these gentlemen thought motion pictures had a different set of criteria. Their logic was based on the fact that a still picture should take in more area of coverage because the eye has plenty of time to scan throughout the frame. They reasoned that the motion picture field of coverage need not encompass as much area and could, thus, be more restrictive, since the camera and composition could move to reveal additional information. As a result, it was decided that a "normal" lens for motion picture applications should be twice the diagonal of the format image area.

Using this formula yields a "normal" lens of about 54mm for Academy 35mm and 25mm for 16mm. Those are the more familiar figures we have come to know and love. But, so what? Exactly what is the significance of the so-called "normal" lens?

To answer this question, I must introduce one more simple formula. A photograph or projected image is being viewed in proper perspective if the viewer is located a distance away from the picture equal to the magnification of the picture times the focal length of the lens on the camera through which the picture was taken. If this criterion was met, the viewer is seeing exactly what the photographer saw from his camera position.

Now, let's move on to the projector in the theatre; if the projection lens is the identical focal length of the camera lens, then it should be obvious that, regardless of screen size, a viewer standing alongside the projector will be at the exact point of proper perspective. Now, if we use a projection lens of twice the focal length of the camera lens, the image receives half as much magnification and the point of proper perspective is now halfway between the screen and the projection booth. By convention, this is exactly what happens. The projectors are fitted with optics equal in focal length to twice that of the so-called "normal" camera lens. By so doing, the majority of the audience in the center of the theatre will be at the point of proper perspective for scenes shot with a "normal" lens. This is basically the gist of the term "normal" lens.

For close-up freaks, like myself, who sit in the third or fourth row, only scenes shot with extremely wide-angle lenses will appear in the proper perspective. All other focal lengths from medium wide-angle, through "normal" and beyond, will appear to have a "telephoto" effect.

FIGURE 65—CALCULATIONS OF A NORMAL LENS

Format	Frame Dimensions	Diagonal inches	Diagonal millimeters	Twice Diagonal
16mm	.404″ x .295″	.500″	12.7mm	25mm
35mm Full-Silent	.980″ x .735″	1.225″	31mm	62mm
35mm Academy	.868″ x .631″	1.073″	27mm	54mm

Likewise, for those misdirected souls who habitually frequent the last rows of the theatre, all scenes shot with focal lengths of "normal" or less will appear to have "wide-angle" perspective.

All this, of course, assumes that the theatre was originally designed with projection optics being twice that of a normal camera lens. However, this is not always the case. Recently, the deplorable trend of bisecting one large theatre into several smaller ones, has totally destroyed these ratios.

The bisected neighborhood theatres have screen sizes almost one half of the original dimensions, yet the depth of the theatre has remained unchanged. Since the projector-to-screen distance is unchanged, the projector must use a lens of almost twice the focal length to shrink the image to fit the smaller screen. As a result, the center of perspective is moved from the center of the theatre to a point about ¼ back from the screen. The audience is thus getting a raw deal. Only those sitting in the front half of the theatre are within the original designed area of viewing perspective. Those sitting in the last rows of these smaller theatres are actually *4 times* the "normal perspective" distance from the screen. Any serious filmgoer should attempt to sit in the front half of these theatres and perferably about ¼ back from the screen to see the film as the cinematographer designed it.

LENS MOUNTS

The professional motion picture industry has standardized on two basic film sizes: 35mm and 16mm. The same 16mm or 35mm film that can run through one brand of camera will work in any other camera of the same format. Isn't standarization nice?

Unfortunately the film that runs through the camera is about the only interchangeable item in the motion picture industry. Motors, matte boxes, batteries, magazines—you name it, and the odds are that it will fit only the camera brand for which it was designed and no other. Standarization is even lacking within the product line of an individual manufacturer. One of the largest camera manufacturers at one time had three basic camera models and each ran at a different voltage. Another manufacturer cannot interchange the expensive magazines of its two models, and yet another company does not offer interchangeability of lenses between its models, which brings us to the topic of this discussion.

The lack of lens interchangeability among camera manufacturers is probably the hardest felt of all the nonstandarizations. This is primarily due to the fact that the lens is one of the most expensive elements in the camera system, often costing more than the camera body itself. Current zoom lenses for 16mm are averaging more than $4,000 and run as high as $7,000. Fixed focal length lenses are not cheap either. One manufacturer lists a set of four fast lenses that total over $10,000. It is a hard pill to swallow when you realize that such an investment in optics will fit only one type of camera.

In the beginning there was the 16mm "C" mount. The mount was simple and adequate. With rare exceptions (e.g., Kodak Cine Special), most 16mm camera manufacturers employed this "standard", and the picture looked rosy for lens interchangeability. Trouble first began with the dawn of the reflex era. The first mirror reflex camera was the Arriflex and being 35mm, it would not employ a "C" mount in any case. Moreover, Arriflex needed more room behind the lens for the reflex mechanism and chose to design a new innovative mount that was strong, practical, and provided a quick-release. When Arriflex designed their 16mm version, it was natural to employ the same lens system and the so-called "Arri" mount became quite popular in 16mm.

As each camera manufacturer developed its own reflex system, a unique lens mount was always part of the package. The reason was part price, part ego, and mostly dollar and cents. Basically, the camera manufacturer wants the purchaser to buy a lens with the camera and not be able to buy the lens anywhere else. The simple solution is to design a unique lens mount and arrange an exclusive O.E.M. contract with the optical manufacturers. So each new reflex camera had its own mount and the ability to interchange lenses began to diminish.

Still, the "C" mount maintained popularity until it was dealt a severe blow by the obvious predominance of the zoom lens. The "C" mount was designed before the zoom lens existed and could not handle the size and weight of these complex lenses. One by one almost every manufacturer had to employ some form of heavy-duty bayonet mount to accommodate the heft of the modern zoom lens. Even Bolex, which for years was exclusively "C" mount, introduced a bayonet option on their popular Rex 5 and designed their new H16EL with a single bayonet lens mount.

Lenses

Probably the strongest indication of the inadequacy of the "C" mount to handle zoom lenses was made by Arriflex. Arri always had one of the strongest mounts in the industry and yet, in 1970, they introduced a new heavy-duty stainless steel bayonet specifically for heavier zoom lenses. If Arri felt that their hefty regular mount was inadequate to support a zoom lens, then the more petite "C" mount certainly could not measure up to the task either.

With every manufacturer having its own bayonet-type mount, the future of the "C" mount and lens interchangeabiltiy would seem bleak. Surprisingly, such is not the case. Some innovative design on the part of camera manufacturers has kept the "C" mount lens alive. Eclair takes the prize with their ACL. It incorporates a universal lens mount system. In addition to the built-in "C" mount, the camera accepts interchangeable bayonet lens mounts for CA-1 (Eclair), Arri and Nikkor. These bayonet mounts are not "adapters" but an integral part of the camera system. The NPR comes with a two-position turret, fitted with one "C" mount and one CA-1 bayonet. In addition, an adapter can convert the CA-1 to an Arri mount.

Bolex offers an adapter to convert their bayonet mount back to a "C" mount, which affords continuity of their product line, and the CP-16R has an optional Arri mount and Arri bayonet converter. There are also many adapters that convert Arri lenses to "C" mount cameras. However, these should not be used for zoom lenses.

In the final analysis, the situation isn't so bad. Certain reflex cameras, because of their design, just cannot accept "C" mount lenses (i.e., Arriflex and CP-16R). However, almost all cameras can, in some way, accept the popular Arri lenses and most newer designs, such as the Eclairs, are making strong attempts to offer greater lens mount flexibility.

Unfortunately, the concept of "lens mount standarization" doesn't even exist in video. Each camera has its own unique mount, and even different models of the same manufacturer may not share the same lens mount. However, this may not be a severe drawback as video takes a different approach to lenses.

ARRIFLEX 16BL AND 16SR LENSES

A quick survey of professional 16mm cameras and lenses reveals that Arri-mount lenses enjoy the greatest popularity, both in terms of quantity and the ability to be used on almost all professional cameras. Both Eclair and Cinema Products offer Arri-type mounts for their reflex cameras, while a wide variety of

Arri "adapters" make these lenses almost universal. However, there is an interesting and quite esoteric paradox to this universality. Certain Arri lenses *cannot* be used with the Arriflex 16BL and 16SR cameras. That's right. While all Arri-mount lenses can be used on almost all cameras, certain Arri-mount lenses cannot be used with Arriflex's own 16BL and 16SR. This incompatability applies only to a very few of Arri lenses. However, the popularity of the 16BL and 16SR, and the potentially horrendous results of a mismatch prompt me to relate the facts (and, in any case, it is an interesting story).

The principle of the mirror-reflex shutter is quite simple. The mirror-shutter deflects the image onto the ground glass during pull-down, while allowing the light to pass freely onto the film during exposure. The crucial point here is that the ground glass must be located at precisely the same distance from the mirror as the film plane. Thus, if the ground glass image is in focus, so is the film plane image. The original Arri 35 design placed the ground glass at 90 degrees alongside the aperture. This is the most effective and simple solution, as the lengths of the light path to the film plane and to the ground glass (via the mirror) are identical.

But there was a problem. Because the ground glass was so close to the film plane, some stray light from the lens could bounce off the ground glass and flash the film. Normally this "flashing" effect is kept to a minimum by making all surfaces behind the lens a "matte black" finish. However, painting the ground glass matte black would undoubtedly reduce its effectiveness for viewing. The solution was to include several matte black vertical baffles. Acting like venetian blinds, they flag the ground glass from stray light and the problem is solved. It is the baffles that account for the vertical black lines you see in the viewfinder of an Arri 35 2C.

When designing the Arri 16S and 16M, the Arri engineers decided to solve the problem in a different manner. They removed the ground glass from the front of the camera altogether and replaced it with a series of lenses. The result is that the image is reconstructed on a ground glass at the *rear* of the camera. Once again the problem is solved; no ground glass near the aperture, no reflection problem.

Now come the Arri 16BL and 16SR. Because of hand-held design considerations, the viewfinder (and ground glass) had to be located near the front of the camera. Thus, the 16S/16M solution of rear ground glass was out. Likewise, the 35 2C solution was equally inappropriate. Because of the much smaller size of the 16mm format, the thickness of the baffles would have been objectionable and distracting in the viewfinder. For this and other reasons, the use of baffles was ruled out. As it turns

Lenses

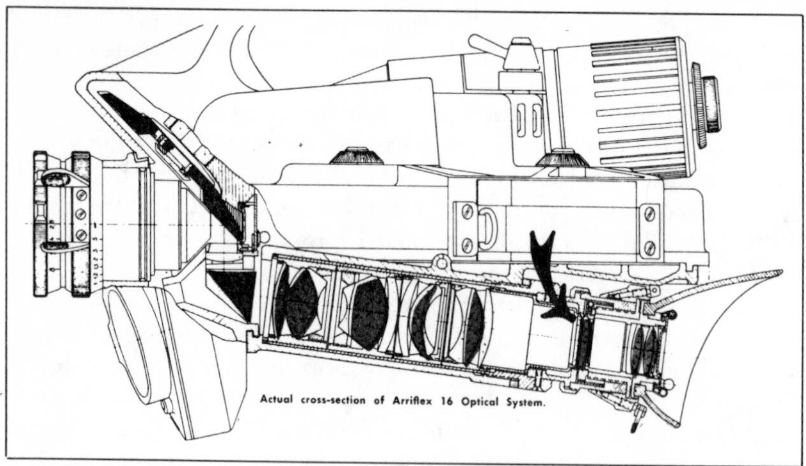
Actual cross-section of Arriflex 16 Optical System.

To eliminate black lines caused by baffles originally inserted to minimize "flashing" effect in viewfinder, Arriflex engineers, when designing the Arri 16S and 16M, removed the ground glass from the front of the camera and replaced it with a series of lenses. The result is that the image is reconstructed on ground glass at the rear of the camera (note arrow).

out, the Arri designers merely moved the ground glass of the 16BL back slightly to recess it from the light path. However, you must remember that the film plane and ground glass must always be exactly the same distance from the mirror. So in recessing the ground glass back, the mirror-shutter had to be moved forward in order to maintain the required distance—and here is the crux of the problem.

The mirror shutter in the 16BL and 16SR is located just slightly forward of the position it normally occupies in the 16S, 16M and 35 2C. As a result, the Arri 16BL and 16SR have just a hair less room between the lens seat and the mirror than the other Arri models. In some cases, the clearance between the rear element of the shorter focal-length lenses and the mirror shutter is extremely small, and while there is sufficient clearance with the other Arri models, the shutter of a 16BL or 16SR can actually hit the back of the lens. The worst case was that of an unlucky cameraman who inserted one such lens into his Arri 16BL. Because the lens was focused at a short distance (racked away from the seat), the rear element cleared the mirror. The camera was turned on and with the mirror spinning, the cameraman began to focus to infinity, screwing the lens slowly backward. He never made it. Before he could reach the infinity position, the rear lens element became very intimate with the rotating mirror.

The Arriflex 16BL and 16SR handle quite well with fixed focal-length lenses. However, check with Arriflex before inserting a lens into your 16BL or 16SR. Arri supplies a list of lenses that can be used with those cameras. The lists consists of GROUP I lenses and GROUP II lenses. The GROUP I lenses can be employed with the Arri 16BL Universal Lens Housing for extremely quiet operation. The GROUP II lenses are safe to use with the 16BL, but cannot be used in conjunction with the Universal Lens Housing and, thus, camera operation will not be as quiet. The 16SR can use lenses from either GROUP I or II.

These two groups include *almost* all Arri lenses, so the problem of incompatibilty is extremely rare. However, those few lenses that do not appear on the list could cause havoc. Lenses that *cannot* be used with the 16BL and 16SR are usually under 24mm and include the old Schneider 10mm and 16mm, as well as some short focal-length Cookes. All lenses above 24mm, as well as all Zeiss lenses, are safe. Check with Arriflex if there is any doubt. The sound of crunching glass will definitely spoil your day.

LENS EQUIVALENTS

There are few cinematographers these days that work in only one format. More often a director of photography will find that there is as much variety in formats as there is in types of assignments. Most features are still shot in 35mm. However, there is a growing popularity for both 16mm and video within the documentary, educational, and industrial markets. In addition many cinematographers, like myself, often employ a 35mm still camera during set preparation and while scouting locations.

It is quite obvious that what is learned from one assignment can often be applied to another, no matter what the format involved. Often I find myself trying to duplicate on one format a particular perspective achieved on another. This usually requires some quick and rough calculations to establish the equivalent focal length. This situation has cropped up with sufficent frequency to motivate my creating the chart reproduced in FIGURE 66. A quick reference to the chart will quickly convert a given focal length from one format to another, as well as give an approximate horizontal angle view.

Note that the 35mm slide column is based on a 1.33:1 format, assuming the width of test slides has been reduced from the full 36mm to 32mm. The 35mm Cine column is based on a full aperture and should be reduced by slightly over 10% to yield an equivalent for an Academy aperture. Of course, most numbers have been rounded off for simplicity.

FIGURE 66

RELATIVE LENS FOCAL LENGTH FOR FOUR FORMATS

HORIZONTAL ANGLE	35mm STILL (32mm x 24mm)	35mm CINE (24.9mm x 18.67mm)	16 CINE (10.16mm x 7.62mm)	VIDEO 2/3″ (8.8mm x 6.6mm)
77°	18mm	15mm	5.9mm	5.1mm
61°	24	19	7.6	6.6
54°	30	25	10	8.7
44°	40	30	12.5	10.8
35°	50	40	16	14
23°	80	60	25	22
12°	160	125	50	43
7.8°	235	190	75	65
5.8°	320	250	100	87
3.8°	470	380	150	130
2.9°	640	500	200	175
1.9°	950	750	300	260
1.2°	1575	1250	500	430
0.7°	2500	2000	800	700
0.6°	3150	2500	1000	865

Critical film tests are always most significant when the actual production camera, lenses, emulsion, and lab are used. As previously mentioned, preliminary tests of location, lighting, sets, etc., can often be conveniently and effectively recorded with a 35mm SLR camera. This process becomes even more meaningful if the same film stock is employed in the SLR camera as will be used on the actual production.

Since most 35mm and 16mm productions employ Eastman color negative (5247/7291), many cinematographers load short ends of Eastman color negative into 35mm SLR containers in order to use this cine stock in their still cameras. In addition to the obvious benefits of a closer match with cine footage, some believe that 5247 emulsion and print systems offer other advantages over the more conventional color still film.

Many photographers must share this view as there are several film labs around the country that specialize in prepackaging 5247 into standard 135-36 and 135-20 cartridges that pop into any 35mm SLR camera. Moreover, these labs offer specialized processing of the negatives.

In most cases the lab will offer a variety of ASA ratings that can be chosen for each roll, usually 100 (normal), 200 or 400 ASA. Each roll is individually color analyzed and can be corrected to any effective color temperature within reason. Thus, no filters need be used under daylight or fluorescent conditions.

Caution should be employed, however, since many labs analyze only the first exposure, not each frame. Therefore, the first exposure on each roll should exemplify both the density and the color balance of the entire roll. Because these services are so economical, it is usually prudent to start a new roll if color temperature or lighting conditions change significantly. In any case, a dialog with a specific lab would be advisable.

Most labs also offer a variety of release formats, including mounting slides, film strip, color prints, or any combination thereof. Costs run approximately $5 for a 36-exposure roll for negative processing and mounted slides. Color prints (3½ x 5) run an additional $7 to $8 for 36 and a replacement 36-exposure roll of negative should not cost much more than $1.50. Most labs offer these services by mail order and can turn a negative into slides in one or two days. Prints usually take an additional day or two.

The projected image from a 5247 slide should be quite similar to that obtained by a 35mm cine answer print taken under similar conditions. With the obvious limitations, the 35mm SLR loaded with 5247 can, thus, be an effective evaluation tool for the cinematogapher.

T-STOPS REVISITED

An "f" stop signifies only the physical dimension of a hole in the lens. It has little to do with the exact amount of light falling on the film plane. As much as 50% of the light can be lost to diffraction, refraction, reflection, and viewfinder optics, before reaching the film plane.

The "T" stop, or photometric aperture, on the other hand, is a true and accurate measure of the light reaching the film plane after the aforementioned optical phenomena have taken their toll. It is obvious that the cameraman is concerned with the light reaching the film plane when setting his exposure and that the arbitrary physical dimensions of the lens orifice are irrelevant and immaterial.

Angenieux deserves a round of applause for the first zoom lenses manufactured with only "T" stop calibrations; there isn't an "f" stop in sight. The only possible significance of the "f" stop is for depth-of-field calculations, which are based on geometric parameters, as opposed to photometric data. However, with modern reflex cameras one rarely calculates depth-of-field. This is especially true of the news or documentary cameraman. When was the last time you saw a news cameraman pull out a tape measure and calculate the distance between the camera and a burning building? The acceptable area of focus is quite visibly apparent on the ground glass. What this boils down to is the fact that "f" stops are virtually useless.

Getting down to some examples, an Angenieux 9.5mm–95mm zoom with reflex viewfinder (for a non-reflex camera) has a maximum aperture of f/2.2, but a maximum "T" stop of T/3. Thus, if a cameraman calculated a T/2.2 stop with his light meter and set the lens to f/2.2, as per the data rings, he would be almost a *full stop underexposed,* as the light reaching the film plane is only a T/3.

Lastly, the amount of difference between the "f" stop and "T" stop will vary from lens to lens and no fixed formula can be employed. Generally speaking, the more complex lenses will exhibit greater differences between "f" and "T" stops. A relatively simple fixed-focal-length lens may have "f" stop calibrations almost identical to "T" stop indices, while a complex zoom lens may have as much as a full stop difference between the "f" stop and the actual "photometric" "T" stop.

FIGURE 67

Type	Focal length	Geometric aperture	T/stop Photometric Aperture
16mm			
R7	5,9mm	f/1,8-f/22	T/2 -T/22
R21	10mm	f/1,8-f/16	T/2 -T/22
S41	25mm	f/1,4-f/22	T/1.5 -T/22
M1	25mm	f/0,95-f/22	T/1.1 -T/22
M2	28mm	f/1,1-f/22	T/1.2 -T/22
S5	50mm	f/1,5-f/22	T/1.6 -T/22
4x17	17 - 68mm	f/2,2-f/22	T/2.5 -T/22
4x17,5	17,5- 70mm	f/2,2-f/22	T/2.5 -T/22
6x12,5	12,5- 75mm	f/2,2-f/22	T/2.5 -T/22
6x 9,5	9,5- 57mm	f/1,6/2,2-f/22	T/1,9/2.4 -T/22
10x 9.5	9,5- 95mm	f/2,2-f/22	T/2.8 -T/22
10x12	12 -120mm	f/2,2-f/22	T/2.5 -T/22
20x12	12 -240mm	f/3,5-f/22	T/4.2 -T/22
35mm			
R62	14,5mm	f/3,5-f/16	T/3.8 -T/16
R2	24mm	f/2,2-f/22	T/2.4 -T/22
S2	28mm	f/1,8-f/16	T/1.9 -T/16
S2	32mm	f/1,8-f/16	T/1.9 -T/16
S2	50mm	f/1,8-f/16	T/2 -T/16
M1	50mm	f/0,95-f/22	T/1.1 -T/22
4x35 T1	35-140mm	f/3,5-f/22	T/4.4 -T/22
6x20 L2	20-120mm	f/2,6-f/22	T/3 -T/22
10x24 A	24-240mm	f/2,6-f/22	T/3.8 -T/22
10x25 T2	25-250mm	f/3,2-f/22	T/3.9 -T/22

As a reference, FIGURE 67 lists some of the more popular Angenieux lenses with both "f" stop and "T" stop maximum apertures. A careful perusal of this list will help the cameraman gain a "feel" for photometric aperture. Note, for instance, that both the 12mm–120mm and the 9.5mm–95mm lenses have a maximum aperture of f/2.2, yet the 12mm–120mm is a T/2.5 and the 9.5mm–95mm is a T/2.8.

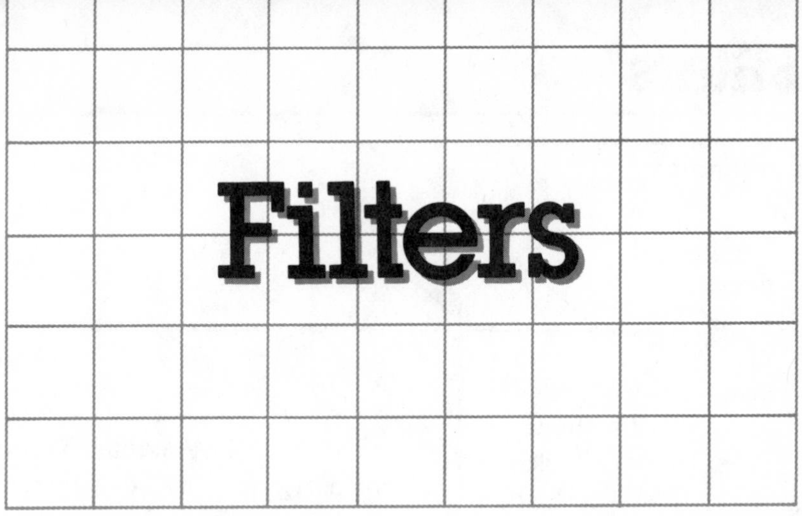

Filters

POLARIZING FILTERS

Most cinematographers are familiar with the properties of absorption filters used for both black and white and color photography. However, for many, the principle of the polarizing filter is a more esoteric subject.

Light waves pulsate or vibrate in all planes perpendicular to the direction of propagation (FIGURE 68). If for some reason, these vibrations are cancelled in all but one plane, the light is said to be *polarized.*

A polarizing filter or "polarizer" is constructed of very fine "optical slits" that cancel all vibrations except in the plane of the "slits", thus polarizing the light that passes through it (FIGURE 69). However, in cinematography a polarizer is rarely used to polarize light, but rather to filter *out* polarized light. If the light passing through a polarizer is already polarized, the filter becomes a variable absorbing filter. For example if the polarizer is oriented with the "slits" of the filter aligned with the polarized plane of the incident light, the polarizer has no effect; it allows this light to pass unchanged. As the filter is turned in such a way as to be out of phase with the incident polarized light, the transmission is reduced proportionately until, when the polarizer is 90° out of phase with the incident light, it will cancel the incident light entirely. Thus, if a polarizing filter is 90° out of phase with a polarized source, it will filter out the polarized rays, while transmitting freely any unpolarized rays. (Actually the unpolarized rays will be polarized after passing through the filter. However, this has no photographic effect.)

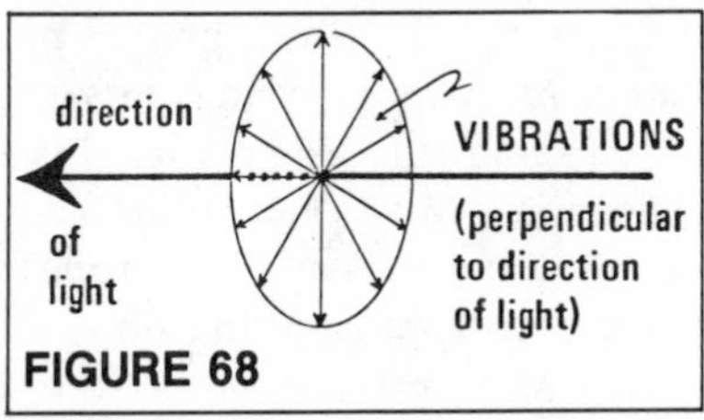

FIGURE 68

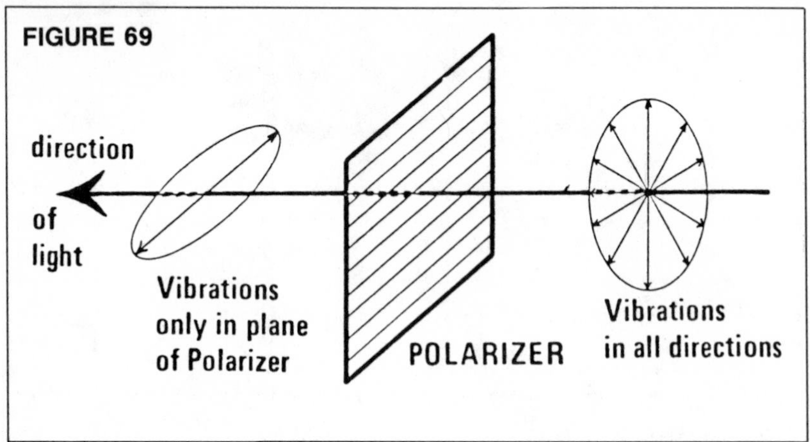

FIGURE 69

There are many cases where it is beneficial to remove polarized light, most familiar of which is "glare." As light reflects off a non-metallic surface, it is polarized.

Essentially as the light hits the surface, its vibrations are cancelled except for those parallel with the surface, which are reflected. Thus the reflected light is polarized in a plane parallel to the reflecting surface, and can be removed by employing a polarizer oriented 90° to the reflecting surface.

Even in cases where glare is not that apparent, the use of a polarizer can produce more vivid colors, especially where most of the objects are in the same reflecting plane. This is due to phenomenon called "spectral reflection". Most photographic illumination is "white" light; it is made up of all colors. An object appears colored by absorbing certain wave lengths and transmitting others. Thus a red object absorbs blues and greens and *emits* red. Notice the word "emits" as opposed to "reflects." The red light that is emitted from a red object is being disbursed by the first few molecular layers of the object (FIGURE 70); it is not being reflected from the surface. This random emission appears as a soft, diffuse light source. On the other hand, a small percentage of the incident light never makes it past the surface and is reflected. Because this reflected light has not been affected by the coloration of the object it is "white;" all colors are reflected equally. This spectral reflection will tend to desaturate or wash out the vivid red color of the object, as can be expected whenever white is added to a pure color. Keep in mind that this spectral reflection is polarized, whereas the red emanating from the object is not. Thus by employing a polarizer at 90° to the surface of the object the vivid red will pass freely through the filter whereas the spectral reflection will be cancelled. Thus a polarizer can prove very beneficial in advertising and other product cinematography where the vivid colors of an object are extremely important. It also helps outdoors where it can improve the saturation of colored foliage, and especially water. A polarizer is also the only way to darken the sky in color photography, as light from a clear blue sky is polarized.

Remember that a polarizer always reduces the amount of light by approximately one to one-and-a-half stops due to the energy it absorbs. Experimentation will determine the correct compensating factors.

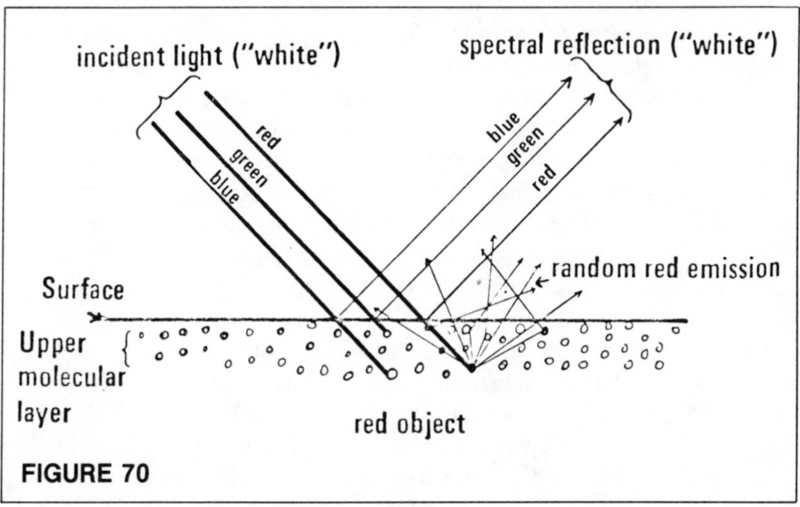

FIGURE 70

THE CARE OF FILTERS

Although most cinematographers have the proper attitude toward filter selection and care, there are many who, unfortunately, think of filters as pieces of colored glass. I have, on several occasions, observed a cameraman spending thousands of dollars on a new camera and lens, and then top off the package with a $1.98 glass filter. It must be understood that a filter, in addition to absorbing certain wave lengths, is also a part of the optical system, and a cheap filter can seriously impair image quality. Theoretically, it is more difficult to grind an optical flat for a filter than a spherical surface for a lens, and the cinematographer should be prepared to pay for a precision optical element, as opposed to a piece of colored glass. When purchasing a glass filter it is best to stay with those few brand names associated with professional motion pictures.

Filters

Once a filter is purchased, it should receive the same care as a fine lens. The proper procedure for maintenance and storage depends somewhat on the type of filter.

There are basically four types of filters used commonly in motion pictures: gelatin, gelatin cemented in optical glass, glass laminate and solid glass. Each type has its advantages and disadvantages and the cinematographer should weigh these against his particular situation.

The gelatin filter has the best overall optical qualities surpassing even the finest glass filters. In spite of this, it is also the least expensive. It is very thin, usually about 0.1mm, and therefore has the least effect on focusing. Unfortunately, gelatin filters are very difficult to handle. Because the slightest touch of a human hand will often irreparably etch the surface, they should be handled only by the edges. A camel's hair brush is about the only cleaning implement that can be employed with gelatins. Any grease, fingerprints, etc., usually means discarding the filter. Gelatin filters are particularly susceptible to moisture which will turn them cloudy. They should be stored flat in a dark dry place, preferably between the pages of a book or two pieces of cardboard. When cutting gelatins, always place them between two pieces of paper and use a sharp scissors.

Cemented filters are easier to handle than film gelatins, yet they still require a considerable degree of care. The filter must be treated just as one would treat a lens; it should be stored in a case where it will not be vulnerable to dirt or dampness. It should be cleaned with a camel's hair brush and, if necessary, a lens tissue moistened with cleaner. Under no circumstances should a cemented filter be washed with water. Water coming into contact with the edge of the gelatin will cause it to swell, thus destroying the alignment of the optical surfaces and possibly allowing air to enter between the glass plates.

Solid glass filters are the easiest to maintain and handle. There is no need to worry about separation or damage due to moisture. They usually have a greater stability or resistance to fading. The major drawback is the difficulty in controlling precise spectral absorption characteristics during manufacturing. The glass laminate filter seems to possess the best qualities of the solid glass and cemented glass.

The specific absorption qualities of all filters are determined by a precise balance of certain chemicals. With age, this chemical balance is disturbed and the spectral qualities will change; this is most noticed as "fade". These chemical changes are aggravated by light, heat and, in some cases, moisture. Therefore, all filters should be stored in a cool, dark and preferably *dry* place. These criteria should be especially adhered to under tropical conditions.

Every uncoated surface of a filter reflects about 4% of the incident light, independent of wave length. If several filters are employed, the light loss can become appreciable. In addition, this reflection causes a certain amount of flare which can affect the image. It is always best to use as few filters as possible. If there is a particular combination that you often use, it may pay to obtain that combination in a single filter, such as an 85N3 which combines an 85 with a neutral density.

In most cases the thickness of the filter is a negligible factor in focusing. Ground glass focusing with a reflex camera will, of course, automatically take into account the filter thickness. There is one case, however, which should be avoided. This is the use of behind-the-lens gels with wide angle zoom lenses (such as a 9.5mm-95mm). A behind-the-lens gel will displace the back focus distance by an amount equal to about ⅓ of the thickness of the gel. (See FIGURE 71) When employing a fixed focal-length lens in a reflex camera, this is automatically compensated for by focusing on the ground glass (the lens will be moved forward an amount equal to the displacement in the process of focusing). However, when using a zoom lens, the back focus distance cannot be altered by focusing and, thus, this displacement cannot be compensated. Because the displacement of one gel is only three or four hundredths of a millimeter, it will remain negligible except for the very short focal lengths (under 15mm) where it could cause softening, especially if the lens seating was not optimally adjusted to begin with. Most modern video cameras are designed with built-in filter wheels behind the lens. These cameras have been designed with the proper back focus distance including these filters.

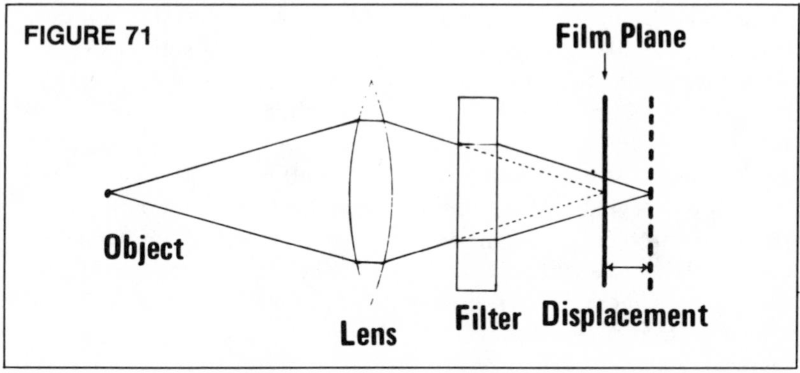

FIGURE 71—A behind-the-lens filter can alter the back focus of a lens. Most modern video cameras that have built-in filters have compensated for this shift.

Filters

NEUTRAL DENSITY FILTERS

It has been established that every lens has a "best" aperture. This is usually two or three stops down from wide open. This is the point where the decreasing aberrations and increasing diffraction reach the best compromise in terms of image sharpness. Attempting to always film at this "best" aperture is not always practical or desirable. To begin with, there are many cases where there just isn't enough light and the lens must be used wide open. The iris is also the main means of controlling depth of field. For a given composition varying the iris is the *only* way to control depth of field. In those instances where there is plenty of light and a small aperture is not necessary for a deep field, the cinematographer should attempt to employ the best aperture for maximum sharpness.

The best method of achieving a particular aperture indoors is to control the lighting. By raising or lowering the foot candles on an interior, the cinematographer can obtain the aperture that will yield maximum sharpness. Outdoors there is usually less control over lighting (unless you have an in). On exteriors the problem on sunny days is usually too much light. When shooting 16mm in the old days, the daylight EI of Ektachrome commercial was 16, which was perfectly matched to a bright sunny day. The faster negatives being used today are more than two stops faster.

Many cinematographers prefer the greater flexibility that the higher exposure indexes provide. While it is a bit fast for bright sunlight, the high EI is welcome in the shade or on overcast days. There are many other situations where the extra speed comes in handy. This brings us back to the original question. How do you avoid f/16–f/22 aperture when using the 100+ EI films in the sun? The variable shutter maybe?

As we discussed some time ago, the variable shutter should seldom be used for exposure control. The decreased shutter opening will cause a very undesirable strobscopic or jerky effect for both subject and camera movements. As it is, the standard 180° shutter records only half the action. By employing a 90° shutter (the smallest you would dare use for exposure control) only ¼ of the action is recorded on the film while the remaining ¾ is lost—and only one stop is gained. Except for a static shot involving no camera or subject movement, the variable shutter should not be used to reduce light levels. In almost all cases one should resort to neutral density filters.

Obviously the best quality N.D. filters should be chosen. It is ludicrous to be using a $15,000 camera, and $3000 lens and a grey lollipop wrapper for a N.D. filter. Whenever possible never use more than one filter to build up greater densities. Carry a complete set of N.D. filters at least an 0.3, 0.6, and an 0.9 density. These will give one, two and three stops of reduction respectively. If an 85 filter must be used also, do not use two filters. An 85N3 or 85N6 will provide one and two stops of reduction respectively in addition to balancing type B films for daylight.

There is another question of filter placement—behind the lens or in front of it? There are two schools of thought here and I can only provide you with the pros and cons of each opinion. The final decisions will have to be made by the cameraman based on his own personal experiences or phobias. If the filter is placed in front of the lens, it should be a glass type filter. These are very expensive, more difficult to obtain and much larger than B.T.L. gels. A different size glass filter may be required for each lens. For extreme wide-angle lenses the size of the front glass filter may be prohibitive or downright impossible to mount. The glass filter is also vulnerable and prone to scratches and dirt.

The behind-the-lens gel, on the other hand, is protected from the elements—one gel will cover lenses of all sizes and shapes—the gel is small and easy to carry—it is cheap and readily available in a wide variety of types—If it is damaged it can be economically thrown out and replaced with a new one. So the B.T.L. gel looks like the way to go? Not so fast.

A neutral density filter is made of colloidal carbon dispersed in a gelatin with dyes. As the light beam passes through the filter there will be a certain amount of scattering effect due to the particle nature of the filter. The purists will argue that the small gel behind the lens will have a greater scattering effect than a large glass filter in front of the lens. Thus the glass in front method should provide the sharper image. Theoretically this is true; however, the amount of image degradation due to this scattering or diffusion effect is minute in the first place and it is debatable whether the effects of either filter would be visually apparent to the audience. The cinematographer should make his own tests under specific circumstances rather than rely on the paranoia or opinions of others.

While the aforementioned scatter effect may be debated, there is another problem with B.T.L. gels that is a cold reality. The back focus distance of a lens will be shifted due to the thickness of a B.T.L. gel. Most gels are 0.01mm thick. The gel will alter the back focus distance about ⅓ of its thickness or about 1½ thousands of an inch. The tolerance of most wide angle zoom lenses (9.5-95, 10-100, 12-120, etc.) is about ± ½ thousandth. Thus the B.T.L. gel will throw the flange-to-focal-plane distance off by as much as *three times* the normal allowable tolerance. There is no debate here—the image is going soft!

If you plan on using B.T.L. gels, the camera should be collimated with a Wratten #0 (clear) gel in the filter slot. Likewise, when shooting with no filter, the Wratten #0 should be placed in the filter slot (or possibly a Wratten #1A skylight). Most ENG/EFP video cameras employ B.T.L. filter wheels which usually include N.D. Filters.

Of course, these video cameras have had the back focus optimized for B.T.L. filters. There are several other precautions that should be noted with B.T.L. filter cameras. Periodically inspect the gel in the camera by removing the lens from the camera. Check the positioning of the gel and ascertain that no oil or grease has been thrown onto the gel by the camera mechanism. Take care inserting and retracting the gels as they are easily scratched. Always carry spare gels and replace old ones as they show signs of wear or if a finger print is present.

By following these precautions the behind the lens gel should give excellent results. It also provides the most convenient method of controlling light level in order to achieve the "best" aperture for a lens.

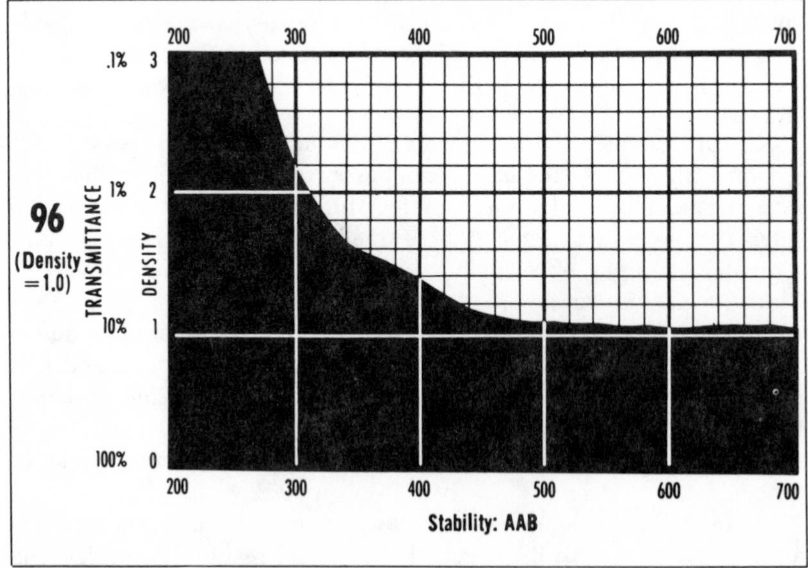

FIGURE 72—The transmittance curve of a typical neutral density filter. In this case, the density is 1.0—or a little more than three stops. Note that the density is more or less even throughout the range of the visible spectrum (400–700).

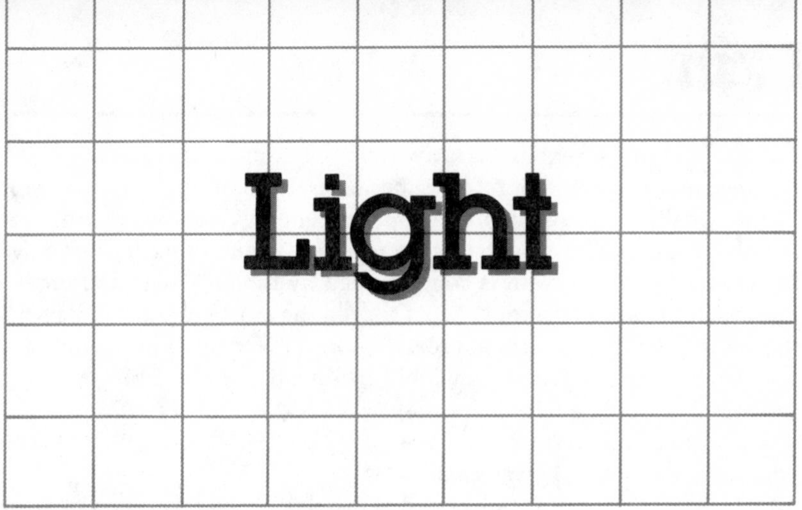

LIGHT

Light is the basic element in every phase of photography. Of all the wavelengths shown on the scale (FIGURE 73), our eyes are only sensitive to a very narrow region which is called the visible spectrum.

A closer look at this region reveals that the human eye can perceive wavelengths from about 400 to 700 mμ and can distinguish different wavelengths as colors. (FIGURE 74).

If more than one wavelength is present, the eye and mind will mix the two wavelengths and come up with an intermediate color. For example, blue and green will be perceived as cyan, red and green as yellow, and red and blue as magenta. If all wavelengths are present, white light is perceived. Objects appear colored by absorbing certain wavelengths and reflecting others. If white light falls on an object that absorbs blues and greens but reflects red, the eye will see a red object. This may seem elementary, but the cinematographer should be aware that the only way the red object can appear red is if red light is included in the original light source.

As an extreme example, take the same red object and illuminate it with bluish-green light (no red). Neighboring objects that are blue or green will appear normal, but the red object will appear black, because there is no red to reflect. A normally yellow object under the same light source will appear pure green because we perceive yellow as a combination of reflected green and red. However, in this case there is no red to reflect, so green is all that will be seen. Thus, the color balance of the light source will determine, to a large extent, the color of the objects on the film.

Although the foregoing is an extreme example, this same effect plagues many cinematographers because the light sources we call "white" really vary greatly in their spectral energy distribution or, more plainly, all colors are present, but the relative amount of each color may be different. This problem is compounded by the fact that the human eye will automatically compensate for even the most gross deviations in the color balance of a light source, thus a source may appear white to the eye, but the results on film could be disastrous, if not bizarre.

Thus, describing a light source as being white is not enough, and the color temperature scale was created as a method of rating so-called "white" light as to its spectral energy distribution (the relative amount of each color).

Most light sources we encounter are incandescent; the light results from heating an object until it glows. Color temperature of a light source refers to the balance of color that is radiated by a non-reflective body heated to a specific temperature. If a piece of steel or a tungsten filament in a bulb (which can be considered a non-reflective body) is heated to about 2500°K, it will glow reddish. It is actually radiating all colors (white) but the amount of red energy is far greater than that of blues and green. At 3200°K the glow will take on an orange hue due to the increased green energy. (Red plus some green yields orange.) If the tungsten is heated to 5500°K, the glow will appear colorless. This is because the amounts of red, greens and blues are about equal. At 7200°K, the radiation will appear bluish because at the higher temperatures there is more blue energy in the radiation than reds or greens. The graph (FIGURE 75) should help clarify the concept of color temperature. It should be noted that in every case all colors are present and the lines are continuous and smooth. This is indicative of what is known as a "continuous spectrum" light source.

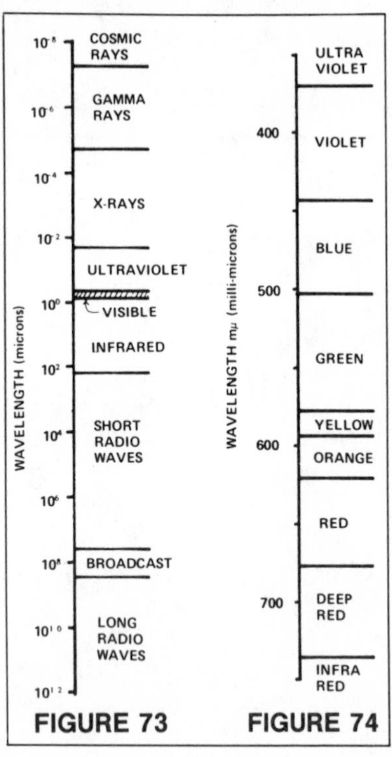

FIGURE 73 FIGURE 74

It is interesting to note that the eye will perceive light from about 2800°K to over 10,000°K as "white" light. If a 2800°K light source were placed alongside a 10,000°K source, the former would definitely appear orange and the latter blue. However, if either of the light sources were present alone, it would appear "white."

Color films are designed to give normal color rendition when the light source is a specific color temperature. Thus a film "balanced" for 3200°K will produce normal color only from a light source of 3200°K. If a film of this type is used with a light source of higher color temperature you can see from the graph that more blue and less red will be present and thus the picture will appear strongly blue with washed out reds.

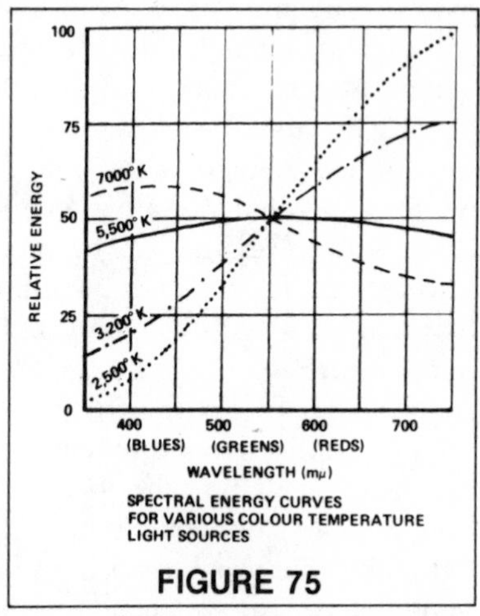

SPECTRAL ENERGY CURVES FOR VARIOUS COLOUR TEMPERATURE LIGHT SOURCES

FIGURE 75

Daylight color films are balanced for a condition known as "photographic daylight" (6000°K) which is a combination of sunlight (reddish) and skylight (bluish). This condition occurs on a clear sunny day from about 9 A.M. to 3 P.M. Near sunrise or sunset, where the sunlight predominates, color temperature drops and an orange hue will appear. On the other hand, on hazy, overcast days or in shadows, skylight will predominate with color temperatures in the 7000-8000°K range. Light from a clear blue sky could reach color temperatures as high as 30,000°K! Thus on hazy, overcast days or in shadows, the film will take on a definite blue characteristic. Under such conditions, which deviate from those for which the film was balanced, compensating filters must be employed to prevent undesirable results, a complete subject in itself.

With a basic understanding of the concept of color temperature and its relation to proper color rendition on film, the next area to explore is the many light sources commonly encountered in motion picture and video production.

COLOR TEMPERATURE

To achieve correct color reproduction, the light source and film emulsion must be matched. The industry has settled on two basic conditions, "photographic daylight" (approximately 6000°K) and "type B" artificial (3200°K). The "type B" films were designed to match the color characteristics of 3200°K incandescent bulbs which have been the predominant source of artificial light for the last 40 years.

The principle of the incandescent bulb is relatively simple. A voltage is applied across a tungsten wire (or filament) and a current begins to flow. The filament is designed with a certain amount of resistance which can be thought of as "electrical friction." As the current flows through this resistance, heat is generated in the same manner as the heat that is produced from mechanical friction. The resistance of a filament in a photographic bulb is carefully engineered to produce just enough heat to raise the temperature of the filament to 3200°K. At this temperature it will glow or incandesce with a continuous "white" light.

It is important to note that the heat is generated by the current passing through the resistance. The amount of current is determined by the applied voltage. If the voltage is raised, more current flows, more heat is generated and a higher color temperature results. Inversely, if a lower voltage exists, less current flows, less heat is generated and a lower or *reddish* color temperature will result. Thus the resistance of the filament in a bulb can only be engineered to produce proper color temperature at a *stipulated voltage*, usually around 120 volts or 230 volts. If the voltage is varied from this amount, the color temperature will vary proportionately. If long extension cords are used, a certain amount of voltage will be "dropped" across these wires, and thus a lower voltage is actually being applied to the bulbs, causing less than 3200°K light. Too many lights on the same circuit can also produce a drop in voltage and subsequently a warm or reddish light. In high industrial areas, it is not uncommon for the line voltage as supplied from the power company to drop below its normal value at certain times of the day. All these effects must be taken into account. A small volt meter is a handy item to have. By measuring the voltage at the lamp socket (not at the wall), referring to the graph (FIGURE 76) will reveal the approximate color temperature.

Some studios are provided with dimmers which actually vary the voltage to the bulb. These can only be employed with black and white films, as the color temperature will also rise and fall with the change in voltage. Therefore, for proper color rendition when using color film stock, the dimmer voltage must remain at the voltage stipulated on the bulb. When dimming studio lights during a video production the video engineer can electronically alter the color balance to compensate for color shift of the light source.

Conventional incandescent bulbs have one serious drawback. They will maintain proper color temperature for only a very short period of time. From almost the instant that the bulb is turned on, it very slowly begins to decrease in both light output and color temperature. At the high temperatures at which the tungsten filament operates, the surface tungsten molecules "boil off" or evaporate in the same manner as water boils and evaporates at elevated temperatures. As these molecules boil off, the filament begins to get thinner and thus its resistance to electric current gets greater. As a result, less current flows, and the heat generated also diminishes, causing a drop in color temperature and light output. This process continues slowly but surely until the bulb eventually burns out. The condition is aggravated by the fact that after leaving the filament, the tungsten molecules are deposited on the inside surface of the glass bulb. This black deposit causes a further decrease in light output.

FIGURE 76

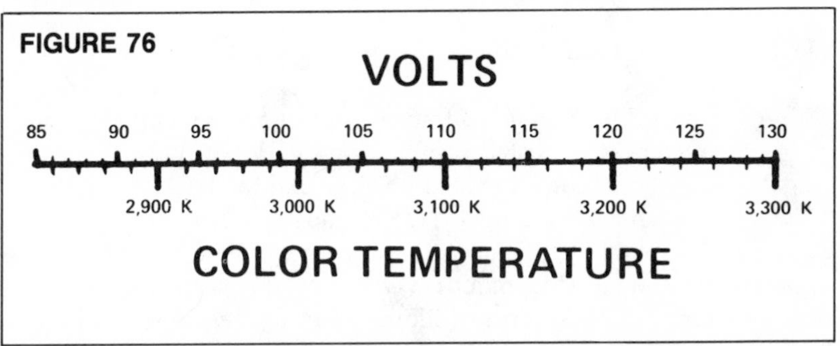

These shortcomings have been rectified with the advent of the tungsten-halogen bulb. As with the conventional bulb, the tungsten molecules begin to evaporate from the filament at operating temperatures. The tungsten-halogen bulb is filled with a halogen gas, such as chlorine, iodine, bromine, etc. As the molecules evaporate they combine with the halogen gas which thus prevents them from being deposited onto the glass envelope. The gas subsequently deposits the molecules back *onto the filament* and the cycle is repeated. Thus, in a tungsten-halogen bulb, the filament does not get thinner and the output and color temperature remain constant for the life of the bulb. The tungsten-halogen bulb is made very compact by keeping the glass envelope very close and tight around the filament. This subjects it to extremely high temperatures necessitating the use of quartz-type glass which has a higher melting temperature. Another advantage of the halogen bulbs is the absence of filament "sing" or vibration that sometimes occurs with conventional bulbs and causes noise in the soundtrack.

Keep in mind that the color temperature and light output of a tungsten-halogen lamp are dependent on voltage in exactly the same manner as a conventional tungsten bulb, and the previous discussion (and graph) on voltage applies without exception. Furthermore, the tungsten-halogen reaction occurs at the normal operating temperatures of the lamp. However, the voltage could be dropped to a point where the temperature is no longer sufficient to facilitate the tungsten-halogen reaction and the lamp will begin to function as a conventional tungsten bulb. Thus, tungsten deposits on the glass could occur at sufficiently reduced voltages. Fortunately, these adverse reactions will be reversed once the bulb is returned to its proper operating voltage.

The tungsten-halogen lamp is one of the greatest achievements in motion picture and video lighting. As long as the bulb is connected to the proper voltage, it will provide constant output and color temperature throughout its entire life.

FLUORESCENT LIGHTING

The principle of an incandescent light source is relatively simple. An element is heated until it glows or *incandesces*. From previous discussions it should be clear that the light emitted from an incandescent source is "continuous". This is reflected in FIGURE 77 where it can be seen that the energy level for all colors is approximately equal. This smooth even color response makes the incandescent source an ideal form of illumination for color film and video production.

Unfortunately one cannot always film by incandescent illumination. With "available light" shooting becoming increasingly popular, many cameramen find themselves facing the cruel world of fluorescent lighting that exists in almost every public, industrial and office building. The fluorescent lamp does not exhibit the smooth color response of the incandescent source due to the fact that it operates on a totaly different and more complex principle called *fluorescence.*

Before discussing practical methods for filming by fluorescent illumination, a short analysis of the fluorescent principle may prove beneficial. The fluorescent tube contains a gas composed essentially of mercury vapor through which an electric current is passed via electrodes at either end. This current causes the electrons in the mercury atoms to jump between several energy levels. Each time an electron jumps to a lower level, it releases a "photon" of light energy whose color is determined by the difference in energy between the two levels. For a given atom, such as mercury, there are only certain energy levels that the electrons can occupy and therefore there are only certain specific colors that will be emitted. (This principle is most familiar in a neon sign where it happens that the only energy level available in the neon atom corresponds to pure red-orange light.) The mercury vapor will emit essentially 5 distinct wavelengths or colors of light which are represented in FIGURE 78 by the five vertical "spikes" at approximately 363, 405, 436, 546 and 578 millimicrons respectively.

It would be impossible to film with this limited spectrum, just as it is impossible to film by illumination from a neon sign. Unlike a neon sign, however, the fluorescent lamp has a phosphore coating on its inner surface. When the lines ("spikes") of mercury vapor radiation strike the phosphore coating, the identical principle occurs again, that is, the electrons in the phosphore begin to jump to higher energy levels and when they jump down, a photon of light is emitted whose color corresponds to the loss of energy due to the downward jump. The only difference is that instead of 4 or 5 distinct "spikes" of color, as was the case with the mercury vapor, the phosphore is an exact blend of chemicals with a multitude of available energy levels and thus the light it emits consists of a myriad of colors that approximates a smooth spectral curve. But not quite. For one thing, an appreciable portion of the light still emanates from the mercury vapor spikes. Secondly, even though the phosphores are blended very carefully, they cannot duplicate the smooth, even response of the incandescent source. (Compare FIGURE 77 and FIGURE 78) As a result the fluorescent source exhibits significant inconsistencies in its color response which make it generally unsuitable for color photography. Furthermore these inconsistencies are random and vary from one type of phosphore to another. Thus a "deluxe warm white" bulb may cause a brown tint while a "cool white" may turn everything green-blue on the film. The term "color temperature" is absolutely meaningless when discussing fluorescent tubes.

The video camera can cope with fluorescent light fairly well. After white balancing under the specific fluorescent illumination, the video camera should give satisfactory results with most popular fluorescent tubes. Remember, there are many varieties of fluorescent tubes, and the camera should be white balanced at each different location or set-up.

There are several ways to circumvent the fluorescent problems with film. Most obvious is to turn them off. If it is possible (and practical) to illuminate the area with tungsten halogen, simply turn off all fluorescent illumination in the area. In many cases this is not practical, as with large factories or office areas.

The second alternative is a filter pack. By analyzing the curve of the "soft white" lamp in FIGURE 78, it can be seen that it suffers from a strong peak in the red region, and a mild peak with a large spike in the blue region. By employing a cyan filter (minus red) and a yellow filter (minus blue) the red and blue peaks can be respectively reduced sufficiently to produce a relatively smooth response curve. Sylvania and GE have analyzed just about every fluorescent bulb in the above manner and publish a fluorescent filter chart which specifically recommends a given combination of filters for each type bulb and film stock.

This system has several serious drawbacks of which you must be aware. First it requires the cameraman to carry a complete set of cyan, magenta and yellow filters. Secondly, both GE and Sylvania stress the fact that their recommendations are just "starting points" for individual experimentation since bulbs change significantly with age. Most cameramen cannot afford to run a test prior to the actual shooting. In addition many rooms are illuminated with several different types of bulbs which make it very difficult to establish the proper filter combination. Furthermore, if one part of the area is illuminated with one type of lamp and the remaining area by another, the color balance will shift as one pans across the two areas. Last, assuming the proper filter combination can be established, the filter factor can be as high as two or more stops, which in many cases renders filming impossible.

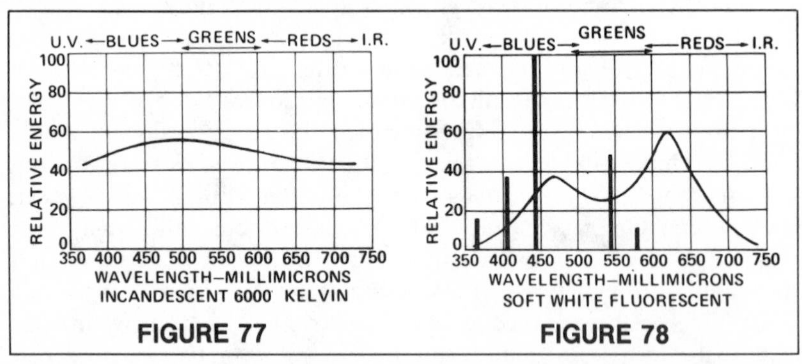

FIGURE 77 **FIGURE 78**

There is one last alternative. There exists on the market several so-called fluorescent filters, such as Tiffen's "FL-B" and "FL-D". The performance of these filters is similar. The manufacturers have attempted to come up with a compromise filter combination that will render decent results with almost any type of fluorescent tube. To the delight of all documentary cameramen, they have succeeded to a large extent. These filters will compensate for almost all types of tubes and combinations of fluorescent and small amounts of daylight or tungsten. In many cases the results are right-on, while in others, a slight color discrepancy is apparent. Most important, however, the results are almost always balanceable; that is, close enough so that most labs will have no trouble in correcting.

In summary, even though fluorescent light may look "white" to the eye, due to its color inconsistencies, the results on film can be a psychedelic nightmare. If fluorescent illumination cannot be avoided, some type of filter compensation must be employed and due to its unpredictable nature, a film test is recommended whenever practical.

Proper color rendition can only be achieved if the color temperature of the light source matches that of the film stock. This prerequisite for good color is easily adhered to in the studio where the inherent color stability of tungsten halogen lamps can be fully utilized. Unfortunately, once outside the studio it is seldom that the cinematographer encounters a lighting condition that is perfectly matched to the film.

In some cases the studio condition can be recreated with portable quartz lighting. However, in most cases the cameraman is forced to shoot with exotic mixtures of tungsten halogen, conventional tungsten, daylight, candlelight, etc. In addition, the cameraman who believes that he is automatically achieving proper color balance by using "daylight" film outdoors is grossly mistaken, for color temperatures during the day can range anywhere from 4000°K to above 25,000°K depending upon prevailing conditions. Light balancing and conversion filters were designed to compensate for those deviations that invariably exist between the light source encountered and that for which the film is ideally designed.

The basic principle of light balancing filters may be most easily understood by taking a closer look at one of the more common conversion filters. Type B films, such as 5247 and 5294 are balanced for 3200°K light. If these films are used outdoors without any filtration the results will have a definite blue cast. This is predictable when the two curves in FIGURE 79 are compared.

The 5500°K light has much stronger blues and less red than the 3200°K light for which the film was balanced. The #85B filter, which is normally used in this situation, is designed to transmit red energy while strongly absorbing in the blue region. Therefore, 5500°K light that passes through the filter will now possess a strong red content with weaker blues due to the absorption and thus closely resemble the color quality of 3200°K light. This is reflected in the 85 series transmittance curves of FIGURE 80 where it can be seen that these filters allow almost 100% of the red energy to pass through unscathed while absorbing 70 to 80% of the blue energy (in the case of the #85B). Notice that the shapes of the #85 series transmittance curves are similar to the shape of the energy curve for 3200°K light.

The #80 series filters are bluish in tint and perform the exact opposite function. By absorbing reds and transmitting blues 3200°K light can be converted to daylight. This practice is not as popular due to the inefficiency of the operation. From the curve in FIGURE 79 it can be seen that 3200°K light has most of its energy in the red region, with very little in the blue region.

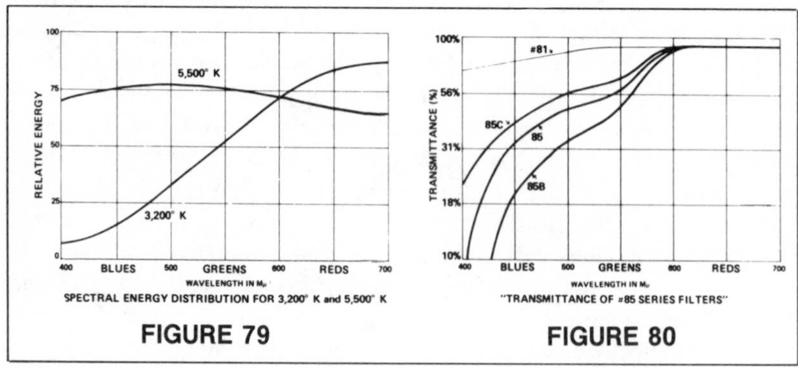

FIGURE 79 FIGURE 80

Daylight has a fairly even energy distribution; its red and blue content are about equal. Therefore, to convert 3200°K to daylight the filter must absorb most of the red energy, leaving only a small amount approximately equal to the original blue content, so that the light transmitted by the filter will have essentially even amounts of red and blue energy and thus resemble 5500°K light. Thus, by bringing the red energy down to the very low level of the blue, the #80 series filter absorbs most of the original energy (about 75%) and an aperture increase of about two stops is necessary to compensate for this loss of light.

The aforementioned #85 series (orange) and #80 series (bluish) are referred to as conversion filters and compensate for great differences in color quality. More subtle deviations in color temperature are handled by the #81 series (yellowish, absorbs excessive blue) and the #82 series (bluish, absorbs excessive red), which are called light-balancing filters. The curve of an 81 filter is included in FIGURE 80 for comparison with the larger compensating factors of the #85 series. The charts in FIGURE 81 should prove helpful in calculating the proper filter for a given deviation from the standard color temperature conditions (3200°K type B and 5500°K "daylight").

A color temperature meter can prove a valuable tool in selecting the correct filter. However, the seasoned cameraman can usually obtain fairly consistent results by relying on his own experience and several basic facts. For example, conventional tungsten bulbs (100-watt household) have a color temperature of 2800°K to 2900°K and would thus give a warm or reddish tint to type B films (3200°K). By employing an #82B or #82C filter, fairly good results can be obtained.

Color	Filter Number	To obtain 5500°K from:	To obtain 3200°K from:
BLUE	82	5210°K	3100°K
	82A	4930	3000
	82B	4670	2900
	82C	4400	2800
	82C & 82	4220	2720
	82C & 82A	4050	2650
YELLOW	81	5780	3300
	81A	6100	3400
	81B	6450	3500
	81C	6800	3600
	81D	7150	3700
	81EF	7700	3850

FIGURE 81

FIGURE 81A

Color	Filter Number	Conversion
BLUE	80A	3200 to 5500
	80B	3400 to 5500
	80C	3800 to 5500
	80D	4200 to 5500
ORANGE	85C	5500 to 3800
	85	5500 to 3400
	85B	5500 to 3200

Conversely, the daylight color temperatures most normaly encountered are usually above the 5500°K for which Kodak "daylight" films are designed. Color temperatures on a sunny day with clear skies are usually around 6500°K in the summer months and about 6100°K in the winter. Totally overcast sky light is about 6800°K while light from a clear blue sky (shadows on a clear day) is 10,000°K to 15,000°K and as high as 25,000°K during the summer months. It should be apparent that a set of #81 filters could be very helpful in these situations to remove the excessive blue. The proper filter for each of the above conditions is reflected in the chart of FIGURE 81.

FLASHING

Flashing", is a simple process of re-exposing the film to a specific amount of white light to reduce contrast and at the same time bring out details in the shadow areas.

The basic principle of flashing is very easy to comprehend after a look at FIGURE 82. Across the top, each vertical line represents one 'F' stop. Below that, row I expresses the same thing in terms of light level. This is very basic; each 'F' stop represents twice as much light as the previous one. Row II defines the approximate exposure range of a reversal film stock, as 6 stops or a light ratio of 64:1.

Row III represents a hypothetical scene composed of objects, A through G. You will notice that each object "happens" to reflect twice as much light, or one stop more than the previous object. This is fortunate, as it makes our discussion a little easier. The numbers above the letters represent the lighting ratio as in row I. However, it will be easier to regard these numbers as "units" of light. Therefore, in the scene, object A reflects 1 "unit" of light; object B reflects 2 "units" of light; C reflects 4 "units"; D reflects 8 "units", etc.

By comparing rows II and III, it is apparent that the scene was photographed one stop underexposed. Had the cameraman opened up one stop on his lens or used a film of double the EI the effect would be that of row IV. Pushing the film one stop would also have approximately this effect. Because raising the exposure one stop doubles the exposure across the board, object A doubles from 1 unit of light to 2 units, B from 2 to 4 units, etc. From row III to IV there is basically no change in contrast or exposure range. Moreover, there is no change in relative exposure between objects.

Now to "flashing". Row V represents another scene, but now with 8 elements A through H. Comparing rows V and II it becomes obvious that the luminance ratio of the scene *exceeds* that of the film by one stop. This is not a problem of underexposure; if row V were pushed one stop, object H would "burn out" and be lost. Flashing is the answer.

Row VI represents the scene as exposed in row V, but after flashing. The flashing is done by exposing the film to a small amount of white light. In the case of row VI, the film was re-exposed to one "unit" of light, or the amount of light being reflected by object A. The cameraman could actually do this himself. The film is rewound and reloaded in the camera. The camera is pointed at a white piece of paper illuminated by a light of the proper color temperature. We want to accomplish approximately a 10% flash, or flash with the same amount of light as object A. From row V, it can be seen that A is 3½ stops down from the center of exposure or middle gray (point m).

Therefore, the cameraman would take a reflected meter reading from the white piece of paper and set the lens aperture 3½ stops down from the reflected reading. This will expose the film to one "unit" of light. Row VI tells the whole story. After re-exposure to white light, object A records an exposure of the original 1 unit plus the 1 unit of white light for a total of 2 units; B jumps 2+1 to 3; C goes to 5 from 4, etc.

Thus object A moves up a whole stop. If the film were processed as in row V without flashing, object A would not have registered at all, but as pitch black. Object B moves up about ⅔ stop; object D only about 1/8 stop; and for all intents and purposes, objects E, F, G and H remain unchanged. Flashing compresses the low end of the film or reduces contrast for the higher densities. It is also evident how flashing brings out shadow details, yet has no effect on the middle or upper exposure areas. Since flesh tones are usually ½ to 1 stop above center (about the same as object E), flashing should have no effect on skin tones.

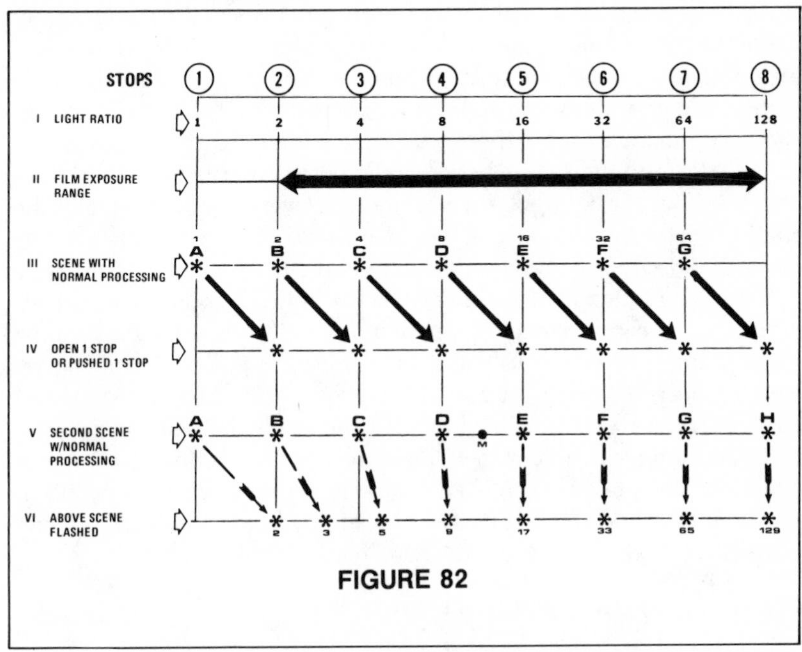

FIGURE 82

Flashing has several interesting applications for the cinematographer. In certain circumstances the cinematographer may encounter a luminance ratio wider than that of the film stock he is using. For example, filming outside, the cameraman may measure a difference of seven stops between the brightest object in direct sun and the darkest object in the shade. The film has a maximum exposure range of six stops (64:1). The obvious solution would be to use some fill light in the shadows or some diffusers on the direct sunlight or both. On some documentary or low-budget productions this may be impractical or impossible. A reasonable solution would involve shooting the scene without fill light and post-flashing the film. The exposure should be set so that the darkest area will actually be slightly below the toe of the film's exposure range; yet, the brightest areas will not exceed the shoulder of the curve. In practice this could be accomplished by taking a reflected reading from the brightest object in direct sunlight, or the skylight, if that is the brightest area in the scene. Using this reading, open the iris an amount equal to one-half the exposure range of the film stock. In our example, the film stock had a range of six stops. Thus, we would open up three stops. If the brightest object indicated an f/11 (reflective) then the iris would be set at f/4. Thus, we ensure that the brightest object will not exceed the range of the film and "burn out." If some dark areas fall below the film's range, the post-flashing will bring out these details. I recently used this technique in a film on camping safely. Filming in the woods, the entire location consisted of areas of deep shade and large shafts or direct sunlight. There was a five-stop difference between the sunlit areas and the shade. I chose an exposure that favored the bright areas, so that these bright areas would not over-expose. Normally the shadow details in the shade would be lost. However, post-flashing brought out enough of these details to make the film acceptable.

A more esoteric use of flashing concerns tinting a scene for a particular effect. By using colored light in lieu of "white" light for the flashing process, the shadow details and darker objects in the scene will take on a tint of the color employed for flashing; yet, the mid tones (skin tones) and upper tones will remain unaffected and render in their natural color balance. Different colors can be used to establish different moods or effects or time periods. This is an extremely interesting use of the flashing technique and the results are very effective, yet subtle. Many creative cinematographers have experimented with this process.

PHOTOGRAPHIC DAYLIGHT

What is the color temperature of daylight? The answer would be simple if there was no atmosphere on our planet, but this might make breathing difficult. As the relatively pure and consistent sunlight passes through the atmosphere it undergoes some pretty strange transformations before it eventually reaches the earth's surface. These transformations depend on time of day, month of the year, weather conditions and latitude. Color temperature can vary anywhere from 5000°K to over 25,000°K. At this point the situation may seem mystically complex and totally unpredictable. Fear not. A few basic facts will shed some light on the subject.

The light coming from the sun is almost a perfectly continuous spectrum of about 5500°K to 6000°K color temperature before it reaches our atmosphere. Molecular and dust particles in the atmosphere act like a dichroic filter and scatter the short wavelengths (blues) while letting the longer wavelengths through (reds). Referring to FIGURE 83, this accounts for the direct sunlight appearing slightly red when compared to the blue sky (scattered light). What we call "photographic daylight" is actually a mixture of the direct sunlight (reddish) and the skylight (bluish). You can gather that the color quality of "daylight" will depend on the relative proportions of these two ingredients.

The direct sunlight is usually about 5000°K to 5500°K, while light from a clear blue sky (no direct sun) is typically 12,000°K to 15,000°K. The resulting "overall" color temperature will obviously be somewhere between, depending on the ratio of these two elements. On a clear day with no clouds, the skylight will comprise only about 20% of the total illumination. Since the sunlight overpowers the blue sky four-to-one under these conditions, the resulting color temperature of the mixture should not be much greater than that of sunlight alone, and the table of FIGURE 84 bears this out. The color temperature of a clear day is typically 6100°K to 6500°K.

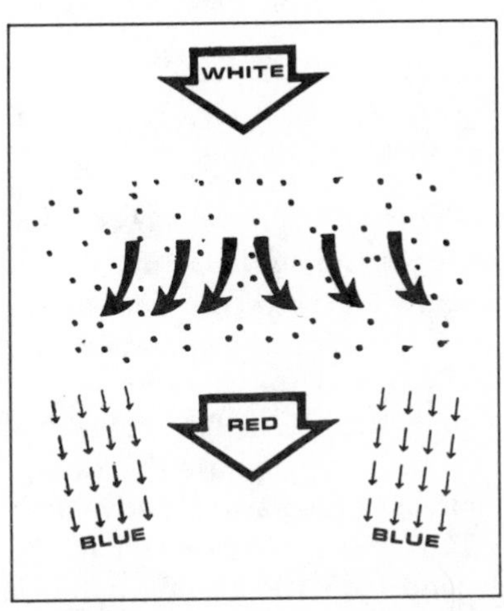

FIGURE 83—White light from the sun (about 6000°K) enters the atmosphere. The short wavelengths are scattered (blues) by particles and molecules in the air. The sunlight emerges minus some blue and, thus, appears slightly red (5500°K). The scattered blue light eventually reflects back to earth as skylight (10,000°K to 20,000°K).

A totally overcast day will reduce direct sunlight by about 75% and cut skylight by only 50%. Under these conditions the skylight accounts for a much greater proportion of the total illumination. As expected, the color temperature will shift upwards (6700-7000°K). The table of FIGURE 84 tells most of the story. In general, conditions with strong direct sunlight and little skylight will go warm. Where the skylight predominates, there will be a cool shift.

In most situations the color temperature will not vary far from the 6000°K mark and will prove fully correctable in the lab. However, there are certain cases that may pose problems. Even on a clear day when the color temperature seems perfect, the key light (sun) will actually be a hair warm, but more important, the shadows may be very cool because they are receiving fill light (skylight) only. This is why shadows thrown on white snow always appear blue. This situation is aggravated at sunrise and sunset when the sunlight is passing through so much atmosphere that a greater than normal amount of the blue waves are filtered out. This accounts for the very red appearance of the sun when it is low in the sky.

	SUMMER	WINTER	SPRING	FALL
Direct sunlight and skylight — no clouds	6500	6100	6500	6100
Direct sunlight and hazy skylight	5800	5700	5900	5900
Sunlight and skylight — about 50% overcast	6700	6200	6400	6300
Totally overcast sky	7000	6600	6700	6800
Very hazy or smoky sky	8200	7700	7500	8400
Clear skylight — No direct sunlight	15000	12000	20000	12000
Direct sunlight w/no skylight	5800	5500	5800	5500

Note: The above figures are relative. Actual figures will obviously depend on geographic location.

FIGURE 84—Typical daylight color temperatures for various seasons and atmospheric conditions.

The biggest problem occurs on *partly* cloudy days where the sun passes in and out of clouds. When the sun is hidden, the blue clear sky that is still exposed could raise color temperatures to over 15,000°K. The condition then reverses when the sun comes out. Now there is direct sunlight and the skylight is partially obscured. Temperatures will plummet to below 6000°K. Smoky or very hazy days will also exhibit a very high temperature (blue cast) but the effect will be consistent in contrast to the partly cloudy condition.

The overall visual effect of these shifts in color temperature will depend a great deal on the nature and color of the elements in the scene as well as camera angle and composition. Reflected light from large colored objects and large areas of background color can have a strong influence on the visual color balance. The cinematographer must weigh these factors together with the atmospheric conditions before a final evaluation can be reached. In most cases, especially with negative stock, color temperature variations can be color corrected during printing. The video cameraman, however, should remember to re-white balance as atmospheric conditions change.

LIGHT METERS

Virtually every cinematographer uses a photo-electric light meter to determine proper exposure. Whether your meter is an incident, reflective, spot or TTL, it invariably operates with one or two types of photo-electric cells.

The most straightforward light meter systems employ a "photo-voltaic" cell. Light striking a photo-voltaic cell produces an electric current. As seen in FIGURE 85, a photo-voltaic type light meter merely consists of a photo-voltaic cell connected to a sensitive microammeter which measures the current from the photo cell. As light falls on the cell, current is generated and measured by the microammeter. As a greater amount of light falls on the cell, more current is generated and a higher reading is produced on the meter, and vice versa. By calibrating the scale on the meter in foot-candles or "f" stops, one has a simple "photo-voltaic" type light meter.

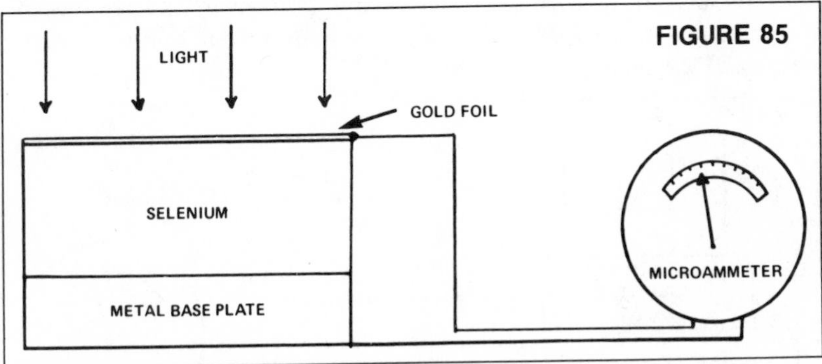

In practice, the photo-voltaic cell is constructed of a layer of selenium mounted on a metal base plate with a thin overlay or film of platinum or gold. Light meters using this construction are sometimes referred to as "selenium" meters. As you can gather, this type of meter is very simple in construction and requires very little maintenance. There are no batteries to wear down and the only two components are the cell and the meter movement. The selenium cell is a rugged and stable unit and should require little attention. The spectral sensitivity of the selenium cell is almost identical to that of film stock and, thus, no color temperature compensation is necessary. The only cautions are avoiding high temperatures, which can damage the cell, and a fall or jolt that would damage the meter movement.

The only drawback of the selenium type meter is its limited sensitivity. The selenium meter is well suited for incident type meters designed for the motion picture industry, where shutter speed is usually 1/50 second and film speed is seldom much above 100 ASA. For situations involving high speed film, fast lenses and low-light levels, the selenium meter may prove to be lacking in sensitivity. In almost all professional situations, the selenium meter is unsatisfactory for reflected, spot and TTL light meter systems due to its limited sensitivity. These applications usually employ a "photo-conductive" type of cell.

The "photo conductive" type cell is usually constructed of cadmium sulphide and thus meters employing this type of cell are referred to as "CdS-type meters". The construction of the CdS type meter is outlined in FIGURE 86. Basically, the CdS cell is a form of semi-conductor that varies its electrical resistance according to the amount of light that strikes it. The more light that strikes the CdS cell, the lower its resistance. Note that, unlike the selenium cell, the CdS cell does not generate any energy and, thus, a battery must be used in conjunction with the CdS cell. The battery provides the current, and the CdS *regulates* the amount of current by its variable resistance. As light hits the CdS cell, its resistance decreases, allowing more current to flow from the battery to the meter and vice versa.

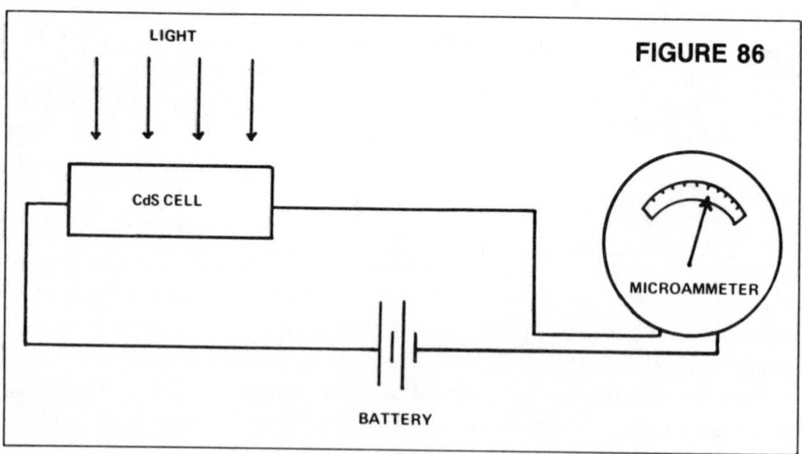

The greatest advantage of the CdS cell is its high sensitivity, about 10 times greater than that of a selenium cell of equivalent dimensions. This makes the CdS cell particularly well-suited for low-light-level situations and meters with limited dimensions or acceptance angles, (i.e., spot meters and TTL meters).

The CdS type meter is quite popular in the professional motion picture industry. Almost all spot meters and through-the-lens metering systems employ the CdS cell. There are, however, certain disadvantages to this system. Because the CdS cell does not generate any voltage, a battery is necessary, which increases the size and weight of the meter and requires a certain amount of maintenance. A mercury battery is usually employed because it maintains an even discharge voltage. However, the more sophisticated systems use an additional voltage-regulating circuit to minimize re-calibrations due to battery voltage differences. The CdS cell also requires some color temperature balancing, as its spectral sensitivity somewhat differs from that of panchromatic film. It should be obvious that the CdS type meter is not quite as simple as the selenium system. In addition, there are other facets of the CdS "personality" that are worthy of mention.

The CdS cell will sometimes "lag" at very low-light levels; in dim situations, the meter is not very quick in responding to small changes in illumination. In low light situations, it is wise to approach the correct reading from two directions and average the readings if they differ. That is, point the meter to an area darker than the area in question (or cover the meter with your hand) and then take a reading in the area in question. Note the reading. Then point the meter into a bright area and again take a reading. If the two readings differ, average them.

Another quirk of the CdS cell is "dark adaptation." When the CdS cell is covered for a long period of time or exposed only to very low light levels, it may give an overly bright reading when exposed to bright illumination. The best defense against this phenomenon is pointing the meter (or camera in the case of a TTL meter) directly into a light source or very bright area for a minute or so before using it. Most modern digital light meters employ a silicon cell instead of the conventional CdS cell. While the silicon cell operates on the same principle as the CdS, it is far more accurate, more stable and has a faster response. It thus eliminates most of the aforementioned quirks of the CdS type meter.

As you can see, the personality of an exposure meter is dependent upon the type of cell it employs. However, the configuration of the meter (i.e., incident, reflective, spot, etc.) is a greater factor in determining exposure technique.

CALIBRATION OF LIGHT METERS

Any discussion of light meters should begin with an emphasis on calibration. One can employ the most expensive light meter using the most sophisticated light measuring techniques and yet obtain an incorrect exposure due to improper calibration of the unit. Firstly, what is calibration and within what limits is a meter considered to be "accurate"?

Light

There are basically two steps in determining the proper calibration of a light meter. Firstly, the individual manufacturer chooses a particular "calibration constant" or "calibration point" that becomes the standard for that particular company. This calibration point is usually determined by the manufacturer's own research department. In some countries, the government stipulates limits for the manufacturer's calibration constant. In England, for example, the manufacturer's calibration constant must be within ± ⅓ stop of the Government Standard. In the United States there is no Government Standard as such, but it is safe to assume that almost all manufacturers have established calibration standards within a ⅔-stop range. In other words, even before a light meter is touched, one company may have set a standard for itself that is as much as ⅔ stop different from that of another manufacturer.

Once the manufacturer has set his calibration point, he now is allowed a manufacturing tolerance, i.e., all the meters he manufactures must be calibrated within certain limits of his chosen calibration point. In practice this is also approximately ± ⅓ stop. This is the second step.

Now, looking at the whole picture, the manufacturer is allowed approximately ± ⅓ stop limits in choosing his personal calibration point, and another ± ⅓ stop manufacturing tolerance on top of this. Thus, considering an extreme condition, a particular light meter from one manufacturer may indicate an exposure difference of as much as 1⅓ stop from a particular meter of another manufacturer and yet both are considered to be "calibrated." This, of course, is a "worst case" example and, in practice, meters of a single manufacturer are usually within ⅓ stop of one another, and meters of different manufacturers are most likely within ½ stop of each other. However, the situation can still exist where two meters may disagree by more than one stop, and yet each is within proper calibration.

I am stressing this point because I believe the cinematographer should not rely solely on the manufacturer's calibration. When using stocks of narrow latitude, the cinematographer cannot afford a calibration tolerance of ⅔ stop. This is why most professional cinematographers own their own light meters and through experience (and trial and error) become acutely tuned to the specific personality and calibration point of their meter. Thus, a cinematographer may find that he gets best results by using a "T" stop of ⅓ less than his meter indicates, or vice-versa.

If a meter is dropped or damaged, it should be sent back to the manufacturer for recalibration. However, the cinematographer will once again have to establish the meter's specific personality. I always have two similar incident light meters as well as a spot meter. I always note the relative calibration between these two meters.—If one goes in for repair, I can always check it against the other when it returns to see if the calibration has been shifted.

FIGURE 87

There are several additional comments on calibration. Many light meters use multiplication or ASA slides to facilitate direct "T" stop readout or allow extended range for high light levels. (See FIGURE 87.) These slides consist of a series of small holes. The manufacturer performs the fine calibration of these meters by adjusting the final dimensions of these holes. It is therefore a good practice to always keep a meter and its slides together and not allow slides from one meter to become confused with those from another. Meters of this type also employ a "photosphere" or disc type diffuser, usually constructed of translucent plastic. This plastic may become discolored with age, which will affect its calibration. Try to keep the sphere or disc as clean as possible and always cover the meter when not in use. If the sphere does become discolored, have it replaced and note the change it produces in exposure indication.

Also check that your meter gives the same readings in both the horizontal and vertical planes. If the movement is not perfectly balanced, the meter can give different readings depending on the position in which it is being held. I am a strong believer in the newer digital meters, especially those with silicon cells. They are infinitely more rugged than meters with mechanical movements. Digital meters are also more accurate and stable and can withstand a few drops without losing calibration.

Last but not least, remember that the exposure meter is actually indicating "T" stops and not "f" stops. An "f" stop refers to the relative size of the aperture in the lens. However, there are light losses in the lens due to absorption and reflection. The "T" stop is a corrected "f" stop, i.e., it takes into account those internal losses. Therefore, when setting the iris of the lens, only the "T" stop has any meaning, the "f" stop scale has no relevancy to exposure. As a matter of fact, some zoom lenses will transmit less than half of the entering light and thus there will be more than a full stop difference between the "f" stop and the "T" stop.

TYPES OF LIGHT METERS

Light meters can essentially be categorized into two basic types: incident and reflective. Every cinematographer seems to have a personal preference as to which type meter he employs. However, each meter has a specific purpose and it is the situation that should determine the proper meter.

The principle of the incident meter is elementary. The meter is placed at the position of the subject, pointed toward the camera position and measures light falling onto the subject. Most incident meters use a "photo-sphere," a translucent hemisphere over the photo cell (see FIGURE 88). This is a device pioneered by Don Norwood and intended to simulate a three dimensional object. The hemisphere will integrate the light hitting from the front, as well as from the sides, above and below.

This type of meter will, thus, give a reading taking into account light falling from all directions relative to the camera position. This reading, however, is based only on light falling onto the subject and does not take into account the subject at all. The subject may be light, dark, yellow or purple, and yet the incident meter will give the same reading for a given lighting set-up. What, then, is the significance of the incident reading? Simply that the incident reading indicates the proper aperture to render an 18% gray subject in the center of the film's latitude. In other words, if the iris is set to the incident reading, those items in the scene that are medium gray (18% reflectance) will be centered in the film's latitude. A white-skinned person (usually 30-35% reflectance) will register as a stop over center, and those darker items (8-10% reflectance) will, likewise, be a stop under. Thus, the incident meter is indicating the proper exposure for a medium gray.

This is a very valid method for determining exposure for several reasons. The average scene has many elements ranging from very dark to extremely bright, and a setting for a medium gray will center these elements within the film's latitude. Moreover, even if a scene is not well balanced and contains mostly bright objects, the incident reading will render these items where they should be, i.e., above center on the film's latitude curve. Probably the most important aspect of the incident meter is *consistency*. By adhering to the incident reading, the cinematographer is assured of consistent rendering of flesh tones and other colors from scene to scene. Because the incident meter measures only illumination falling onto a subject, any given object, regardless of its color or shade, must be rendered at a specific spot on the film's latitude from scene to scene, location to location. When working with actors or other elements where scene-to-scene matching is imperative, the incident meter is undoubtedly the best choice.

The reflective-type meter works on the exact opposite principle from that of the incident meter. In practice, the meter is positioned at the camera, aimed at the subject, and measures light reflected from the subject. What is the significance of the reflective reading? The answer is a little tricky. First, it should be stated that, compared with the incident meter, the reflective meter is an extremely ignorant device. It takes the intelligence of the cameraman to properly interpret the reflective reading. Actually the reflective meter thinks everything is a medium gray (18% reflectance) whether it is or it isn't. If one were to literally follow a reflective reading, everything would come out the exact same shade of gray. Essentially the reflective meter has no idea what the subject is and is calibrated to assume it is a medium gray (18% reflectance). You might say that the reflective meter is the ultimate liberal; no matter what shade or color the subject is, the reflective reading will put it dead center in the middle of the film's latitude.

Obviously the reflected reading (unlike the incident reading) is not meant to be taken literally. Because the reflective meter does not know the color or brightness of the subject, the cinematographer must add this information to arrive at the proper iris setting. The reflective reading will put the subject in the center of the film's latitude (medium gray). It is up to the cinematographer to decide if this is the best place for it. As an example, a scene is to be shot in a snow-covered field. A reflective reading is taken and indicates an F/11 reading. If the aperture is thusly set, the snow will be rendered tattletale gray. The cinematographer knows his particular film stock has a latitude of ±1½ stops and would like the snow to be high on the latitude curve, but not into overexposure. In this case, he would probably shoot at F/8, one stop open from the reflective reading. Thus, the snow will come out white, while still leaving about a half stop of latitude above the snow for highlights. Likewise, if the subject were a forest of dark trees and a reflective reading indicates an F/5.6 reading, the cinematographer would stop down about one-half stop from this because he wants the subject to be darker than the medium gray which would result if the F/5.6 reading were used.

When using a reflective-type meter, one must take into account the angle of acceptance of the photo-cell. Most reflective meters have an acceptance angle of approximately 30-40°. There are narrow angle meters (10-20°), spot meters (½-5°) and variable angle meters, such as a TTL with a zoom lens. With an understanding of the principles of the incident and reflective light meters, we will next examine spot meters. TTL exposure systems and automatic iris systems.

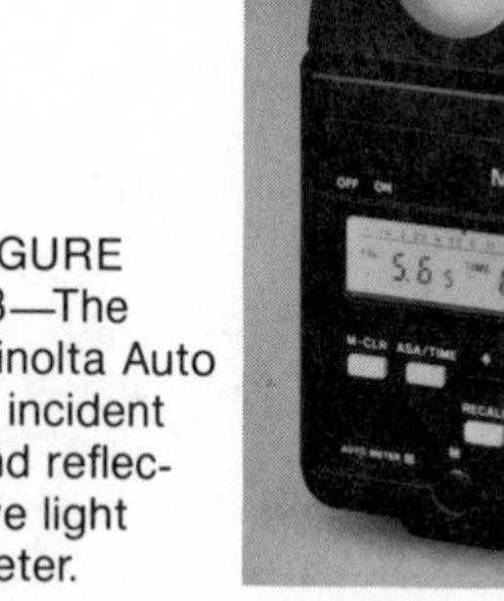

FIGURE 88—The Minolta Auto III incident and reflective light meter.

FIGURE 89—A Minolta LCD memory spot meter.

LIGHT METERS—PART IV

The incident meter seems to have achieved the greatest popularity among cinematographers. Its basic design ensures accurate exposures and guarantees scene-to-scene matching of skin tones. There are several instances, however, where it is either impractical or impossible to obtain an incident reading. For example, the subject may be a great distance from the camera, as when using a telephoto lens. In some cases the cinematographer may feel that the taking of an incident reading may disturb the subject, as when working with children, animals or politicians. Certain manufacturing processes in a factory may prohibit the close proximity necessary for the incident reading. Other cases where an incident meter would be impractical include: shooting sports from a press box at a stadium, concerts or other performing arts that are spotlit and the lighting changes during the performance; subjects which are luminous or transluscent and backlit, such as neon signs, a lighted Christmas tree, stained glass windows, etc.; subjects with an extremely high ratio of highlights to shadows. In almost all these cases a spot-type meter will provide the easiest and most accurate exposure.

The spot meter is essentially a reflective-type light meter and everything we have discussed about reflective-type meters will pertain to the spot meter. The main difference is the angle of acceptance. Most spot meters will have an acceptance angle of ½° to 5°. However, the most popular units seem to be those with the most narrow angle, usually around 1°. Because the measuring angle is so small, there must be a critical method of aiming the meter. All spot meters must have a viewfinder, in many cases, one of single-lens-reflex design.

In practice, the cameraman can take a reading from the camera position by sighting the critical areas of the subject in the measuring area of the viewfinder. As with any reflective meter, the color and brightness of the subject must be taken into account. If a reading is taken from the face of a fair-complexioned performer on the stage, the cameraman should *open up* approximately ⅔ to 1 full stop from the spot reading. A light-complexioned person reflects about twice as much light (1 stop) as medium gray (18% reflectance).

The TTL metering systems actually belong in the spot meter category. I am, at this point, referring to the professional type match-needle configuration and not the fully automatic iris. The match-needle system allows the cameraman full control of the iris, such as the APEC system for the Arriflex cameras. This match-needle system has been most popular with professional still photographers for over ten years.

These new TTL systems are of fully professional quality and are capable of the most accurate readings. I have no doubt that, like the still industry, every professional motion picture camera designed in the future will incorporate a TTL system. This is not to say that the TTL replaces the incident reading. Simply stated, there are many cases in normal everyday shooting where the TTL system will provide the quickest, most accurate or *only* method of obtaining correct exposure. For documentary or *cinema verité*, the TTL is almost a necessity. Essentially, all the cases stated above for use of a spot meter are equally suited to the TTL system. By zooming in to the longest focal length, a 12-120 zoom lens (16mm) or a 25-250 (35mm) lens will have an acceptance angle of only 4°. Most TTL systems are center-weighted, that is, they read only the center portion of the frame area. Thus, the effective angle of acceptance of the TTL Is approximately half that of the entire frame. (See FIGURE 90). Thus, the above lenses would effectively be 2° spot meters when zoomed tight. On the other hand, by zooming wide, the TTL becomes an averaging reflective meter of over 60° acceptance.

The TTL is perfectly suited to zoom lens technique. The cameraman zooms in to the subject, opens wide, focuses, stops down to the needle match and then zooms out to compose. In one step he has achieved critical focus at wide aperture and maximum focal length, obtained an accurate spot reading, set iris and composed, *without removing his eye from the finder.* In addition, the TTL allows follow-iris technique. If the lighting changes during the scene or the camera is panned or zoomed to alter the overall brightness of a scene, the cinematographer can follow iris, similar to following focus on a traveling shot. Another advantage of the TTL is the automatic compensation of filters.

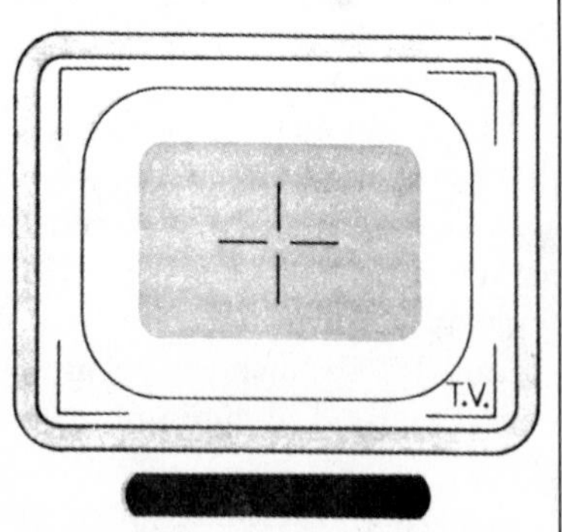

FIGURE 90—Most TTL metering systems are center-weighted, the effective angle of acceptance covering approximately half of the frame.

The fully automatic exposure system which is standard on almost all video cameras, has reached the film industry also. This device couples a TTL system with a servo-motor that sets the iris to the proper setting. It essentially by-passes the cameraman and uses its own information. Of course, the cameraman can override the servo-system. The better of these lenses are definitely of professional caliber; however, they must fall into the special-purpose category. For certain types of documentary, hard news, sports coverage, *cinema verité*, etc., these lenses can prove to be invaluable. A professional automatic iris lens (see FIGURE 91) performs its function flawlessly. In recent tests, this lens smoothly tracked from an F/2.2 to an F/22 during a pan. The results were accurate, consistent and smooth.

Its placement into the special-purpose category is not due to any shortcoming of the automatic iris system *per se*, but rather to the inadequacies of the reflective-type light meter principle which we have already discussed. The iris will faithfully and accurately follow the reflective reading. However, the cameraman's brain is not in the servo system to interpret the reflective readings. Thus, a closeup of a light-skinned person may be too dark, or the iris will shift on a static subject due to changes in the background brightness. This could occur while panning a subject walking down an evenly lit street. The light on the subject will remain constant, yet the iris will compensate as the subject passes in front of a light-colored building and then a dark one. It is for these reasons that *the automatic iris should always* be put in the manual mode on all film *and video* cameras.

FIGURE 91—Angenieux 12–120mm professional automatic-iris lens

Amateur and semi-professional automatic iris systems suffer from conditions known as "hunting" and "overshoot". Hunting occurs when the iris tends to oscillate back and forth at approximately the proper exposure point. It appears that the iris knows the correct spot but cannot quite make up its mind. Overshoot usually occurs when the lens is panned from one extreme of illumination to another. The servo motor whips the iris to the new positon, but gains too much momentum in the process and overshoots the proper stop and then slowly comes back. An automatic iris lens can easily be checked for these shortcomings. Truly professional automatic lenses have almost entirely eliminated these problems.

THE GREAT F-STOP MYSTERY

An interesting predicament occurred recently when a cinematographer called out a stop of T/9. The operator asked if he meant halfway between T/8 and T/11. The director of photography confirmed that the T/9 was indeed meant to be the half stop. The first assistant then added his opinion that the correct designation for the half stop between T/8 and T/11 should be T/9.5. Immediately a controversy arose and, at the first available moment, there was a flurry of activity. Each member of the camera department went for his own personal reference, be it a cinematographer's manual, cameraman's lens chart, cinema workbook or a handi-dandi f-stop wheel. Lo and behold, these trusted sources did not agree with one another. Moreover, many of the values presented did not fit the logical progression one would intuitively expect. This was massive trauma, as lifelong faiths stood to be shattered.

With so much at stake, I humbly volunteered to engage this paradoxical mystery.

I must admit that I had never given the matter much thought. I had always assumed that "T-stop" engravings were based on divine origin, and the precise designations for fractions of a stop never concerned me, as I usually call out stops as "T/8 and ⅓" or "T/4 and ½", etc. However, this particular controversy intrigued me. Something inside me said that there was more to this than met the eye. There were two major clues staring right at me. The accepted sources did not agree and the fractional intervals were not spaced evenly. I knew immediately that there was only one way to clear up this paradox—the computer.

Starting with the basic formula for f-stops, the computer derived the complete set of f-stops from f/0.71 to f/32, including ¼, ⅓, and ½ stops. The results gave me quite a jolt, and for an instant I relived the childhood trauma of realizing that Santa Claus was a fake.

Would you believe that T/5.6 is really T/5.7 (5.6569), that T/11 is really T/11.3 (11.3137) and that T/22 is indeed T/23 (22.6274). No wonder the ⅓ and ½ stops seemed unevenly spaced; the f-stops themselves were inaccurate. I had undoubtedly stumbled onto a clever cover-up of massive proportions. But before notifying the *Washington Post* and Ralph Nader, I decided to re-check my calculations and research the situation more thoroughly.

My calculations proved correct and accurate and the numbers that appear in FIGURE 92 were actually derived by Nobel laureate, economist and mathematician Milton Friedman on his Hewlett-Packard micro computer. However, the massive cover-up plot quickly dematerialized as these same figures appear in the government's ANSI booklet on photographic standards.

The bottom line is that the numbers that appear in FIGURE 92 are the actual f-stop (T-stop) values to four decimal places. FIGURE 93 is a fairly accurate simplification derived by rounding off to one decimal place above f/1.4 and to full integers above f/16. These are the exact figures as specified by ANSI. (The values in parentheses are to an additional decimal place where I felt the accuracy was needed.)

The popular misconception of actual f-stop values stems from an over-simplification. Apparently the f/1.4142135 (which is actually the square root of 2) was rounded off to the popular f/1.4. Thus, the f/2.8, f/5.6, f/11 and f/22 were derived by doubling the f/1.4 one, two, three and four times respectively. The original rounding-off error is compounded along the way until the f/22 is really an f/22.6274 which, when properly rounded off, yields an f/23, not f/22.

Now that the great f-stop mystery is solved, what does it all mean? Well, for me it doesn't mean much at all. I still call out stops as X and ⅓, and the numbers engraved on the lenses are correctly indexing the iris for full T-stop apertures. In other words, the T/11 mark is actually the T/11.3 aperture, as specified by ANSI standards, so there is no cause for concern. (So don't call for a T/11.3 or you'll drive the operator and assistant nuts.)

For those who like to call out the interval fractions by their actual numerical values, then FIGURE 93 will prove invaluable. A T/9.5 can be called out with the full confidence of knowing that the operator will precisely place the iris halfway between T/8 and T/11, assuming, of course, that he has read FIGURE 93.

f-stops & ⅓ stops	½ stops
32.0000	
28.5088	26.9087
25.3984	
22.6274	
20.1587	19.0273
17.9594	
16.0000	
14.2544	13.4543
12.6992	
11.3137	
10.0794	9.5137
8.9797	
8.0000	
7.1272	6.7272
6.3496	
5.6569	
5.0397	4.7568
4.4898	
4.0000	
3.5636	3.3636
3.1748	
2.8284	
2.5198	2.3784
2.2449	
2.0000	
1.7818	1.6818
1.5874	
1.4142	
1.2599	1.1892
1.1225	
1.0000	
0.8909	0.8409
0.7937	
0.7071	

FIGURE 92

f-stops & ⅓ stops	½ stops
32	
28-(28.5)	27
25	
23	
20	19
18	
16	
14.3	13.5-(13.45)
12.7	
11.3	
10.1	9.5
9.0	
8.0	
7.1	6.7
6.3	
5.66	
5.00	4.8-(4.76)
4.5	
4.0	
3.6	3.4
3.2	
2.8	
2.5	2.4
2.2-(2.25)	
2.0	
1.8	1.7
1.6	
1.4	
1.26	1.2
1.12	
1.0	
0.89	0.84
0.79	
0.71	

FIGURE 93

INCIDENT ILLUMINATION

Very frequently on location the question comes up: "How many footcandles do you need for this shot?" At this point most cinematographers will do what I do, make a reasonable estimate from experience or take a peek at the footcandle scale found on most light meters. Recently one of my colleagues rang me up and asked if I knew the quickie formula for accurately determining footcandles, given the 'T' stop of the lens and EI rating of the film. I was embarrassed to admit that I was not aware of it. However, it was quite obvious that one must exist, as the 'T' stop, EI, and footcandles must follow some simple mathematical relationship.

Some quick figuring came up with the quite simple formula to determine the footcandles necessary for a T/2.8 aperture, assuming a 175° shutter at 24 fps, yielding an exposure of approximately 1/50th of a second. The formula is this: merely take the number 10,000 (ten thousand) and divide it by the EI. The result is the footcandles necessary for a T/2.8 exposure at that EI. What can be more simple? For any stop other than T/2.8 merely double the result for each stop above T/2.8 or halve the result for each stop under T/2.8. For example, how many footcandles do you need for a T/5.6 exposure at 125 EI? Dividing 10,000 by 125 (EI) results in 80 footcandles for a T/2.8 exposure. Doubling the result once yields 160 footcandles at T/4 and doubling again yeilds the final result of 320 footcandles at T/5.6. This is a simple system for determining footcandles and the only thing that need be remembered is the number 10,000.

Further thought on the matter revealed an even better formula that will directly yield the required footcandles, given EI and 'T' stops. This formula is based on the number 1250 (one thousand two hundred fifty) and works as follows: divide 1250 by the EI and multiply the result by the square of the 'T' stop. That's it. The answer is the footcandles necessary to achieve proper exposure at the prescribed EI and 'T' stop. This formula is even easier than it sounds, since the odd 'T' stops have very easy squares, i.e., (1.4^2) is 2, (2.8^2) is 8, (5.6^2) is 32, and (11^2) is 128. (See FIGURE 94) Taking the previous example of T/5.6 at 125 EI: 1250 divided by 125 is 10. Multiplying this by the square of 5.6 (which is 32) yields 10 x 31, or 320 footcandles.

I prefer the second formula because it directly yields the proper footcandles for any 'T' stop and EI. The squares of the 'T' stops are easy to figure and even if one forgets the proper square for the odd 'T' stop, just remember it is double the square of the preceding even 'T' stop. Thus, the square of T/5.6 is twice the square of T/4 or 2 x 16, which is 32.

These formulas work equally as well for television cameras. Determine the effective ASA of the camera (as described in the video chapter) and just plug it into the formula. So take your pick; whichever formula appeals to you. For those choosing the second formula, the number 1250 is easy to remember as it was the year a little-known German engineer named Gustav Schpruked invented the sprocket hole. (Unfortunately his invention lay virtually unnoticed for over 600 years until film was invented.)

'T' STOPS AND THEIR SQUARES TO BE USED IN FORMULA TWO

'T' Stops	Square of 'T' Stops
'T' 1	1
'T' 1.4	2
'T' 2	4
'T' 2.8	8
'T' 4	16
'T' 5.6	32
'T' 8	64
'T' 11	128
'T' 16	256
'T' 22	512

FIGURE 94

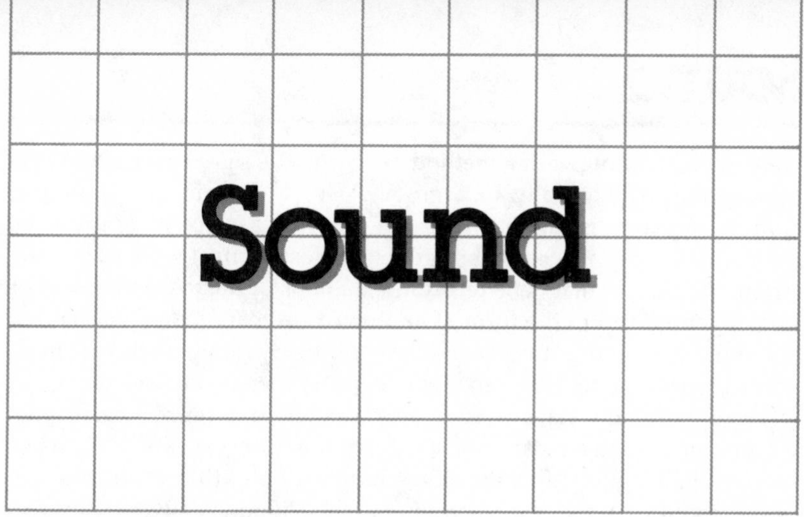

MAGNETIC SOUND RECORDING

The next several chapters cover sound recording and recorder maintenance. Before delving into the technical procedures, an elementary review of magnetic recording principles may prove helpful.

The perception of sound is caused by fluctuations of air pressure near our ears. The magnitude of these fluctuations (amplitude) is perceived as loudness, and the speed of the fluctuations (frequency) is perceived as pitch or tone. There is no way of capturing or recording these fluctuations in their existing state of air pressures. Therefore, they must first be converted into some other form.

The microphone is the converting device, changing fluctuating air pressures into fluctuating electrical voltage. The resulting electrical signal is directly proportional to the original sound; changes in loudness are reflected in the amplitude of the electrical signal, and the frequency of the electric current matches that of the sound. This electrical facsimile of the original sound, however, is still not in a form that can be stored or recorded. Another conversion is necessary. In the case of a phonograph record, the electrical signal is converted once again into a mechanical signal that is ultimately recorded in a soft wax or plastic. The electrical signal is fed to the coil of an electromagnet. As the signal fluctuates, the magnetic field will fluctuate proportionately and a cutting stylus, which is under the influence of this field, will fluctuate likewise. The cutting stylus cuts a path into the soft recording material, and the result is a squiggly-looking groove that is an exact replica of the original air pressure fluctuations or sound.

The phonograph disc has its limitations. It is susceptible to dirt and scratches, and it is almost impossible to edit. As early as 1888 scientists were experimenting with a method of storing the signal magnetically as opposed to mechanically in a groove. The basic principle is simple. Almost everyone is familiar with the fact that a piece of iron can be permanently magnetized by bringing it in close contact with an existing strong magnet. In magnetic recording, millions of microscopic pieces of iron are employed in the form of an iron oxide coating on an acetate or polyester tape. In the erased condition, those tiny iron particles are in an unmagnetized state. The recording head is merely an electromagnet with an extremely narrow gap, very similar to a horseshoe magnet whose open ends almost, but not quite, touch. Because the gap is so narrow, the magnetic flux density is very strong in this small area.

Meanwhile, back at the microphone, the sound is converted into an electrical signal which is amplified and sent to the recording head. The recording head, as mentioned, is an electromagnet that will convert the electrical impulses into magnetic energy. Thus, the strength and polarity of the magnetic field in the gap of the head is directly proportional to the original signal. While this is happening, the tape, with its emulsion of iron oxide particles, is brought tightly against the gap in the head and moved at a steady rate. At any given instant, the magnetic field in the gap will magnetize the iron oxide particles on the tape that happen to be at the gap at that instant. Furthermore, these particles will be permanently magnetized, that is, they will retain this magnetism even after they pass out of the region of the recording head. Thus, on the tape, is a long series of microscopic permanent magnets whose polarity and magnitude vary proportionately with the strength of the field in the head gap at the instant they passed. The original sound is now recorded in the form of millions of tiny magnets. If you could "see" the magnetism in the tape, you would see the tiny magnets closely spaced (many to the inch) for high tones, and loosely spaced for low notes. These magnets would be strong for loud passages and weak for quiet ones. For example, when recording at 15 i.p.s., a 60 Hz tone would be recorded as eight magnets per inch (alternating North, South, one cycle is recorded as two magnetic impulses, a North and a South). Likewise a tone of 15 KHz would be recorded as 2000 magnetic impulses per inch. Like film, resolution becomes a problem at higher frequencies. The emulsion must be very fine to record 2000 impulses per inch. The problem is even greater at slower speeds. For example, the 15 KHz signal would be 8000 impulses per inch for a tape speed of 3¾ i.p.s.

The playback process is merely the direct inverse of the recording procedure. The tape is moved past the play-back head, which is constructed almost identically to the recording head. As the tiny magnets in the tape pass by the head gap, they induce an electric current in the head coil. This electric signal is proportionate in both frequency and amplitude to the spacing and strength of the magnetic impulses on the tape. This electrical signal can now be amplified and can drive a speaker or another recorder.

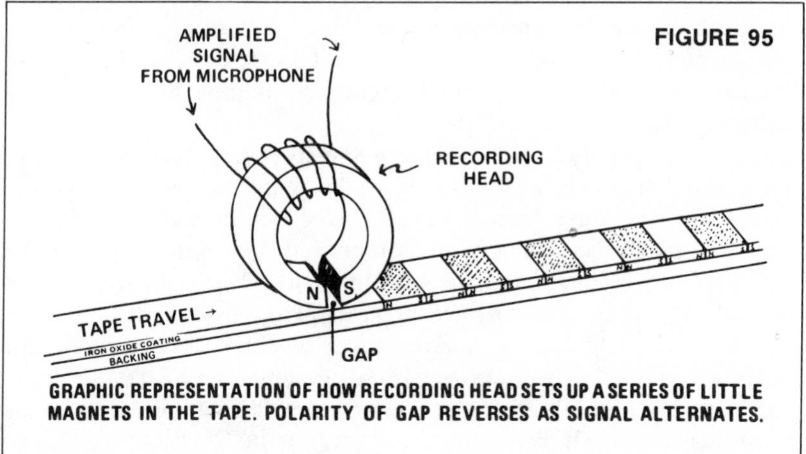

GRAPHIC REPRESENTATION OF HOW RECORDING HEAD SETS UP A SERIES OF LITTLE MAGNETS IN THE TAPE. POLARITY OF GAP REVERSES AS SIGNAL ALTERNATES.

SOUND RECORDING TAPE

The portable magnetic tape recorders used by the motion picture industry are considered the finest machines available. Reflecting the most recent state-of-the-art electronic designs, they are capable of producing recordings of extremely high quality. In fact, these recorders have achieved such a high level of sophistication that, in many instances, the recording tape becomes the limiting factor in terms of overall quality of reproduction. To ensure optimum results from the recorder, the magnetic tape should be selected with great care. An improper choice will not only impair the quality of the recording, but can also damage the machine and recording heads.

The recording tape consists of basically two parts; the magnetic layer and the base or "carrier." The base determines the mechanical properties of the tape while the magnetic layer actually retains the recorded signal.

The magnetic layer consists of an emulsion of iron oxide particles. A professional recording tape must not only incorporate a high quality of iron oxide, but the size and shape of the particles and the distribution of these particles will also determine the recording characteristics of the tape. The iron oxide is usually processed into tiny "needles" only one micron in length. This oxide is then dispersed in a vehicle which contains binders and adhesives. The resultant liquid is used to coat the base material. This is a very critical process, for the coating must not only maintain a precise and uniform thickness, but the oxide must also be oriented in the longitudinal direction. During this process it is also critical to maintain uniform density of the oxide particles within the emulsion. If careful control is not maintained at this point, the particles may group together forming pockets of high density with corresponding areas of almost plain vehicle, while continuing to maintain the uniform thickness.

On a high-quality professional tape the coating is then polished to a super mirror smooth finish. This is a very important step. It is critical during the recording process that the tape maintain a very intimate contact with the recording head. A tape that does not have a smooth finish will not maintain a consistent, close contact with the head (much like an old car on a bumpy washboard road). A tape with a mirror-smooth surface will slide smoothly over the head and maintain the necessary contact. This improves high-frequency response and eliminates dropouts. Another important aspect of polishing is its effect on the recording head itself. Premature head wear is the typical result of tape abrasion which is caused by inferior polishing.

It is the magnetic layer that determines the recording quality of the tape. Almost all brands incorporate similar backing materials, but it is the magnetic layer that separates a professional tape from that which is mediocre and inferior. It is false economy to purchase an off-brand or "discount" brand of tape. Invariably these tapes are not well polished and will irreparably damage the recording and playback heads. In addition, the frequency response is not as flat or consistent as the professional product. The professional tape is usually more sensitive; that is, it will retain a stronger signal for a given set of conditions. Upon playback, this tape provides a higher output signal requiring less amplification—thus providing a better signal-to-noise ratio and a greater dynamic range.

The base material is the carrier of the oxide coating. It must be very supple to facilitate an intimate contact with the head, and yet it must possess considerable strength to withstand the stress and shocks of fast rewinds and sudden stops. Audible range magnetic tape is available in two types of base materials: acetate and polyester. Some recordists have arbitrary preferences. However, there exist major differences in both stability and strength of these two materials.

The base material should maintain dimensional stability throughout changes of both temperature and humidity. Both acetate and polyester are thermally stable to the extent that this aspect becomes relatively unimportant. However a significant difference does exist in the respective reactions to humidity and moisture. The acetate is eight times more sensitive to relative humidity than the polyester. For example, with a change of 60% in relative humidity, an 1800-foot roll of acetate tape will change more than five feet, or almost 20 seconds (at 3¾ ips). This reaction to humidity has other adverse effects. At high relative humidity the moisture absorbed by the acetate backing will tend to curl or cup the tape. In this condition the tape will not rest flat upon the head and, thus, the important tape-to-head contact is impaired. This stretching and shrinking with humidity changes will also cause an overly loose or too tightly wound condition on the spool. The polyester base, on the other hand, is relatively insensitive to moisture and exhibits the aforementioned problems to only a minimal degree.

Differences also exist in strength. FIGURE 96 gives a lucid picture of the relative strengths of the two materials. Both materials show a yield point of approximately 5% elongation. This means that both materials can be stretched to 5% without permanent deformation. (This is the so-called elastic region—once the stress is removed, the tape will return to its normal dimension.) If either tape is stretched beyond 5%, it will be permanently deformed. Note, though, that the polyester is 15% to 20% stronger; it will withstand a greater stress before permanently deforming. Also, the polyester can deform to twice its length before breaking, whereas the acetate will break at 25% elongation.

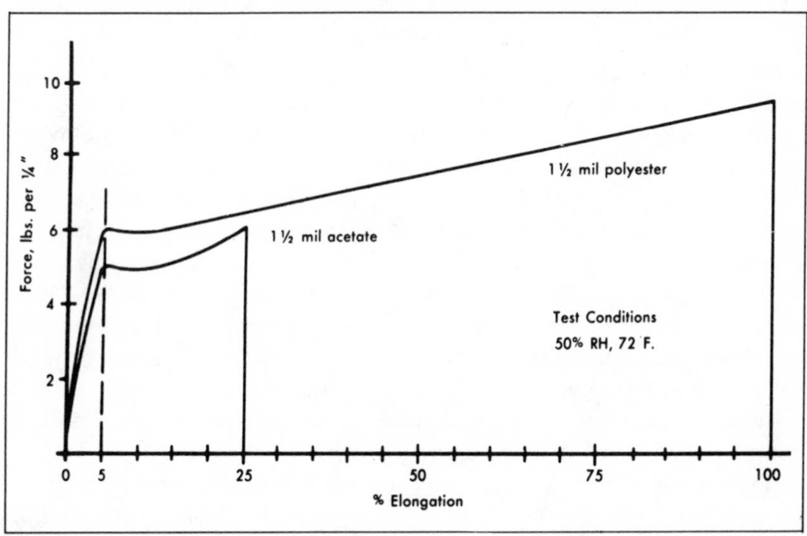

FIGURE 96—TENSILE PROPERTIES OF 1½ MIL BACKING

The ability of the acetate to absorb shock is greatly affected by humidity. At high humidity its impact strength is much greater than under dry conditions when it becomes brittle. The polyester, however, maintains a higher impact strength regardless of relative humidity. In addition acetate is greatly weakened by slight nicks or notches in the edge of the tape. The polyester tape, in contrast, can maintain its full yield strength in spite of minor nicks or edge imperfections: Lastly, acetate has a tendency to "age" or become brittle with time due to loss of moisture content, while polyester exhibits no such phenomena.

It should be clear that the polyester backing exhibits superior performance in almost all respects. Some recordists still prefer acetate for editing reasons. However, where ultimate strength, stability and quality are vital, especially under rough or adverse conditions, the polyester backing will provide the greatest reliability and consistency. (It is interesting to note that polyester backings are used almost exclusively in video, instrumentation and computer applications.)

CARE OF MAGNETIC TAPE

It is general knowledge that the camera original footage should be treated as a delicate, fragile and priceless commodity. It is kept clinically clean and treated only with white editing gloves, etc. Unfortunately, it is not general knowledge that the original ¼-inch sound tape requires equal respect and attention if optimum results are to be expected.

The latest generation of magnetic recording tapes are capable of retaining information for an infinite period of time. The recorded signal will not deteriorate, fade, distort or weaken with age. A magnetic recording is, thus, a precise and virtually permanent record of the sound track. Considering only the magnetic properties of the recording tape, one may form the erroneous impression that the tape is a very rugged and stable medium, invulnerable to abuse. Alas, such is not the case. The physical properties of recording tape are susceptible to the same everyday hazards that plague film: dust, fingerprints, humidity, heat, etc. With proper handling and storage techniques, the adverse effects of these common problems can be held to a minimum.

Dust and dirt are among the most common problems that impair sound quality. Dust or dirt particles on the tape will cause amplitude dropouts and attenuate high frequency response. The particles intrude between the oxide coating and the head, lifting the tape slightly off the head. For optimum recording quality, it is essential to maintain a smooth and consistently intimate contact between tape and head. This random intrusion of foreign particles between tape and head is definitely not going to help maintain such intimacy. Fingerprints on the tape will aggravate this condition. While the oil of the skin will not directly affect the oxide coating, it does form an excellent adhesive that will attract and hold dust and dirt in a manner quite similar to fly paper.

Much like a contagious disease, the dust and dirt particles spread their contamination. Even fingerprints or dirt on the base side of the tape will cause problems. As the tape is wound tightly on the take-up reel, particles on the base are pressed firmly into the oxide coating. On each subsequent playing of the tape, the particles of contamination will spread. Some will become dislodged from the tape and contaminate the tape deck, (heads, rollers, guides, capstan, etc.), which will, in turn, recontaminate the same or a different tape. This could continue to epidemic proportions.

A few basic rules of cleanliness can preclude the foregoing. *Always keep tapes in their boxes.* This is true for both storing and carrying extra reels on location. As one reel is finished, replace it immediately in its box, and do not remove the next reel until it is ready to be loaded on the recorder. Many professional tapes come in a plastic bag within the box. It is a good idea to retain this bag and always replace the tape in it after each use. This practice will protect the tape not only from dirt, but also against extremes in humidity. All professional motion picture tape recorders are equipped with protective lids on the deck. *These should be kept closed at all times, especially on location.* It is also good practice not to smoke or eat while operating the recorder, as ashes and food particles have a way of winding up on the tape. Fingerprints can be held to a minimum by simply not touching the tape.

Even under the most ideal conditions, dirt and oxide particles will build up on a deck. *It is imperative that the parts of the machine which touch the tape be thoroughly cleaned after each day's shooting and preferably after each reel.* A piece of cotton or other lint-free material moistened with Freon TF (Du Pont), or a similiar solvent, will remove most contaminants from heads, rollers, guides and capstan. Be certain that the cleaner is completely dry or evaporated before resuming use of the machine.

Do not forget to clean the empty take-up reel each time it is used. At the same time, inspect it carefully for warpage, cracks or rough edges. A worn or distorted take-up reel is the cause of the most common tape failure; edge damage. The cracked or warped reel will rub or snag the edge of the tape, creating a series of nicks or waves along the edge of the tape. Not only will this cause severe amplitude modulation and dropouts, but the damaged section will tend to lose some of its oxide coating, which will be deposited on the deck and eventually recontaminate the entire width of the track. An excessive amount of oxide on the machine is a certain indication of either a warped, cracked reel or a misaligned guide or roller.

Tape cinching is another problem that can cause permanent tape damage. When tape is fast-wound or rewound, the tension may be uneven, causing the tape to shift on the reel. This results in the tape bunching up or cinching as in FIGURE 97. If left on the reel in this state, cinched tape will develop a permanent "wash board" deformation that renders the tape useless. Another problem that inevitably occurs when tape is fast-wound or rewound is uneven edge winding. As seen in FIGURE 98, uneven edge-wind leaves random tape edges protruding. These edges are susceptible to various types of damage and contamination. There is a simple procedure that can prevent both cinching and uneven edge-winding. *Do not* rewind the tape after recording or playback. Leave it in the unrewound state until just prior to its being used again. The tape is wound very evenly and with an almost constant tension during recording and playing, resulting in a perfect condition for storage.

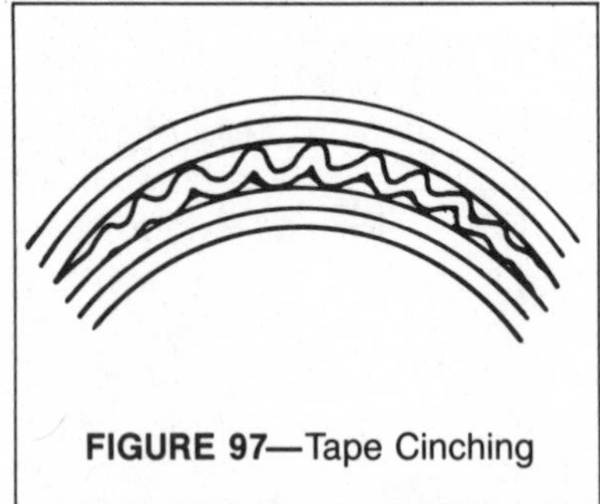

FIGURE 97—Tape Cinching

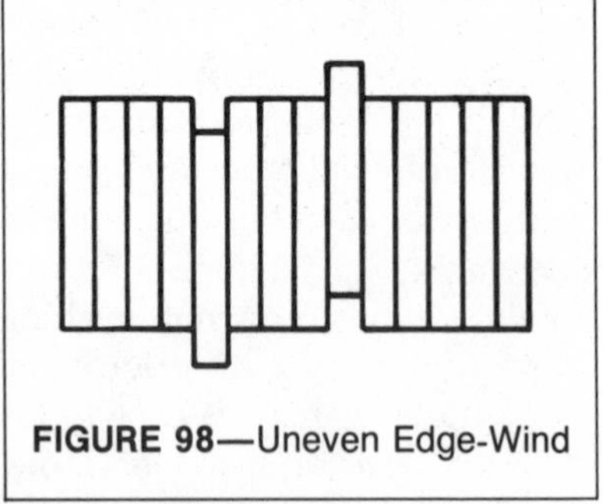

FIGURE 98—Uneven Edge-Wind

Accidental erasure by stray magnetic fields, which is the greatest fear of most producers, turns out to be the least of recording worries. It takes quite a strong magnetic field to erase a tape, and the strength of the field is greatly weakened by distance. A bulk eraser produces a field of 1500 oersteds. At as little as three inches aways, this is reduced to less than 50 oersteds, too slight to affect the tape. It is safe to assume that, in normal transit, a magnetic source as strong as a bulk eraser would not be encountered. However, even if it were, the field could be reduced to a harmless level by packing the tape in a box with approximately three inches of bulk (newspaper or cardboard) on all sides. The chance of accidental erasure is thus virtually eliminated.

RECORDER ALIGNMENT

The tape recorder is usually referred to as an electronic piece of equipment. Ironically, however, most of the problems that occur with recorders are mechanical in nature. Poor adjustment of tape guides or heads can cause amplitude drop-outs, loss of high frequencies, oxide build-up on heads, tape contamination, premature head wear, permanent tape damage, etc. A simple program of inspection and adjustment can keep the recorder performing at optimum and protect expensive or irreplaceable tapes.

The first prerequisite that must exist on all tape transports is a common tape-path center line. If an imaginary line is drawn from the center of the feed spool to the center of the take-up spool, all components that guide or contact the tape must have their centers exactly on this line. (See FIGURE 99). If one of the reel pedestals or tape guides is not adjusted to this common line, it will produce an excessive side or edge pressure on the tape. This can cause permanent deformation or nicking of the tape edge, resulting in loss of high frequencies and excessive amplitude drop-out. In addition, this condition causes the oxide to flake off the tape base, resulting in oxide build-up on the guides and heads and recontamination of the tape itself. Furthermore, the tape will not be properly positioned over the heads. This will affect cross-talk, signal-to-noise ratio, pilotone level, and azimuth adjustment. It should be clear that improperly aligned guides and rollers can cause a lot of headaches.

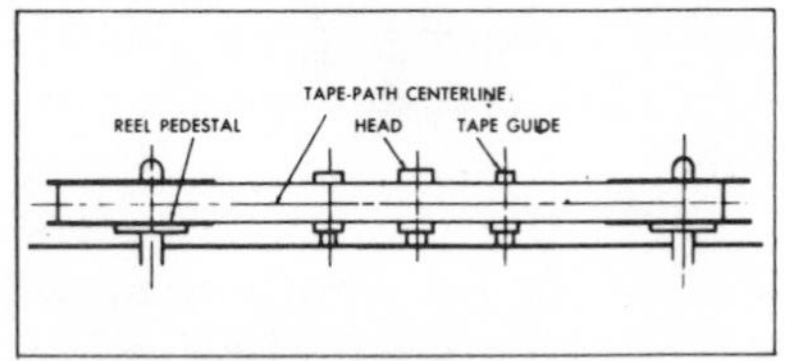

FIGURE 99—SIMPLIFIED TAPE PATH CENTERLINE

I use a very simple method to visually check the center line adjustment of guides and rollers. On a paper cutter or using a straight edge and a razor, cut a strip of paper just under ¼″ in width. Ideally this strip should be about 1/64″ under ¼″, or 15/64″ wide, and about a foot long. Tape each end of the strip to the feed and take-up spools respectively, so that they are centered between the two flanges. Put the reels on the recorder and thread the paper through the machine. With the pinch roller open, twist the reels so that the paper strip is very taut. With the strip in this taut condition, carefully inspect each roller and guide in the transport path. Because the paper strip is slightly under size, it will not fill each guide and there will be a slight space or gap on both sides of the paper strip. If the guide or roller is properly adjusted, the two gaps will be of identical size. If the space on one side is larger than the other, the guide or roller must be realigned.

Once the guides, rollers and reels are adjusted to a common plane, the heads must be aligned. Basically there are five separate adjustments, the three axes and two planes (the third plane is the actual location of the head in the tape path. This is usually not critical). FIGURE 100 best explains these adjustments. The three axes movements are (A) Tilt, (C) Tangency and (E) Azimuth. The two planes of alignment are (B) Height and (D) Contact.

TILT—The first head alignment is to establish that the head is truly parallel to the tape transport plane. If the head is tiled (A—FIGURE 100), tape tension will not be even across the length of the gap resulting in possible reduction of both signal-to-noise ratio and high frequency response. In addition, if this misalignment is excessive, the tape will have a tendency to slide off its proper center line. This adjustment is best made visually with the aid of a square against the transport deck.

HEIGHT—Height is very easily checked. (B, FIGURE 100). With the machine threaded, adjust the height of the head so that the tape perfectly covers the gap length top to bottom. Improper height adjustment will result in uneven head wear, loss in signal-to-noise ratio, loss of pilotone level and (in stereo) cross-talk.

TANGENCY—Like the height adjustment, tangency is usually determined visually. It involves squaring the head to the tape (C—FIGURE 100). In other words, in a top view, the axis of the head should be perfectly perpendicular to the tape. The result of improper tangency is both a loss of high frequencies and an increased susceptibility to drop-outs.

CONTACT—The contact adjustment (D—FIGURE 100) affects the amount of tape "wrap around" on the head. This adjustment is usually designed into a professional recorder and seldom requires any attention.

AZIMUTH—Last, but certainly not least, is the azimuth adjustment. This is by far the most critical of all the alignment procedures. The azimuth adjustment determines that the head gaps are precisely perpendicular to the tape center line (E—FIGURE 100). Because the head gaps are so narrow, it is impossible to align azimuth visually, and a special azimuth alignment test tape must be employed. This test tape is simply a high-frequency signal recorded by a machine with a critically adjusted azimuth. The procedure is simple. Play back the test tape on the recorder. Note the level reading on the VU meter. Then adjust the head azimuth *very slightly* to either side and note the level reading on the meter. If the level increases in one direction and decreases in the other, keep turning in the direction of the increased reading until a peak level is reached. This is the optimum adjustment, (Note: also check gap visually, as there could be smaller, secondary peaks in level on either side of the main peak or proper adjustment.)

Once the playback head is adjusted, the record head is aligned in a similar manner. Record a steady tone onto a blank tape, monitoring off the playback head. Adjust the azimuth, as before, for a peak reading on the VU meter. Heads with improperly aligned azimuth will suffer from severe loss in signal strength and exhibit poor signal-to-noise quality.

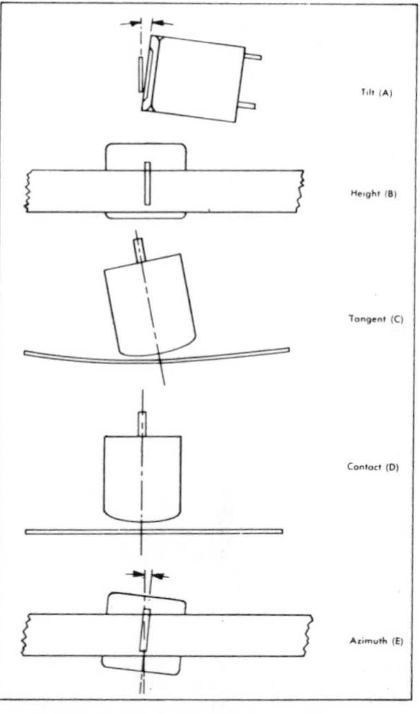

FIGURE 100—HEAD ALIGNMENT

SOUND BASICS

The most often mentioned audio specification must be "frequency response". Whether it be an audio amplifier, speaker, or tape recorder, the question of frequency response will most probably be posed first. This specification alludes to the range of frequencies from the lowest notes to the highest that the piece of equipment or tape/track can handle. This specification has little meaning if deviation limits are not given. For example, in FIGURE 101, both manufacturers claim 20-20,000 Hz. frequency response, which is excellent and, for all practical purposes, the ultimate frequency range. Most adults can't even hear frequencies as high as 20,000 Hz. and a range of 30-16,000 Hz. is in most cases considered perfect. However, a closer look at FIGURE 101 reveals that the curve for item B rolls off severely at the upper and lower ends of the frequency range. At 20 Hz. and at 20,000 Hz. the response is down almost 10 db. Item A, on the other hand, exhibits a very "flat" response curve. When response limits are quoted, the difference between these two items becomes apparent. Most often the response limits of professional equipment are ±1 or ±2 dB. With

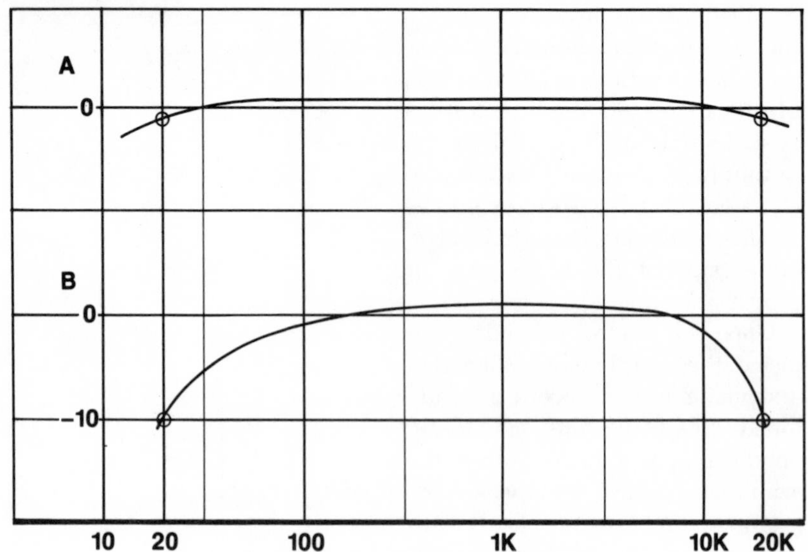

FIGURE 101—Both A and B claim 20-20,000 Hz. frequency response. However, with ± 1 db tolerance, A remains at 20-20,000 Hz., while B is actually 100-10,000 Hz. This diagram reveals that item B rolls off severely at the upper and lower ends of the frequency range. Item A, on the other hand, exhibits a very "flat" response curve.

limits of ±1 dB. deviation, item B becomes only 100-10,000 Hz. ±1 dB, while item A remains at 20-20,000 Hz. ±1 dB.

The specifications of an item indicate only its maximum capabilities. There are cases in which a wide frequency response is not necessary or even desirable. The sound recordist must know the frequency range of the subject he is recording, as well as the frequency capabilities of the final product such as a 16mm optical track or a 35mm magnetic track, et cetera.

FIGURE 102 shows the frequency range of several sounds and musical instruments. While the range of 20-20,000 Hz. is considered the full human hearing range, most important audio information occurs in the lower frequencies. With the exception of the organ and several deep bass instruments, most musical fundamentals occur in the 50-5,000 Hz. range. Even the violin, considered by most a "high frequency" instrument, only extends to 3,000 Hz. in the fundamental range. Note also that speech fundamentals fall within a very limited range of about 300-to-3,000 Hz.

With few exceptions, the frequencies above 5,000 Hz. are essentially harmonics or "overtones" of the fundamental frequencies. I am not implying that these harmonics are unimportant. The entire high-fidelity industry is based on preserving and reproducing these harmonics to the limits of audibility. These harmonics add to the unique "sound" of each particular instrument. A "low-fidelity" system that did not reproduce high-frequency harmonics would sound relatively dull and flat. However, these harmonics are usually very low-energy signals compared with the fundamental notes and, thus, comprise only a small portion of the overall signal for most instruments (usually only 5% to 20%). While the loss of the high-frequency components of the signal will undoubtedly knock some of the "brilliance" off the recording, it will not seriously affect the overall performance. All fundamentals will still be present. Each and every note that is played will be heard, and each instrument easily identifiable. The loss of high frequencies will obviously have a greater effect on those sounds that are comprised essentially of harmonics, such as cymbals, bells, and hand clapping.

It is important for the recordist to know the frequency range of his subjects for several reasons. Selection of microphones and other components depends on the frequency range. Tape saturation and signal overload are affected by frequency range, particularly high-energy harmonics at slower tape speeds. Probably most important to the motion picture soundman is the problem of background noises on location. By knowing the frequency ranges of both the subject and the unwanted noise, the recordist can usually reduce the objectionable noise by altering the frequency response of the recorder. This is usually done by

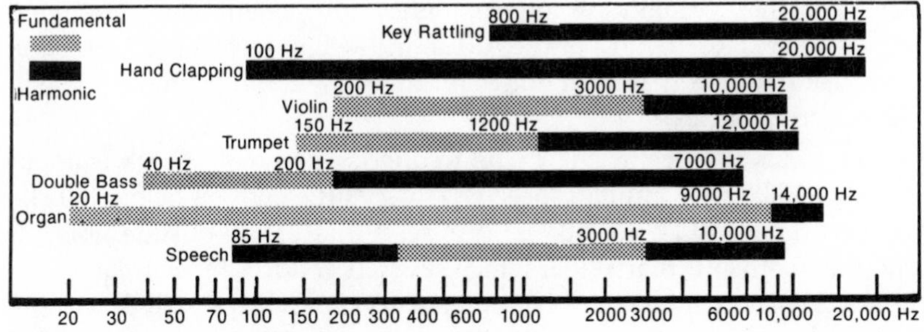

FIGURE 102—Chart illustrating frequency ranges of various sound sources, including Key Rattling, Hand Clapping, Violin, Trumpet, Double Bass, Organ and Speech. While the range of 20-20,000 Hz. is considered the full human hearing range, most important audio information occurs in the lower frequencies.

means of filter circuits. Rather than plunging into a theoretical discourse of filters, a common example will probably best explain this principle.

An interview is taking place in an office. The subject is obviously the human voice which has a frequency response of about 150 Hz to 3,000 Hz with the most significant information occurring in the 300 Hz to 2,000 Hz range. Now for a look at the noise in the room. Objectionable noises emanating from within the room can usually be eliminated. Refrigerators, fans, air conditioners, etc. can be temporarily turned off. In most cases, then, the noise is coming from outside the room. Under these circumstances, the noise is almost always comprised of low-frequency components in the subaudible (10 Hz) to 150 Hz range. This is due to the transmission of low frequencies by the walls of a building. Because of the great mass of the walls, the higher frequencies will bounce off and be reflected. Very strong low frequencies, however, can cause the walls to vibrate or resonate, and these low tones or rumbles can be transmitted to the most interior areas of a structure.

Most people who live in an apartment house have experienced this phenomenon when a next-door-neighbor is playing a hi-fi unit loudly. Often the melody, most of the instruments, and vocals are inaudible, and the tune is unrecognizable; however, the rhythm and beat of the bass drum and bass guitar is quite distinguishable. The walls between the apartments will reflect or absorb the higher frequencies, yet the very low frequencies will cause the wall to vibrate, and those low frequencies will be transmitted into the next apartment. In many cases a good neighbor need not lower the overall volume of his hi-fi but merely lower his bass control. This is also why a portable AM radio can usually be cranked up quite loud without offending neighbors. The portable AM radio has virtually no low-frequency components, and assuming windows are closed, most of the AM sound will not leave the room. The conclusion here is that most noises reaching the room from outside will be low frequencies.

Now, back to our interview. The frequency range of speech is about 150 Hz to 3,000 Hz. Human speech has very little content below 150 Hz, yet this range (10 Hz to 150 Hz) is exactly that of the outside noise. It should be obvious that a filter which severely reduces those frequencies below 200 Hz will have little or no effect on speech, yet will drastically reduce low-frequency noise reaching the recording room. Almost all professional recorders, both single- and double-system, employ some form of low-frequency attenuation for exactly this purpose. Sometimes called roll-off or speech-music controls, these switches will provide a flat response in the normal or "music" position, while offering a reasonable amount of low-frequency attentuation in the roll-off or "speech" position.

FIGURE 103 represents the actual group of curves for the Nagra SL recorder. The "speech" position begins to attenuate at 200 Hz, but is only -2db down at 90 Hz, and will, thus, have virtually no effect on audible speech quality. Yet this curve provides -8db of attenuation at 50 Hz, which should reduce low frequency noises and rumbles quite effectively. The three curves marked "S & LFA" (speech and low-frequency attenuation), "M & LFA (music and low-frequency attentuation), and "roll off" appear quite severe, but in reality, the effect on speech quality is relatively subtle. In any of those three positions, the quality of speech is only altered by an almost inperceptible loss of the "bassy" aspect of the male voice. A higher female voice is hardly affected at all. While these three filters begin to roll off at 2,000 Hz, they are only 3db down at 350 Hz and do not have a great effect on the major portion of the speech spectrum. However, in the sub-speech area, they provide an enormous amount of low-frequency attenuation. The roll-off position is most effective with almost 10db of reduction at 100 Hz, and about 20db at 30 Hz.

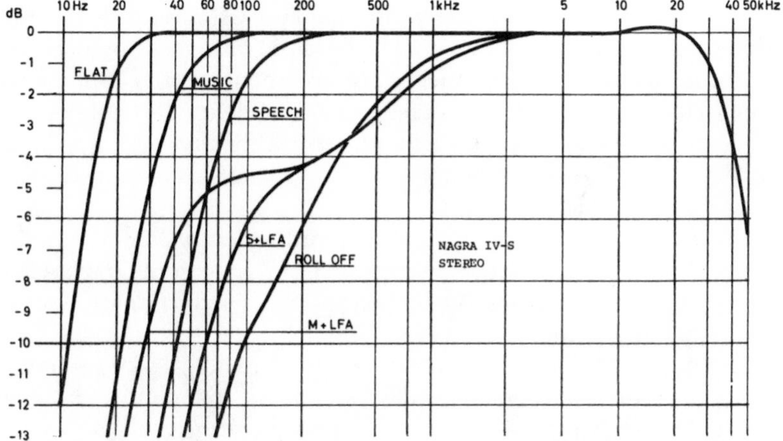

FIGURE 103—Low-frequency filter curves for a two-track Nagra recorder.

A recent assignment included recording inside a house. Outside, a bulldozer was busily at work and although closing all the windows dampened most of the noise, the low-frequency rumbles almost shook the house. Switching in the "roll-off" filter rendered the bulldozer almost inaudible.

In many cases the low-frequency filtering can be done when transferrring the tape. However, where the low-frequency noise is quite severe, it could drive the tape into overload and distortion and under these circumstances the filtering should be done before the recording process.

QUALITY LIMITATIONS

A soundperson, like any craftsman, should always try to obtain the best results possible. However, there are certain circumstances that might prevent optimum results. Under these less-than-ideal conditions, a compromise in quality may be acceptable for particular applications. A soundperson is definitely at an advantage if he knows the specific application of his track and, in addition, the demands and limitations of that specific end-product.

For example, 35mm film travels through the projector at 90 feet per minute or 18 ips (inches per second). This is actually faster than many studio tape recorders which run at 15 ips. Thus, a 35mm magnetic track, and even a 35mm optical track, is capable of studio-quality sound. Moreover, with the introduction of Dolby and "dbx" noise reducers and color sensitive multiple-channel optical techniques, many 35mm audio playback systems can be considered true high-fidelity. Last but not least, a 35mm theatrical release usually plays in a theatre with reasonably good acoustics, low ambient noise, and large speakers capable of wide-frequency reproduction.

The point here is that the sound recordist on a 35mm theatrical project has little room to compromise quality. Noise in the track will be easily heard, and any loss in frequency response or fidelity will undoubtedly be noticed.

The demands of a 16mm print are, unfortunately, less stringent. A 16mm print travels through a projector at 36 feet per minute or 7.2 ips. While this is still a respectable speed for magnetic recording, it is rather slow for an optical track and the upper-frequency response suffers drastically.

FIGURES 105a and 105b represent the actual frequency response curves for a well-known professional 16mm mag/opt projector. The magnetic response (FIG 105A) is relatively flat, being $\pm$2db from 40-12,000. This is a very good response and just within the realm of "high-fidelity." The optical response of FIG 105B is a different story. The curve begins to roll off rapidly above 3,000Hz and below 100Hz.

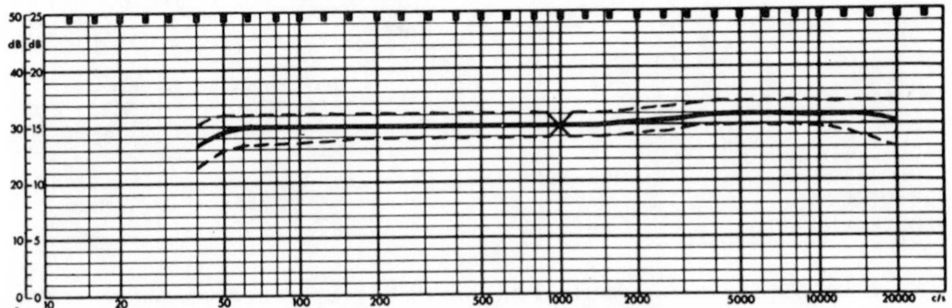

FIGURE 104—Frequency response curve of a top-of-the-line condenser microphone. Note extremely flat response from 40 to 20,000 Hz. The capabilities of the microphone and Nagra recorder far exceed those of the projector.

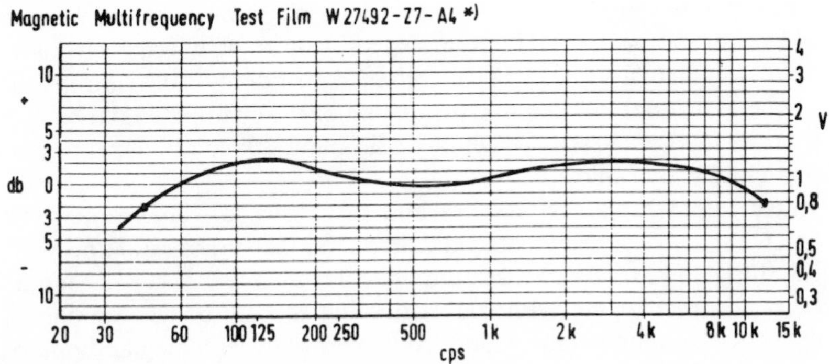

FIGURE 105A—The playback frequency response of a magnetic 16mm projector. The response is ± 2db from 40 to 12,000 Hz, which is quite good and can be considered to be just within the realm of "high fidelity."

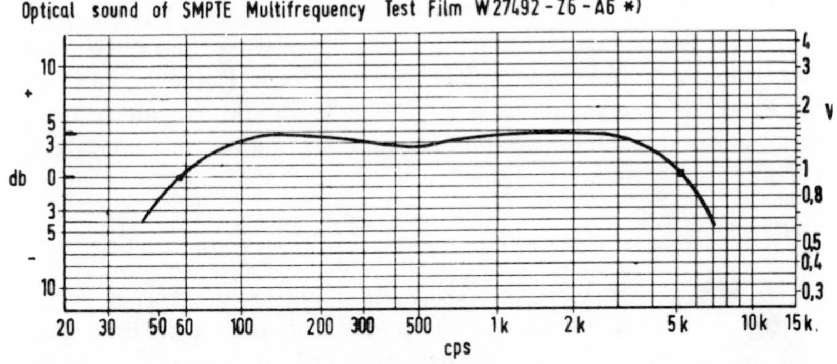

FIGURE 105B—The playback frequency response of an optical 16mm projector. The response is only ± 2db from 60 to 5,000 Hz. This is acceptable for speech and most music fundamentals, but it is certainly not "hi-fi."

FIGURE 106

	Nagra	Microphone	S/S Camera	Projector Mag	Proj. Opt.
Frequency Response in Hz, ±2 db	30-20k	40-20k	50-8k	40-12k	60-5k
Signal/Noise Ratio Record/Playback	70db	71db	50db	—	—
Playback only	83db	—	—	38db	50db
Wow & Flutter	.05%	—	.45%	.40%	.40%

The ±2db response is about 60-5,000Hz. This is an acceptable response, as far as the reproduction of speech and music fundamentals is concerned. However, it is a far cry from "high-fidelity." Moreover, a 16mm print is most likely played back in a classroom or auditorium where acoustics are less than ideal and room ambience is quite high (often including the noise of the projector itself).

If the 16mm print is to be viewed via television, the above arguments hold double in spades. The audio quality of most telecine chains is deplorable (actually they are capable of high fidelity). While much of the blame belongs at the transmission end of the chain, the fatal blow is struck at the home receiver where audio playback components resemble a child's toy radio.

Most 16mm projection systems and single-system cameras also fall somewhat short of the ideal in the area of signal/noise ratio and wow and flutter. FIGURE 106 lists the specifications for a current-model Nagra recorder, along with top-of-the-line models of a microphone, single-system sound camera, and a projector with both mag and optical playback. FIGURE 104 diagrams the frequency response of the microphone. Note that the capabilities of the microphone and Nagra far exceed those of the projector.

The point of this dissertation is *not* to imply that 16mm and television sound reproduction should be considered second-rate. The soundperson should always strive for the best possible results. The Lord knows a 16mm track needs everything possible going for it. However, when less than ideal conditions exist, the soundperson should consider the final format before inordinate amounts of time and money are spent trying to achieve the ultimate in soundtrack fidelity.

LOUDNESS

We have been discussing the quality and accuracy of various types of audio equipment from microphones to speakers. Regardless of the amount of effort spent in selecting the best audio components, there is always one device in the audio chain that exhibits specifications far below all others—the listener's ear.

The human ear does not perceive all frequencies with equal loudness. Moreover, the magnitude of this inaccuracy is dependent on the loudness level of the sound.

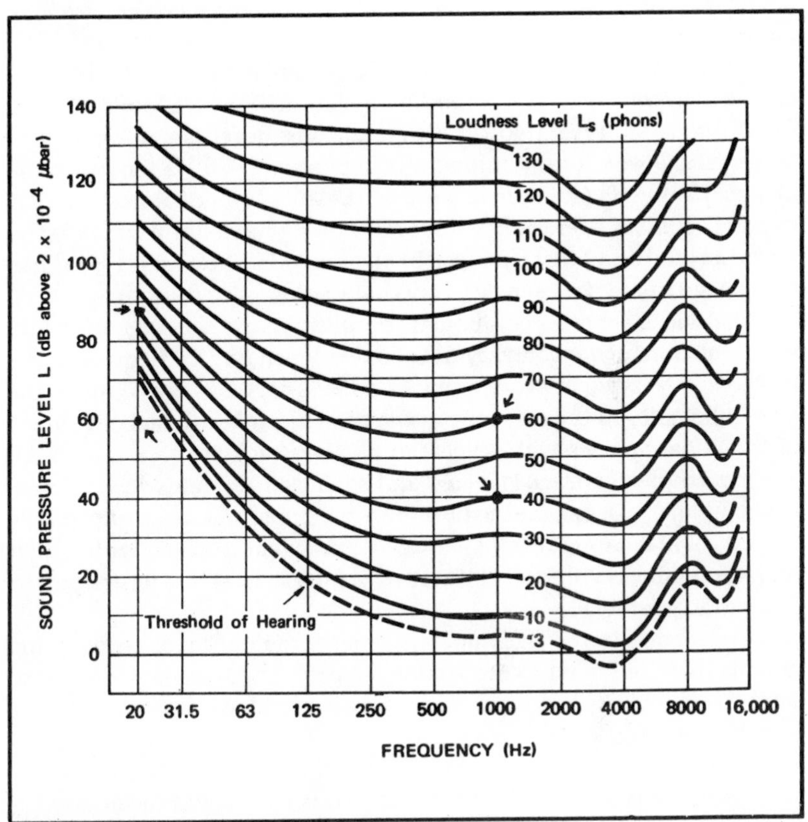

FIGURE 107—Loudness Contour Curves of the Human Ear. These curves exhibit the so-called "Fletcher/Munson Effect." The numbers on the left are Sound Pressure Levels in decibels (dB). This is the actual energy reaching the ear. The numbers on the curves themselves are "phons" or the *perceived* loudness, the sensation of loudness that registers with the brain. Note that at 1,000 Hz the S.P.L. in dB is equal to the Loudness Level in phons for any value of loudness. However, as the frequency varies from 1,000 Hz, the ear and reality are definitely on different paths.

Most obvious is the ear's lack of sensitivity at low frequencies. More important, however, is the fact that this lack of sensitivity becomes more acute as the loudness is reduced. As an extreme example, a 1,000 Hz signal at 60dB will be quite audible at 60 phons (normal conversation level). Yet a 20 Hz signal at the same 60dB will be totally inaudible to the human ear, being below the threshold of hearing.

A series of curves expressing the relationship between frequency and loudness was first published in 1933 by Fletcher and Munson, and this loudness/frequency dependency is most often called the Fletcher/Munson effect. The revised curves in FIGURE 107 best explain the Fletcher/Munson phenomenon.

Most obvious from these curves is the ear's relative lack of sensitivity at lower frequencies. For example, a tone of 1,000 Hz at a loudness level of 40 phons requires a 40 dB sound pressure level (sound energy or power). However, for the human ear to perceive a 20 Hz tone with the identical loudness (40 phons), a sound pressure level of almost 88 dB is required. It takes over 65,000 times more energy to make a 20 Hz signal sound as loud as a 1,000 Hz signal at 40 phons. The human ear is far less responsive to low frequencies, especially at low sound levels.

It is ironic to consider equipment specifications on the order of ±1 dB when the human ear can vary over 60 dB, depending on frequency and level. However, the important point on these curves is not so much the lack of linearity in the response of the human ear but the inconsistency of these inaccuracies with respect to playback volume.

For example, if a track is mixed and equalized at a fairly low volume, it will sound "bassy" and exhibit a slight upper midrange dip if it is played back at a loud level. Likewise, a track that is mixed with a high monitor loudness will be significantly lacking in bass when reproduced at a more quiet level.

Some models of reproduction equipment employ "loudness contour" circuits that are linked to the volume control. These circuits attempt to alter the frequency response with respect to volume according to the Fletcher/Munson curves. However, most of these circuits are approximations at best.

In terms of practical sound recording, this Fletcher/Munson effect is only noticeable when the playback volume differs significantly from the original, usually a matter beyond the control of the sound recordist. However, I believe that an understanding of our hearing mechanisms is interesting, and one never knows when the information may prove helpful.

LEVEL METERS

The audio level meter is probably the most basic tool in sound recording. Every professional recordist, and even most amateurs, have a basic feeling for these meters. The general rule of thumb seems to be, "Keep the needles kicking up around 0 VU, but don't let them go over." This is like a cameraman saying, "Point the camera at the subject and push the button." While neither of these statements is false, they are obviously gross simplifications. Yet, for many sound recordists, the former statement represents the extent of their knowledge of level meters.

What is a level meter really telling you? To begin with, there are two different types of level meters in use today, and each displays entirely different information.

The older type of device is called a VU meter, while the modern trend is toward the Peak Reading Meter or Modulometer. An understanding of the VU meter requires a quick look into its history. In the old days of recording, before solid-state microelectronics, a meter had to be direct and simple. What could be more simple than a basic voltmeter, reading the level of the audio signal? That is basically what a VU meter is—a voltmeter connected to the recording amplifier. However, the VU meter turned out to be *too* simple. A voltmeter is partly a mechanical device, and the moving pointer has a definite mass, inertia, damping, and friction. All these characteristics are called its "ballistics". The audio signal is often comprised of quick transient peaks on the order of a milli-second which the mass of the VU pointer couldn't possibly register. The mass of the pointer is great enough that many extremely short peaks can be there and gone before the pointer even begins to budge.

What this boils down to is the following: If the audio signal is a long, sustained note, the VU meter gives an accurate indication of the signal. It has plenty of time to reach the maximum level of the signal and stabilize. If the signal is of extremely short duration, the VU meter may not register at all or, at best, give an indication significantly below the actual maximum level. If the signal is comprised of a series of peaks and dips (human voice, music), the VU meter will give an *average* reading somewhat below the peaks. In this respect, the mass of the VU pointer acts like a mechanical flywheel displaying the average energy being fed to it.

To make the matter even more complicated, the various audio manufacturers incorporated meters with different ballistic characteristics and different calibration points. Eventually a standard had to be agreed upon.

Since the human voice seemed to be the most prevalent signal in the early days of broadcasting, the VU meter was calibrated with voice as a reference. Once the ballistics of the VU meter were standardized, it was found that the quick peaks of the human voice (to which the meter does not respond) were actually 8 to 10 dB above the *average* reading that the VU meters displayed. As a result, the 0 VU point on a VU meter was (and is) set 8 to 10 dB below actual 100% modulation. In the case of tape recording, the 0 VU point is actually 8 to 10 dB below the point of tape saturation. FIGURE 108 best explains this fact. Note that the line representing actual tape saturation is 8 to 10 dB above the 0 VU meter point for the most significant portion of the audio spectrum. This 8 to 10 dB area is sometimes referred to as *recording headroom.*

In practical terms, the two important points to remember are, one, that the VU meter has mechanical mass that prevents it from responding to quick peaks. As a result, it will *average* quick fluctuations of volume. Point two is that the VU meter is usually calibrated such that 0 VU is really 8 to 10 dB *down* from actual tape saturation or broadcast overmodulation.

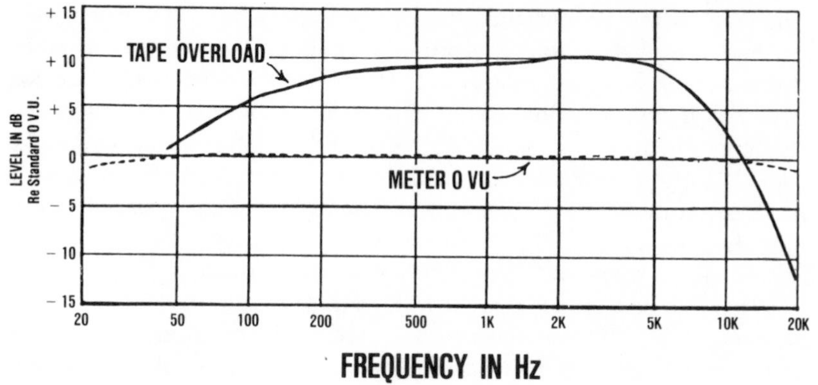

FIGURE 108—Note that for the major portion of the audio spectrum, tape saturation is actually 8-10dB above 0 VU. This 8-10dB distance above the meter 0 VU is called recording headroom.

When recording voice, the needle should be kept close to 0 VU and rarely should it be allowed to dart much above the 0 VU point. This practice is based on the definition of the VU meter. Since we know that the peaks of the human voice are 8-10 dB higher than the average reading of the VU meter, these peaks will "use up" the 8-10 dB headroom. Therefore, the average reading of the VU meter should not be allowed to go above the 0 VU mark.

Where the signal is relatively sustained and not peaky, the VU meter can actually be allowed to go significantly above 0 VU. For example, an opera soprano hitting a sustained note can put the needle up to +3 VU easily. As a matter of fact, if the VU meter was marked up to +8dB, the needle could be allowed to reach this point. The reason should be clear. On sustained notes, the VU meter has time to display the actual peak or maximum level, and, by calibration, the maximum level is 8 to 10dB above 0 VU on the meter.

On the other hand, recording musical instruments most often involves the exact opposite technique. Instruments in the percussion or plucking family such as drums, piano, guitar, et cetera, often contain peaks that are 15 to 20 dB above their average signal as displayed by the VU meter. Keeping in mind that the VU meter is based on 8-10 dB headroom (for the human voice), it should be obvious that these musical instruments require an additional 5-10 dB of headroom (or peak room). Depending on the amount of peakiness, these instruments should therefore be recorded with a VU maximum of -5 to -10dB. This will yield a total of 15 to 20 dB of headroom to accommodate those signal peaks to which the meter is unresponsive.

The use of the VU meter requires a knowledge of its principle as well as constant awareness of the nature of the recorded signal. Mastering the technique of the VU meter usually requires a significant amount of experience.

The peak meter or modulometer, in contrast, is far less mysterious and does not exhibit such a complex personality. While in many cases, the modulometer or peak meter is still a mechanical meter, it is connected to a complex electronic circuit.

This electronic circuit receives the audio signal that is being applied to the recording heads. Because this circuit is purely electronic, it can sense instanteous peaks in the audio signal as short as a millisecond. The circuit is designed to "memorize" these peaks for about one second or so before "forgetting" them. This memory signal is then sent to a somewhat standard voltmeter or L.E.D. display. The combination of this "memory" circuit and the fast-responding voltmeter becomes a peak meter or modulometer.

In practice, an audio peak comes along and is gone before any mechanical meter could possibly respond to it. But, in this case, the peak-reading circuit "holds" the peak long enough for the mechanical voltmeter to respond fully to the maximum amplitude of signal. Even though the audio peak has long since gone, the peak-reading circuit remembers it long enough for both the meter and the recording engineer to respond.

In essence, the mystery is gone. The peak meter presents an accurate and precise picture of the maximum amplitudes being recorded. The type of signal rarely has to be considered in interpreting a peak meter. Whether it be voice, music, sound effects, etc., the meter will follow maximum levels and, thus, prevent overloading on peaks. Likewise, on signals with little or no peaks, the meter will allow higher recording levels, making use of the headroom that might have been unused with a VU meter. This results in a quieter recording (improved signal-to-noise ratio).

One thing is important to understand with a peak-reading meter: THERE IS NO HEAD ROOM! The meter is calibrated to indicate tape overload at 0 dB. (See FIGURE 109) Remember that the VU meter is calibrated in such a way that 0 VU is actually 8-10dB *under* actual tape saturation. Not so with the modulometer.

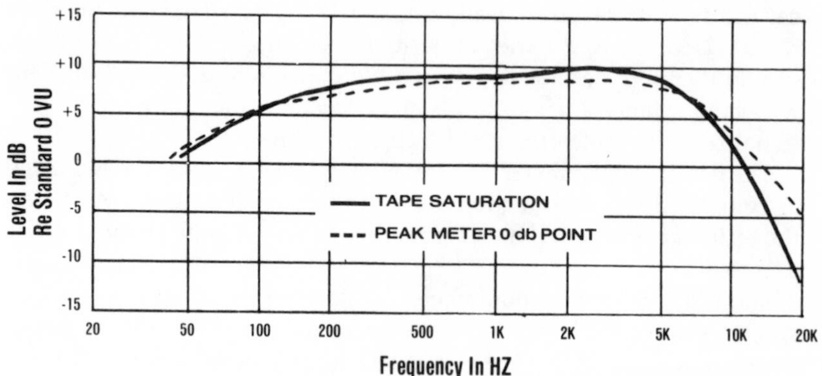

FIGURE 109—The 0dB point on a peak meter or modulometer does not correspond to the standard 0 VU level. The 0dB point on a modulometer follows the level of actual tape saturation. It is important to understand that there is NO headroom with a peak meter.

When the peak meter says 0dB, it means it. That is the limit. (Compare to FIGURE 108) As a matter of fact, when transferring from a VU-metered recorder to a peak-metered machine, the 0dB reference tone on the VU meter should be set to a −8dB on the peak meter. The distance between the −8dB and 0dB (8dB) on the peak meter thus corresponds to the 8dB of headroom built into the VU meter. It should be clear, then, that 0dB on the peak meter is the bitter end.

I should mention that at 0dB, the tape doesn't become instantly distorted. As the signal exceeds the 0dB point, distortion slowly increases (FIGURE 110) with level. A top-quality recorder employing the latest tape formulations can usually tolerate a +2 to +4dB signal before distortion really approaches the objectionable point. However, in normal practice, this 2 or 3dB should be kept for emergencies, and the 0dB point should be considered as maximum. A quality modulometer should facilitate optimum recording levels under almost all circumstances.

FIGURE 110—Distortion does not commence the instant 0dB is exceeded. It gradually builds up from insignificant amounts to about 1% at 0dB. Above 0dB distortion rises quite rapidly. However, at +3dB the distortion may still be acceptable on some high-quality recorders.

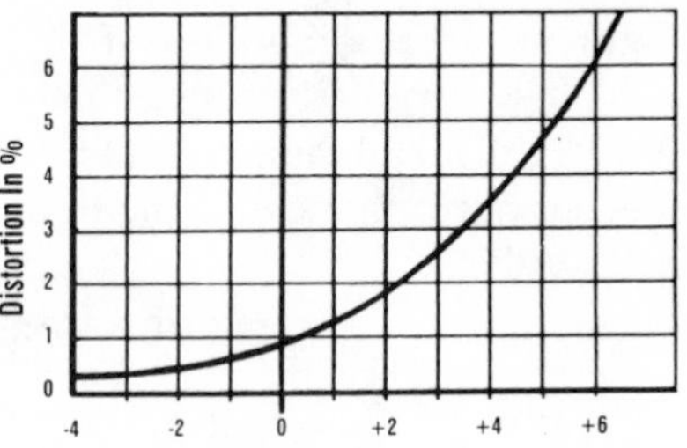

MICROPHONES

The first link in the recording chain is the microphone. It is the device that initially converts the mechanical sound waves into electrical impulses that can be mixed, equalized, and ultimately recorded and re-recorded. There are currently hundreds of microphones from which the cinematographer can select, and, to all but the most knowledgeable sound technicians, this wide choice can be confusing.

There are basically three types of microphones: the *crystal* or *ceramic*, the *dynamic*, and the *condenser (capacitor)*. The crystal-type microphone is seldom used for professional sound recording. The crystal mike requires extremely high input impedances which restrict both cable length and low-frequency response. Because they are inexpensive to manufacture, this type is usually supplied with home tape recorders. For all intents and purposes, the cinematographer can rule out the crystal or ceramic microphone for sound track recording.

The dynamic microphone is the most widely used of the three types. It combines high quality, rugged construction and reasonable cost. Mechanically, the dynamic microphone is constructed like a miniature loudspeaker. The sound waves strike a diaphragm and coil assembly, causing it to vibrate. This vibrating coil is in a magnet structure and thus generates a small voltage. The dynamic mike is simple and rugged, and requires no special power supplies or oscillators.

The ribbon microphone falls in the dynamic class. It is a very high quality device, but, because it is so delicate, its use is usually restricted to recording studios. Ribbon mikes are seldom used in the motion picture industry for this reason.

The condenser microphone has gained great popularity in the motion picture industry over the last ten years. Condenser microphones employ a tiny feather-light membrane instead of a heavy coil assembly and are considered to have superior electro-acoustical characteristics. The very light membrane, because of its low mass, produces a "clean" sound which is especially noticeable at higher frequencies. Unfortunately, this light membrane also very delicate, and for this reason, the condenser microphone, like the ribbon mike, has usually been restricted to the studio.

MICROPHONE CONSTRUCTION

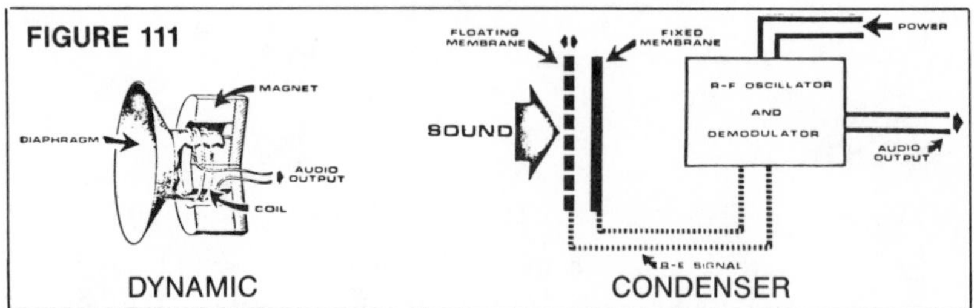

DYNAMIC MICROPHONE

The principle of the dynamic mike is similar to that of the loudspeaker, only in reverse. Sound waves striking the diaphragm cause it, and the attached coil, to vibrate. The coil assembly is immersed in a magnetic field and, thus, the vibrations cause an electric potential (voltage) to be generated. This vibrating voltage is connected (via the leads) directly to the pre-amp input of the recording amplifier, where it is amplified.

CONDENSER MICROPHONE

The condenser mike is not quite as simple as the dynamic mike. The dynamic mike is essentially a generator; the moving elements actually generate the audio signal which merely has to be amplified. The condenser mike uses two thin membranes as the active mechanical elements. These two thin membranes by themselves cannot generate any signal and, thus, additional electronics have to be employed. A r-f condenser mike, in addition to the two membranes, employs an r-f oscillator, a power supply, a demodulator and an audio pre-amplifier. The r-f oscillator-demodulator system needs power to operate, and since no power is generated within the system (unlike the dynamic mike), power must be supplied from an outside source. Some tape recorders have built in power supplies for condenser mikes. In other cases a battery is connected in the microphone line and supplies a D.C. voltage to the mike over the two audio output conductors, thus precluding the necessity for additional or special mike cables.

With the oscillator powered up, a r-f signal is applied to the two membranes which are essentially a capacitor or condenser. As the sound waves hit the moveable membrane, it will vibrate, thus fluctuating the distance between the two membranes. This will, in turn, cause the capacitance of the two membranes to vary accordingly. This capacitor, however, is part of the r-f system and will cause the r-f voltage or in some cases the r-f frequency to vibrate respectively. These vibrations are isolated in the demodulator section of the mike, amplified, and emerge as a clean audio sound.

Recent technical advancements, however, have made the condenser microphone more versatile and rugged. Probably the biggest breakthrough has been the r-f condenser mikes (Sennheiser 415, 815). These microphones employ an extreme high-frequency signal on the membranes. The sound pressures will then modulate this high-frequency (r-f) signal and the audio signal ultimately results from demodulating this r-f signal.

This may appear to be a roundabout method, but the results are quite impressive. For openers, the r-f condenser mike is very rugged and is less sensitive to physical shock, humidity and temperature when compared to conventional condenser microphones. Most astonishing is the extremely low noise level of the r-f condenser mike, which approaches the theoretical noise limit. (The mike can actually register the movement of free air molecules when compared to a vacuum.) The audio output of the r-f condenser is very high and thus high gain in the pre-amp stage is unnecessary, thus further enhancing its low noise characteristics. Because of the inherent superior characteristics of the condenser mike, and in light of the recent technical advancements, the r-f condenser mike is fast becoming the most popular device for those demanding the ultimate in recording quality.

On the negative side, the r-f condenser is usually very expensive. It also requires an external power supply. However, on the latest models this merely consists of a tiny battery that attaches to the mike itself. Most basically, a dynamic mike is usually available that will be more than adequate for the particular situation. In other words, in many cases, the quality of an r-f condenser mike will grossly outclass the other components in the recording chain and, thus, nothing is actually gained above that which a good dynamic mike would have provided. (Keep in mind that a 16mm optical track has a response of approximately 70-6000 Hz and typical S/N of 40-45db. Not exactly what would be considered the ultimate in high fidelity.) In general, the quality of the microphone should be equal to, but not necessarily superior to, the other components in the sound chain including the final product.

DIRECTIVITY OF MICROPHONES

Among the many microphone specifications, by far the most distinctive is the directional characteristic. This refers to the relative sensitivity of the microphone to sounds arriving from various directions. The test procedure for determining the directional nature of a microphone is simple and direct. The mike is placed in an anechoic (soundproof) chamber with a sound source. With the axis of the mike facing the source, the output of the mike is set to a relative value of 1.0. The mike is then slowly rotated, and the output (or volume) of the mike is plotted as a function of its axial position relative to the sound source. This test is then repeated once for each of several different frequencies as a sound source. The results are plotted on a polar diagram (see FIGURE 112).

Microphones can basically be categorized into three direction types: Omni-directional, directional (cardioid and super-cardioid), and ultra-directional. The omni-directional mike is virtually non-discriminating as to the direction of a sound source. The recorded level of a sound will be the same whether it is in front of the mike or directly behind it. This type of mike usually operates on the "pressure" principle and, thus, sources close to the mike will far outweigh those sources at a greater distance. Due to these indiscriminate characteristics, the omni-directional mike usually picks up much unwanted room presence and background noises and, as a result, finds little application in the motion picture industry.

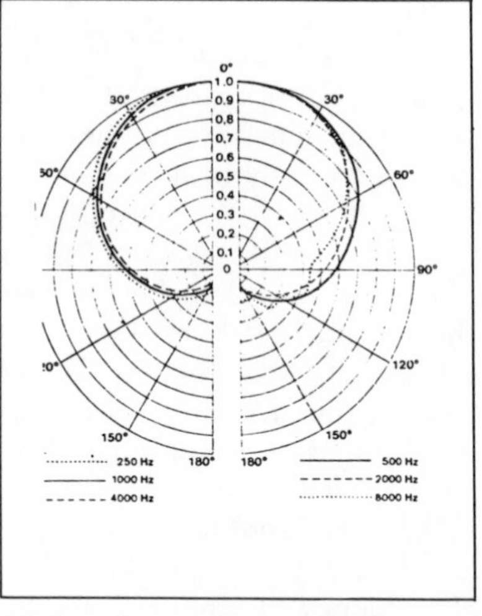

FIGURE 112—Polar diagram of a directional (cardiod) microphone

The cardioid or directional microphone is represented by the polar diagram in FIGURE 112. On axis, the sensitivity of the microphone has a value of 1.0 by definition. From 0° to 60° to either side, the response remains fairly constant. Around 90° (directly to the side) the response begins to fall off and by 120° the response has dropped to a value of only 30% of the on-axis response. Note that the higher frequencies exhibit a greater directional characteristic. A good directional mike can have a front to back rejection ratio of as much as 10:1 or 20 db. The cardioid is very popular in motion picture sound recording for these reasons. The mike will pick up all sounds from the front while rejecting to a large extent unwanted noises from behind. The cardioid mike operates on the "pressure-gradient" principle, as opposed to the "pressure" principle, and thus has a greater "throw." That is, the cardioid can operate from greater distances while still maintaining some sense of intimacy or closeness.

From the polar pattern in FIGURE 113 can be seen that the directional characteristics of the ultra-directional microphone are similar to the cardioid, only more severe. Again, response is maximum on axis. However, roll-off begins at only 30° off axis, and by 60° almost all frequencies are down 10db to 20db. Thus, the ultra-directional mike has a tendency to pick up only those sounds at which the mike is pointed, while rejecting those sounds approaching from both sides and the rear. This narrow beam of acceptance has given rise to the nickname "shot gun" to this group of microphones. The ultra-directional mike operates on the "interference" principle and is physically characterized by the long narrow "interference tube." As expected, the ultra-directional mike has a tremendous throw, and can pick up "on-axis" sounds from great distances while rejecting closer sounds that are off axis, that is, to the side and rear.

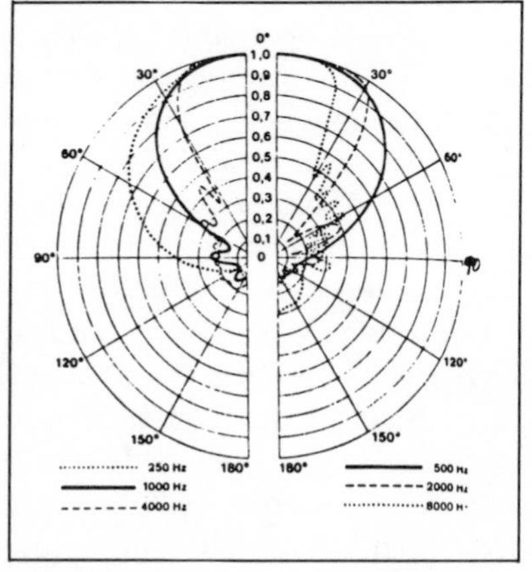

FIGURE 113—Polar diagram of an ultra-directional (shot-gun) microphone

The directional and ultra-directional microphones account for the great majority of sound track recording for motion pictures. They are especially useful on location where ambient noises are high and their directional characteristics can almost isolate the essential sounds. They are also advantageous when using an unblimped camera on location. In many high ambient noise conditions, such as a city street, busy store, etc., the noise of an unblimped camera will blend into the background if it is kept a reasonable distance from the subject, and an ultra-directional mike is employed in close proximity with the sound source. Of course, the mike should be oriented with the subject on-axis and the camera well to the side or rear.

Likewise, one can sometimes use a so-called "self-blimped" camera in very quiet locations, such as a hotel room, and still maintain studio quietness by employing a highly directional mike to reject any slight camera noise.

It should be kept in mind that reflecting surfaces (i.e., large bare walls) behind the subject will drastically reduce the effectiveness of a directional microphone. Sounds from the rear will bounce off the surface and enter the microphone on-axis. Placing the subject next to a large sound-reflecting surface should be avoided, or the surface should be deadened with a drape or other sound absorbing material. In the extreme case, a cardioid or even or super-cardioid microphone will be rendered totally non-directional in a small "live" room. This situation should obviously be well avoided.

ELECTRET CONDENSER MICROPHONES

What *is* an electret condenser microphone? I am being asked that question more frequently these days, which is probably indicative of the growing interest of professionals in this relatively new type of microphone. In light of this expanding popularity, a brief discription of the electret microphone seems appropriate.

The dynamic microphone operates on the basic principles of a generator. The voice or sound waves strike and vibrate a diaphragm/coil assembly. The vibrating coil is housed within a magnet. The moving coil within the magnetic field generates an electric current that is proportional in amplitude and frequency to the original sound. What could be more simple? Nothing, really. However, for the purist seeking the highest degree of sonic reproduction, the dynamic microphone can be improved upon.

This is where the condenser microphone comes in. In lieu of a relatively heavy diaphragm/coil assembly, the condenser microphone employs an ultra lightweight diaphragm only. Because this represents much less inertia, the condenser microphone usually exhibits superior sonic characteristics, including a flat, smooth frequency response, precise directional qualities and a low sensitivity to mechanical vibration. In addition, the output of a condenser microphone can be as much as 20dB higher than that of a dynamic unit, allowing longer cables to be employed without danger of noise pick-up. These benefits do not come without a price, both figuratively and literally.

The diaphragm in a DC condenser microphone cannot "generate" an electric current. As a result, it requires a power supply. In practice, a DC bias voltage is applied to the diaphragm which is one of the two plates forming a capacitor. As the sound causes the diaphragm to vibrate, the capacitance will fluctuate proportionately. This minute signal must then be amplified before it can be useful. FIGURE 114 represents a condenser microphone. It is obviously more complex than a dynamic mike, requiring a power supply, voltage converter and audio amplifier.

The rf condenser microphone operates on a similar principle, but is even more complex and costly. The diaphragm condenser is part of an rf tuned oscillator, (typically 8MHz). The audio vibrations thus frequency modulate this rf signal. A demodulator isolates the audio portion, which is then amplified. The rf condenser microphone thus requires not only a power supply, but an rf crystal and demodulator, as well as an audio amplifier. These components have kept the DC and rf condenser microphones both complex and costly.

Space-age technology and modern production methods have recently resulted in a major simplification of the classical condenser microphone. The main breakthrough was the development of thin plastic foils with a permanent electric charge. Charged foils have existed for almost fifty years and are called *electrets;* however it was only recently that a technique was developed for maintaining a polarizing charge over long periods of time and under extremes of temperature. The electret condenser microphone uses an electret foil as a diaphragm, thus eliminating the need for a voltage converter or DC power supply. Moreover a miniature integrated circuit (IC) performs the entire audio amplification function. Because this IC draws only a minute current, a miniature battery can be incorporated right into the microphone. FIGURE 115 represents an electret microphone circuit. The electret microphone re-

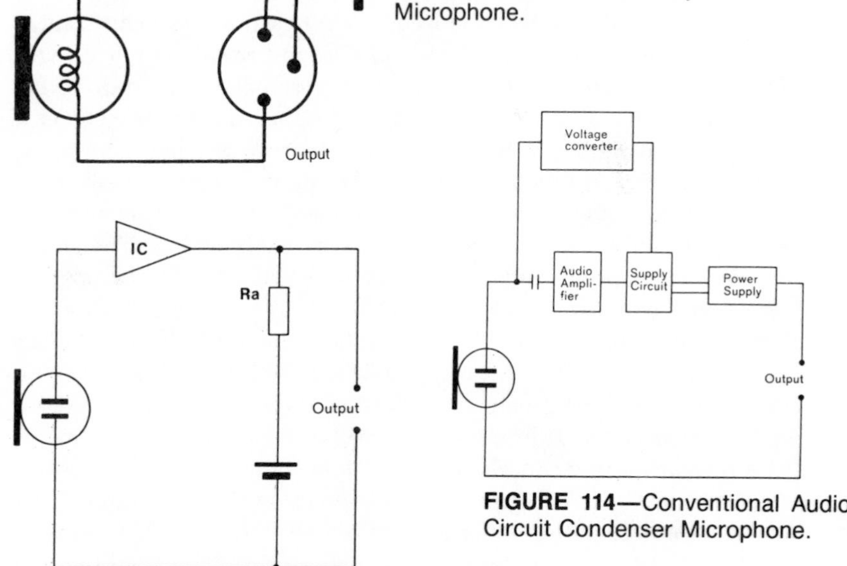

FIGURE 113—Standard Dynamic Microphone.

FIGURE 114—Conventional Audio Circuit Condenser Microphone.

FIGURE 115—Electret Condenser Microphone.

tains most of the advantages of the standard condenser microphone, but at a fraction of the cost. In addition no external power is necessary and in most cases the electret microphone can interface with most audio devices, as if it were a standard dynamic microphone.

HAND MICROPHONES

Microphone designers have long since succumbed to the age of specialization. Today there are cardioids, hyper-cardioids, electret lavaliers, rf condenser shotguns and a myriad of other special types to perfectly match any specific sonic applications. Most soundmen today carry several electret lavaliers, a shotgun or shorty-shotgun hyper-cardioid and at least one old standby "hand mike", either omnidirectional or cardioid. Before the newer exotic microphones were invented, most applications had to be met with the more conventional hand (or stand) microphone. However, with a little expertise, those microphones could handle most situations.

An interview between two people can sometimes be best handled with a single omnidirectional mike, assuming the room is not too live. The mike is simply placed between the two persons. This achieves matched tonal balance, as well as good sonic perspective. Two cardioid microphones could also be employed, one for each person. This configuration (FIGURE 116) has its drawbacks. Sound from one person will reach the other's microphone. This secondary signal will not be in phase with primary signal, due to the longer distance it must travel. As a result, the two signals will cancel each other at certain frequencies, yielding an unnatural hollow, or possibly "tinny", sound quality. One cardioid placed between the two people may give better results, again assuming a fairly dead and quiet acoustical environment. The single cardioid can be positioned straight up, as in FIGURE 117, or pointed down from a boom or, as in FIGURES 118 and 119, pointed down using a desk as a reflecting surface. If the microphone is used facing up, it must be placed as close to the desk as possible (FIGURE 120). Otherwise, the situation in FIGURE 121 will result. Similar to the condition in FIGURE 116, the reflected sound from the desk will arrive out of phase with the direct sound, causing cancellation of certain frequencies. The problem can be rectified by placing the microphone close to the desk (FIGURE 122). The cardioid pattern does not roll off much before 90° from axis. The microphone is just as receptive to the sound coming from the side (FIGURE 122) as it is to the front (FIGURE 121). Thus, the setup in FIGURE 122 should not impair quality nor increase noise; yet it will reduce the possibility of phase cancellations, due to multipath. An alter-

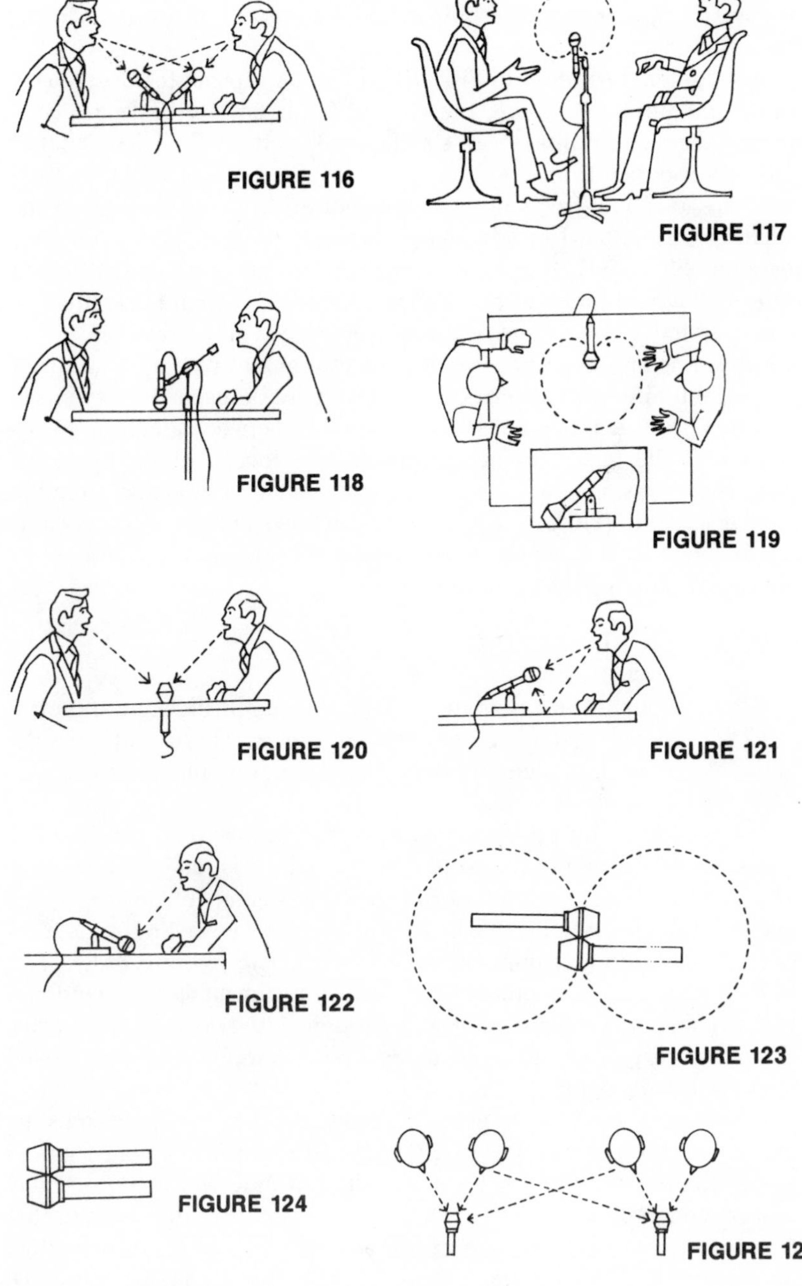

FIGURE 116

FIGURE 117

FIGURE 118

FIGURE 119

FIGURE 120

FIGURE 121

FIGURE 122

FIGURE 123

FIGURE 124

FIGURE 125

nate solution would allow the position of FIGURE 121, but with a piece of foam or other sound absorbing material under the microphone to kill the reflected sounds.

An additional solution to FIGURE 116 is the capsule-to-capsule cardioid configuration. Placing the two cardioids back-to-back and connecting them out of phase yields a "figure 8" pattern (FIGURE 123) that will reject sounds from the side.

Where loud low-frequency ambient noise is a problem, phase cancellation can be used to advantage. Taping two cardioids (or omnies) together (FIGURE 124) and connecting them out of phase with each other will cancel much of the ambient sounds; yet sound presented in close proximity to *only one* of the microphones will be received.

When it is impractical to use one microphone to pick up a group of people, multiple microphones must obviously be used. However, the trick here is to maintain a distance ratio of 3:1 between adjacent microphones. If the microphones are placed one foot from the speaker's mouths, the next microphone over should be at least three feet from the speaker's mouth (FIGURE 125). This will achieve at least a 10db separation between microphones, which should preclude any impairment of the sound due to phase cancellations.

TWO-TRACK RECORDING

About ten years ago, several manufacturers introduced professional portable stereo tape recorders. These units, for the most part, went unnoticed by the motion picture industry—who needs stereo?

The reason many professionals have not bothered to consider the stereo models is due to the word "stereo" which is really a misnomer. True, some visionary producers will record in stereo, anticipating stereo television, which is undoubtedly on the horizon. However, for the most part, these stereo machines should be called "two-track recorders".

Why a two track-recorder? Under most circumstances a soundman will double mike. Whether it be an interview with two or more persons, a documentary, or an industrial, at least two microphones are employed to cover the dialogue.

When using a full (single) track recorder, these microphones must be mixed on the spot into the single track. In essence, the soundman is forced to perform a mix as he is recording. It may be found on replay that one microphone was at too low a level relative to the other, or that two people (one on each mike) talked at once, drowning out each other. Or possibly one microphone pick-up required some equalization while the other did not. At this stage there is little that can be easily done to rectify these problems, as the whole ball of wax is in one track. In addition, it is difficult for the soundman to properly ride gain, as both microphones are being read on one modulometer; he can never be sure which mike is actually peaking the meter.

Now consider the two-track recorder. The two-track recorder (such as the Nagra SL in FIGURE 126) is the same size and weight as comparable full track recorders. Surprisingly, the quality of each of the two tracks is the equal of the full track recorder in terms of signal-to-noise ratio and

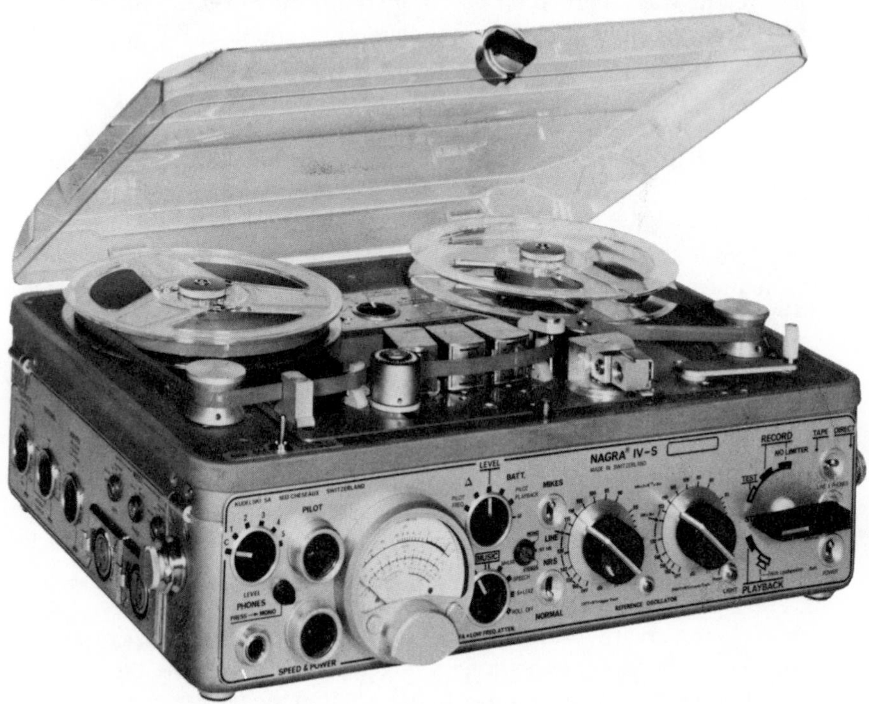

FIGURE 126—The Nagra IV-S Stereo recorder, a "two-track" system

frequency response. Thus, if only one microphone on one track is employed, the quality would be comparable to that experienced with the more conventional full-track recorders. But the fun comes when two microphones are employed. Each microphone is recorded on a totally separate track. In addition, a double modulometer is employed, an indicator for each microphone level. The soundman can adjust to the optimum level of each mike to obtain maximum signal-to-noise ratio. On the Nagra two-track recorder the two indicators are superimposed on one scale and color-coded red and green to correspond to the respectively colored level knobs. This feature is really great, since the soundman doesn't go crosseyed trying to keep his attention on two separate level meters. Thus, recording with the two-track recorder is easier for the soundman. He doesn't have to worry about mixing or relative levels of the two microphones. He just rides gain for best signal-to-noise ratio (100% modulation) and lets the mixer in the studio worry about relative levels.

Meanwhile, back at the studio, the mixer is ecstatic. Because each microphone was recorded on a separate track, the mixer has full control of relative volumes and can independently equalize the individual tracks. Take our previous example where two people talk at the same time and both voices are garbled by each other. In the two-track instance, the mixer just kills the gain on the less interesting of the two voices and the remaining track comes through relatively clean and intelligible.

There are other advantages to the two-track recorder. In lieu of a neopilotone track, the two-track recorder employs a third center track (sometimes called synchro-tone) to facilitate sound sync. The center track performs the same function as the neo-pilotone track, namely the recording of the 60 HZ pilotone or crystal signal. However, because it is a conventional type head as opposed to the push-pull double-gap neopilotone head, the center track can record a broader frequency spectrum. It can be used to record voice cues or other pertinent information in addition to the pilot signal. This could come in handy for inaudible start-stop cues when using multiple cameras with radio slating. Because of this difference in pilot recording, a tape recorded on a two-track machine must be resolved on a two-track machine.

The two-track recorder not only solves a lot of old problems, it encourages the creative soundman to explore new techniques. On documentary productions two wireless mikes can be used, one on each of two subjects. The two receivers can fit right into the pocket on the Nagra case, each plugged into its separate track. When covering a live event, one track can be used for the dialogue while the second track is used for ambience. For example, at a recent political event I used a two-track Nagra. The recorder and soundman were stationed by the podium with one mike on the speakers platform picking up the clean and pure voice track of the speaker. The second input (and track) was connected to a wireless mike receiver. The wireless mike was on me, the cameraman. As I moved through the crowd, my mike picked up the ambient sounds of the crowd in the vicinity of the camera.

Back at the studio the mixer used mostly the speaker's track. However, when the camera went wide to pick up crowd reaction (applause or jeers as the case may be), the mixer would bring up the ambience track which gave the audience a great feeling of presence that would have been lost if just the single speaker's track were employed throughout.

The two-track recorder makes the soundman's job easier, enables the sound lab to do an infinitely better mixing job and encourages new and more effective techniques. Two tracks *are* better than one.

PILOTONES

The pilotone sync signal had gone through several stages of evolution before the industry standardized on the present neo-pilotone system. The neo-pilotone technique consists of a dual "push/pull" head arrangement, (FIGURE 127). Unlike the earlier systems, these head gaps are perfectly perpendicular to tape travel, as are the audio heads. The trick is that the two small head gaps are precisely on the same line and wound with opposing polarity. When one is positive the other is negative. The impulses left on the tape are likewise equal but opposite. The audio head, because it spans the full width of the tape, reproduces these two sets of impulses simultaneously, which causes them to cancel each other out, yielding no sync pulses at all. Only the sync head can reproduce the pilotone signal, due to its dual gap inverted design. In the same way the neo-pilotone head cannot reproduce the audio signal because the inverse polarity causes the audio signals to cancel.

The neo-pilotone system works like a charm and by the mid-sixties virtually all manufacturers of ¼″ recorders adopted the system. Transfer and sound studios installed the proper neo-pilotone resolving systems and it appeared that stability had finally come to motion picture synchronization. However, life is never that simple. Enter the era of stereo and the corresponding two-track recorder.

Remember that the principle of the neo-pilotone isolation was the fact that the audio head read the two impulse tracks simultaneously causing them to cancel. Now with the two track head, one neo-pilot track falls into the left channel while the other is reproduced by the right. There is no cancellation (unless, of course, the two channels are mixed into mono with exactly equal proportions). The 60 Hz or 50 Hz pilot signal will be blended into the audio signal, rendering it useless.

Clearly a new system had to be devised for the two-track recorders. As I have mentioned, the two-track recorder offers many decided advantages over the more conventional mono units. While the motion picture community in general was rather reluctant to part with its old standby, the percentage of two-track recorders has slowly but steadily increased, and now it appears that the video industry is swinging very much in the favor of the two-track machines. All this means headaches for the audio houses, because there are now three different types of pilotone systems and none are compatible with each other.

There is a space between the two audio tracks to prevent cross-talk between the two channels (FIGURE 128). This was the most logical place to lay down the sync track. Both Nagra and Stellavox use a third narrow track in this area for the pilot signal. However, it would be too easy for these two companies to use the same technique.

Stellavox chose the most direct method and put the 60 Hz or 50 Hz pilot signal right down the middle of the tape between the audio tracks. Nagra, on the other hand, was concerned that the relatively low frequency sync signals might bleed into the closely adjoining audio tracks. Because higher frequencies have less of a tendency to bleed, the Nagra technique employs a 13,500 Hz carrier frequency which is frequency modulated with the pilot signal. The resulting signal on the tape thus deviates from approximately 8,000 Hz to 19,000 Hz. In addition to recording the pilot signal, this center track can record audio cues in the 0-2,500 Hz region.

What all this boils down to is: an audio tape must be played back and transferred on the same type of recorder as it was recorded upon. Tapes must be labeled clearly with the type (mono or stereo) and brand of the recorder. If this advice is not followed, the following problems will arise:

A—Nagra Stereo tape reproduced on a mono system: high-pitched whine in the audio.

B—Stellavox Stereo tape reproduced on a mono system: 60HZ (50Hz) pilot signal reproduced clearly in the audio.

C—Mono sync tape reproduced on any stereo machine: 60Hz (50Hz) pilot signal reproduced clearly in the audio.

In addition to the pollution of the audio tracks, it should be obvious in the above examples that resolving is impossible. Moreover, a Nagra stereo cannot be resolved on a Stellavox and vice versa, although the audio tracks will remain relatively clean.

It appears that these various formats will be coexisting for quite some time to come. Good practice should include careful labeling of tapes, as well as pre-arrangements with transfer studios to assure compatibility.

If it is any consolation, the three aforementioned formats are relatively compatible if no sync signals are recorded.

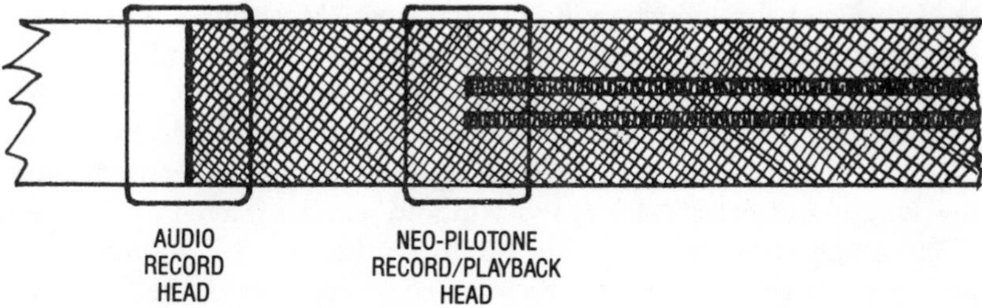

FIGURE 127—Conventional mono ¼″ recorder with neo-pilotone-sync system. Neo-pilotone technique consists of a dual gap head that puts two impulse tracks over the audio information. These two impulse tracks are equal, but of opposite polarity.

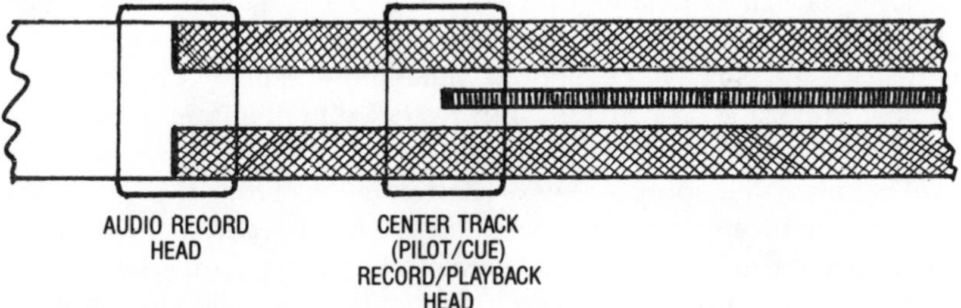

FIGURE 128—Stereo or "two-track ¼″" recorder with sync track. The Nagra uses a 13.5KHz carrier frequency for the sync track, onto which the sync tone is FM-encoded. Most other manufacturers use the direct method of placing the 50Hz or 60Hz tone directly into the center track.

NOISE REDUCTION

Over the past few years, it has become more and more common to hear the term "noise reduction" mentioned by professional recordists. Almost every professional recording studio employs some form of signal processing to reduce noise, and even consumer items, such as hi-fidelity cassette decks, almost exclusively employ Dolby B circuitry. Brand names such as "dBX" and Dolby have become household words, and dBX has two models of noise reduction units designed specifically for the Nagra SL and Nagra 4.2 respectively. The reasons for this current popularity are not as simple as the term "noise reduction" may suggest.

Each application has a different purpose for such circuitry, and, moreover, these circuits do more than just reduce noise. Any discussion of noise reduction must begin with the concept of "dynamic range", Cinematographers should be familiar with this concept as it is identical to the latitude or luminance ratio of a film stock. Most film stocks have a luminance ratio of 6 or 7 stops. This is in essence a "window"—only objects within this range will be recorded on the film. All objects brighter than this range will be burned out and have no detail, and all objects below this range will be black and indistinguishable on the film. By changing EI or "T" stop, this "window" can be moved up or down to favor lighter or darker objects; but the width of the "window", the 6 or 7 stops it can distinguish, remains constant. This is the "dynamic range" of the film.

Magnetic recording tape is identical in this concept. The upper end is limited by tape saturation. Once the signal exceeds this level, it will be distorted. On the lower end, the tape recording process has a residual noise level usually referred to as "tape hiss". A signal must be substantially above this inherent noise to be usable.

Once again we have a "window" situation: a ceiling of distortion and a floor of noise. The signal must be restricted to fit within these limits, the dynamic range of the tape.

The cinematographer is always confronting the problem of "dynamic range". Quite often a scene exceeds the luminance ratio of the film, and reflectors and fill light must be employed to bring up the low end or compress the range of the scene to that of the film. The same problem exists with sound recording.

FIGURE 129 represents a typical situation. The subject being recorded might be a symphony orchestra. This is an extreme situation where the difference between a flute solo and a fortissimo of the entire orchestra can be on the order of 100dB. The problem is the tape has a range of only 50dB. The recordist can set the level to favor either the loud or soft

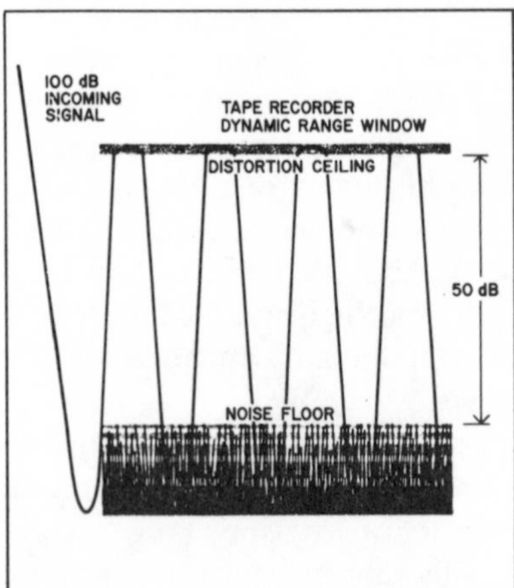

FIGURE 129—In this illustration, the recording tape has a dynamic range of 50dB. Between tape saturation (maximum recorded signal) and the residual noise, the tape can accept a program with a maximum range of 50dB. It can be seen in this example that a program with a range in excess of this 50dB (in this instance, the program has a 100dB range) will not "fit" on the tape. The loud passages will distort, and the softest passages will be lost in the noise.

portions, but the range remains at 50dB. From Figure 129, it can be seen that the loud peaks will be clipped off, causing considerable distortion and the softest passages will be totally lost in the residual noise. In addition, the reproduced signal will only have a range of 50dB between the loudest and softest passages, hardly the equivalent of the original 100dB.

Like the cinematographer, the recordist would like to employ some means of reducing the dynamic range of his subject so that it will fit within the limits of his tape. Moreover, even if the subject had had a range of 50 dB, the softest passages would still be so close to the residual noise, that his noise would be quite prominent during playback. It is this aspect of the problem that has given rise to the somewhat narrow expression "noise reduction". Thus, in practice, the goal is not only to compress the subject to enable it to fit unscathed within the range of the tape, but to include an extra margin of compression to ensure that even the softest passages are recorded significantly above the residual noise.

The reasons for employing so-called noise reduction circuits depend somewhat on the application. The professional recording studio may use as many as 16 or 32 individual tape tracks in preparing a final cut. Many of these tracks are recorded during the original performance by employing an individual microphone (and track) for each instrument and vocal. This practice provides the mixer with full flexibility in combining and adjusting the individual elements of an ensemble. The mixer has full control of the "sound" of the recording. Additional tracks may be used for "overdub" where the same or different musicians, at a later date, can add parts while listening to the previously recorded tracks. Theoretically one could record an entire symphony orchestra without any two musicians being at the same place at the same time.

The point here is that somewhere along the line, these 16 or 32 tracks must be mixed down to one (or two) tracks for the final mix. While the signal-to-noise ratio or dynamic range of an individual track may be acceptable, the noise content of each track will *add* during mixdown.

The final cut will not only have 32 musical instruments, but also 32 noise tracks. The resulting music will sound as if it had been recorded in front of a waterfall. Thus, in the case of multiple-track recording, some type of noise reduction circuitry must be employed during the original recording to preclude a horrendous build-up of noise during the mixdown.

The reason for the almost universal association of Dolby B with consumer cassette recorders is entirely different. The cassette recorder uses a very narrow track width (about 1/32″) and an extremely slow tape-speed of only 1⅞ ips (as opposed to professional speeds of 7½, 15, and 30 ips). These two factors contribute to an extremely poor signal/noise ratio, usually about 10dB poorer than a reel-to-reel machine of equal quality. The inclusion of Dolby B circuitry in essence restores this 10dB of dynamic range to the cassette machine, making it competitive with the best reel-to-reel recorders.

Now we consider an application close to home—the dBX units for the Nagras. Unlike the recording studio, the Nagra soundtrack is not going to be one of 16 or 32 tracks involved in a massive mixdown. Nor does the Nagra suffer from an inherently poor signal-to-noise ratio like the cassette deck. (On the contrary, the Nagra exhibits one of the finest signal-to-noise ratios ever.)

The reason for using dBX with a Nagra is somewhat different from both those cases. The basic name of the game here is increased dynamic range.

The restricted dynamic range of the recording process is the real nemesis of the location recordist. In many instances the recorded subject has a dynamic range exceeding that of the tape. Under these circumstances the problem is similar to the proverbial 10 pounds of material into the five pound can. The recordist will usually employ gain riding and peak limiting to enable the program to fit within the range of the tape. In practice the levels are set slightly high, such that the occasional peak will slightly overload. A peak limiter is activated that will reduce the amplitude of these peaks before the tape actually distorts. This practice can add 3-to-6dB to the signal-to-noise ratio, but at the expense of having the loudest peaks in the program lopped off.

Gain riding involves boosting the level controls during soft passages to get these low sounds up away from the noise. While this practice does keep the soft passages out of the noise, it also destroys the original relationship between the quiet and loud passages. After gain riding/peak limiting, the loudest peaks have been lopped off, the quiet passages made louder and the net result is that the original sound with a range of 70dB has now been emasculated to a dull 40dB.

In essence, the peak limiting/gain riding compresses the giant signal, enabling it to fit the petite range of the tape. This practice does get the entire signal onto the tape and, in this respect, is better than nothing.

However a second look at this process poses an interesting question. Suppose the soundman could somehow note down precisely when and how much the gain was altered during recording? Now, upon playback, the gain is altered an equal but opposite amount. This would totally negate the gain manipulation employed during recording and restore the original dynamics. Now you have the best of both worlds. The signal is compressed to fit the tape and then the dynamic range is restored by uncompressing.

This phenomenon is reflected in FIGURE 130 and is precisely what a "dBX" system does. The original source is compressed 2:1, allowing 100 dB of dynamics to fit a tape with a dynamic range of only 50dB. If the tape was played back without expansion, the subject would sound dynamically flat, the soft and loud passages would be "closer together". However, when played back through the corresponding expander, the original loudness relationships are restored.

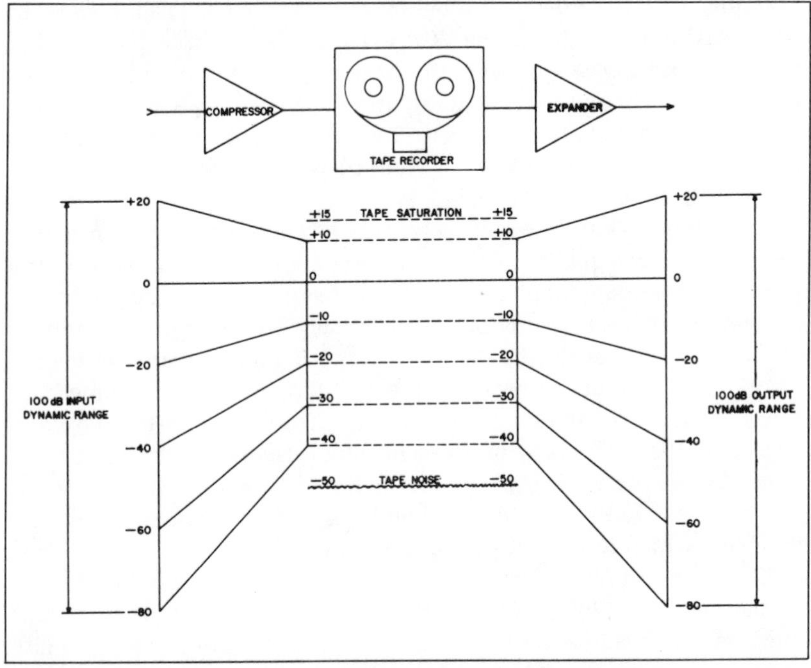

FIGURE 130—The basic concept of the compressor/expander: The 100dB input is compressed down to a dynamic range of only 50dB, which fits nicely onto the tape. Note that the loudest peaks are below saturation and the softest passages are well above the noise. Upon playback, the expander restores the original 100dB dynamic range.

In theory this compression/expansion process seems uncannily simple. While tape and recorder manufacturers are striving for that extra 2 or 3dB of dynamic range, this simple process virtually doubles the dynamic range and, in most cases, represents an increase of 30-to-50dB. The results of this process are so impressive, and the idea so logically simple that one can't help but wonder why Leonardo DaVinci didn't think of it (or at least Thomas Edison).

While the compressor/expander is a relatively simple and direct concept, the electronic execution of the theory is quite complex. Manipulating the signal with a 2:1 compression and a corresponding 100% expansion can get quite hairy if precautions are not taken. A block diagram of a "dBX" unit appears in FIGURE 131. The heart of the system (and a breakthrough for "dBX") is the Voltage Controlled Amplifier (VCA) and the Root Mean Square (RMS) detector. Essentially the RMS detector monitors the incoming signal and controls the VCA. For example, if the RMS detector senses that the signal has just increased in volume by 10dB, it calls for the VCA to *reduce* its gain in such a way that the 10dB louder passage comes out of the VCA being only 5dB louder. Likewise *any* change in level going into the VCA comes out with only half the original change in level. Thus, the original dynamic range is compressed 2:1. The expansion during playback works in a similar but opposite fashion.

While the VCA and RMS detector circuits are complex in themselves, there are other equally complex considerations. One of these is the problem of residual tape "hiss". All tape has a certain amount of background noise. Because this hiss is essentially a constant, the playback expander could cause this hiss to become louder or softer as it goes about its job of uncompressing the signal. This effect is sometimes referred to as "pumping" or "breathing". The "dBX" system virtually eliminates these effects by introducing a high-frequency "preemphasis" circuit before the VCA. This boosts the high frequencies during recording by about 12dB. A similar deemphasis circuit is employed during playback which attentuates these same high frequencies by the same 12dB. As a result the program is unaltered, but the hiss is reduced 12dB, rendering it inaudible. Notice also that similar preemphasis circuits must be employed before the RMS detectors to preclude the possibility of high-frequency overload of the tape.

It should be obvious that this system depends upon perfect "tracking" between the compressor during recording and the expander during reproduction. Certain subsonic signals could cause the expander to mistrack. To preclude this, bandpass filters are employed on the RMS detectors as well as the input. These filters do not affect the audible range, but they effectively eliminate those spurious signals that could mislead the detectors.

In reality, the compression/expansion system is quite complex, relying heavily upon state-of-the-art integrated circuit technology. Ironically, all this electronic complexity is designed to make the recorder appear to do nothing. What goes in must come out—exactly. No noise, no distortion, no lost dynamics.

The "dBX" type noise-reduction system is, in reality, a dynamic range expander. Its circuits allow the tape to accept almost twice the normal dynamic ratio. Under most circumstances this also translates into a major reduction in residual tape noise. The benefits of such a system should be obvious to the studio multi-track recordist who must cope with the cumulative noise problem associated with multiple-track mix-downs. Likewise, a classical concert recordist can surely appreciate a dynamic range of 90dB. (No longer must he live with the guilt of performing those cardinal sins of limiting peaks and riding gain.)

The motion picture soundman benefits from the "dBX" system in a slightly different manner. The biggest problem facing the location motion picture recordist is the unexpected. Particularly on documentary and industrial films, it is difficult to predetermine exactly what the sound will be during the actual take. If levels are set close to 0dB to gain the best signal-to-noise ratio, most assuredly someone will raise his voice or yell once the take has begun, resulting in a 15dB overload of the tape. The problem is even more acute for documentary or news style filming. Usually employing a Sennheiser 815 shotgun or similar microphone, the documentary soundman must cover an entire group of people with just one microphone. It is almost impossible to ride gain during the conversation as it shifts back and forth from persons close to the mike who speak loudly, to soft-spoken people (who are invariably farthest from the microphone.) The soundman usually compromises, or attempts to ride gain, but inevitably some loud voices will distort or some soft sections will be lost to the noise, and the net result will be a disaster. In almost all cases the swishing effect of gain riding will be heard, as the soundman can't possibly react instanteously to level changes.

The "dBX", under these circumstances, is a godsend. The technique I use with the "dBX" is quite simple and the results consistently excellent. The recordist adjusts the level in such a way that the loudest peaks normally encountered do not exceed −10dB. The Nagra or similar professional recorder is capable of delivering clean sound up to a recording level of +3 to +5dB on the modulometer, when used with the newer tape formulations. By restricting the peaks to −10dB, there is, thus, a total of 15dB of "headroom". But the dbx compresses the signal 2:1 resulting in a total of 30dB of effective headroom instead of the usual 4 to 5dB (without dbx and the normal 0dB maximum levels). Thus, by restricting "normal" peaks to −10dB, an unexpected super peak, such as a shout or yell, can exceed normal maximum levels by as much as 30dB and still be recorded undistorted on the tape. Moreover, the signal-too-noise ratio, even at this −10dB level, is superior to a 0dB level without dBX.

At a 0dB level, the signal is typically 50dB or better above residual noise. Assuming this 50dB ratio, recording at a −10dB level would reduce this s/n figure to only 40dB. But the dBX will effectively double this to 80dB. Thus, by employing dBX and a −10dB reference, the recordist has a whopping 30dB of headroom *and* an exceptional signal-to-noise ratio of 80dB relative to the −10dB point. (The signal-to-noise ratio would actually exceed 100dB relative to a 0dB peak if one should occur.) Armed with this system, the soundman has a dynamic range that exceeds almost any sonic situation that could possibly arise (with the possible exception of a New York City subway train).

In practice, by employing the dBX and a maximum level of −10dB, the soundman is ready for just about anything. He can almost forget about gain adjustments and concentrate on optimum microphone placement and establishing a closer rapport with the cameraman. (Most cameramen will welcome this aspect).

Using this dBX technique, the recorder will easily accept signals both 30dB above and more than 60dB under the −10dB reference point. A faithful recording of almost any location situation is thus facilitated without having to manipulate the gain during the recording. Once back in the transfer room, the signal can be compressed, expanded, or otherwise processed at will. In essence, the soundman delivers to the transfer a precise and unadulterated recording of the sound exactly as it existed on location. The sound can then be tailored for the final soundtrack in the transfer department under controlled conditions and with the proper equipment.

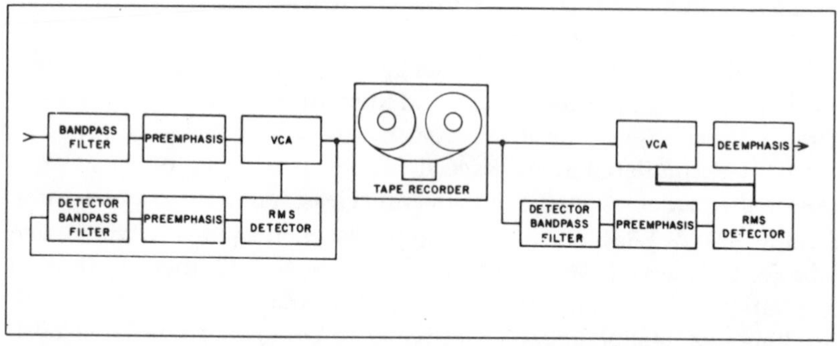

FIGURE 131—Block diagram of a "dBX" compressor/expander. While this theory appears quite simple, the electronic execution is very complex. The heart of the system is the RMS (Room Mean Square) detector and the VCA (Voltage Controlled Amplifier). The additional circuits prevent any possible side effects (see text).

HEADPHONES

Bless the sound stage. The command is given: "Quiet on the set!", and silence permeates every cranny of the studio. The recordist is in his element, a 24dB acoustic fortress of thick concrete walls and double doors that protects him from the most severe sonic attacks. In this environment the soundman can forget the mundane sounds that plague the real world. He is free to concentrate on his technical and more creative tasks. What a trauma it is when the soundman is thrust from the sonic security of this walled womb. What a shock to confront the plethoric sounds of a myriad of diabolical devices.

Deprived of his massive fortress, the recordist must now engage in jungle warfare, employing guerrilla tactics and the latest sonic weaponry: shotgun microphones, condenser lavaliers, diversity radio mikes, dynamic-range expanders, et cetera. An entirely new set of problems exists in the outside world and an entirely new set of techniques must be developed to cope with it.

The most important piece of equipment the soundman has is his ears. It follows that the second most important element is his earphones, which connect those ears with the remainder of his sound system. The soundman will undoubtedly spend inordinate amounts of time and spare no expense in selecting a recorder, mixer and microphones. Yet it is the headphones with which the recordist ultimately defines the quality of the recording. It is fairly obvious that good monitoring headphones have a wide and smooth frequency response and low distortion. However, the most important aspect of monitoring headphones is often overlooked; *acoustic isolation.*

By employing directional microphones and close microphone techniques, the soundman can greatly modify existing sonic conditions. In order to evaluate the effectiveness of his efforts, the recordist must be able to differentiate between the sounds coming through the system, and those that hit the ear directly by "leaking" around the headphones. There is really no way to tell which is which. This can be an exasperating problem. Recently I was shooting a documentary piece near La Guardia airport in N.Y. for a T.V. network. This particular shot was an outdoor interview between a network personality and a single subject. My soundman used a condenser lavalier on each, placed very close to the mouth. One would think that this technique would allow the voices to override any extraneous noises. Yet, every time a plane flew in the distance the soundman aborted the take, due to the intrusion of the noise into the track. This occurred a half-dozen times. Needless to say, this put a damper on the proceedings, as well as wasting film and time. Ironically, upon later examination, it was found that the sound track was absolutely clean. In not one instance did the sound of the planes come even close to being objectionable. What is the mystery?

It turned out that the soundman was using stethoscope-type headsets with foam ball earpieces. These offer *no* isolation whatsoever. The soundman was hearing the sounds of the planes directly, not through the microphones. He obviously could not tell the difference, thinking the sounds of the plane were actually in the sound track. In this case, the soundman thought a noise was in his track that, in reality, wasn't. However, the opposite condition is more disastrous. An unwanted sound can slip by the soundman into the track, masked by a loud ambient condition and headphones with poor isolation. Back in the preview room these unwanted sounds will be quite obvious.

There is an obvious solution to this problem. Because it is impossible to tell the difference between off-the-tape and direct sounds, the direct sounds must be virtually eliminated. The recordist is then assured that what he hears is definitely in the track and can evaluate accordingly. The first step is selecting a set of headphones with good isolation. This is the ability of the mechanical design to reduce the level of ambient sounds reaching the ear. "Open Air"-type headphones should never be used for location monitoring. These units are characterized by open foam-type ear cushions. While they are quite comfortable and provide excellent sound for later studio or home playback, they offer absolutely no isolation. In addition, they can actually cause an echo in the sound track due to off-the-tape sounds leaking out of the headphones and back into the microphones.

Almost all non-open-air headphones offer at least 10dB of isolation. For monitoring purposes an isolation of 20dB or better is preferable. Some headsets provide in excess of 30dB of isolation. However, a compromise may have to be reached between size, weight and isolation. Certainly a reasonable balance of attributes can be found in a headset that still provides 20 to 25dB of isolation.

While isolation figures are seldom published, a close physical examination should provide a reasonable idea of isolation effectiveness. The ear cushions will have substantial padding, effectively sealing the area around the ear. The pads should be covered with soft leather or vinyl. The cushions should be ruggedly affixed to the headset. Most important, the headband should be metal and offer a substantial clamping force between the two earpieces. A good seal is impossible if the headband does not compress the ear cushions against the head. Lastly, try the headphones on, without connecting them to any device. The ambient sounds in the room should be substantially reduced. This last test is best accomplished in a relatively noisy environment and by trying several prospective headsets in succession.

Reduction of ambient sounds is both a function of headphone isolation and monitor volume level. In general, I usually crank the monitor volume up as high as I comfortably can. (Of course, too high a level is also undesirable, causing distortion and acoustic fatigue.) Discretion and experience will usually determine the optimum level. As an example, employing headphones with 25dB of isolation and a monitor volume about 15dB above actual ambience yields a total of 40dB between the monitored signal and leakage of room ambience. This is quite a significant amount and should allow the off-the-tape sound to stand out easily from the almost insignificant ambience.

FIGURE 132—The table below illustrates in numerical terms why some headphones are better than others for monitoring the recording of location sound tracks. The first step is to select a set of headphones with good isolation. This is the ability of the mechanical design to reduce the level of ambient sounds reaching the ear. ''Open-air''-type headphones, which offer virtually no isolation, should never be used for location recording.

ATTENUATION OF AMBIENT NOISE	DEGREE OF ISOLATION
10 dB	— Minimum isolation for circumaural type headphones
11 — 15 dB	— Fair isolation — not for monitoring applications
16 — 19 dB	— Fair to good isolation — May be acceptable for certain monitoring applications
20 — 25 dB	— Good isolation — Sufficient for most critical monitoring
26 — 30 dB	— Superior isolation — maximum amount of isolation commercially available

HIGH-FREQUENCY BIAS

The magnetic recording process stores information in the form of tiny magnets on a base or tape. For the moment, however, consider any recording medium as a mirror with a memory. It will receive a signal, and at a latter time "reflect" back that same signal. In line with this analogy, the perfect recording medium, like the finest optical mirrors, would reflect an undistorted image of the original subject. Unfortunately the magnetic recording medium does not fulfill this criterion. On the contrary to continue the analogy, the magnetic recording process would be similar to a "fun house" mirror, that delivers quite a distorted version of the original object.

FIGURE 133 represents the curve of a perfect recording medium. The x axis (horizontal) represents the incoming signal, and the y axis (vertical) signifies the resulting signal that remains on the tape. The "curve" is actually a straight line, as the incoming signal is exactly proportional to the recorded information.

FIGURE 134 represents the *actual* recording curve of a magnetic tape. It can be seen that the curve is indeed not a straight line, and the resulting recorded signal is not proportional to the original.

Note, however, that the areas labeled A and A' are quite linear, and if the recorded signal could be restricted to these areas, a relatively clean and undistorted image of the original information could be reproduced.

This is not a new concept to cinematographers. Film behaves in the identical fashion. In magnetic recording the linear portion of the recording curve (A or A' in FIGURE 134) is called its *dynamic range.*

In film, this linear region is called its *latitude.* A hypothetical exposure curve for film appears in FIGURE 135. It can be seen that an accurate representation (exposure) of the original scene (light) can only be accomplished for objects reflecting light energy between the 3 and 7 levels. Objects in the scene darker than the 3 level will all register as black on the print. The negative begins to reach its minimum density at approximately the 3 level and cannot register anything darker. Likewise, any objects that reflect a large amount of light (exceeding level 7) will fully expose the film and appear as white (maximum negative density). Thus, details cannot be accurately recorded for objects that reflect light lower than 3 or greater than 7. Within the region of the curve labeled "B", objects will be recorded in their proper perspective. That is, objects reflecting light in the 3 to 7 range will appear relative to one another as they do in reality. Objects reflecting light around 3 will appear dark, those around 4 to 5 medium gray and those around 6 will appear light, etc.

An accurate representation of the original scene can only be accomplished if the light levels reflected by all pertinent objects remain in the linear region (3 to 7). This scene will be "distorted" if objects are below or above this linear region.

The term "distortion" implies that the resulting recorded information contains less or more elements than the original. For example, a window in a scene contains a beautiful panorama of the New York skyline. Unfortunately, the light in the room is very dim, and it is very sunny outside. If proper exposure is taken for the room, the outside will be completely washed out. Thus, what was a beautiful panorama in reality, is recorded as a blob of white light. This is "distortion." While it is not that objectionable in photography, it is intolerable in sound recording.

In FIGURE 134 the recording curve is very similar to the density curve of the film. For a given input signal or volume level, you expect an equal strength magnetic "image" to be recorded on the tape. (The tape has a positive and negative portion to its curve, corresponding to the plus and minus current from the microphone and North and South magnetization on the tape. Each half by itself is similar to the film density curve.)

As mentioned before, this can only occur in the linear portion of the curve. If the signal should go below level 3, the magnetization is no longer proportional to the input. Levels above 7 will saturate the tape so that, like a fully-exposed film, it will no longer be able to record additional information. The trick, of course, is to make certain that the volume levels remain within the region b to d or, in other words, 3 to 7, at all times.

In the case of film, the set is lighted and an aperture chosen such that a medium gray will register a level 5 (point 'C') or exactly in the center of the linear portion of the density curve (FIGURE 135). Furthermore, the lighting, props and costumes are designed within a certain lighting ratio so as not to exceed the linear portion of the curve (latitude of the film). In other words, the median or starting point of the light level variations is adjusted or "biased" to a point midway on the linear portion of the curve. (Level 5 or point C).

In sound recording, the exact same principle is employed. Referring to FIGURE 134, we would like to move the operation point from zero to level 5. If this were not done, very soft sounds that register between 0 and 3 would be in the distortion region. If we move the starting point to 5, then the volume can swing from a value of zero (5) up to a maximum of 2 (7) and never enter the distortion region. (An equal area, 3-5, is necessary below the starting point, as sound is an AC signal requiring an equal minus signal space.) Like lighting a set to the middle of the latitude scale, the magnetic recording must be "biased" so that the starting point is at the center of its linear portion.

This is accomplished by high-frequency bias. Very simply, the recorder generates an extremely high frequency signal that is added to the audio signal before it reaches the recording head. (FIGURE 136) The level of this h-f bias signal is adjusted to exactly point C or, in the example, level 5. Thus, the signal reaching the record head is always the audio plus 5. The original criterion for undistorted recording is thus satisfied; the starting point of the audio can now be considered as 5 or point C. The h-f bias does not alter the audio playback signal because of its high frequency, which is usually 4 to 6 times above the human audible limit.

FIGURE 136 sums up the entire h-f bias recording process. It can be seen that the audio signal appears to "ride" on top of the h-f bias, thus remaining in the linear regions A and A'. Only the h-f bias is required to pass through region D, the distortion area. Note, also, that in FIGURE 136 the audio is at its maximum value or 100% modulation (0db). If the audio signal were increased, it would enter the non-linear distortion region. This is what determines the upper limit of recording level.

The lower limit of volume is not determined by distortion, as is the upper limit. There is always a certain amount of residual noise inherent in the record playback process. The audible signal must remain a significant level above this noise to be usable. Thus, the lower limit of the volume is determined by the signal-to-noise ratio. As the signal approaches the noise level, it will begin to blend with the noise and be unusable.

The foregoing discussion has been primarily an academic explication of high-frequency bias and its importance in the magnetic recording process. However, there are also important practical aspects of this system that are of great concern to the soundman. Most prominent is the fact that the VU meter, or *modulometer,* of the recorder is absolutely meaningless if the bias is not properly adjusted. Furthermore, every brand and type of magnetic tape displays unique magnetic characteristics, and the bias must be adjusted to each type. If a recorder has been adjusted to a low noise-high output type tape, it will not deliver optimum results with a standard tape, and conversely.

The modulometer or level meter can only respond to absolute values of level. It is calibrated with respect to a *proper bias adjustment.* Thus, when the meter indicates 100% modulation (0db), it signifies the maximum acceptable signal only if the bias is in its proper center position. If it is not, the signal will go into the distortion region, even though the modulometer seems to indicate safe levels. This is evident from FIGURE 134. In this hypothetical recording curve, the h-f bias is at level five, and the modulometer reads 100% (0 db) for levels of '2', that is volume with amplitude from 3 to 7 (5, ± 2). If the bias level is incorrect, say at level 6, the same safe reading in the level meter will now actually be 4 to 8 (6, ± 2). It is evident that this is a serious incursion into the upper distortion region. It should be clear that the audio signal and the h-f bias signal are added together before going onto the tape (FIGURE 136). It is the sum of the two signals that determines the actual recording level. However, the modulometer only reflects the level of the audio and not the h-f bias. The only reason this is valid is due to the assumption that the h-f bias is an absolute constant at its proper level. If it is not, the entire VU or modulometer system is rendered invalid.

To compensate for slight miscalibrations in bias levels, most recorders will incorporate a safety factor into their VU meter or modulometer. This, a reading of 100% modulation, or 0db, is in reality 3db, 6db, or sometimes even 10db down from the actual 0db level. The bias can be incorrect by these small amounts and the modulometer will still be valid. In practice, if a tape is employed other than the type for which the recorder is calibrated, a recording should be made with a maximum of −5db or so, to compensate for a bias level mismatch.

For best results, the level of the h-f bias should be periodically calibrated and an attempt should be made to always employ the type and brand of tape for which the calibration was made.

FIGURE 133

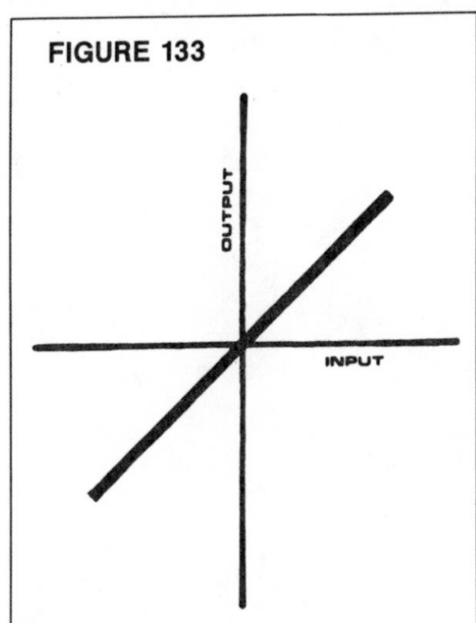

FIGURE 134

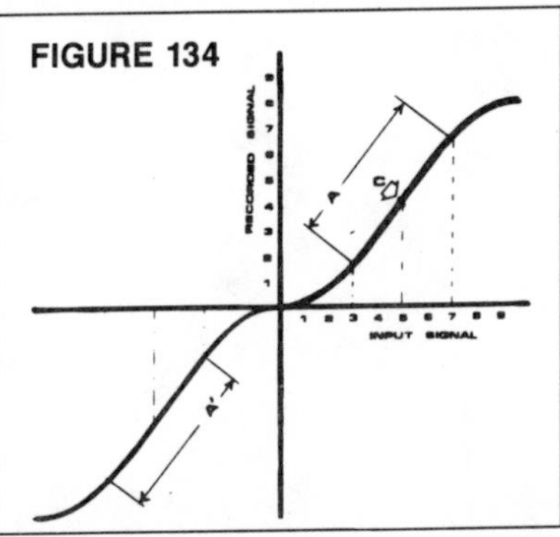

FIGURE 135

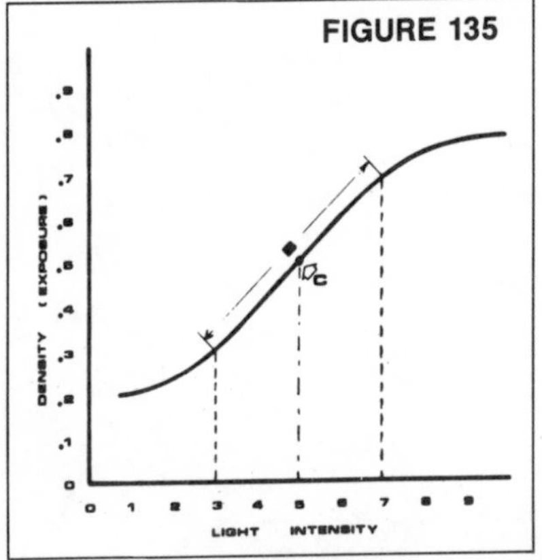

FIGURE 136A

FIGURE 136B

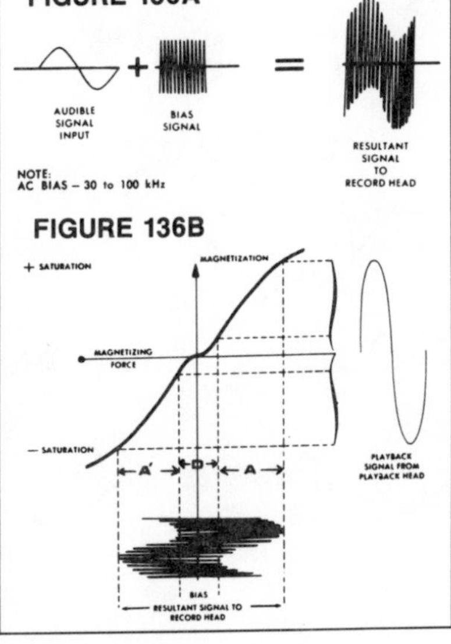

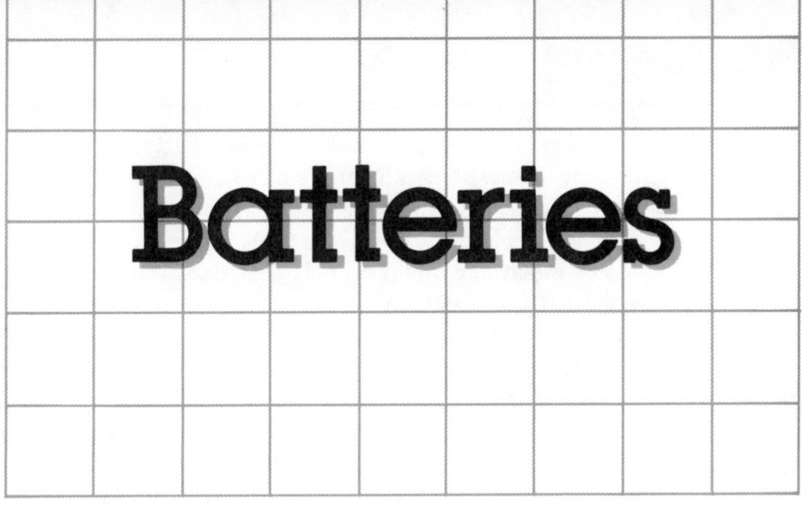

BATTERIES

It is a fact that all professional motion picture and video cameras require a battery. It is also a fact that this battery is the most frequently cursed piece of camera equipment. Every cameraman has experienced some sort of battery failure which undoubtably occurred at a most inopportune moment.

Batteries have thus gained an infamous reputation as fickle and unreliable pieces of equipment. In truth, this reputation is quite undeserved.

Most battery supplies used in our industry are constructed of sintered plate, sealed nickel-cadmium cells. These cells are the most rugged and reliable battery cells available and are truly a product of modern state-of-the-art technology. The problems encountered with these batteries are not due to their design or construction, but rather to the method in which they are used and charged.

Nickel-cadmium batteries have a very complex "personality." To get the most from these cells and to assure trouble-free operation, the cameraman should fully understand the many facets of this personality. In the case of high quality professional video and motion picture batteries almost all battery failures can be traced to some type of procedure error on the part of the cameraman during the charging, discharging or storage of the battery. In light of this fact, we will take a close look at the nickel-cadmium battery and try to cover those points most closely associated with battery failures.

This discussion will apply exclusively to premium sintered plate, sealed, rechargeable nickel-cadmium batteries. Most all quality power supplies used in motion picture and video are of this type of construction.

CONSTRUCTION—The sealed nickel-cadmium battery is an extremely rugged device, both physically and electrochemically. (See FIGURE 137) The construction is relatively simple. The cell consists of a positive plate, a negative plate and two separators. These four sheets are then rolled up very much like a jelly roll. The plates are nickel-plated steel strips to which an extremely porous plaque is sintered. This plaque is then impregnated with the chemicals which form the active plate materials. All connections are securely welded and the cases are nickel-plated steel. All this adds up to a design that is straightforward and rugged. The cells exhibit excellent resistance to shock and vibration and can be operated over a wide range of temperatures.

SEALED CELLS—The entire case of the cell is tightly sealed. This means that the battery is virtually maintenance-free. All gases and chemicals are held within the cell. The cells can be fully enclosed in a molded plastic case or metal container. Moreover, they can be operated, charged and stored in any position. (Almost all sealed cells have some provision for venting if an emergency arises. This will be discussed later.)

LONG-LIFE—Sealed nickel-cadmium cells have an extremely long life—whether measured by charge/discharge cycles or years of operation. The exact life of a Ni-Cad battery is greatly dependent on the methods by which it is charged and used. This important relationship will be the topic of a complete chapter. Under proper conditions one can expect a range of 300 to 1000 charge/discharge cycles. If the battery is not frequently used, the cells will maintain their ability to cycle over a period of many years.

OVERCHARGE PROTECTION—The sealed Ni-Cad battery is designed to accept an indefinite overcharge at the C/10 rate. For a battery rated at 2 amp-hours, the 'C' rate charge/discharge would be 2 amps. Thus the C/10 rate charge would be 2/10 of an amp, or 200 milliamps. At this rate, the battery will fully charge in 14–16 hours and can withstand an overcharge of days with no permanent damage. In addition, the charging mechanism is very simple.

HIGH RATE CHARGE/DISCHARGE—The Ni-Cad battery is capable of delivering very high rates of discharge, even as high as 30C or 60C. Thus, a 4 amp-hour cell can deliver over 200 amps under certain conditions without any damage to the cell. The Ni-Cad can also take fast charge cycles as short as one hour or even 10 minutes. (Special sophisticated chargers are required for charging Ni-Cads at anything above the C/10 or "overnight" rate. This is why the "overnight" rate remains the most popular.

LONG STORAGE LIFE—Ni-Cads can be stored for several years with no appreciable loss in capacity. After several charge/discharge cycles, the cell will regain full-rated capacity.

FLAT DISCHARGE CURVE—The Ni-Cad battery will maintain a relatively constant voltage as it is discharged. It is only after the cell is over 80% depleted that the voltage will begin to drop. Many other battery types will display a voltage curve that is continually decreasing as the battery is discharged.

CHARGE RETENTION—Charge retention is the ability of the battery to hold its charge during storage. Ideally, a battery should hold its charge indefinitely under open circuit conditions. Unfortunately, due to "self discharge", a battery will slowly lose its charge when left for extended periods. The rate at which a Ni-Cad battery will self-discharge is very dependent on storage temperatures. This fact is reflected in FIGURE 138. A fully charged Ni-Cad battery left at room temperature (20°C) for three weeks will lose about 20% of its capacity. If the temperature were 50°C, the battery would have lost over 50% of its capacity during this same three-week storage period. The self-discharge rate increases with age and use. Some cells may self discharge in a matter of days at room temperature.

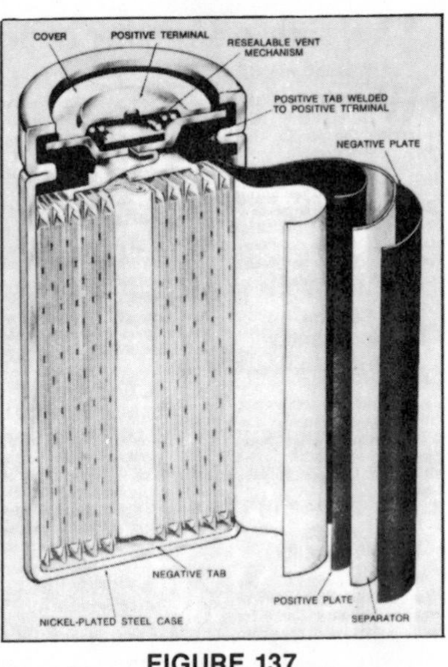

FIGURE 137

As a general rule, Ni-Cad batteries should be stored in a cool or cold area for best charge retention. Below 0°C, (freezing), the batteries will maintain 90% charge almost indefinitely (3–6 months and longer). When Ni-Cads are stored at room temperature for a couple of days, it is always a good idea to top them up with a few hours of charging. If they have been stored for longer than three weeks, *definitely* charge them for at least four to ten hours to insure a 100% available capacity.

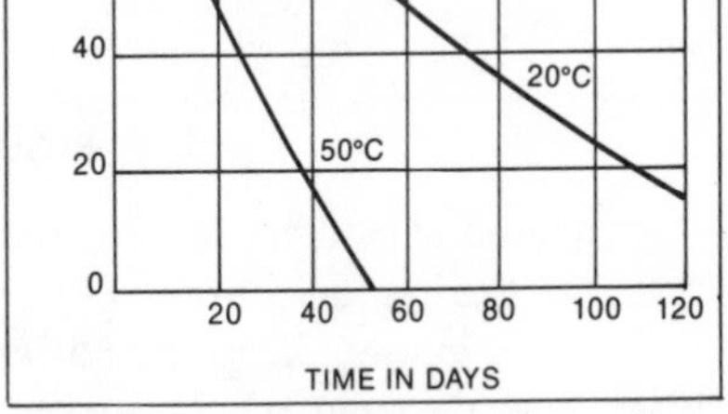

FIGURE 138—Charge Retention Vs. Battery Temperature

Actually, Ni-Cad batteries can be stored at temperatures as low as −40°C. However, the most practical storage temperatures are between 0°–10°C. Storage temperatures above 45°C–50°C should be avoided. While the Ni-Cads can be stored at a wide range of temperatures, the temperatures at which they can be charged or discharged are somewhat more restrictive.

CHARGE/DISCHARGE TEMPERATURES—A Ni-Cad battery can be discharged over a fairly wide range of temperatures (−20°C to +40°C). However, in practice, temperatures below 0°C (freezing) should be avoided. Low temperatures during discharge will not damage the cell, but will seriously reduce the available capacity. FIGURE 139 is a typical chart of a sealed Ni-Cad battery showing the relationship of available capacity as a function of temperature. Curve "A" is for light discharge currents while curve "B" is for a "C" rate discharge. Curve "B" represents most motion picture applications. It is evident that maximum capacity is available at approximately room temperature. Below 50°F, available capacity begins to drop off quite rapidly. At 20°F, only ½ of the rated capacity is available to power the camera. Available capacity also drops off at higher temperatures, but this is minimal when compared to the adverse effects of low temperature operation.

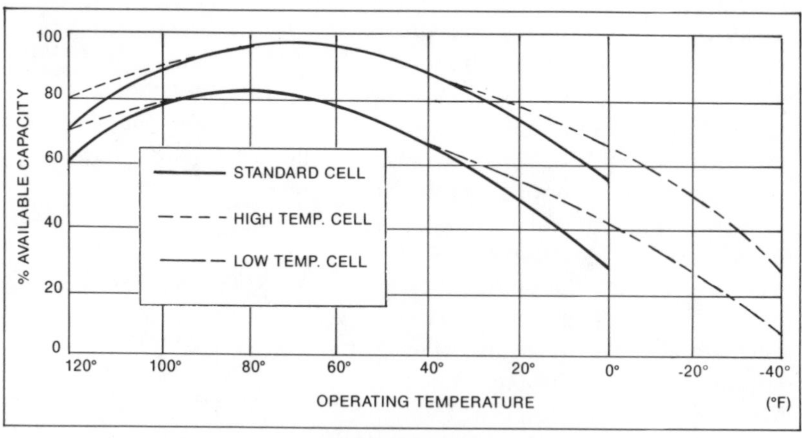

FIGURE 139

As a general rule, try to keep batteries as close to room temperature as possible during discharge. Under cold temperature conditions (near freezing or below), keep the batteries under a coat and as close to body warmth as possible. Also keep batteries in a warm house or car until the last possible moment before exposing them to the cold temperatures.

The most critical temperature range is associated with the charging of a Ni-Cad battery. A Ni-Cad battery must be *above* +5°C (about 45°F) during charging. *If a battery is brought in from the extreme cold, allow it to approach room temperature before throwing it on charge.* Under no circumstances allow a Ni-Cad to be charged in a room that is below 45°F. At these low temperatures, the chemical activity of the battery is reduced, and cannot keep up with the input charge current. Gassing and venting will result, and the cells will ultimately be destroyed.

High temperatures should also be avoided, but this is not too critical, except with fast charging systems. With conventional overnight chargers, temperatures can run as high as 40°C. However with fast-charging systems, temperatures should remain as close to 20°C. (70°F) as possible. If a battery comes in from a hot condition (direct sunlight, desert, etc.) let it reach room temperature before putting it on a fast charge.

In addition, a battery that is much above room temperature will exhibit a "reduced charge acceptance". That is, it will not reach a state of 100% charge.

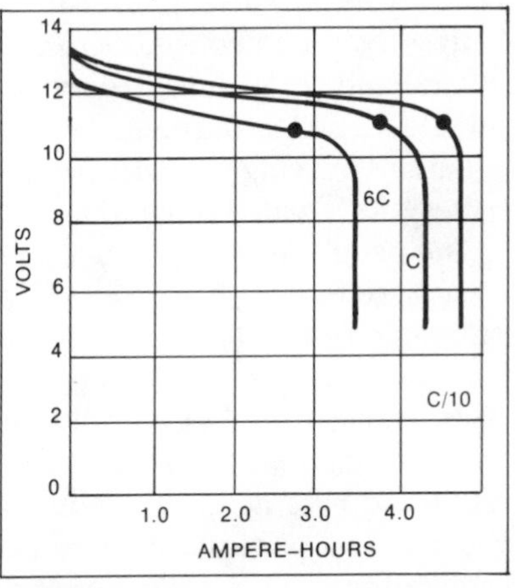

FIGURE 140—Typical Discharge Curves

CURRENT AND CAPACITY—A Ni-Cad battery is usually rated as having a particular ampere-hour capacity. This rating is valid only for a particular discharge rate, most frequently the "ten-hour rate" or 0.1 C rate. At higher discharge currents, the efficiency of the battery is reduced, and it will exhibit a lower effective capacity. FIGURE 140 is a capacity versus voltage plot for a 4-amp-hr. Ni-Cad battery at three different discharge rates. Note that the battery does exhibit the claimed 4 ah at the 0.1 C rate [400ma], but at the C rate [4 amps] the effective capacity is reduced to 3.5 ah. This is not that great a loss. However, at the 6 C rate [24 amps], the capacity is reduced to only 2.7 ah, almost a 35% loss in capacity. As a general rule, a Ni-Cad battery will give best performance and efficiency at discharge currents of approximately C rates or less. As currents exceed the 2C rate, efficiency and capacity take a nose dive. Choose a battery that can handle the current the camera will need.

Batteries

BATTERY CAPACITY

The first most basic step in choosing a battery is determining the necessary capacity. This is not quite as simple as it may seem. The philosophies are entirely different for film and video. The film camera only draws significant current when it is running. It draws virtually no power while the cameraman sets up his shot or practices his moves. As a matter of fact, the cameraman can do all the preliminaries without a battery at all. The capacity of a battery for a film camera can thus be directly related to film capacity, i.e., this battery will run three 400′ mags while that one will run seven 400′ mags, etc.

The video camera is an entirely different animal. Without a battery or external power source the video camera is just an expensive anchor. The camera draws full power whenever the cameraman wishes to look through the lens or check the various camera functions. There is thus *no* correlation between camera battery capacity and the amount of tape that can be recorded. This makes choosing a video battery a little tricky. In one instance, the camerman may have his camera 'hot' for over an hour as he sets up, lights and practices an intricate shot. An entire battery may be depleted before a single second of tape rolls. On the other hand, the same battery and camera may run four or five 20 minute cassettes during a fast breaking ENG situation. With actual situations varying so widely, is there any rule of thumb for choosing a battery for a video camera?

The people at Anton/Bauer have come up with some recommendations based upon their research. Anton/Bauer employs a special computer that fully evaluates every battery that is manufactured. This same computer analyzes every battery sent in for repair. The data is stored on discs and can be periodically analyzed to determine any trends or chronic situations in returned batteries. Over the years, one very definite trend became quite evident. There was a high rate of complaints concerning a particular battery that was supposed to run its associated camera for one hour. An inordinate percentage of these batteries were returned with almost identical complaints; "the battery only ran the camera 10 minutes" or "it didn't even make it through one 20 minute cassette". Well, lo and behold, almost everyone of these returned batteries ran over one full hour on the computer and in some cases as high as one hour and 20 minutes. The batteries were returned to the customers with the request that they fully charge the battery, and then put it on the camera, turn it on, and return an hour later. In every case the customer would acknowledge that the battery did, indeed, run over an hour but he couldn't understand why it only ran 15 minutes or so the last time he used it.

The answer is very simple. Nobody really keeps track of the 'on' time of a video camera. The cameraman will turn it on to check registration (while he has a cup of coffee), then he may roll some bars and check the various electronics with a chip chart. Fifteen to twenty minutes are easily consumed. Out at the location the camera is fired up as the cameraman checks composition and lighting and maybe practices an intricate move. Another twenty minutes can easily be consumed. The talent requests several walk throughs which the cameraman follows with the camera obviously on. Of course, no one realizes that the camera has been 'hot' for almost an hour, and so comes the complaint, "gee, we weren't even through the first cassette and the battery went dead".

The folks at Anton/Bauer have proved beyond any doubt that this situation is very prevalent and occurs more often than not. Moreover, they have been able to pinpoint, through the computer data, the optimum capacity to minimize the aforementioned phenomenon.

As described above, most complaints centered around a battery/camera combination that provided about 1 to 1¼ hours of continuous operation. Most interestingly, this very same battery was also coupled with another camera which drew half the power of the first and thus provided a two hour battery/camera combination. In the latter case there were virtually no complaints or problems with low capacity, even though it was the same battery. By analyzing data from other camera/battery combinations a clear pattern developed and several conclusions could be made.

The following recommendations have proven to be quite valid. The ideal situation is a battery that will run the video camera for two hours or more. A battery that will run the video camera between 1½ hours and 2 hours will usually be satisfactory, but the 1½ hour point is considered marginal. The 1 hour to 1½ hour battery/camera combination is bound to prove unsatisfactory even though an hour or so seems like it should be sufficient. And lastly, anything significantly under a "one hour battery" will undoubtedly be a disaster.

Also keep in mind that these capacity ratings are for new batteries under ideal conditions. As the battery ages, or under low temperature conditions, the available capacity will be reduced. As a matter of fact, according to industry accepted conventions, a battery has reached the end of its useful life when it no longer delivers 50% of its rated capacity. A video battery that provides 1 hour of running time when new will only deliver ½ this capacity (30 minutes) at the end of its useful life.

Most modern ENG/EFP cameras and camera/VTR units draw between 15 and 30 watts and should be matched to 4 amp hour NiCads or better. A battery smaller than a 4 amp hour NiCad should only be considered if the camera draws *under* 15 watts where a 2 amp hour NiCad would be quite sufficient. Those cameras drawing more than 30 watts would be better matched with dual paralleled 4 AH (8 AH) NiCads or a 12 AH silver zinc battery. If a camera in the 30 to 50 watt range is used with a 4 amp hour NiCad, conscious effort should be made to turn the camera off if it is not in actual use.

As a matter of fact, in general, the best advice to prolong any video battery capacity is to turn the camera off whenever your eye is away from the eyepiece or monitor, even if it is only for a few moments. Remember, that modern ENG/EFP cameras come up to operating specifications within seconds of being turned on, so there is no reason to leave them fired up when there is no eye on the finder. Even with smaller cameras drawing under 15 watts, the 4 AH NiCad is the preferred battery. It provides better balance and stability than smaller batteries, as well as providing the convenience of over 3 hours of operation.

CHARGING NICAD BATTERIES

There are basically two ways to kill a NiCad battery: improper discharging and improper charging. Of these improper charging is definitely the more prevalent crime. In many cases the person charging the batteries may be an unwitting accessory to the crime by not understanding proper charging procedures. In other cases the manufacturer of the batteries and/or charger may be an accomplice by employing insufficient protection circuits in both units or by using improper or marginal charging routines.

SLOW CHARGING—What is slow charging? Slow charging is also called "overnight" charging (14–16 hours) and is actually a constant current charge rate that is 1/10 of the ampere hour rating of the battery. The reason slow charging is popular and inexpensive is that it is also the "maximum continuous charge rate" of most NiCad cells. That is, the sealed NiCad cell has a built-in overcharge protection capability. Once fully charged, the continuing charge current produces oxygen and heat within the cell. The cell can reabsorb all this oxygen as long as the charge rate does exceed this "overnight" (C/10) rate. If the charge rate *were* to exceed this rate, oxygen would be produced faster than it could be absorbed and the cell would eventually "vent" and be destroyed. By staying at the "overnight" rate, the charger can be a simple constant current device without any concern for overcharging, as the cell is protected up to this charge rate. It appears that slow charging is a simple, straightforward, and foolproof method of charging. Guess again.

Slow charging has several potential problems. Upon reaching full charge, the charging energy is being dissipated as heat within the battery. The internal temperature of the battery pack can typically reach 45°C to 55°C, which is above the upper safety limits of most NiCads. More important, NiCads should be stored at *cool* temperatures, usually room temperature or lower (0°C–20°C). Thus leaving a charged battery on slow charge for any length of time unleashes the number one killer of NiCads: heat. Instead of being stored at a cool temperature, the battery is being cooked to death. Extended slow charging will typically age a battery *10 times* faster than normal. (See FIGURE 141) It can also reduce charge acceptance and lower discharge voltage.

This potential problem can obviously be avoided by removing the battery from the slow charger as soon as possible after a full charge has been achieved. This practice, however, is sometimes impractical and can create an additional problem. As NiCads age, they begin to self-discharge faster than normal. With most NiCad batteries being made of 10 cells or more, the law of averages (and Murphy) will result in at least one or two cells self-discharging in as few as 2 or 3 days. So if the battery is removed from the slow charger and left on the shelf for a few days there is a good chance that it will not deliver full capacity. In worst cases the battery will appear stone dead. Lastly, the "overnight" charger has a problem with its name. The "overnight" rate requires 14 to 16 hours for a complete charge, yet very few ENG/EFP crews sleep 14 to 16 hours each night. More typically a crew will return to the studio or hotel room at 10 or 11 PM and have to be up by 7 AM the next morning. Under these conditions the batteries will only be half charged.

Most of these problems can be avoided with correct procedures or proper equipment. Most obviously, don't leave batteries on slow charge longer than necessary. If a fully charged battery is removed from slow charge and allowed to sit for more than a few days, it should be given an additional "overnight" charge the evening preceding the day it is to be used in order to bring up any cells that may have discharged. Even if the battery were still 100% charged, this additional overnight charge will not adversely affect battery life.

The exclusive technology of the Anton/Bauer Lifesaver™ chargers eliminates these two problems automatically. Firstly, a logic controlled circuit monitors the charge current. When the charger has delivered a full capacity charge to the battery, the constant charge current is terminated, preventing any extended heat build-up that would reduce battery life. Simultaneously, the charger enters the "Lifesaver™ mode" which is a maintenance charge routine that keeps the battery cool yet negates any self-discharge. Thus the battery is safely kept at full charge, ready to use, for days, weeks, or even months.

The slow charger, by definition, cannot charge quicker than 14 to 16 hour rate. To overcome this limitation requires a quick charger or fast charger which is an entirely different animal.

FAST CHARGING AND QUICK CHARGING—A fast charger and quick charger are essentially similar devices technologically, differing only in charge rate. By industry convention, a charger that fully charges a battery in one hour or less is dubbed a "fast" charger while one that requires longer than one hour but less than the 14 to 16 hours of the slow charger, is termed a "quick" charger. In either case, these chargers must include some means of determining the full charge status of a battery and immediately terminating the fast charge current. Remember, the NiCad cell cannot fully absorb overcharge oxygen when the overnight rate is exceeded. If the fast or quick charge current were allowed to continue past full charge the battery would eventually be destroyed.

Developing a reliable method to sense the full charge state is the first step in designing a safe fast or quick charge system. There are three things that happen when a NiCad cell approaches full charge; the voltage rises, the pressure increases and the temperature rises. Sensing the rise in voltage, though used in some fast charge systems, is of dubious reliability. The rise in voltage of each cell is only temporary. Once the cell enters overcharge the voltage actually *decreases*. Because a NiCad battery always includes 10 or more cells, Murphy again predicts that they will reach full charge at slightly different times, thus the voltage sensing charger operates under the fairy tale belief that all cells will reach full charge at the same time; when they don't, the battery could be severely damaged.

Sensing the pressure rise is totally impractical, which leaves temperature sensing as the preferred fast charge method. Most fast charge batteries use regular NiCad cells and implant one or two thermal sensors into the pack. When the battery reaches full charge these sensors will pick up the rise in temperature and cancel the fast charge current. Simple? Guess again.

There are two major flaws with a conventional TCO (temperature cutoff) fast charge battery. Remember that it is the pressure from the oxygen that causes the cell to vent. Unfortunately, in a standard NiCad cell the pressure rises to venting levels *before* the temperature can reach the TCO point. So the temperature sensing system is like closing the barn door after the cow is gone. The solution is a special (and more expensive) premium NiCad cell that is currently available from only three cell manufacturers in the world. This cell has been designed for TCO fast charging by optimizing the oxygen absorption system within the cell. It is the oxygen absorption that produces the heat (exothermic reaction), so in this special cell the temperature *always* rises to the TCO point well *before* the pressure gets near the venting level. While this special cell is necessary for safe TCO fast charging, there is still one other problem. Because cells can self-discharge at different rates, a battery can become unequalized. A condition can actually exist where some cells are fully charged and others are stone dead within a single battery. If only one or two thermal sensors were employed, the probabilities are good that the sensor could be on a cool discharged cell while a fully charged cell is being destroyed by the fast charge current. Again there is a solution. Every Anton/Bauer battery employs an exclusive multiple sensor system that monitors the temperature of *every* cell within the battery. As soon as even a single cell reaches full charge, the fast charge current is terminated to protect that cell. This combination of the special TCO NiCad cell and a sensing system that monitors every cell has resulted in the first truly foolproof and 100% safe fast charge system.

EQUALIZING—Assuming that the battery is unequalized and has some cells more charged than others. A battery with all-cell sensing will safely terminate the fast charge current as soon as the first cell reaches full charge. But then how do the lesser charged cells get to be fully charged? The answer is simple. After the fast charge current terminates, the battery is given the "overnight" (C/10) charge rate. This does not hurt the fully charged cells yet will bring up all other cells to full charge. This, however, ends up with the potential problems of slow charging, i.e., extended heat build-up if left on the charger or self-discharge if taken off. The solutions are the same. Don't leave the battery on the fast or quick charger for more than 12 hours. If a battery remains unused for several days, give it a *slow* charge the evening before the day it is to be used.

Again, the Anton/Bauer Lifesaver™ Quick Chargers and Fast Chargers eliminate these problems automatically. These chargers employ 3 separate charge modes. When the very first cell within the battery reaches full charge, the charger drops to the equalizing rate (C/10) automatically. Because the logic circuit is monitoring the amount of charge the battery has received, it knows exactly how much charge is necessary to bring the most discharged cell up to full charge. Thus the equalizing mode continues just long enough to get all the remaining cells up to full capacity safely. When all cells are fully charged, the logic circuit terminates the constant charge current and activates the Lifesaver(TM) maintenance charge which keeps all the cells in the charged battery fully charged with no heat build-up. The battery can safely remain on the charger until ready for use, for weeks, months or even years! This is the ultimate charging system.

FICTION, MYTHS AND FACTS—Most people are under the impression that fast charging or quick charging is damaging to the battery or "stresses" the battery. This impression results from the proliferation of poorly protected fast charge batteries employing improper cells and the equally abundant number of poorly designed fast charge systems that are in use. Inherently, fast charging and quick charging are no more stressful to the cell than slow charging if the proper cells and protection are employed. Aside from choosing a well designed battery/charger system, there are several other considerations.

The quick charger usually makes most sense as the nucleus of a good ENG/EFP battery system. While the quick charger shares the technological sophistication of a fast charger, it can be made smaller, lighter and less expensive because it only has to pump about 15% as much current as a fast charger. In one case a 4 position 8 hour quick charger is about the same size, weight and cost as a single position one hour fast charger. The quick charger charges all batteries in 8 hours which is ideal for normal circumstances. A conventional slow charger takes too long (14–16 hours) and the 1 hour charger is faster than really necessary in most cases.

The prudent ENG/EFP battery package should include enough batteries to run all equipment for a normal day without the necessity to recharge during the day. There should be an 8 hour quick charger available for *each* battery so all batteries can be charged simultaneously overnight (8 hours). A single fast charger may be included for the unexpected.

In general, fast charging should be considered an exigency process. That is, no one should buy just two batteries and figure to charge one while using the other, or use two in the morning and charge them both at lunch for afternoon use. Such procedures are both foolish and impractical. Firstly, one never knows if an assignment will present access to AC power for charging even during lunch. Secondly, it is easier to carry around two extra batteries than a fast charger or two. Lastly, the two extra batteries cost virtually nothing. This is due to the fact that NiCads have an almost indefinite shelf life. Thus, if you normally bought two batteries every two years, it would cost no more to buy four batteries every four years and have the luxury of having two extra batteries for those times when you need them. Crews should always carry enough batteries to see them through any assignment. If they expect to shoot 8 hours and they get 2 hours per battery, carrying anything less than 4 batteries is foolhardy. You cannot count on being near AC power, you cannot count on having time to recharge, even if it is only 1 hour or as little as 20 minutes, and lastly you cannot count on fast chargers in many situations.

For example, a battery that has been fully charged and not used for a few days may not remain fully charged. Some cells in the battery may still have full capacity while some others may have partially discharged, while yet others may be stone dead. This battery will not run a camera for even one minute. This is just one of those unexpected situations where the fast charger could come in handy. Right? Wrong! This battery *cannot* be fast charged. Because several of the cells may still be fully charged, they cannot accept the high fast charge current which would destroy them. A well designed battery system will prevent this battery from receiving a fast charge and thus protect the fully charged cells. A poorly designed fast charger or battery may not sense that some cells are fully charged and commence the fast charge current which will destroy those cells. So just when you think the fast charger will come in handy, it doesn't do a thing, or worse yet, may destroy the battery.

Another situation finds you short on power on a cold day, you run inside and pop the battery into the trusty fast charger for a quickie. Guess again. A NiCad battery should not be charged when it is much under 55°F. As a matter of fact, the battery not only will be damaged if fast charged at low temperatures, but, to add insult to injury, it will not even accept the fast charge current. You are left with an uncharged damaged battery. The situation is similar in hot climates. The battery tends to self-heat during discharge. This heat coupled with either hot direct sunshine or high ambient temperatures can easily yield temperatures in excess of 110° that is considered the maximum fast charge temperature. A well designed fast charger and battery will sense these excessive temperatures and prevent the fast charge circuit from being activated. If the high ambient condition persists, it may take quite a long time before the battery is cooled to a safe fast charge temperature. Once again the fast charge is not available when you need it.

Having covered some of the limitations of fast charging there are certain situations where fast charging can come in handy if done properly. Firstly, fast charging must only be done at or near room temperature. During very hot weather, a battery should be fast charged in an air conditioned room. If the battery is hot enough to trip the 'hot' protection circuit of the fast charger, it can be put in a refrigerator for a few minutes to reduce the battery temperature to within charge limits. If the battery comes in from a cold climate, it must be allowed to reach room temperature *before* fast charging is attempted. If the battery is at freezing temperatures, this can take from one to three hours.

Most important, a battery must have its cells equalized in order to successfully accept a fast charge. The only way to equalize the cells of a battery is to give it an overnight charge the night before an assignment. Even in as little as two or three days a battery can become unequalized due to certain cells self-discharging. Taking all these factors into account creates a realistic picture of proper fast charge technique. One, slow charge or Lifesaver™ charge the batteries the night before using. Two, take enough batteries to cover the assignment under normal circumstances. Three, try to keep batteries at or near room temperature both before and *after* use. Four, if at the end of the day you are caught short, the room temperature, equalized batteries can be successfully fast charged in a well designed charger without any problems.

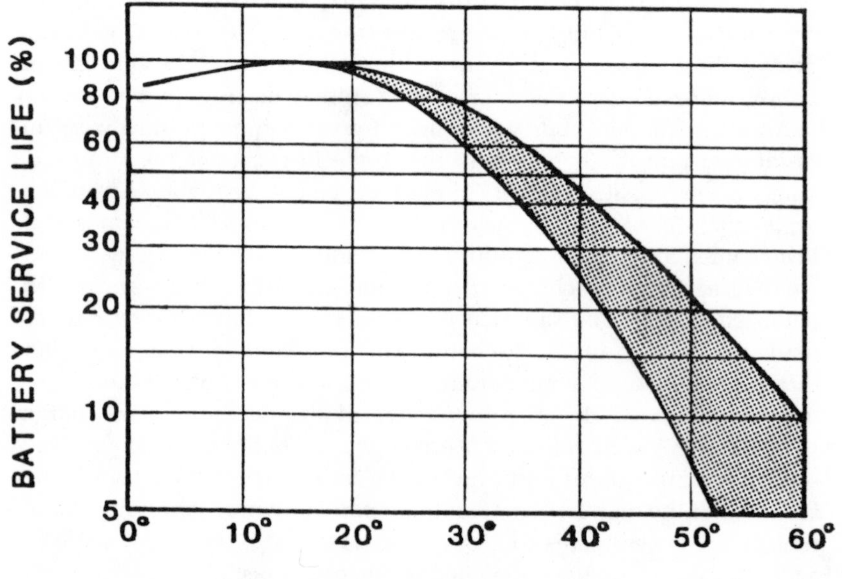

FIGURE 141

Constant slow charging can raise the internal temperature of a battery to 45°C to 55°C. At these temperatures, the battery will only deliver 10% to 20% of its normal service life. The battery is thus aging up to 10 times faster than normal.

NICAD BATTERY LIFE

After spending $500 or more on a NidCad battery system, most people feel it should last forever. But alas, like most of us the NiCad battery will eventually die. The battery can at least be comforted knowing its owner will be grieved by its demise. And with good reason, as passing of one battery means a new one must be purchased. It is thus understandable that one of the prominent questions always asked while shopping for batteries is "How long will it last?" This is a very valid question as the ultimate cost-per-hour of the battery is obviously a function of its initial cost divided by its length of service. Unfortunately, that question is very similar to asking a doctor in the maternity ward to what age a particular baby will live.

This analogy has many parallels. There are many "diseases" that can affect the life of a battery as well as "coronaries" that can kill it almost instantly. Certain ailments can be cured while others are most certainly terminal. Lastly, there are certain guidelines that will definitely help to achieve a longer and healthier life for a NiCad.

Most people relate to NiCad "life" in either years of service or number of charge discharge cycles. Paradoxically, the tendency of a NiCad to "wear out" is not directly dependent on either of these parameters. NiCads have been known to last up to ten years under ideal test parameters and minimum cycling. Likewise, NiCads can survive up to ten-thousand cycles under strictly controlled conditions. So where can you buy cells like these? Unfortunately, the life expectancy of a battery is almost totally dependent on the way it is used and its environment. In the real world, NiCad cells rarely achieve anywhere near the length of service of which they may be capable under laboratory conditions. The elements that actually account for a NiCad "wearing out" are prominently temperature, over charging conditions, and, to a lesser degree, depth of discharge. These factors are obviously tied in to the number of cycles and the age of cells. Thus both time and cycling indirectly become elements in determining the ultimate life of the battery.

Figure 142 shows the wide range of life expectancy that a NiCad can experience. If one considers 80% or more as optimum capacity, then a NiCad can survive anywhere from 250 to over 10,000 cycles. Video and motion picture applications unfortunately fall somewhat toward the lower end of this spectrum and Figure 143 is a more realistic outlook. Figure 143 is an approximate bell curve of distribution of NiCad life expectancies based on data compiled within our industry. Basically, the average life expectancy is around 400 to 500 cycles, while the full range runs from 300 to over 800. Only under the most adverse conditions should a NiCad deliver fewer than 250 cycles and conversely, it would require divine intervention to exceed 1,000 deep discharge cycles.

When is a NiCad considered deceased? For convenience, the battery industry considers a cell to have reached the end of its useful life when it no longer can deliver 50% of its rated capacity at a "C" rate discharge at room temperature. This concept has interesting implications. A new battery that is rated to run three film magazines may run only one magazine in its old age. Likewise, a new battery rated to run a video camera for one hour will only squeak out a half hour close to its demise.

Before discussing the actual reasons for battery failures, it should be made clear that there are basically three categories of failures. The "permanent failure" needs little clarification. The cell has bought it. It cannot be reconditioned or revived. In other cases, the cell may cease to meet proper performance levels but it can be revitalized or reconditioned back to an acceptable state of health. Such a malady would be labelled a "nonpermanent" or "reversible" failure. The third classification is the "functional failure". In this case, the cell still has life, but its performance has slipped below that necessary to properly run the piece of equipment to which it is matched. This is not really a battery problem but rather a case of an improperly designed piece of equipment or an incorrect battery selection.

Reviewing, there are three categories of battery failure:

1. The "permanent" failure,
2. The "temporary" or "reversible" failure, and
3. The "functional" failure.

There are remedies for the latter two conditions but "permanent" failure is death to a NiCad cell. The permanent failure usually results from either an internal short circuit or an open circuit. The short circuit can either be a "dead" (low resistance) short or a high impedance short. In the case of a dead short, the cell in essence becomes a piece of wire. It will not accept a charge nor will it contribute any power to the battery. The symptoms of a shorted cell are typically an open circuit (no load) voltage 1.3 to 1.4 volts lower than normal and a voltage under load that is about 1.2 volts lower than normal. Note that capacity of the remaining cells in the battery is not seriously affected assuming that the device being powered can still function on the reduced voltage. By the way, this is one of the big benefits of the modern wide range "switching type" regulators found in most state-of-the-art video equipment. Such equipment will usually function on voltages from 10.8 up to 18 volts. Thus a 14.4 volt NiCad can lose one or even two shorted cells and still power one of these devices without any problems. On the other hand, if a 12 volt NiCad battery is employed, the device being powered will cease to function as soon as even one cell becomes shorted.

The "high impedance" short circuit can be considered a "partial" or "slow" short circuit. This partial short provides a small path that will slowly self discharge the afflicted cell. Such a cell can be charged if the charge current is significantly higher than the current being dissipated by the slow internal short. However, even if the cell is charged, it will slowly lose all its capacity in a few days or even hours depending upon the severity of the short. The symptoms of a battery afflicted with a high impedance cell will vary depending upon the time elapsed since charging. Immediately off charge, such a battery will behave normally with little or no reduction of capacity or voltage. However, with longer interims between charging and actual use, the battery will exhibit progressively less capacity. The best way to combat the high impedance short problems is to fully charge or recharge a suspect battery at the *slow overnight* rate, the evening immediately preceding the day of use.

These internal short circuits are the most common cause of death for a NiCad. As with all things, death is inevitable, but certain conditions and practices will certainly speed its arrival. The internal short is usually caused by the 2 plates inside the cell coming into contact with one another. This could be the result of a physical shock or a direct hit that dents the cells. The two plates are kept apart by a tissue thin separator material. A dent in the case can pinch the separator material and cause the 2 plates to touch (dead short) or almost touch (high impedance short). Obviously the best defense is not to bang batteries about. Despite the best of intentions, batteries in our industry are bound to experience some rough handling and in anticipation of such, a battery should offer some protection to the cells inside. Choose batteries with hard outside cases as opposed to soft coverings. The construction should not transmit the shock of a fall directly to the internal cells.

The other main cause of internal short circuits is separator breakdown caused by excessive or elevated temperatures. Prolonged exposure to high temperatures will accelerate the decomposition of the separator material and other organic elements within the cell. Obviously, the best defense is to keep batteries cool. Do not leave them on overnight charge longer than 16 hours. Extending the overnight charge rate for days or even weeks will not "damage" the battery due to over charging (venting), but the elevated temperatures resulting from this continuous charge current will drastically reduce the life expectancy of the battery. As a matter of fact, the heat from extended slow charging can age a NiCad battery 10 times faster than normal. Even a battery that is just slow charged on weekends can age 4 times faster than normal. Anton/Bauer Lifesaver charges automatically eliminate this problem by terminating the constant charge current upon full charge and putting the battery on the Lifesaver maintenance charge routine. This keeps the battery safely topped with no heat build up. Because charge routine can be a major factor in determining the life of a NiCad the chapter on charging should be read carefully. Do not leave batteries in a hot trunk or van. Do not leave batteries in direct sunlight whether indoors or out. Brief exposure to higher temperatures will have little affect on life, but frequent excursions to elevated temperatures that result in the raising of the average battery temperature will most assuredly have an adverse effect on life expectancy. Heat is the biggest enemy of batteries. So whenever possible keep batteries in the coolest available place. In hot climates batteries that will not be used for an extended time should be charged and then stored in an air conditioned room or refrigerator (while heat is the number one killer of cells, very low temperatures must likewise be avoided during charging).

There is also a certain amount of heat generated within the cell during discharge due to its internal resistance. This is usually negligable at low current drains but can become significant at higher relative currents, especially in hotter climates. For example, a camera drawing 2 amps will discharge a 4 ampere hour battery ("D" size) in two hours at the ½ "C" rate. This same camera will discharge a one ampere hour (sub "C") battery in ½ hour at the 2 "C" rate. Because the smaller one ampere hour sub "C" cell has a higher internal resistance, it will generate more heat during discharge. One can thus expect longer life and more dependable service from the larger "D" size 4 ampere hour battery. Likewise, "D" size 4 ampere hour batteries in portable lighting service (8 amps/2 "C" rate) should not be expected to give the same length of service they would if used with a portable ¾" VTR (one amp/¼ "C" rate).

Over discharging a battery can also invite a short circuit. Because a short circuit is a direct path from the positive to negative, tremendous current will flow through this internal path the instant it forms. Assuming the cell has some charge left this high current can often vaporize internal short circuits as they develop. This self correcting phenomenon cannot take place if the cell is discharged close to zero volts. Therefore, it is good practice not to over discharge a battery.

Change to a fresh battery at the first indication of depletion and charge depleted batteries as soon as possible after use. Batteries should be stored in the charge condition and should receive an additional slow overnight charge the night preceding re-use. I have heard some people mention that they have corrected an internally shorted cell by charging it for a few seconds with a tremendously high current. While this

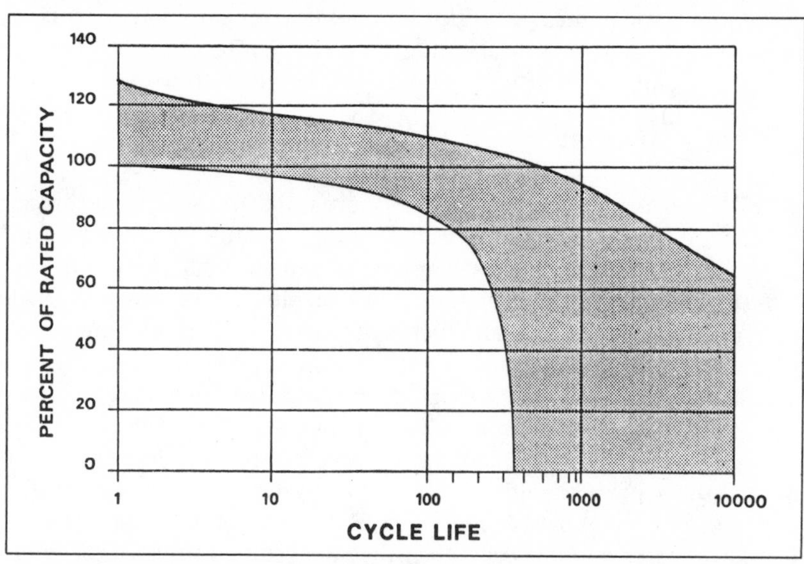

(ABOVE) FIGURE 142—NiCad Life Expectancy Range, Relative to Capacity. Depending on environmental conditions and application routines, a NiCad cell can deliver acceptable performance for over 10,000 cycles or die after as few as 300 cycles. (BELOW) FIGURE 143—Approximate Bell Curve for NiCad Life Expectancy of Batteries Employed in Motion Picture and Video Application. While average life is around 400 to 600 cycles, the gamut is from 300 to 800 cycles. Proper use and maintenance can shift the life expectancy of a battery from the low end to the high end of this curve.

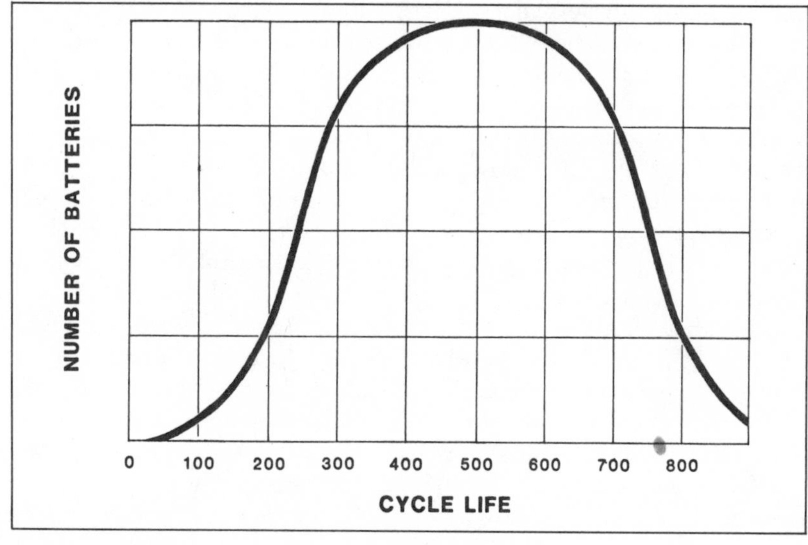

procedure is sometimes successful in zapping away the short, it actually burns a larger hole in the separator. Thus the rebirth of the cell is only temporary and the short will undoubtedly be quick to return.

BATTERY MEMORY

There is no doubt that batteries are unlike most other technical devices. They do not adhere strictly to the precise "laws of operation" as most users and designers might wish. On the other hand, most battery types exhibit a "personality" that battery engineers can plot, and thereby remove most of the mystery and uncertainties from battery performance.

One of these "personality traits" is the so-called memory effect. Despite the fact that this memory phenomenon is quite clearly defined by battery engineers, battery memory has become the most misunderstood of all battery phenomenon. This memory hysteria is inadvertently aggravated by several battery manufacturers who have been selling "dememorizers" or touting cell types that allegedly do not suffer from memory. It appears that most battery users do not have a clear understanding of what memory is, where it comes from, or how it affects performance. Most ironically, the memory effect is quite rare, and even in those isolated cases where it may be present, it will have little effect on the performance of a properly designed piece of equipment.

The cause of the so-called "memory effect" can be attributed basically to two situations. The first is a *precisely* repetitive partial discharge, followed by a full slow charge. Here is the first area of misunderstanding. The key word here is *precisely.* This effect was first noticed in a satellite where the battery was discharged only partially to the exact same point and recharged. As the process continues, the battery will eventually "memorize" this point of partial discharge. If the battery is partially discharged to various and random depths of discharge before recharging, the memory effect is not encountered. Repetitive partial discharge can be avoided by labeling batteries "A", "B", "C", etc. Batteries should be rotated so that each successive day begins with a different battery. For example, on Monday start with battery "A" and run it to depletion (low battery warning) and then proceed to battery "B" and "C". On Tuesday start with "B", etc. At least the first battery is run to depletion on most days and this rotating technique will thus assure that all batteries will get a deep discharge at least once or twice a week, which will prevent any memory problems.

The second cause of a "memory type" phenomenon is long term overcharge at the overnight rate. If the battery is left on a slow charge for many days or weeks, an undesirable secondary alloy of nickel cadmium (Ni_5Cd_{21}) begins to form causing an effect similar to "memory" (See Figure 145). This situation can be avoided by removing batteries from slow charge after 16 hours or using an Anton/Bauer Lifesaver Charger which automatically terminates constant charge current upon delivering a full charge. This latter method is preferred as the Lifesaver charger prevents self discharge that would occur if a battery is simply removed from a conventional charger. The aforementioned techniques will prevent any memory problems, but even if a memory problem is suspected, it can be erased by two or three deep discharges (up to, but not past low voltage warning).

Now that it is clear where it comes from and how to get rid of it, what exactly *is* memory? Contrary to popular belief, memory does *not* usually involve a significant loss of cell capacity. What it does is cause a "jog" in the discharge voltage curve. (See FIGURE 144). This jog or dip in the voltage curve (about one tenth volt per cell) will occur at the time where previously and repetitively the discharge had been terminated. Hence the term memory.

In the case of long term slow rate overcharge, the jog point will move from the end of the discharge curve to a point progressively sooner in the discharge cycle depending on the length of overcharge time. (See FIGURE 145). In the extreme case of weeks or months of overcharge the jog point can be right in the beginning of discharge and hence not be noticeable. It will just appear that the entire discharge curve is lowered by approximately one tenth volt per cell.

It should be obvious from both figures that the major result of the memory effect is a jog in the discharge voltage and not necessarily a loss of capacity. If a cell does have a memory, it will still deliver most its capacity but merely at a slightly lower voltage. Thus cell memory is rare, and does not significantly effect performance of a properly designed piece of equipment. So where's the problem?

Unfortunately, not all electronic equipment is properly designed. One would think that in today's world of sophisticated LSI chips and microcomputers, it would be duck soup for an electronic engineer to interface with a simple battery. Alas, such is not the case, and in more than one instance an otherwise perfect piece of portable electronic equipment has been rendered almost useless because the design engineer overestimated his own knowledge of batteries. The problem is basically one of voltage range. Most users think that a 12 volt NiCad battery puts out 12 volts. In most cases it doesn't. Unfortunately, this naivete is shared by electronic design engineers. For example, one manufacturer of audio visual electronics has numerous portable devices that are designed to

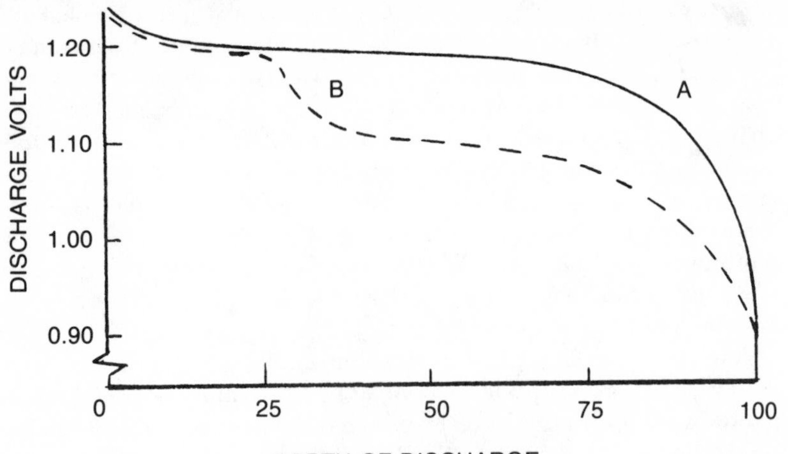

FIGURE 144

Effect of cell "Memory" is a jog or dip in the voltage discharge curve. Solid line represents a new cell. The dotted line is a cell that has memory approximately ⅓ into the discharge curve. Note that there is usually little loss of capacity but merely a slight lowering of the discharge voltage which will have no effect on a properly designed piece of equipment.

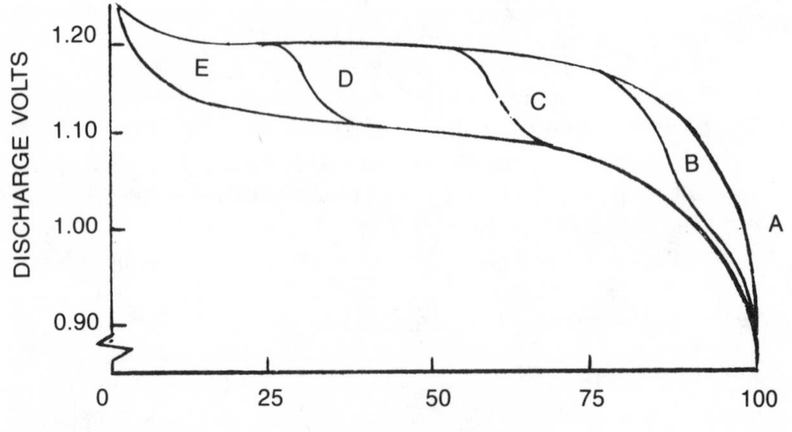

FIGURE 145

This chart graphically presents the "Memory Type" phenomenon associated with long periods of overcharging at the overnight or trickle rate—Curve "A" (top curve) represents a new cell. Curve "B" results from excessive overcharge. As the length of overcharge time increases, the jog in discharge voltage occurs sooner as in curve "C" and "D". Eventually the overcharge time can reach a point that causes the jog to occur immediately upon commencement of discharge. This is represented by curve "E" which looks identical to curve "A" except about 1/10 volt/cell lower.

run on "12 volt batteries". A close look at the spec sheet states: "12 volts ± 1 volt". A check of the equipment confirms that the device poops out if the voltage goes much below 11 volts. The irony is that there is no such conventional battery that can maintain 12 volts ± 1 volt. Even more ludicrous is the fact that the manufacturer in question supplies it's own battery that, like all other batteries, doesn't even come close to maintaining it's own tolerances.

A NiCad cell is rated nominally @ 1.2 to 1.25 volts/cell depending on discharge current. The key word here is "nominal". If you look it up in the dictionary, the word nominal means: "Existing in name only; not actual", and the use of this word as it applies to the voltage of a NiCad cell is quite apropos. In reality a NiCad cell can be as high as 1.45 volts/cells immediately off charge (at small discharge currents) or as low as 1.0 volts/cell near end of discharge at higher current rates or under adverse conditions. The 1.0 volts/cell is an important figure because it is the end of the discharge basis for most capacity measurements. In other words, the cell manufacturer is saying that he will guarantee full capacity only if the cell can be taken down to 1.0 volts/cell. (Some cell manufacturers specify even lower cut-off voltages such as 0.95 or 0.90 volts/cell)

In most cases a "12 volt battery" means a 10 cell NiCad battery. Using the previous figures, this 10 cell pack can put out as much as 14.5 volts or as little as 10 volts. This is 12 volts ± 2 volts, or even more conservatively, ± 2.5 volts. It should be clear that a 12 volt ± 1 volt battery is the figment of a design engineer's imagination and any piece of equipment designed around this fictitious power source is destined for problems. The properly designed 12 volt device can take up to 14.5 volts for short periods without being damaged and can still function flawlessly on as little as 10 volts, or preferably 9 or 9.5 volts.

Now back to cell memory. Remember that the aforementioned improperly designed device will poop out at 11 volts while the properly designed instrument will function down to 10 volts. Under ideal conditions the discharge voltage of a new NiCad will stay above 11 volts, however, as the cell ages and conditions become less than ideal, such as cold temperatures or a memory situation, the voltage can easily dip into the 10-11 volt region. This is graphically demonstrated in FIGURE 146. Camera 1 in FIGURE 146A calls for a 12 volt battery yet ceases to run below 11 volts. The discharge Curve A is typical of an older battery under actual use. Note that halfway through, the discharge curve dips below 11 volts. At this point the camera will cease to run, yet the battery is only half discharged. The other half of the energy in the battery is called "unavailable capacity". The capacity is there but the camera cannot get to it. This is not a problem with the battery, as it is normal for

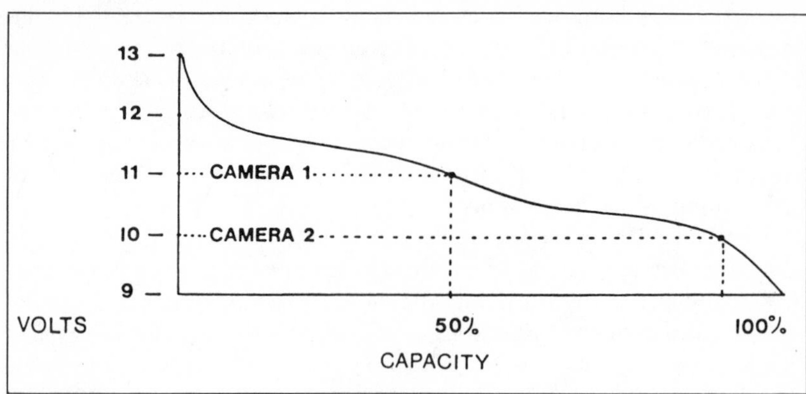

FIGURE 146

CURVE A

This represents a typical 12 volt NiCad battery that has been in the field for sometime. Note that Camera #1 ceases to run below 11 volts. The battery still has 50% capacity left, but Camera #1 cannot get to it. Camera #2 can run down to 10 volts and will get a full 100% capacity from the same battery. Likewise, camera #1 will operate perfectly with a 14.4 or 13.2 volt NiCad, which has a low end cut-off of 12 volts or 11 volts respectively. Almost all modern video equipment will perform better with a 13.2 or 14.4 volt battery.

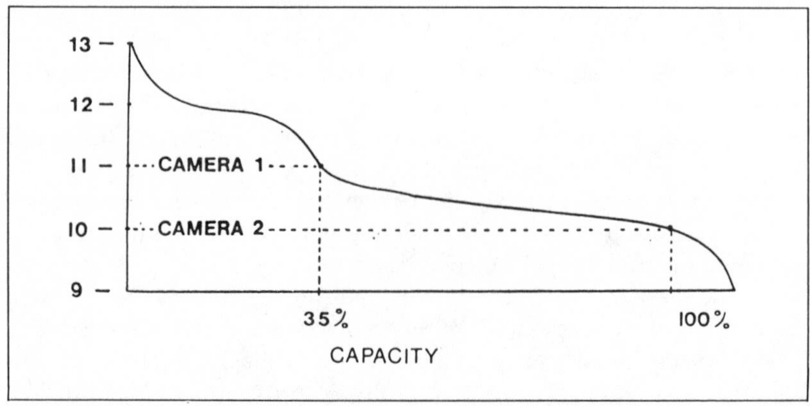

CURVE B

This represents the so-called "Memory" discharge curve. The memory is really a jog of about 1.1 volts in the discharge curve, which is arbitrarily drawn here at approximately ⅓ into discharge. Camera #1 ceases to function past the memory point as the voltage dips below its cut-off.

Camera #2 doesn't even see the memory point and runs for its full 100% capacity. Once again Camera #1 should be matched with a 13.2 or 14.4 volt battery which will solve the problem.

a NiCad to go down to 10 volts. The problem is the design of the camera.

Now look at Camera 2, a properly designed camera, run on the very same battery. It continues to run for the full capacity of the battery.

Curve B represents a so-called "memory" curve. Note that for this example the memory point is ⅓ into the discharge curve. Camera 1 will quit as soon as it hits the memory point because it dips below its cut-off point. Note that the memory point has no effect on Camera 2. This is the major point. The main reason memory affects a camera or any other portable instrument is if the device was improperly designed in the first place. Note that such an improperly designed camera will also suffer what appears to be a loss of capacity whenever the voltage drops slightly, as in cold weather.

Hopefully such problems are a thing of the past. While there are still one or two manufacturers who employ inferior and improper regulator design, almost all modern cameras and recorders employ the state-of-the-art wide range switching type regulators. These devices can usually accept anything from 11 volts up to 18 volts, and, moreover, are constant power devices. That means as the voltage goes up, the current drain goes down and the battery lasts longer.

Most new cameras are usually coupled with a 14.4 or 13.2 volt battery. So even if these batteries go down to 1.0 volts/cell due to adverse conditions (such as cold or memory) they still deliver 12 volts or 11 volts respectively. This is more than enough to drive any of the newer cameras which usually cutoff at about 10.5 to 10.8 volts. This is why it is important to use the 13.2 or 14.4 volt battery and *not* a 12 volt battery on these cameras. It should be clear that virtually all the new cameras and recorders, when coupled with the proper battery, are impervious to most memory problems. As a matter of fact, even if your battery were experiencing the memory phenomenon you probably wouldn't even know it, nor would it matter.

SEPARATE POWER SOURCE FOR CAMERA AND VTR

Many consumer or home video users employ one battery internally within the VCR and power the camera from this same battery via the camera/VCR cable. While this practice may make sense for the amateur, it has several drawbacks for the professional. Before a professional makes a final decision on this matter, he should consider the following points:

VOLTAGE—Unlike most consumer cameras which are designed for 12 volt supplies, virtually all professional Video ENG/EFP cameras are designed to operate with a 13 to 14 volt nominal battery source.

While some of these professional cameras may operate marginally with a 12 volt battery, they clearly provide optimum performance with proper 13–14 volt battery. This is due to the fact that all professional cameras employ advanced switching type (constant power) regulators. These regulators convert excess voltage into power, thus the 14 volt battery will provide more than 20% more power and more than 3 times the reserve voltage of a 12 volt battery. Moreover, under adverse conditions, or as batteries age, the benefits of the 14 volt battery become increasingly important. Under certain circumstances, the 12 volt battery may cease to operate altogether where the 14 volt can still deliver full capacity.

The problem is that all portable VTR's require 12 volts, not 14. Thus if the camera is being powered by the VTR, it is only getting 12 volts. As a matter of fact, with the combined current load of both camera and VTR as well as the voltage drop of the cable, the camera will typically get only 11½ volts or so. This totally defeats and nullifies the advantages of the camera's wide range switching regulator and thus greatly increases battery problems.

The bottom line is that a 12 volt (BP-90 type) battery *cannot* be a universal battery. Even with separate batteries for camera and VTR, the camera battery must be 13.2 or 14.4 volts to optimize performance and minimize problems.

The preferred method is to use a 14 volt battery on the camera and a 12 volt battery on the recorder, thus optimizing each unit. Another approach is represented by the Anton/Bauer Pro Pac 14 Snap-On™ batteries for both camera and VTR applications. The custom Anton/Bauer Snap-On™ brackets for all portable VTR's employ solid state devices that drop 14 volts to 12 volts. Thus the user can standardize on its Anton/Bauer Pro Pac 14 Snap-On™ battery for all applications. When snapped onto the camera, it delivers the proper 14 volts, yet when snapped onto the VTR, it delivers 12 volts.

FLEXIBILITY—There are many times when the professional may disconnect the VTR/camera cable yet still need the camera to be powered. In deciding camera angles or placement, the cameraman will use the camera as a director finder, sampling different camera positions. In such a case the VTR need not be lugged around if the camera has its own battery.

In addition, there are instances where the cameraman may wish to climb to a relatively inaccessible vantage point such as the roof of a building or a catwalk. In such cases the VTR is usually left in a convenient location and the short VTR/camera cable is replaced with a length of BNC/BNC coax. Once again this flexibility can only exist if the camera carries its own power.

BALANCE—Because an ENG/EFP camera is designed with the idea that a battery will be mounted on the camera, it is significantly front heavy without the camera. This is very fatiguing on the camera operator's arm. In almost every case the cameraman agrees that the extra weight of the battery is negligible compared to the comfort, improved stability and perfect balance that the rear mounted battery provides.

CAPACITY & CONVENIENCE—When employing a single battery to power both camera and VTR, the combined current drain is 50% to 100% greater than would normally exist with individual batteries. This causes less effective capacity per battery. In practical terms, if a camera and VTR each draw 2 amps, by employing a 4 AH battery on each individually, 2 hours of uninterrupted service will be delivered. If the same 4 AH battery were used to power both units simultaneously, it would run them *less* than the one hour you would expect, the loss of capacity resulting from the derating caused by the increased current.

Thus simultaneous powering of both VTR and camera from a single battery is inconvenient for two reasons: 1) more batteries would have to be carried to compensate for the aforementioned loss of capacity and 2) the obvious inconvenience of having to change batteries up to twice as frequently.

In the final analysis, the separate battery for camera and recorder is the professional's choice; optimum voltages, improved battery performance, greater flexibility and better balance and comfort, and in virtually all cases, the professional camera should be powered with a 13.2 or 14.4 volt battery.

ELECTRIC CURRENT

The cameraman traveling abroad can easily determine the local voltage by using a simple voltmeter. The frequency (either 60Hz or 50Hz) can be easily ascertained from local authorities or by using an electrical frequency meter that is available from most industrial electrical suppliers. Once the local voltage and frequency is known, the cinematographer must check his equipment and determine if a mismatch exists. The odds are that an American crew traveling in

Europe or Asia (or vice versa) will encounter both a voltage and frequency mismatch. One should not fret, however, as there are several simple solutions to this mismatch problem.

Although there is basically no simple way to convert frequency, the difference (50Hz to 60Hz) in most cases, will have a negligible effect and can be ignored. The exception, of course, is with synchronous motors or other sync equipment. As stated previously, traveling crews should stick with governor motors/pilotone cable or crystal-sync and thus eliminate all frequency mismatch problems. With the frequency problem out of the way, the prime concern is mostly matching voltages.

There are several different types of devices available to the cinematographer that will convert voltages. It is most important to understand that the type of voltage converter that should be employed is totally dependent on the type of equipment being used. A device that will match voltage for a lighting unit may not work at all for a battery charger. Basically, voltage-dropping devices can be broken down into two categories: transformers and diodes.

The diode voltage-dropper is becoming popular with gaffers. The most important thing to remember is that the diode device can be used *only* with lighting gear.

It cannot be used for battery chargers nor motors. When you see a little box (1½″x1½″x3″) that weighs three ounces and sells for $10.95 and claims 1000 watts of conversion from 220v to 110v, you can be certain it is a diode device. If it were a transformer device, it might have the same size and cost, but it would have a rating of only 25 or 30 watts at most. A 1000-watt transformer would be quite inconvenient—unless your grip happened to be King Kong.

The diode device works on a simple principle (see FIGURE 147). The diode is a rectifier that lets electric current pass only one way. The bulbs in the lights are designed to operate on 120 volts. FIGURE 147A shows the normal 120-volt 60Hz AC current. You can see that the 120 volts is actually an average (or root-mean-square) voltage rating. In reality, the current consists of sinisoidally alternating plus and minus 170-volt pulses.

In FIGURE 147B, the 240-volt current has pulses twice as large (double the amplitude). The diode lets through only the plus pulses and cancels the minus pulses. With the diode device, the pulses are still twice the peak of the 120 pulse (approximately 340 volts), but the diode cuts the number of pulses in half by eliminating every other one. Thus, these two facts cancel each other and you end up with an *average* of approximately 120 volts. This a very nifty way to get 240 down to 120; small, light, cheap. There is a catch. Because the diode lets through only plus pulses, the current is actually rectified to D.C. While this is fine for lights, obviously it is not compatible with any device designed for A.C.—such as battery chargers or motors. Normally, D.C. is desirable for lighting because it does not consist of the 60Hz pulsations that cause the "sing" which can be a problem on the quiet sound stage. The D.C. from the diode voltage-dropper, however, is *not* free of pulsations. As a matter of fact, the pulses are twice as big and half as frequent. The "sing" might be even more pronounced.

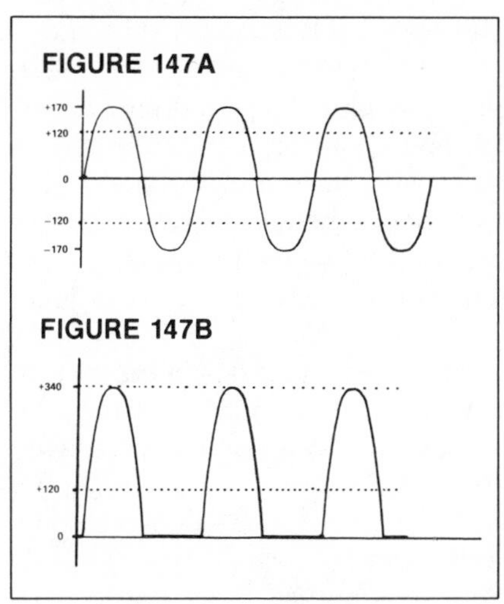

FIGURE 147
(a) Regular 120 volt AC consists of plus and minus 170 volt pulses that average to 120 volts.
(b) Normally, 240 volt AC consists of plus and minus 340 volt pulses that average to 240 volts. The diode cuts this average in half (120 volts) by eliminating every other pulse (minus pulses).

A crew that travels internationally might be wise to carry two sets of lamps, one 120v and the other 240v. This is the most convenient and economical way to go. For the occasional trip to a foreign country, the diode device is a simple and economical way to drop 240 to 120 for lighting purposes only.

A transformer is used for almost all voltage changing applications, either up or down, and does not affect the wave form of the current, other than changing the amplitude (voltage). Thus, a transformer device can safely be used on any type of equipment. The only thing you must check is the power rating in watts. If you use a transformer of insufficient power rating, the unit will heat up and possibly burn out. In addition, it will not put out the full rated voltage.

Since almost all professional motion picture and video cameras, and recorders are battery operated, the battery charger is probably the most vital electrical device the cameraman will plug into the wall. Most battery systems that use separate chargers employ a transformer-charger system with a 110/220 switch. In essence, the step-down transformer is built in. Most battery belts and self-contained battery systems use a capacitive charging circuit. These circuits, in many cases, do not have built-in provision for 110/220 operation. In addition, the capacitive system draws about 10 times more power from the wall than a transformer-type charger (on a 12-volt battery). As a rule of thumb, an overnight capacitive-type 120-volt battery charger will consume 10 times its ampere-hour capacity in watts. Thus, a four-amp-hour battery belt will draw approximately 40 watts. If a fast charger is employed, this figure has to be multiplied again by the speed of the charge. Thus, if the charger will charge the battery in one hour instead of 12 hours, it is obvious that the charge rate must be twelve times as high. In the above example, the four-amp-hour belt with a one-hour-capacitive fast-charge will draw (4x10x12) 480 watts! That would take a pretty hefty size transformer. On the other hand, some of the better compact "electric shaver" type transformers can handle up to 40 watts (the cheaper ones are rated at 20-30 watts) and will, thus, accommodate a four-amp-hour battery belt at the overnight rate.

If the charger employs a 110/220 switch, make sure it is in the correct position. If it is in the wrong position, the battery will not charge or a fuse will blow. If the charger does not have a 110/220 switch, check with the manufacturers who will recommend the proper size transformer to handle the application.

UNDERWATER TECHNIQUE

Filming underwater can be a cameraman's dream. Where else can you float "weightless" with your camera and maneuver yourself over, under and around your subject at will? These moving camera shots are actually quite easy. The cameraman's movement through the water gives him an element of stability. It is the static shot that poses problems. A cameraman with neutral buoyancy will tend to bob around with the slightest movement.

A simple solution is an inflatable life vest known as a BC or buoyancy compensator. The cameraman carries extra weight to give him a definite negative buoyancy. He then partially inflates the vest which counteracts the extra weight to achieve neutral buoyancy. When a static shot is desired, the vest is totally deflated, which plants the cameraman firmly on the bottom. The vest can also be fully inflated in an emergency which will shoot the cameraman rapidly to the surface.

Another trick when filming on the bottom is the use of a wet suit that incorporates little booties. When on the bottom, the cameraman removes his flippers (heavier than water) which could kick up sediment into the camera view, and can walk around in the booties.

The biggest problem in filming underwater is suspended sediment and particles in the water. These particles cut down the light and severely limit the distance through which you can film. It is very similar to filming in a perpetual and dense smog.

This brings up two obvious points. Try to film in the clearest body of water you can find. The areas around the Bahamas are a favorite. Secondly, film at the shallowest depth you can get away with. If the scene is supposed to be at 300′, you don't want surface ripples in the scene. A depth of ten feet is ideal, but usually impractical, due to surface

Jordan Klein maneuvering with one of his underwater rigs. Because action seems to move so much more slowly underwater, most cinematographers shoot at 22 frames per second. Camera governor motors should have the points or electronic circuits recalibrated for this speed. The best natural lighting conditions occur underwater between 10 a.m. and 2 p.m.

effects. The range from 25′ to 15′ is probably the most workable. Things begin to go downhill past 30′.

First there is the time factor. Below 30′ divers must go through a decompression procedure upon ascending and must not exceed certain time limits, depending on depth. These considerations do not exist above the 30′ level. In addition, light levels and color saturation fall off rapidly below 30′.

Light being at a premium, it is best to film between 10 a.m. and 2 p.m. for optimum results. Actually, high noon is not quite as good as the late morning and early afternoon.

Artificial light should be employed only when absolutely necessary, as in a cave. Artificial light always looks like exactly that. The suspended particles will kick the light back into the lens, much like headlights into a dense fog. If lights must be used, they should be placed to the side or above.

The color of the bottom is also a factor. Bright sandy bottoms will reflect a good deal of light. Some divers are surprised to find the water actually gets brighter as they near the bottom of a deep dive.

Color balance is a big problem, as the reds begin to disappear quickly as depth increases. Almost all reds are gone at only 10 ′ and oranges vanish at about 30′. Some cameramen employ color-compensating filters, such as CC20-50 reds or magentas. But this can be overdone. Not only will it reduce light levels, but the result may be *too* well-balanced and not look "underwater." Jordan Klein uses no correction filters at all. He is always able to achieve the desired results at the printing stage.

In almost all cases, the timer can correct the color balance. This brings up an important point. You should choose your laboratory carefully. Its technicians should be very familiar with underwater footage. A proficient timer who turns out excellent studio footage may not know what good underwater quality should look like. As previously stated, the color balance problem can be miminized by staying close to the surface.

Because action seems to move so much more slowly underwater, most cinematographers use 22 fps camera speed. Actually, a slower speed of 18-20 would be even better, but the air bubbles will appear to rise too fast, revealing the in-camera trickery. Thus, the 22 fps rate is a conservative compromise. The governor motors should have the points or electronic circuits recalibrated for this speed.

UNDERWATER LENSES

The photographed underwater image will suffer from a diffusion effect due to the underwater particles. The effect, again, is similar to photographing in a dense fog. As distance is increased between subject and camera, the subject will lose resolution and saturation. At distances considered normal on the surface, subjects underwater could be totally indistinguishable.

Which brings us to point number one: work as close to the subject as practical so as to cut through a mimimum of suspended particles. This brings us to point number two: a wide angle lens must be employed to take in all the action at these close distances. The beginner who goes down with a normal or telephoto lens will most likely come back with either murky ghost-like images in the distance or clear sharp pictures of earlobes and eyeballs.

Choosing underwater optics requires the cinematographer to shift his thinking to the short focal lengths. Thus, in the 16mm format an 8mm to 10mm lens would be considered a "normal" lens, while 16mm lens would be considered a "telephoto". For a wide-angle effect, a 5.9mm would have to be employed. Likewise, in the 35mm format an 18mm objective would be considered "normal", a 28mm lens would perform the telephoto function while a 9.8mm lens would be considered a "wide angle." In general, almost all underwater shooting could be accomplished with an 8mm lens for the 16mm format and a 18mm for the

35mm format.

When a closeup is required, the camera rig is just brought in tight with the "normal" lens. About the only reason for going to a logner focal-length would be an extreme close-up where the presence of the camera rig would block the light or cast a shadow. Such a shot might be a cutaway of a wrist watch or pressure gauge, etc. A telephoto might also be appreciated when the subject is less than friendly, such as a killer shark.

There are other reasons for employing wide angle lenses underwater. The refractive index of water is 1.33, which will make objects appear 25% closer than they actually are. This will effectively *increase* the apparent focal length of a lens. The use of wide angle lenses will neutralize this phenomenon. The short focal length objectives will also minimize the visual effect of camera unsteadiness. Of course, wide angle lenses also minimize hand-held unsteadiness on the surface, but camera unsteadiness seems to be a consistent problem underwater.

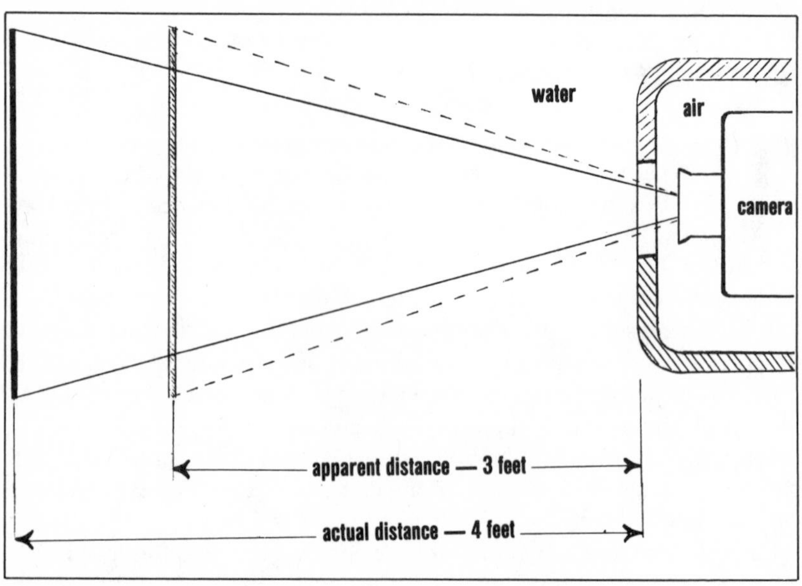

FIGURE 149—Diagram illustrating the difference between the refractive indexes of air and water. The refractive index of water is 1.33, which makes objects appear 25% closer than what they are. This will effectively increase the apparent focal length of a lens. The use of a wide angle lens will neutralize this phenomenon, as well as allowing the underwater cameraman to work closer to his subject, thus minimizing the effect of particles suspended in the water.

The fact that water has a refractive index of 1.33 will also affect focus calculations. As stated previously, objects will appear 25% closer. This poses no problem if the distance is approximated visually, as the observer and camera lens are similarly affected. The cinematographer can just set the lens to the distance where the object *appears* to be (as if he were on the surface). Similarly, a reflex camera will be focused in the normal fashion. However, if a tape measure is employed, the lens must be set to only 75% of the indicated distance.

Some underwater housings use a "dome port" or curved glass for the lens window. This minimizes the foreshadowing effect and fields a wider effective angle under water.

One last point. The colors of costumes and props should be chosen with care. Poor judgment here could completely negate all other efforts for good underwater footage. Stay away from reds and oranges as they will quickly desaturate at even minimum depths. They will appear mud-brown or even black. Bright chrome yellow will show up best. Bright greens and blues also work well. Pure white usually produces less than ideal results, due to a halo or haze effect.

In summary, film in as shallow an area as possible (10′ to 25′ ideal), the clearest water, use a wide angle lens and stay close to the subject (7-15 feet), film at 22 fps, chose good colors for subjects and make sure your laboratory is proficient in correcting underwater footage.

UNDERWATER CINEMATOGRAPHY

Location filming is definitely in. Elaborate sets and intricate process photography have been forsaken in favor of the more credible realism of the location, not to mention the significant savings of both time and money in most instances. Of course, the word "location" can mean anywhere, and often does. Among the more exotic locations, underwater sites seem to be gaining in popularity. Industrials, documentaries, as well as theatricals and television, are employing more and more underwater footage. In light of this, it is not unlikely that a cinematographer will eventually find himself with an underwater sequence to shoot. Being basically a land mammal, the average cameraman may find working underwater somewhat alien. Some pertinent pointers on filming underwater may thus prove wise.

I have filmed in many diverse and unusual locations but above sea level. We once had an assignment to film in the Hudson River, but we wound up simulating the sequence in a tank filled with muddy water and two bags of garbage. This experience hardly qualifies me as an underwater expert.

The expert on underwater cinematography is without a doubt Jordan Klein. Jordan has logged almost a year of his life underwater. His screen credits include "THUNDERBALL", "20,000 LEAGUES UNDER THE SEA", "CREATURE FROM THE BLACK LAGOON", the TV series "FLIPPER", and more than a hundred other films of all types. I visited Jordon some time ago at his Miami factory where he designs and builds underwater equipment, including camera housings. My visit was most enlightening.

FIGURE 150—The underwater housing recently introduced by Image Devices for use with the Eclair ACL camera, with 400-foot magazine—thus allowing this basically topside camera to double as an underwater rig.

Certain cameras are better suited to underwater applications than others. For 16mm, the Arriflex 16M seems to be the first choice of professionals. The small size, quick-change magazine and reflex system make it ideal for this work. The 16S Arriflex is not as well suited, due to its bulkier and more complicated magazine system, and the excessive current drain of its two motors (drive and mag torque). There are, of course, other cameras that can be used underwater. Bolex makes an underwater housing for the H-16 cameras that is ideal for certain semi-pro applications. Image Devices has an underwater housing for the Eclair ACL 400′, thus allowing this topside sound camera to double as an underwater rig. (FIGURE 150) There are also several underwater housings available for video cameras including the one piece camera/VTR combinations such as the Sony Betacam.

The Arriflex 35 is almost always the choice in the larger format. It is usually employed with the flat offset motor base. FIGURE 151 shows Jordon Klein with one of his own Arri 35 underwater units.

FIGURE 151—Underwater cinematography expert Jordan Klein, shown with one of his own underwater housings for an Arriflex 35mm camera. This is the camera most favored in the large format.

The design of the housing is very important. It must be perfectly matched and coordinated with a specific camera/battery combination. The center of gravity must be concentric with the center of buoyancy; otherwise the camera will have a tendency to twist on axis, or pitch forward or backwards. The complete rig should have a slight negative buoyancy when fully loaded. Some cameramen prefer a neutral buoyancy, but never a positive one. This may sound strange, as the camera will slowly fall to the bottom when let go. This is actually preferable to the camera floating to the surface. Rarely is a crew working in an area so deep that the camera cannot be recovered from the bottom. As a matter of fact, it is normal to leave the camera on the bottom when going topside to get instructions. The camera doesn't have to be hauled up and down unnecessarily. In addition, it is easier to spot a camera on the bottom than it is to locate one looking up at the back-lit rippling surface of the water. The slight negative buoyancy is also more natural to work with.

Designing and building an underwater housing is an exacting science. In addition to proper balance and buoyancy, a housing should have a finder system and a means for determining footage. The better housing will have magnified reflex viewfinders, allowing the cameraman a through-the-lens view, even with his face mask on. There are several firms that make professional underwater housings for both sale and rental. Check the features and, if possible, try one before the actual shoot. It is also a good idea to check with a cameraman who is familiar with the unit in question. He may be able to give you an insight into the particular "personality" of the unit.

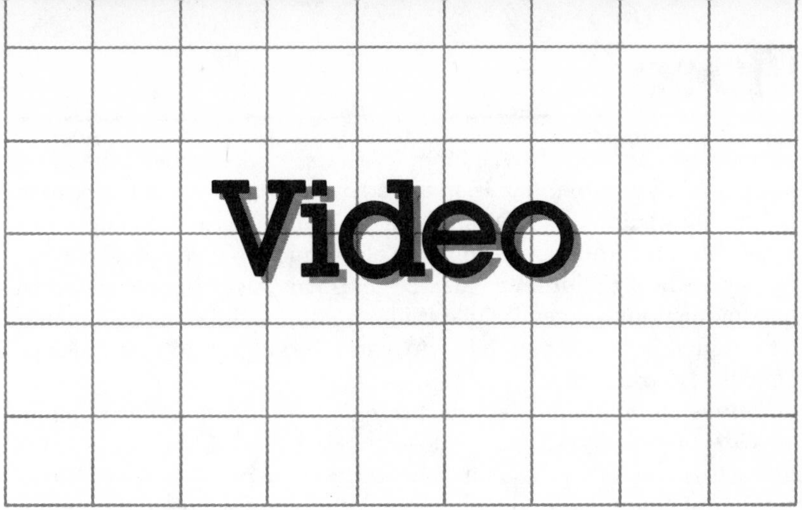

THE "FILM LOOK"

There is always lively debate when the relative virtues of film and video are discussed. In almost every arena of comparison the controversy rages. Whether it be production, post-production, special effects or long-term storage, each medium can be argued to have its specific advantages. The advent of the new electronic cinematography cameras is sure to add fuel to the already fiery debates on the subject by making differences between these formats even more subtle. However, before extolling the relative advantages of either medium, a very basic question comes to mind: Exactly what is it that makes film look different from tape on television? That is not an easy question and the complex answer has mystical, as well as technical, elements.

The "film look" enigma on television is even more intriguing when it is understood that a film to be displayed on television is rephotographed by a video camera. The "film chain" and "flying spot scanner" are the usual devices for converting a film into the video format for taping or broadcasting. Both these devices are essentially a video camera taking a video picture of the film. A hasty analysis of these facts could lead to the erroneous conclusion that film on television is somehow inferior to video tape. If film on television is nothing more than a video camera taking a picture of the film, why not have the video camera take the picture of the original subject in the first place, and save one generation? If film is just an extra step in the process, it seems logical that it must somehow detract or subtract something from the quality of the image. After all, who has ever seen the quality of an image improve with subsequent generations?

This train of thought, if continued, would lead to the belief that the video camera and its VTR yield the "live look" or the highest obtainable image quality, and that film is an extra or additional step in the process that can only subtract something from the image. These two beliefs then suggest that the "film look" could be electronically synthesized by manipulating the signal from a video camera. This supposition is based on the aforementioned premise that if film does not add a mystical quality, but rather subtracts something, why can't the subtracted entity also be removed electronically?

There is an intrinsic fallacy to this logic. Yes, film is an extra step in the video process, and yes, it does subtract something, but what it subtracts is certainly not quality, but rather some of the inherent shortcomings of the modern video camera. It is not true that a subtraction from an image necessarily means a reduction in quality. A filter is also a device that in most cases subtracts something from the image, yet, in most cases, the results are improved. A polarizer, for example, by subtracting certain rays of light, can yield a superior image from a scene with an otherwise excessively bright sky. A closer analysis of the subject adds greater significance to this analogy. Indeed, for the video process, film appears to be "anti-lag," "comet-tail eliminating," and a "low contrast" filter all in one. Film seems to be a buffer for these inherent problems that plague the modern video camera. What exactly are these problems and how does film help?

Film has some very nice inherent qualities relative to video. Most important, every frame of the film image starts on a virgin canvas. This may seem like a sophomoric statement, but it accounts for one of the biggest differences between film and video. After a frame of film is captured, the shutter closes and a brand new piece of film is advanced to the aperture. Thus, whatever happened during one frame cannot possibly affect any subsequent frames. The video camera, on the other hand, has only one target from which every frame is scanned. Thus what occurs during one frame can (and does) affect subsequent frames. Film is similar to drawing each frame on a new slate while video makes use of the same slate over and over again merely erasing each image with a less than ideal eraser before each subsequent frame. As a result, video is vulnerable to certain excessive conditions.

Video is very sensitive to overexposure. Very bright areas will "burn" into the target and not be completely erased, showing up as after images in subsequent scenes. Because of the electronic nature of the process, overexposed areas tend to "bloom" or "bleed" into adjacent areas. Indeed, areas even a half f-stop over maximum brightness will yield a "burned out," overexposed look. The inherent problem of incomplete erasure causes excessively bright areas to have a cumulative effect from frame to frame, thus aggravating the problem. Bright practicals or other lights that may get into the scene will "comettail" if the camera is moved rapidly. Thus, a round fresnel can appear shaped like an egg or teardrop if the camera is swiftly panned. The most limited aspect of video is its extremely narrow luminance ratio and abrupt transition into under and overexposure. Video can only tolerate a luminance ratio of about 25:1 to 32:1. This is only 4½ or 5 f-stops. Moreover, shadow details below this range are usually lost, as are highlights that exceed maximum brightness. Film negative has a far broader luminance ratio of over 128:1 or more than seven stops. Equally important, film exhibits smoother transitions into over and underexposure. The gamma of film has a gradual knee and shoulder that helps capture shadow details and highlights by compressing the extremities of exposure.

Taking all these facts together, film becomes the perfect buffer for many of the shortcomings of the video camera. The video problems of lag, burning, blooming and comet-tailing are all precipitated by excessive highlights. Film absorbs these highlights and compresses them to levels that can be handled by the video camera without incurring the aforementioned side effects. Film can also bring up some shadow details that can be captured in the film chain, but that otherwise might have been lost in a pure video production. In general, a greater tonal range can be created by shooting film and transferring to video than can be achieved by a video camera. A more subtle color quality is also attributed to film. I believe all these effects add up to the elusive "film look" which quite often yields a far more pleasing image than that obtainable with a pure video production.

The technology of video is by no means standing still and video engineers are attempting to correct the weaknesses of the video process without the help of film, as we shall see.

ELECTRONIC CINEMATOGRAPHY

Most studies indicate that an all-electronic production will cost less than film and can be completed in a significantly shorter time with fewer hassles.

Many producers still prefer to shoot film, even though the production will eventually become a video tape. This preference for film is based upon two factors: The superior "look" of film and the refined techniques associated with film production. Addressing themselves to these two aspects, Ikegami Electronics has designed a new camera to lure film producers into video production.

The design intent of the Ikegami EC-35 is quite evident. Its initials stand for Electronic Cinematography and the "35" undoubtedly indicates its intended purpose to replace 35mm film cameras on productions destined for television. Ikegami spent much time researching and developing the EC-35. After three years and five generations of prototypes, the present EC-35 incorporates many unique circuits and innovative features that should appeal greatly to the film community. The EC-35 succeeds in achieving both design goals; i.e., to come closer to a "film look" and to handle more like a film camera.

Don't let anyone in the video industry fool you. The buzz term "film look" is nothing more than an euphemism for an image that is free from the problems that make most video look plastic or "electronic." Problems occur, such as lag, comet-tailing, white clipping and lack of luminance range. The reason film looks better on television than an electronically produced image is that film acts as a buffer or filter that removes those extreme exposure elements that would otherwise precipitate the aforementioned video vices. The camera designers can say they are trying to achieve a "film look," but they are really just continuing the evolutionary process of perfecting the video camera.

The goals are to increase the luminance range, eliminate comet-tailing and blooming, and achieve the tonal subtleties of the film image. The Ikegami EC-35 represents a major step toward these goals.

The EC-35 starts with ⅔" low-capacitance diode-gun Plumbicon® pick-up tubes. These are the latest technology tubes and are capable of extremely improved resolution and detail. A dynamic beam focus circuit produces sharp pictures from corner to corner by improving corner focus. The image enhancement circuits of the EC-35 also represent improvements to the state-of-the-art. Out of band aperture correction signals are proportionately mixed with image enhancement to produce a very sharp, yet pleasing image. More conventional image enhancement produces an artificial edginess which most cinematographers consider "plastic" or similar to a child's coloring book. The EC-35 produces a well detailed, yet natural picture. The entire camera circuitry, including the pre-amps, makes prolific use of low noise devices, resulting in a S/N ratio of over 57db rms, which means a very quiet image with little noise (grain). The method used to calibrate or "set-up" the EC-35 will be covered later, as that has more to do with the unique and innovative handling of the camera. However, the set-up procedure incorporates some very ingenious new technology that facilitates more accurate camera alignment. This results in consistently optimal image quality. For example, registration can be easily set up with exceptional accuracy, due to a new type of geometry corrector based on quadrant control.

These improvements create a higher quality image, but what about those video evils of comet-tailing, blooming, lack of shadow and highlight details, et al.? The EC-35 attacks each of these problems with some very unique circuitry, resulting in an unusually wide dynamic range.

One of the desirable features of film is its gradual gamma curves. Film does not abruptly lose detail at the extremes of exposure. The gamma of film rolls off at either end, compressing the extremities of exposure. The result is a pleasing visual transition from the linear portion of exposure into the regions of under or over-exposure. Much detail can still be discerned within shadows and highlights. Video, on the other hand, tends to go abruptly black in the shadows. Even more disconcerting is the tendency of video to "burn-out" or "white-clip" in areas that exceed maximum allowable illumination. The EC-35 incorporates special technology that produces gamma curves that more closely simulate film. In addition, the set-up box allows push-button selection of three different gamma correction curves. These can be used to facilitate a particular look or to compensate for high-key or low-key lighting problems. These gamma options can effectively stretch the shadow areas or conversely stretch the brighter areas of the scene. By proper manipulation of these gamma options plus the normal master pedestal control (similar to flashing), the cinematographer can surely create a pleasing "film look" to the shadows and darker areas of the image.

The opposite end of the exposure classically poses the biggest problems for the electronic camera. If any area of the scene goes much above 2–3f stops over medium gray, the conventional video camera will abruptly "white-clip" the signal, which appears as a burned-out white homogenous blob on the screen. Moreover, if the camera is moved, this white blob will "comet tail" or "tear" as it moves across the screen. The EC-35 combats these anomalies two ways. First, it incorporates a knee compression circuit that can compress a signal that is 600% over the rated level down to the 100% level. This further modifies the gamma curve to react more like film. Thus, highlighted areas that may have "burned out," are now brought down or compressed into a region where they can be recorded with detail.

Comet-tailing, as well as severe blooming, occur when an overexposed area is not fully "erased" by the electron beam after each frame of the image has been captured. If the overexposed area is stationary, blooming can result, as the effects of incomplete "erasure" become cumulative after each successive frame. If the overexposed area is moving, comet-tailing results, as the image now includes not only the overexposed area, but the ghost of its previous position. The EC-35, like most modern broadcast quality cameras, employs an automatic beam control circuit that senses an overexposure situation, calculates the extent of overexposure, and increases the strength of the electron beam in that area to assure complete "erasure" of the image. While most beam control circuits can handle two to three stops of overexposure, the EC-35 incorporates a new dynamic beam stretch circuit (DBS) that can stabilize highlight signals as much as four stops in excess of normal peak video level. This DBS, together with the knee compression circuit, creates for the cinematographer a more natural "film-like" rendition of highlights.

All these unique features, as well as a new color masking circuit, make the EC-35 a camera uniquely suitable to cinematographers and the film industry in general. Not only does it deliver an image of exceptional quality, but it comes uniquely closer to "film-like" rendering of a scene. In my opinion, however, these facts do not make the EC-35 an "electronic cinematography" camera. What these facts do make the EC-35 is a damn good video camera; the next generation video camera. These new EC-35 features would be welcome on *any* video camera, as they create a superior image, as well as eliminating or minimizing many of the visual anomalies inherent in the video process. What *does* make the EC-35 an "electronic cinematography" camera is its unique and innovative packaging, and its new high definition format.

Originally the EC-35 was conceived to use film-type fixed focal length and zoom lenses. However, the relay optics necessary to facilitate the use of cine lenses would have limited image quality. Ikegami, therefore, commissioned both Canon and Fujinon to create an entire set of high quality fixed focal length and zoom lenses specifically for the EC-35. The Canon set includes five fixed focal length lenses of 6, 10, 15, 24 and 35mm focal lengths, all with a maximum aperture of T 1.5. The set is completed with a 10.5–50mm T 1.6 zoom lens. FIGURE 152 gives the equivalent focal lengths for 35mm cine lenses with similar horizontal angles of view.

These lenses have been designed to yield optimum performance at maximum aperture, unlike most video lenses which are optimized for medium openings. This will, of course, provide sharp, well-exposed images, even under very low light conditions, but less obvious is the matter of depth-of-field. The format of ⅔″ video is less than half the size of 35mm film. This means that for a given scene and f-stop, the ⅔″ video camera will have significantly more depth-of-field. Thus, if a cinematographer wants to achieve a specifically narrow depth-of-field,

LENS EQUIVALENCES

EC-35 Lens	Horizontal Angle	35mm Lens
10.5-50mm Zoom	45.5°-10.1°	24-120mm
6mm	72.5°	15mm
10mm	47.5°	24mm
15mm	32.7°	38mm
24mm	20.8°	55mm
35mm	14.3°	85mm

FIGURE 152

the ⅔″ video camera lens would have to be opened more than a full stop, compared to a 35mm film camera recording the identical image. The ability to yield a sharp image at wide apertures can, thus, be more important with a ⅔″ video camera, and this set of Canon lenses has been optimized for the task. It should also be remembered that ⅔″ video, like 16mm film, has a decided advantage over 35mm film when a deep focus or extreme depth-of-field is desirable.

The cinematic aspects of the optical system are further enhanced by a choice of two types of follow-focus mechanisms, as well as a motorized joystick zoom control. A professional matte box completes the system. The viewfinder system is another Ikegami achievement. Not only can the viewfinder be attached at four different points on the camera, but it can be oriented a full 360° to accommodate even the most bizarre camera angles.

Moreover, there is provision for two viewfinders so that the assistant cameraman can view the image also. The viewfinder also incorporates several additional features. A "super peak" button activates a circuit that magnifies the image in the viewfinder as a focusing aid. The "peak" control creates an artificial edge on objects in the scene. This occurs only in the viewfinder and is also an aid to critical focusing. The viewfinder incorporates the standard brightness and contrast controls, as well as a unique zebra circuit that will indicate those areas in the viewfinder that are precisely at the proper skin tone level (79 IRE units) or at peak video level (100 IRE units). A digital display indicates remaining tape time. The EC-35 incorporates auto white balance, as well as auto black balance which will automatically adjust the camera for perfect color bal-

The Ikegami EC-35

ance under any illumination.

The most unique feature of the EC-35 is the microprocessor set-up box and built-in memory system. This system allows the EC-35 to be anything you want it to be. For those who desire a video camera that requires absolutely no adjustments in the field, the EC-35 is it. Before production begins, the video technician plugs the set-up box into the EC-35. The camera is adjusted to optimum image specifications and at the same time the director of photography can have the technician tailor certain controls for any particular "look" desired. All the adjustments are then memorized by the microprocessor in the camera. The set-up box is then unplugged from the camera. No further adjustment of the camera is required during the entire duration of the production. The set-up box can be left behind, as the camera maintains its memory of the set-up parameters for *months*. During production, the camera can be optimized by merely pointing it at a special test chart and pressing the "auto-set" button. When the set-up light goes out, the camera has automatically set itself by recalling all the proper calibrations from the memory. You don't need a crew of engineers with the EC-35. For all intents and purposes it functions as easily as a film camera and you don't even have to clean the gate.

At the other extreme, for the cinematographer who likes the creative flexibility of video, the EC-35 can accommodate unlimited possibilities. On location, at the D.P.'s option, the set-up box can be plugged into the EC-35, facilitating access to the camera's internal controls.

The cinematographer can have a creative field day with the myriad possibilities. Control of master pedestal is similar to flashing. Individual red/blue pedestal can create "pastel shadows," both gamma and knee compression can be adjusted to create an endless variety of tonal effects, and the detail threshold and gain can be manipulated to soften or sharpen the image. It is like having Kodak design a special film for each scene. For the *pièce de resistance*, each control has a digital readout so it can be returned to precisely the desired level, assuring consistency.

The EC-35 thus offers the best of both worlds. The built-in microprocessor/memory/auto set-up system provides a camera that requires virtually no attention whatsoever, yet with the set-up box attached it can provide an unlimited array of creative possibilities.

The technological advancements and refined operating features of the Ikegami EC-35, when combined with the already acknowledged advantages of electronic post-production, yield a very strong argument in favor of the all-electronic production. With an estimated 75% of the production in the major studios destined for television, the era of electronic cinematography is most assuredly upon us.

LIGHTING FOR TELEVISION

There are two schools of thought on video lighting, and as usual, diametrically opposed. The first believes that lighting for television is no different from lighting for film, and the other, that television lighting requires an entirely different technique. I tend to take an intermediate position, favoring the former. The basic art of film lighting applies equally to television and I am convinced that cinematographers and film directors of photography also make the best lighting directors in video productions. They have learned the art of painting with light, as opposed to the practice of illuminating an area to so many foot-candles. There are, however, several factors that must be considered, due to the particular nature of the video process.

Under normal circumstances, the television process has a much smaller luminance or contrast range than film. Most cinematographers are accustomed to a luminance ratio of 64:1 to 128:1 representing 6 to 7 "f" stops. Television, on the other hand, cannot cope with ratios much above 32:1—or about five stops. As a result, lighting ratios seldom exceed 2:1 and care must be taken outdoors to avoid dark shadows caused by direct sunlight. Exteriors usually call for sunlight diffusers, reflectors and often fill light in the way of the newer HMI-type lights. Attention must also be given to background lighting, as the television signal does not pick up shadow detail well, nor does it cope well with large homogenous dark areas which tend to show noise and recording imperfections, particularly on later generations.

One may draw the erroneous conclusion that lighting for video is synonymous with low contrast or flat lighting. Such is not the case. Ironically, low contrast situations, particularly predominantly light or dark scenes, must also be avoided. Most home TV receivers have poor (to abominable) DC restoration. What this means, is that the TV signal will tend to center itself about a medium gray.

For instance, on a recent documentary called *"The Cocaine Connection,"* I filmed two users injecting cocaine by candlelight in an otherwise unlit room, using fast lenses and high speed film. I was ecstatic when I viewed the film on a Steenbeck. The blacks were like velvet, the faces were perfectly illuminated by the candle and the room details could just be made out in the shadows. The effect was perfect—on film. Once in the film chain, this scene could have become a disaster. Firstly, the chain camera would not pick up the shadow detail, so the entire background would go black, and then when the signal got to the home receiver, the black would become a medium gray. The result: two dimly-lit faces amid a fog of gray. The reason for the gray-out is poor DC restoration. Everything in the original scene was between black and medium gray, using only the lower half of the total range available on the film. Thus, it had room to "float" up to the center position on the home receiver. The trick here is to "fill" the video range completely by including a "white reference." In the above example, I purposely included the candle in most of the shots. While the scene was still occupying the lower half of the signal, the candle flame was right up there at the top. Thus, there was no extra room for the signal to float around, even in the absence of proper DC restoration. The blacks were black, the faces were properly dim and the bright candle even helped aesthetically to justify the dimness of the scene. For most dark or flat scenes, the obligatory white reference can be provided by strong back or rear side light that creates highlights without diluting the dark or flat ambience of the scene. A hard light in the scene—such as a lamp, candle, neon sign, etc—will also serve the purpose.

The exact opposite situation must also be avoided. A face in front of a back-lit window will work on film, but not on tape or through a video receiver. Here, all the information is in the upper half of the range. The result is that the signal will "float" downward to center itself, with the face going almost black and the window becoming a light gray. In this instance, a black reference is necessary.

The bottom line in video, whether it be film or tape, is filling the 5-stop range by including a black and a white reference, and yet not exceeding this range with high luminance ratios. As video camera technology improves, as with the new "Electronic Cinematography" cameras, the differences between film & video lighting may all but dissappear.

VIDEO VS FILM

We have been discussing many aspects of the video process which has raised some philosophical as well as practical comparisons between the various film formats and the video process. Therefore, this may be a good time for a retrospective of these two media. Having now worked extensively in both formats I have obviously formed some pretty strong impressions and opinions based upon observations, experience and frustrations.

First, I believe that film is without a doubt a far more powerful medium when projected on a large screen than video. As a matter of fact, video is not even in the same league with the projected film image. Viewing film in a darkened room or theater is similar to the process of dreaming. The large bright moving forms are viewed in a darkened environment where no other frame of reference exists. The motion picture is "experienced" as well as viewed. The audience is taken on a trip through time and space. The video image on the other hand is viewed on a small screen in a box. (Large screen TV is nowhere near acceptable at the present time). It cannot come close to having the impact, power or visual splendor of the "silver screen." Moreover, there are other important differences. The video process is restricted to a luminance range of about 25:1 or 32:1 at best. The film process, on the other hand, is capable of a range in excess of 125:1, which, when properly exploited, can yield a depth and subtlety of texture totally unobtainable in video. A prime example of the difference in media is Coppola's THE GODFATHER. Coppola created the magnificent "underworld" texture by extensively exploiting the shadow detail capability of film. Most of the action in many of the interior scenes existed in the lowest regions of the exposure curve. In my opinion this subtle feel of the texture was lost when the film appeared on television as the medium could not cope with the range of exposure, especially the shadow details.

For these reasons I always attempt to persuade my industrial and educational clients to use the film medium. The projected motion picture is just far more capable of moving an audience. Whether it is an idea, an emotion or thought or a feeling that must be conveyed, or an attempt to motivate, excite, outrage, shock, impress or scare, the projected film image with its sheer size and many subtle textures is by far the obvious choice. I believe there is no debate here. Assuming the finished product can be exhibited as a projected motion picture there is only one logical direction: shoot it on film.

Now enter the realities of life. Much of what is shot today cannot be exhibited as a projected film. Obviously everything shot for television whether a network, independent, cable program or video disc, will be displayed on a CRT (television set). Moreover, many industrial, commercial and educational centers are set up for closed circuit video taped television and can no longer accommodate or wish to accommodate projected film. I am sad to say that the majority of my clients distribute their visual products almost exclusively via videotape. Most large corporations have complete inhouse closed circuit studios and a cassette video player in almost every executive office and work location.

Once it becomes obvious that the product will be viewed primarily on television with very little chance of ever being projected on a screen, doing the production in the video format presents some distinct advantages over film. I acknowledge that film still holds some advantages over video production even when the finished product will be a tape. However, I believe that in most cases it would prove beneficial to execute a video product completely in the video format, from pre-production through production and post-production. There are many reasons for this conclusion—not the least of which includes cost, expediency and creative control.

I have no doubt that most cinematographers will be quite intrigued when they realize that the visual control is actually possible right inside the video camera. All those hundreds of little controls and adjustments inside the video camera are primarily there for the video technicians to calibrate the camera to some predetermined "standard" or "specification." However, the cameraman can use some of these controls to create an unlimited variety of visual subtleties. By departing from the standard parameters the cameraman can visually manipulate the image in much the same way as the film laboratory when they modify the standard development parameters as set down by the film manufacturer.

Imagine a film stock that allows you to change color balance at will for each scene if desired, or verify that it doesn't change even under varied lighting conditions. Imagine a film stock that you can tint to any of an infinite number of hues repetitively and accurately, for any given scene. Imagine a film process where you could flash selected scenes within the same roll while you are shooting and select any degree of flashing by instananeously viewing the results. Moreover, imagine that you can tint the flash without tinting the rest of the scene much like was done in YOUNG WINSTON, again with an infinite range of tints and the ability to preview the results before any film was shot. Imagine a film stock with a gamma curve to be manipulated at the time of shooting for selected scenes on the same roll. This could be used for "day for night" or any of an infinite number of visual effects. Moreover, imagine you can manipulate the gamma of each of the red, green and blue layers *independently* to create intentional color effects and, of course, be able to view the results instantaneously as the adjustments are made. Consider the ability to manipulate color saturation to create a plastic Kodachrome look or soft pastels. All this can be accomplished to a reasonable degree in the video camera.

The video process is just as intriguing during post-production as it is during shooting.

All the aforementioned manipulations can be equaly achieved during post production. Video technology is advancing at a frenzied pace in this area. Super sophisticated switchers with memories, multichannel digital effects generators, computer controlled character generators and computer animators all provide limitless post production creativity.

If all this sounds like "Star Wars," let me reduce this back to practical reality by relating a recent experience when two of our productions went into post production at the same time. One was filmed and the other was video. The details of the saga may prove illuminating.

The 16mm film project was for IBM. It was approximately 15 minutes long and the subject was the introduction of a new computer. The video project was an employee motivation tape for AT&T of about the same length. First the film project. I am sure that the story will sound familiar.

—The creative aspects of the rough cut have been finished; now we have to work on the supers, titles, credits and opticals.
—The client was quite precise as to the size, shape and color of the title, especially the logo. All morning is spent with the graphic artist at the effects house going over details.
—Next day another trip into the city to approve the artwork before it is shot. Changes are made and the art work goes to the camera.
—Two days later, into the city to check the titles and supers; no good. The positioning is off as well as the colors. I wanted orange and the color was too yellow. Moreover, the supers did not "pop" onto the screen at the right time. The camera operator admitted it was his error and he would try again. Come back in two days.
—A week later all titles and supers are approved. The original goes to the negative cutter for A and B rolls.
—The next day a call from the negative cutter. He is not sure about one scene, would I come over.
—Two days later A and B rolls go to the lab for timing and first answer print.
—Three days later first answer print is ready. Despite explicit instructions and directions it is no good. Color balancing is not perfect. One group of scenes that was supposed to be darkened dramatically was printed up, and one or two of the dissolves did not work well (our fault).
—Four days later, second answer print; not perfect but okay.
—Four days later first answer print from CRI.
—Final result, after almost four weeks and more than a half-dozen trips into the city (plus related aggravation and frustration), we've got a product that is still a compromise, but it does get client approval.

While the foregoing melodrama was ensuing, I found one day to get our AT&T project into the video editing room. This relaxing, clean and modern facility included a CMX computer editor, a Chyron character generator, a Quantel digital effects generator and a CDL 480 switcher, all built into one console. The dialog went something like this:

EDITOR: How do you like this type face for the title? (Shows me title *already* supered on the scene.)
ME: A little bolder and make it lower on the screen.
ED: (Pushes a few buttons) How's this?
ME: Fine, but the green color is too yellowish.
ED: (Turns knob) How's this?
ME: Perfect. Now fade the title in; four-second fade in.
ED: (Executes four-second fade in. How's that?
ME: A little slow. Let me see a three-second fade.
ED: (Does three second fade) You like?
ME: Looks good. Let's do it.
ED: (Presses edit botton) Next?
Later
ED: What about the transition into this next scene? Instead of a dissolve, how about a wipe?
ME: What did you have in mind?
ED: (Shows me three different wipes, a page turn, a multi-split screen wipe and a flip-out, each with the actual scenes involved so that I can evaluate exactly how it will look.) Which one?
ME: I like the page turn, but can you speed it up?
ED: (Turns knob) How's this?
ME: Do it!
Later
ME: This scene looks a little bright and pale.
ED: (Turns down video level, turns up chroma on TBC) How's this?
ME: A little more color saturation but not too much red.
ED: (Turns knobs) How's that?
ME: Okay.
Similar dialog continues.

Results of video edit: In one day (10 hours) I have an edited master and dub, the equivalent of a CRI and first answer print from CRI. In one day I have a perfect product with almost no compromises, complete with titles, credits, supers, sophisticated opticals and sound mix, not to mention perfectly timed and color corrected (and no gray hairs).

I am convinced that I have achieved superior results in one-twentieth the time that would have been required had this production been done on film. Agreed that the project would have had more impact as a film on a large screen. However, once the client stipulated video distribution, doing this project in video was the only way to go, both creatively and financially (and it's easier on the the ulcers).

VIDEO LENSES

The most popular location production television cameras fall into the category known as ENG/EFP, respectively "Electronic News Gathering" and "Electronic Field Production". These cameras invariably employ the popular ⅔" Plumbicon® or Saticon® type tubes. The latest generation of these cameras has achieved the size, weight and portability of the most compact 16mm cameras and thus an analogy between the 16mm film format and the ⅔" EFP camera should prove interesting.

The 16mm camera aperture is .292" x .402" or 7.4mm x 10.2mm which yields an image diagonal of .497" or 12.6mm. Since this diagonal is approximately ½", one would naturally assume that the ⅔" tube video format was actually larger than the 16mm negative area and that lenses used with these ⅔" television cameras would cover a wider angle than the same focal length lens on a 16mm camera. These assumptions are quite incorrect. Despite its ⅔" name, the target area of the ⅔" format is actually 8.8mm x 6.6mm yielding a diagonal of 11mm, slightly under ½". Thus the ⅔" television format is slightly smaller than the 16mm film although the aspect ratios are identical (1.33:1)/

The 16mm format is approximately 15% larger in linear dimension that the ⅔" video field. As a result, a lens of a specific focal length will cover *less* of an angle on the television camera. In other words, to cover the same angle of view on both a 16mm film camera and a ⅔" video camera, the ⅔" video camera should use a lens with a focal length of about 15% less than that on the film camera. As an example, a 10mm to 100mm zoom lens on a ⅔" EFP camera would be roughly equivalent to a 12mm to 120mm zoom lens on a 16mm film camera. The film cameraman who is beginning to use video should remember, that for a given visual perspective, the video lens will have to be about 15% shorter than one that would be selected for the 16mm format.

While on the subject of lenses, there is an entirely different philosophy toward optics in the video industry. The concept of interchangeable lenses and matched sets of fixed focal length lenses still enjoys popularity and prestige in the motion picture industry, yet the fixed focal length lens is virtually nonexistent in the video industry, as is the entire concept of interchanging lenses. While the new "electronic cinematography" cameras such as the Ikegami EC-35 and Panacam feature interchangeable lenses, it remains to be seen if the video community will adopt this technique. The more typical EFP camera is ordered with a specific zoom lens that rarely, if ever, is removed from the camera.

Although these ⅔″ video cameras are virtually married to a single zoom lens they do not suffer from a lack of optical versatility. An entire new breed of zoom lens, or more accurately zoom lens "system", has been developed for the ⅔″ EFP camera. For an example, Fujinon has a 17 to 1 zoom lens with a range of 9mm to 153mm and a maximum aperture of f/1.7. The built-in 2x extender converts the lens to an 18mm to 306mm for a combined range of 9mm to 306mm or a 34 to 1 range. The lens weighs only 2.5 Kg. But that's only part of the story. An accessory 0.8x retrozoom attachment affixes to the front of the lens creating a 7 to 122mm zoom lens with virtually no loss of light and a similar 1.83x adaptor alters the zoom range to 280mm. If you have been keeping score, the combination of the basic 17 to 1 zoom lens with the built-in 2x extender, 0.8x retrozoom and 1.83x teleconverter covers a range of 7mm to 560mm, a ratio of almost 80 to 1. Both Canon and Angenieux have similar lens systems for the ⅔″ video format. As mentioned earlier, these focal lengths should be increased by about 15% when drawing comparisons with 16mm camera lenses.

Lastly, the interchangeability of 16mm lenses and ⅔″ video lenses between broadcast quality EFP cameras and 16mm film cameras is nonexistent. The video lenses will not cover the film format. Likewise, the film lenses have much too short a back focus distance to mate with a prism type video camera which requires large back focus distances and correspondingly large rear clear apertures.

THE VIDEO CAMERA

The power and impact of the projected motion picture remains supreme. No miniscule picture in a box can even begin to challenge the spatially spectacular and emotionally awesome potential of the silver screen. Nor can any electro-*nouveau* process hope to duplicate the creative potential and sophisticated subtleties that can be achieved on film using techniques that have been perfected by cinematographers for over 75 years.

Unfortunately, only a small and decreasing percentage of production ever makes it to the silver screen. Whether it be an action series, TV feature, commercial, industrial, educational, training or documentary film, the odds currently predict that it will be viewed on a TV screen. Once this unfortunate but nonetheless realistic conclusion is accepted, an even more depressing fact must be confronted: electronic production offers many decided advantages over film, not the least of which is the "live" quality when displayed on the CRT television "screen".

Realizing these advantages, many producers of television-destined materials have already switched to the electronic medium. As a result, many cinematographers have also made this transition and many more are destined to follow. Although this change is often approached with reluctance, most cinematographers are pleasantly suprised to find that their cinematic artistry and creativity can be applied equally as well to the electronic format. While the two media are very similar from a cameraman's point of view, there is a significant reorientation that should be mastered if the cinematographer wishes to fully exploit the potential of video.

Optically the two formats are virtually identical. They both form an optical image at a specific "film" plane. However, here the similarity all but vanishes and the cameraman must learn an entirely new video language.

Almost all broadcast quality cameras employ three image-forming tubes. These are usually Plumbicon tubes or a variation called a Saticon tube. The reason for three tubes can best be explained by drawing an analogy to the 3-strip Technicolor process which was the mainstay of color motion picture production from 1933 until the early '50s. During that period, film could only record degrees of light and dark (B&W) and not color. It was known, however, that for human beings of this planet all colors could be represented reasonably well by combining varying proportions of three colors: red, green and blue. The Technicolor process employed a beam splitter and filtering system, such that the image coming through the single lens was split into red, green and blue components and recorded on three separate B&W film strips. Each of the three B&W images represented the red, green and blue elements of each frame respectively. In the process of making the release print, each of the B&W strips was used to dye transfer their respective color onto the release print in succession, much like a color printing press.

The modern video camera works on an almost identical principal. The Plumbicon tube is like a B&W film stock that is sensitive to only light and dark but otherwise color blind. Behind the single lens is a beam splitter that trisects the image into three paths, each with a corresponding color filter (red, green and blue) and terminating at the target screen of a Plumbicon tube. Thus, three separate signals are generated, one from each of the Plumbicon tubes, representing the red, green and blue elements of the image.

In motion pictures, the term "registration" pertains to image steadiness or the ability of each *successive* frame to register exactly the same spot relative to the aperture. In video, the term pertains to the ability of all three color components to coincide into a single image. If registration is not correct, the image exhibits color fringing and appears soft. Registration must be percise for all three tubes, both horizontally, vertically and rotationally on axis. The mounting of the three tubes and the prism assembly is one of the most critical elements of the video camera. The prism/tube assembly must be ruggedly constructed and shock-mounted to the outside case. If the camera is jolted or jarred severely, mechanical realignment may be required, but in most instances minor registration errors can be corrected electronically with adjustment pots located inside the camera. While modern EFP/ENG cameras rarely require adjustment, it is usually the registration that ultimately needs attention.

This three-tube design may appear "old fashioned" and troublesome, but in reality it is remarkably easy to maintain and affords the cinematographer a flexibility not found with film. Eventually the red, green and blue signals are combined to form a single composite video signal. However, the cameraman has access to the three individual color signals before they are combined. With controls provided, the cameraman can "paint" the scene by varying the gain of the individual red, green and blue components. Additional controls facilitate optimization of white and black levels as well as contrast. Combining a firm command of the nuances those adjustments provide with existing knowlege of filters and lighting give the cinematographer extensive control of the video "look".

The "image plane" in the film camera is obviously the raw stock, where the image is actually recorded as optical information. The television camera first splits the image formed by the lens. Each of three resulting image paths passes through a color filter before it finally focuses on the respective red, green and blue television tubes. The image is not recorded by the tubes, but instaneously transformed into an electronic signal. This is the most basic difference between a film camera and a television camera.

In video terms, the film camera is actually both camera and recorder, as it both forms the image and permanently records it. The television camera, on the other hand, only forms the image and transforms it to an electronic signal. This output signal must be connected to some external recorder or fed to a monitor or transmission system. The image from a television camera that is not connected to some external system is like the sound of one hand clapping.

This point may seem very basic. However, it is important for the cinematograher to conceptualize the two-stage process of recording the video image. The camera converts the image to a complex electrical signal and then the VTR records this signal. Image quality is a function of both elements: camera and recorder. Even the simple concept of format size must consider this duality.

The cinematographer uses film in 16mm, 35mm and 65mm formats. This film format number really defines two properties: the size of the formed image at the image plane, and the size of the recorded image (or the area of raw stock consumed to record each frame). In film these two parameters are obviously one and the same, but in video they are quite distinct and different. The size of the video tubes employed in the camera would correspond to the first aspect of format size, i.e., the size of the formed image at the image plane. The VTR would correspond to the second aspect of format size. The term "size of recorded image" is not applicable because it is not an "image" that is actually being recorded, but rather an electronic signal representing the image. However, the concept of "area of raw stock consumed to record each frame" does have a reasonable correlation with the quality of video recording. The size of the tape track, as well as the method of recording, defines the video tape format and level of quality to be expected. The point here is that film format is dependent on only the gauge of film, whereas in video both the camera design *and* VTR type must be considered to obtain an equivalent concept of format.

There are many factors that affect the quality of a video image. The camera tubes, where the image is transformed into an electronic signal, is probably the single most important element. Almost all modern broadcast quality cameras employ three Plumbicon® type tubes, one each for red, green and blue. These tubes come in three basic sizes for broadcast quality applications: ⅔″, 1″ and 1¼″. As might be expected, the ultra compact ENG/EFP cameras employ the ⅔″ tubes, while the larger, more sophisticated studio cameras make use of the 1¼″ tubes. An intermediate class of camera designed as a "portable studio" camera makes use of the 1″ tube.

The current rage of "film style" video production usually involves the ENG/EFP compact ⅔″ cameras. The cinematographer drawn into the video service will most likely find his head next to one of these sophisticated devices.

It may be tempting to draw an analogy with film, comparing ⅔″ video with 16mm; 1″ video with 35mm, etc. However, attempting such an analogy at this point would be hasty and ultimately erroneous. There are other factors that enter into the picture.

For a given film format, say 16mm, there are many different raw stocks available with respectively different qualities. A specific fine-grain, high-resolution stock may be available in the smaller format and yet not be available in the larger. This was exactly the case with Kodak ECO Ektachrome Commercial. Kodak developed this fine-grain, high-resolution ECO reversal stock specifically for their 16mm format, realizing the greater demands required of the smaller image area. This same technology was *not* applied to the larger gauge raw stocks, due to the greater image area available. As a result, the difference in quality between 16mm and 35mm was not as great as the difference in their respective image areas might suggest. There is a similar technological situation in video. The ⅔″ tube, being the smallest of broadcast quality devices, has received a lot of technological attention. In addition, the ⅔″ tube is used in virtually all broadcast-quality ENG cameras and most EFP cameras. This adds up to a lot of tubes. As a matter of fact, the ⅔″ tube accounts for the great majority of all broadcast tubes being manufactured and sold for new cameras. This represents quite a lucrative market which has understandably resulted in a very competitive atmos-

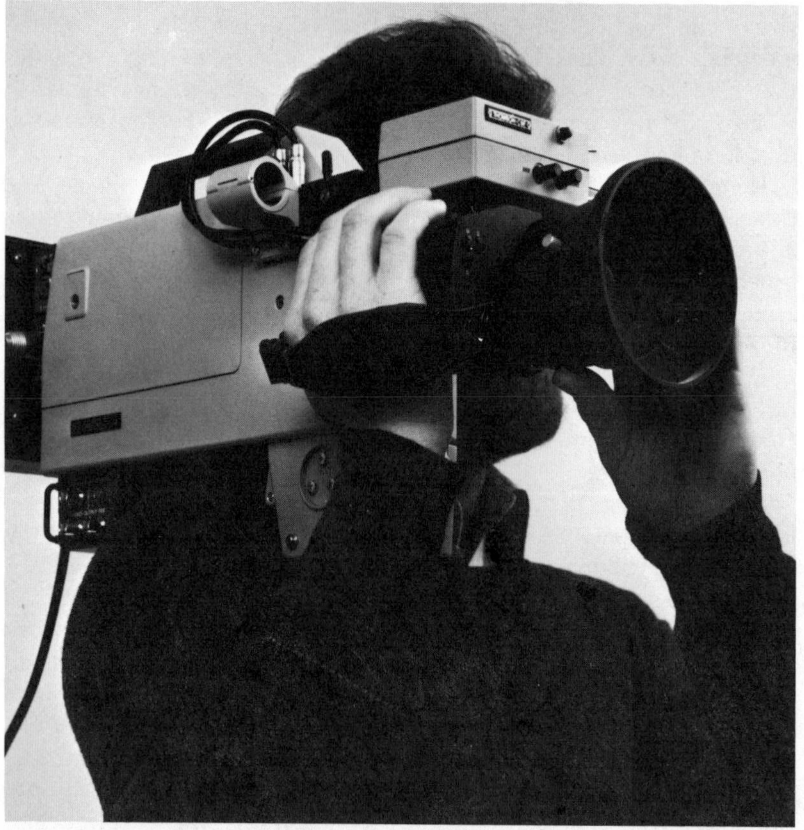

FIGURE 153—This Thomson ENG/EFP MICROCAM weighs only 12 pounds and delivers a picture that rivals the best studio cameras.

phere among tube manufacturers. As any student of the free enterprise system will tell you, competition yields a better product for the consumer. Broadcast tubes are no exception and it is not surprising that the ⅔″ tube has been the recipient of the highest state-of-the-art technology, such as low capacitance diode gun Plumbicons and the new mixed field image tubes. The implication is clearly that the difference in quality between the ⅔″ tube and its larger brethren may not be as great as the difference in size suggests.

Although the actual conversion of the optical image into an electronic signal occurs in the Plumbicon or Saticon® type tube, there is an unbelievable and staggering quantity of sophisticated electronics associated with the formation of the final composite video signal. It is obvious that the quality and sophistication of these electronic circuits will also have a great effect on the final video product. Lastly, it should be understood that video has a finite maximum performance level, unlike film projected on a screen. There are 525 horizontal lines, no more. Vertical resolution (band width) is usually limited by the monitor/receiver, VTR, or transmission, whichever is worse. In most cases the camera exceeds the performance parameters of the other elements in the system. The bottom line is that the current state-of-the-art ⅔″ ENG/EFP cameras can deliver performance very close to the theoretical limits defined by the overall system.

It should, of course, be realized that the latest generation of 1¼″ studio cameras have also reached new heights in image quality as well as picture control and the use of computer technology to optimize electronic parameters. The signal from one of these cameras will obviously be superior to that from even the best ⅔″ camera. However, once the two signals are retrieved from even the best VTR's and displayed on a monitor, only a well-trained eye would be able to distinguish a difference. In many cases it is the VTR that is the limiting factor in an EFP production.

VIDEO RECORDING

A television camera and video recorder must be chosen as a system. Ideally each should have the same caliber of quality, as the final video product can only be as good as the weakest link. As with film, there are different VTR formats or types and some definitely deliver superior quality over others. However, the situation is not quite as cut-and-dried as it is with film, such as: "65mm is superior to 35mm which is better than 16mm." Before delving into the technical workings of the VTR, a brief familiarization of the more popular VTR types may prove helpful.

The first acceptable broadcast quality VTR was the 2″ quad. Introduced back in the mid 1950's, it is still the backbone of most broadcast television operations. The 2″ quad machine has been the standard of VTR quality and not until very recently have there appeared new VTR formats to challenge the superiority of the 2″ quad. The term "quad" comes from the fact that the video signal is put onto the tape by a high-speed rotating head assembly containing four video recording heads. It was this rotating head concept that was the major technological breakthrough enabling quality video recording. The tape is two inches wide and travels through the machine at 15 inches per second, which requires about a 10-inch reel of tape for a full hour's program. Broadcasters were pleased with the professional quality of the 2″ quad and were willing to overlook the extreme size, weight and cost of these machines. Outside the broadcasting industry, however, these undesirable aspects and the exorbitant costs for maintenance and tape proved prohibitive.

Recorder manufacturers thus developed the Helical Scan VTR. The low price and relative compact size of these helical machines were designed to fill the rapidly growing demand for VTR's among industrial, commercial and educational institutions. The helical scan machines come in all sizes and shapes and use tape widths of ¼″, ½″, ¾″ and 1″. While all helical machines operate on the same basic principles, the method and quality of construction, number of heads, tape paths and recording electronics can vary so widely that the cheapest ½″ helical machines are considered consumer electronics while the best 1″ machines are considered broadcast quality. The U-matic format, which is basically a ¾″ Helical VTR in a cassette, has achieved a great popularity among industrial producers and ENG units of virtually every TV station in the country. The U-matic format was originally developed for industrial applications and can not be considered broadcast quality. However, its compact portable size and ease of operation and editing made it ideal for ENG applications. It was the development of the "time base corrector" that enabled the U-matic machines to be used in broadcast applications. While the quality is still inferior by broadcast standards, the extreme portability and efficiency of the U-matic system is attractive enough to make it the first choice of most broadcast ENG operations. The ¾″ U-matic format may be challenged soon by several new ½″ formats that record luminance and chrominance channels separately. The quality of these new formats are said to be far superior to ¾″ and almost as good as 1″.

The most recent development in VTR standards, is the "broadcast quality" high-band 1" helical scan recorder. Recent technological advancements in the field of servo mechanisms and micro electronics have resulted in this new generation of ultra-sophisticated broadcast machines that exhibit quality equal to, and in most cases superior to, the long-revered 2" quad machines. This high quality comes in a significantly smaller, lighter and much less expensive package with far greater flexibility and features—not the least of which is film-style editing, including still-frame, slow motion, frame-by-frame jogging and the ability to maintain an image at even 30 times normal speed. These 1" Broadcast High-Band recorders have virtually made 2" quad machines obsolete and while quads will be around for a long time due to the sheer number of machines in existence, broadcasters have already begun the changeover to the more flexible and less costly 1" format.

It should be mentioned at this point that there is no compatibility among helical formats even if they use the same tape width. Every manufacturer uses its own design for angle of the tracks, tape speed, writing speed, placement of the audio and control tracks, placement of the heads, etc. Thus, a tape has to be played back and edited on the same type of machine upon which it was recorded. Imagine if all film shot on an Eclair could only be projected on an Eclair projector, and so on with each camera/projector manufacturer. The helical VTR market was and is quite hectic. Not until the overwhelming popularity of the U-matic did standardization begin to create some order. The developers of the U-matic format allowed franchises to other manufacturers and a standardized format was created.

Because of the pressures from the broadcasters a similar standardization now exists with the new 1" broadcast formats through the efforts of the SMPTE. Unfortunately, there are currently two popular and totally different and incompatible one-inch broadcast formats—the SMPTE Type C and the SMPTE Type B—and so there is still controversy within the industry, with the usual compatibility problems. The SMPTE Type C format is exemplified by the Sony BVH 2000 and the Ampex VPR-2, both of which are also available in portable models. Hitachi also has a 1" Type C portable. The SMPTE Type B format is also called the BCN format and was developed by Bosch-Fernseh. The BCN system not only includes studio consoles and a one-hour reel-to-reel portable, but also a 20-minute cassette portable, all with the same high broadcast quality. The choice between the Type B or Type C format is a difficult one. Specific features must be carefully compared and compatibility with other systems must be considered. The BCN Fernseh Type B system has a very good track record and is quite popular in Europe, and to a lesser extent in the States. While the Type C format is relatively newer, it appears that the major U.S. networks and production houses are fairly well committed to the Type C system.

At the present time in the U.S. most broadcasters are making the transition from 2″ Quad to 1″ Type C. Virtually all new professional production and post production houses are 1″ Type C, with limited ¾″ U-matic interface. Almost all ENG hard news and TV documentary is ¾″ U-matic as is most professional, industrial and educational production. Some low budget in house industrial and educational producers make use of so called "industrial grade" ½″ VHS and Beta VCR's.

While the 1″ Type C is quite firmly the choice of professional broadcast quality production, the new one piece cameras utilizing the new high quality component ½″ formats may replace both 1″ and ¾″ for location EFP. Likewise the recently introduced component ¼″ cassette format exhibits an image superior to ¾″ U-matic and may become the new standard of ENG operations.

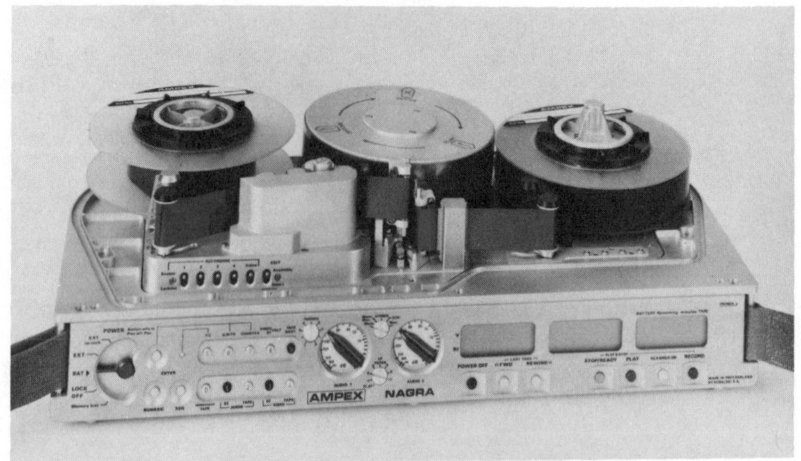

The Ampex Nagra VPR-5 1″ VTR weighs 15 pounds.

THE VIDEO TAPE RECORDER

The VTR or video tape recorder is quite a complex device. This is mainly due to the high frequencies involved in video recording and the high degree of signal stability necessary for quality reproduction. A comparison between conventional sound recorders and a video tape recorder will illustrate the greater demands placed on the VTR and the reasons for the complex design.

The typical sound recorder must record the full spectrum of audio frequencies, which is usually considered to be 20Hz to 20KHz or more realistically 30Hz to 15KHz. The high-band video recorder must record signals up to 10,000 KHz(10MHz). Thus, while the audio tape recorder does not have to record signals above 20 *thousand* Hertz, the VTR must record signals up to 10 *million* Hertz. This is not twice the frequency or even 10 times the frequency but over 500 times the high frequency capabilities of an audio recorder.

The high frequency capability of any tape recorder is a function of both tape head gap and tape-to-head speed. It was determined by video engineers that the optimum tape-to-head recording speed for the high frequency video signal would be approximately 1000 inches per second, which is roughly 100 times faster than the 7½ ips or 15 ips associated with audio recorders. If the tape in a VTR were to travel past a stationary tape head in the same fashion as an audio recorder, the 1000 ips speed would use up tape so fast that a full 10½″ reel of tape would last less than one minute! Clearly this method would be unacceptable, but, how else could the 1000 ips tape-to-head speed be maintained.?

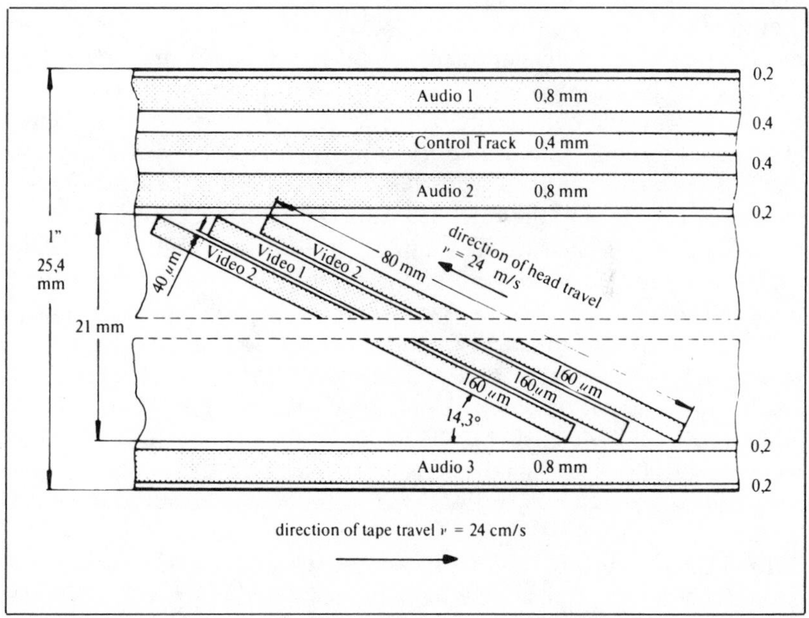

FIGURE 154—Track layout of the SMPTE "Type B" (BCN) 11″ Broadcast highband helical scan VTR. The three audio tracks, as well as the control track, are recorded conventionally by stationary heads. The video tracks are recorded by a high-speed rotating head assembly that spins at a specific angle (see FIGURE 155).

The answer is the rotating head. In a helical-scan VTR, the tape is wrapped around a rotating drum that contains a tiny video recording head. The drum spins at high speed while the tape itself is pulled slowly around the drum. In the "Type B" and "Type C" broadcast 1" VTR's, the tape moves at approximately 9.6 ips, yet the spinning head whizzes across the tape at about 1000 ips.

FIGURE 154 illustrates the track layout of the BCN (Type B) 1" broadcast highband helical format. Note that the figure is *not* drawn to scale, that the helical video portion of the tape has been compressed to conserve diagram space. A quick reference to the left edge of the diagram will show that the helical video portion of the tape occupies 21mm of the full 25.4mm tape width. The video signal thus accounts for almost 90% of the usable tape width, while the control track and three sound tracks all together occupy little more than 10%.

It should be obvious where the name "helical-scan" VTR originated. Because the tape is wrapped at an angle to the axis of the rotating head drum (FIGURE 155), the narrow video tracks recorded by the spinning head are oriented on the tape with a respective angle. It should be noted that the three individual sound tracks, as well as the control track, are recorded by a separate stationary head assembly and thus appear as conventionally recorded tracks perfectly parallel to tape direction.

At this point the complexity of the VTR should be apparent. However, the recording process is duck soup compared to VTR playback, which is even more difficult. Those little helical video tracks are only 160 *micro*meters wide, and there are 300 scans per second. During playback, the whizzing playback head, scanning at 9000 rpm and almost 1000 inches per second, must perfectly align itself with the prerecorded tracks 300 times every second. As you can imagine, without a road map this is no easy task. The most complex tape tension circuits and servo-feedback techniques are employed to assure perfect track alignment and accurate color rendition. Upon playback, most minute residual errors in the video signals can be easily cleaned up by the time base corrector, or TBC. The digital TBC is really a digital video computer that can analyze certain flaws in the video signal and automatically correct them.

The BCN or "Type B" VTR we have been discussing uses a segmented format. This means that it takes more than one pass of the video head to record a full picture field. Referring to figure 154 it would thus take more than one helical scan track to store a complete field. For example, 2" quad requires 16 successive scans to record one full picture field. The advantage of segmented formats is smaller head drums. The major disadvantage is that most segmented formats are a nightmare to edit as there is inherently no stable picture except at sound speed—no still frame, no slow scan, no jog and no high search.

The 1″ Type C, ¾″ U-matic, ½″ VHS and Beta formats are all non-segmented or full field VTR's. As the name implies, it only takes one pass of the video head to record or play back a full picture field. Thus a complete picture is stored in a single video track. While this requires a larger head drum, the advantages are heaven to an editor. The non-segmented formats edit just like film in a modern flatbed, complete with still frame, jog, fast or slow scan in either direction and of course, sound speed. In some cases, such as the Sony BVH2000, much of the variable speed range actually yields a broadcast quality image.

FIGURE 155—Scanner assembly for Bosch-Fernseh BCN "Type B" 1″ Broadcast VTR. Precision guide rollers maintain exact angle between tape and rotating head assembly. Spinning heads rotate at 9,000 rpm and scan 300 tracks per second at a head-to-tape speed of nearly 1,000 inches per second. Yet, the tape moves forward at only 9.6 inches per second.

THE VIDEO SIGNAL

Motion picture film captures the entire image in one fell swoop. The lens forms the image, the shutter opens, and the image is captured in the film emulsion. So what's new? The point is that all elements of the image are captured by the film emulsion simultaneously and in the same instant. This is *not* the case with the video process. This difference in image forming technique is the very essence of the principle of television.

Any picture or image is really made up of many "bits of information." In film these building blocks are grains of silver and a newspaper or magazine picture is made up of dots of ink. If a picture is comprised of two few "bits of information", the image will appear coarse and grainy with a lack of fine detail. Ideally, the image should be comprised of "bits" significantly smaller than than the finest detail of the picture. The

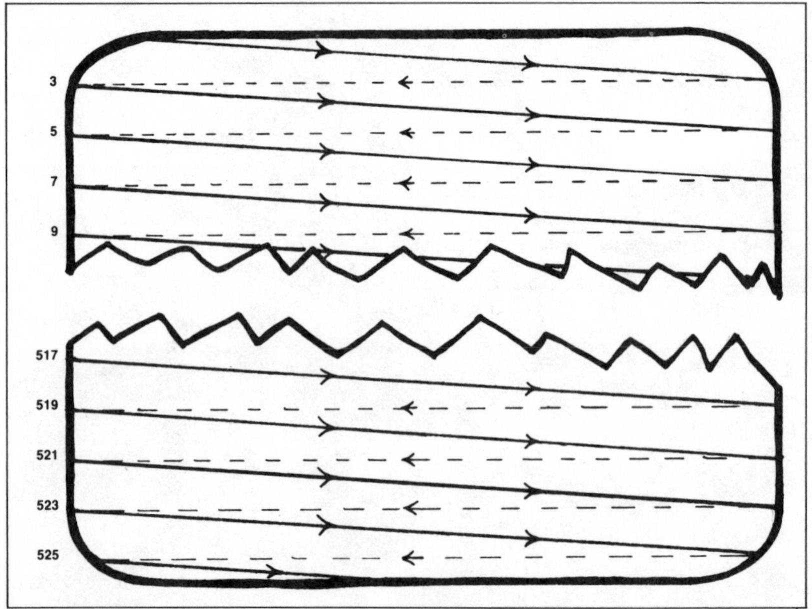

FIGURE 156—Scanning Pattern of an odd field. Starting at upper left, the electron beam in the camera tube scans the entire image left to right. Upon reaching the right edge, the beam goes into the blanking mode and then rapidly retraces back to the left edge to scan the next line. This continues until all 262½ lines of the field have been scanned. The image is reconstructed in the monitor by the reserve process. The scanning electron beam creates light and dark information on the receiving tube phosphor target proportional to the instantaneous signal level.

television picture can also be considered to be made up of bits of information, as many as 250,000 in a high-quality image. For simplification, these bits may be thought of as dots that can be black, white, or any shade of gray between, similar to grains of silver on photographic film. (For the time being, only a B & W picture will be considered.)

The lens on the television camera forms the image on the target of the tube in the same manner as a motion picture camera lens forms the image on the film. While the entire image is present on the target of the tube during the "exposure" of one "frame", the image is captured one bit at a time sequentially.

A beam scans the target image looking at each dot of information. Starting at the upper left hand corner, the beam scans horizontally to the right. When it reaches the right hand side of the screen, it quickly retraces back to the left, moves down a slight amount and begins the next scan. It makes 262½ horizontal scans before reaching the bottom of the image. This scanning process is really made in two stages. In reality, the television image is comprised of 525 horizontal lines. The scanner first scans the 263 odd lines and then goes back and scans the 262 even lines. Thus the television "frame" is comprised of two interlaced "fields". Each field takes 1/60th second to scan, so 1/30th second is necessary to scan a complete video "frame". See FIGURE 156.

The output of the television tube is merely a fluctuating voltage. As the beam scans the image, this voltage will reflect the brightness of the dot that it is scanning at that instant. A white dot will cause the voltage to reach its maximum, while a black dot will result in zero voltage for that instant. Likewise, shades of gray will result in respective intermediate voltage levels. See FIGURE 157.

This fluctuating voltage is, thus, the essence of the video signal. There are other elements that are added to the signal to assure proper synchronization and other functions. However, this fluctuating voltage is all that remains of the visual image. It is this fluctuating voltage that is sent to a monitor for viewing. It is this same signal that is recorded on tape for future viewing. And it is this same signal that is sent through the air to home receivers.

While this description is extremely simplified, the principle is valid and accurate, and will suffice as a basis for our future discussions on video process.

The waveform monitor: FIGURE 158 represents a typical image and the corresponding "waveform" for the one horizontal scan (of 525) indicated by the black horizontal line in the image.

Several things should be noted from these figures. Most obvious is the manner in which the signal fluctuates with brightness. The height of

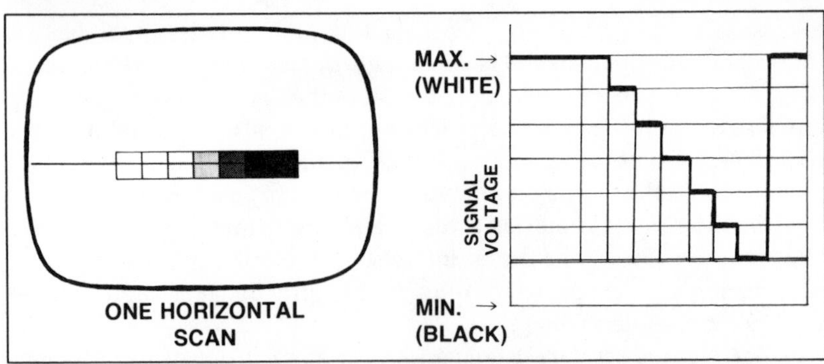

FIGURE 157—Voltage output of camera during the single horizontal scan through the gray scale depicted above. As the beam scans the image, the instantaneous camera voltage is proportional to the brightness of the image at that point.

the waveform is divided into 140 IEEE units (Institute of Electrical & Electronic Engineers). The picture information falls in the positive voltage area from 0 to 100 IEEE units. Peak white level is 100 IEEE units while black is 0. In actuality, the darkest elements in the scene are held at about +7½ IEEE units, slightly above theoretical black level.

Notice that even though the scene has a light background, the signal goes to theoretical black (0 level) at the very end of the scan and before the beginning of the scan. This is called blanking level and causes the electron beam in the monitor to shut-off so as to render it invisible as it retraces rapidly across the screen to begin the next scan. (See FIGURE 158).

The waveform monitor scale also includes –40 IEEE units below the 0 black level. This is the so-called blacker-than-black area and is used for the sync pulse. In FIGURE 158, the sync pulse can be seen at the right on the waveform. It is this pulse that triggers the electron beam in the monitor to retrace back to the left of the screen to start another horizontal line. All viewing monitors and home receivers are adjusted to overscan so that the black blanking areas on either side of the picture will not be visible. Most of us at one time or another have seen a TV with insufficient overscan, and the black blanking areas are indeed visible to the left and right, as well as the top and bottom , of the picture.

Putting this all together, the fluctuating voltage represents the picture information (brightness) for that particular horizontal line left to right. When the beam reaches just beyond the right hand edge of the monitor, the signal goes to blanking (black) level, making it invisible. The sync pulse then triggers the beam to begin the rapid retrace back across the screen to the left side. Notice that the signal remains at blanking level well after the sync-pulse in order to give the beam enough time to

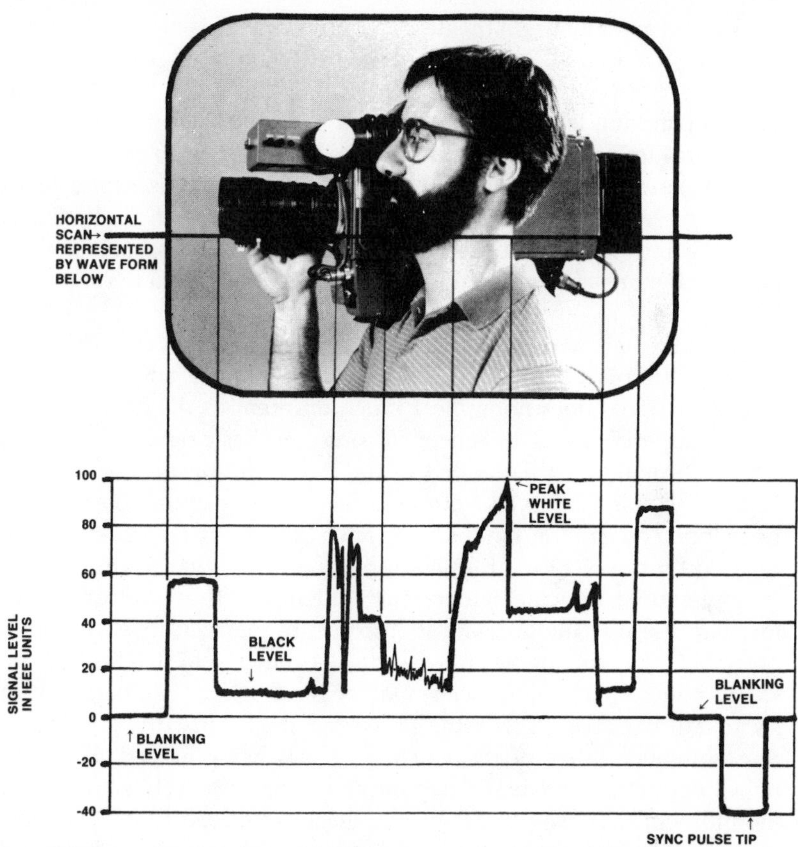

FIGURE 158—The waveform monitor visually displays the instantaneous video signal level and is the ideal graphic representation of the video process. The picture of the cameraman has one black horizontal line through it. This represents the one line out of 525 that we have singled out to analyze. While some waveform monitors can actually display one particular horizontal scan in this manner, most display all 525 lines continuously in real time. Due to persistence of vision and the slow decay time of the monitor screen phosphors, it usually appears that the waveforms for all 525 lines are superimposed on one another. Note that before the picture information begins, the signal is at blanking level (0). As the picture information begins, the signal goes to an intermediate level (50 to 60 IEEE units) representing the gray background. The black lens causes the signal to go to its minimum level. Note that the minimum black level is not quite 0 level, but usually adjusted slightly higher to approximately 7½ IEEE units. In a similar fashion the signal continues to respond to the light and dark portions of the scan. Upon reaching the right edge, the signal goes to blanking level, and then the sync pulse triggers the electron beam to rapidly retrace to the left edge for the next scan.

retrace and actually begin the next scan invisibly. This process continues line after line until all 262½ lines of the field have been scanned. At this point the signal goes into the vertical blanking interval. Here the signal goes to blanking level, also. However a slightly larger (width) vertical sync pulse triggers the electron beam in the monitor to retrace all the way to the top of the screen to begin another field. As would be expected, the vertical blanking interval is much longer than the horizontal blanking interval and consumes the equivalent of approximately 20 horizontal scans as the beam travels invisibly back up to the top of the screen.

Basically, the B&W television signal consists of this waveform which contains the picture information, blanking intervals and sync pulses. The color signal does not appear much different as the color information is "superimposed" or "encoded" onto this basic signal. Other reference information can be added to the signal during the horizontal or vertical blanking intervals without affecting the picture. These signals need not conern the cinematographer, as his attention should be focused on the picture information portion of the waveform.

Why should the cinematographer understand the waveform monitor? Because it is the ultimate spot exposure meter. It displays the exposure of *every* spot in the entire scene at a glance, all 250,000 of them. It shows percisely where the scene may be too bright or two dark or if the scene is well balanced with the proper contrast ratio. It will indicate if the luminance range of the video system is being exceeded or if the obligatory white and black references are present. While the picture monitor will obviously reveal most of these same aspects, the waveform monitor (scope) provides significantly greater quantitative information enabling the cinematographer to more accurately control and develop his visuals.

AUTO WHITE BALANCE

Every cinematographer is familiar with color temperature and the fact that every film made is balanced for one specific color temperature only, usually 3200°K (tungsten) or 5600°K (daylight). It is also common knowledge that if lighting conditions do not match one of these two standards, color correction or conversion filters must be employed to ensure proper color rendition. Murphy's law seems to hit hardest in this area as every location seems to have a mixture of window daylight and overhead fluorescent, while the light kit is always tungsten. Despite the best color temperature meters, color compensating filters for the camera, and dichroics or gel for the lights, perfect color balance is difficult to achieve and there is still the chance of a horse of a different color. Even outdoor locations employing "daylight" film or filters run the risk of gross color errors, as outdoor conditions can range from 3000°K to more than 20,000°K. Of course, most labs can color correct to a certain extent. However, they still request that the cinematographer balance as best he can on location. At the very least, color balancing has always been a necessary nuisance for the cinematographer.

Now, imagine a new film stock that will automatically adjust its color temperature rating to perfectly match the prevailing lighting conditions of each shot. Whether the illumination be candlelight, sunset, open shade, or a mixture of daylight, tungsen and fluorescent, the results would always be spot-on, without the necessity of external filters or gels on the lights. This may seem like a far-out fantasy, yet virtually every professional ENG/EFP video camera does just that.

The tiny button is usually labeled "auto white balance" and is inconspicuously grouped with the several other buttons and switches found externally on all video cameras. The process takes anywhere from 5 seconds down to ½-second on the newest cameras. The principle behind his miracle is really quite simple and a short explanation of the auto white balance process is sure to be a thrilling revelation.

Color is determined by the specific wave length or frequency of light. There are myriad colors in the rainbow, ranging on a continuum from infra-reds through ultra-violets. Yet, we as human beings determine color only by the relative amounts of reds, blues and greens. The eye is thought to be made up of three basic sensors, which repsond to blues, reds and greens respectively. Even though a particular object or surface may be emitting or reflecting many different frequencies, the eye just registers the relative strength of these frequencies in groupings of reds, blues and greens. The brain then "averages" these three signals and comes up with a "color" for the object. It should be realized that in many cases this "color" that the brain comes up with may not have any resemblance to the actual "colors" of the object according to frequencies of light.

The important point is that the ultimate color, as perceived by the brain, is created by merely registering the red, blue and green content of the image.

Color film makes use of this fact and is constructed of three layers, one each to register reds, blues and greens—just like the human eye. (Of course this terrestrial film may not provide acceptable color rendition for other cosmic creatures. However, that is a problem Kodak will have to face when the situation arises.) The color temperature rating of a film stock merely reflects the relative sensitivities of the three layers. For example, "daylight" balanced films have color layers of approximately equal sensitivity, due to the fact that "daylight" is composed of relatively equal amounts of red, blue and green. Tungsten balanced film, on the other hand, is designed with a more highly sensitive blue layer relative to the red layer to compensate for the fact that tungsten light is weak in blue wave lengths. So color temperature ratings describe the relative sensitivities of the three color layers.

As we now know, the professional color video camera operates on the same principle as color film employing three light sensitive tubes, one each for reds, blues and greens. Because the output of these tubes is an electrical signal, the color temperature rating of the video camera can be made to *any* value by merely adjusting the relative gain or "volume" of these three signals. Thus, if the illumination is weak in the blues (as is a tungsten light source), the signal from the blue tube can be turned up. Now comes the amazing auto white circuit.

The video camera is merely pointed at any white surface. A plain white piece of paper is usually sufficient. The auto white button is pressed. Inside, the camera knows that "white" means exactly equal amounts of red, blue and green. So, while holding the gain of the green tube constant, the camera automatically adjusts the gain of the outputs from the red and blue tubes so as to perfectly match the output level of the green tube. *Voila!* The outputs of all three tubes are identical, so the white card will reproduce white. Thus any anomalies in the light source are automatically compensated. The process takes as little as ½-second and an indicator light in the viewfinder usually tells you that the process is completed. Once the button is released, the gains of the three tubes are locked and the "color temperature rating" of the camera will remain unchanged until another lighting situation is encountered and the button is once again pressed.

Even if the source is a mixture of daylight, fluorescent and tungsten, merely place the white card in the position of the subject, zoom in on it, adjust the iris and press the white balance button. That's it. Flesh tones, as well as other colors, will be perfect.

In addition, most video cameras employ built-in color filters for gross adjustments of color temperature. There is usually a 3200°K and 5600°K position and, in some cases, an intermediate position of 4500°K. The cameraman should first approximate the color condition with one of these three filters and then auto white balance. The results are amazingly accurate and even the most bizarre lighting mixtures can yield perfectly balanced images.

Recently I mentioned that the video camera inherently offers the cameraman many interesting, creative techniques. Most of these techniques involve the prudent manipulation of the camera controls and adjustments that were actually meant for the video technican and not for the cameraman. While most of these controls enable the video technician to calibrate the camera circuits to the manufacturer's precise specifications, the astute cameraman can in many cases alter some of these controls to his creative advantage. One of the simplest of these alterations doesn't even require changing any controls on the camera per se.

There are many instances where the cinematographer may wish to "warm" or "cool" a scene or add a specific color tint to achieve a particular effect. In most cases this would be done by controlling the lighting with gels on interiors or placing filters over the lens. For example, if the cameraman wishes to warm up a scene, he can employ straw gels on the lights or a light yellow/orange filter on the lens. To achieve a full range of subtle effects, the cameraman would have to have dozens of filters or a warehouse full of gels. The video camera can accomplish this without filters or gels.

The method involves the auto white balance circuitry of the camera. As you will recall, during auto white balance the camera is pointed at a pure white card that is being illuminated by the same source as the scene to be photographed. The auto white balance button is pressed and the camera automatically equalizes the outputs of the red, blue and green circuits, which is the defintion of pure white: equal amounts of red, blue and green. Thus, anything white in the scene will be perfectly white and all other colors will fall into place.

An interesting point to ponder, however, is that the camera is taking it upon faith that you are indeed directing its lens at a pure white card when you activate the white balance circuit. This fact is the basis of the tinting technqiue which, in reality, amounts to lying to the white balance circuits. Taking the former example where a scene is to be warmed up, the video camera is pointed at a card that is not white but tinted in the opposite direction of the desired results. If a straw tint is desired, the camera is pointed at a pale blue card which is the color that is 180° opposite the straw on the color wheel. This should, of course, be under the illumination of the scene to be shot. The white balance button is activated, and presto, the bluish card is now perfectly white on the color monitor. The white balance circuit has boosted the yellow/orange gain in the camera to change the bluish card to white (not realizing that it has been tricked.) Now when the scene is viewed, it will have a straw tint to it, and the effect can be instantly evaluated on a color monitor.

By carrying a small patch book of various pastel tints and shades, the cameraman has at his fingertips a complete palette of color subtleties. He can instantaneously add to any scene. This technique is superior to gels and filters for several reasons. It is obviously cheaper and easier than carrying filters and gels and automatically balances the changing lighting conditions. For example, if filters were used, the camera would first have to be white balanced on a white card without the filter, and then the filter would be inserted. With the tinted card technique the tint is achieved at the same time the balance circuits compensate for any changes in lighting conditions. Moreover, there is nothing in the optical path to impair image quality.

INSIDE THE VIDEO CAMERA

The professional motion picture camera represents the ultimate in mechanical precision. Yet, in the realm of modern technology, the film camera is a relatively straightforward and simple device. Despite the recent plethora of digital tachometers, TTL metering, and other electronic accoutrements, the film camera is still the

FIGURE 159—This simple, unassuming white balance button found on virtually all ENG/EFP video cameras can do more than just create true whites. The astute cameraman can use this button to create a wide variety of color tint effects. (See text)

basic intermittent movement with its rollers and sprocket wheels.

I am not attempting to impugn the dignity of the motion picture camera. Its precision and simplicity make it an accurate, reliable and dependable instrument. However, the cameraman who is accustomed to opening a camera and seeing a couple of rollers and guides may experience cardiac arrest upon viewing the inside of a modern video camera for the first time.

FIGURE 160 is a view of the left side of an Hitachi SK-90, a modern EFP camera, with its cover removed. For anyone interested in counting, there are more than 70 adjustment pots and switches in the picture. This is just the surface. Removing individual boards (FIGURE 161) reveals even more pots and switches mounted internally on the face of the circuit boards. And if this is not enough, removing the right camera side panel exposes even more of the same. The final score? Most ENG/EFP cameras will employ well in excess of 200 individual adjustments and switches. In addition, there are usually at least 50 designated "test points" on the circuit boards with corresponding waveform and voltage specifications.

FIGURE 160—Removing the side cover of a modern ENG/EFP camera reveals more than 70 adjustments.

Before you run out and enroll at M.I.T., or jump under the blankets and assume the prenatal position, it must be said that very rarely, if ever, is the cameraman required to come into contact with any of the aforementioned adjustments. Quite the contrary. With few exceptions the cameraman should *not* mess with the pots inside the camera. I have seen a video engineer spend two days attempting to realign a camera that was suffering from the results of a cameraman who had "just turned a couple of watchamacallits slightly". In most cases one adjustment affects another, and the unskilled tinkerer can easily start a chain reaction of misalignment that is most difficult to define and correct.

The point here should be clear. The video camera is a different breed of animal altogether. Its electronic complexity is light years apart from a film camera and requires highly skilled electronic engineers or technicians and sophisticated test equipment to facilitate proper adjustment. Many EFP productions and almost all studio productions employ a video engineer as a standard member of the crew. Under circumstances where a video engineer is not present during production, the camera should be thoroughly checked out and calibrated prior to departure. Just because the picture "looks good" on the monitor does not mean that the camera is perfectly adjusted. There are many aspects of the video signal that can deviate from optimum specification and only built-in or external test procedures can reveal these anomalies.

Every video camera should be treated like the sophisticated electronic instrument that it it is. Every video camera should have an "electronic godfather" somewhere who can tweak the camera to optimum performance on a regular basis. Lastly, for those cameramen who do not have the luxury of a resident engineer, there are fairly simple built-in test procedures on most ENG/EFP cameras. By learning these procedures and the corresponding adjustments, even the most un-

(LEFT) FIGURE 161a—Removal of a printed circuit board reveals even more adjustment pots. (RIGHT) FIGURE 161b—A peek behind the right side cover show the remaining adjustment pots and switches. The grand total is usually in excess of 200.

electronically oriented cameraman can keep his camera delivering optimum picture quality. In reality the modern EFP/ENG camera is a reliable and stable device, and aside from these very few adjustments, the more than 200 or so pots rarely require attention.

Next we will look into some of the more basic diagnostics that a cameraman can perform for himself.

REGISTRATION

Camera registration to the film cameraman means image steadiness. Does the camera register each successive frame in precisely the same position relative to the aperture? If the registration was poor, the image would appear to weave when projected. This condition is particularly intolerable during dissolves, titles, or split screen. Very rarely does a professional motion picture camera develop poor registration (unless it is dropped or shipped by air), and even if it did, there is nothing the cameraman can do about it except send it to the manufacturer for major surgery.

Registration is an entirely different animal in a video camera. Not only is it the most prevalent and frequent misalignment in a video camera, but the cameraman can usually correct it himself with no other special tools than a small screwdriver and a registration chart similar to that in FIGURE 162. But first, what is registration?

The video camera has three light sensitive tubes, one each for blues, greens and reds. Similarly, color film has three light sensitive layers or emulsions one each for the same three primary colors. When the film is manufactured, these three color layers are bonded to each other and to the celluloid film base. They cannot move relative to one another throughout the exposure, developing or printing processes. Likewise, future prints or generations also have this color position stability. In other words, even though the color image really exists on three different emulsion layers, they are, and remain, perfectly registered to one another for a perfect color rendition.

The old three-strip Technicolor process, as well as modern 4-color printing presses, do not enjoy this inherent stability. In each case, the separate color information is recorded and retained on totally separate pieces of film or printing plates, respectively. It now becomes imperative that these three or four separate pieces of color information are perfectly superimposed or registered to insure that the original color image is precisely recreated. Most people are familiar with the results of poor printing registration. One color is positionally off from the others, which appears as color fringing.

The video camera shares with the printing industry this same vulnerability. Because the image is split and directed to three separate tubes, there is always present the possiblity that these three images can get physically out of registration. As in the printing industry, the precise physical location of the three tubes is mandatory, and is called mechanical registration. The tube mounting assembly in the camera usually allows for rotational movement and an in/out movement to adjust back focus.

Because video is essentially an electronic process, all other registration parameters are dealt with on an electronic basis. Movement of the image left or right, up or down, shrinking or enlarging and various other image shaping functions can be adjusted with electronic controls. Failure to properly register a camera will result in color fringing and overall image degradation.

One of the first rules a video cameraman learns is: Never touch any control in the camera that affects the green image circuit. In almost all cases the green tube and all its associated electronic circuity are set up in the engineering lab with sophisticated test gear and precision reference equipment. Once this is accomplished, the red and blue tubes and circuits can be adjusted to perfectly match the green reference. In most cases, a nail polish type paint is put on all green circuit adjustment pots by the manufacturer to prevent accidental destruction of precise calibration, and the external centering registration adjustments found on many cameras don't even include a pot for the green channel. (Obviously the camera designers are quite aware of people who turn screws first and ask questions later.) Thus, for the cameraman in the field, the name of the game, for the most part, is keeping the red and blue images perfectly aligned with the green. Before going into the practicalities of field alignment, it may prove beneficial to look at the various ways in which an image can be electronicallly manipulated and, more specifically, what the lab does to set up the green tube to deliver optimum results.

In almost all instances a home TV receiver operates with the identical principles as the television camera and many of the circuits and adjustments are quite similar. This is especially true of scanning circuits, and almost all of the camera adjustments to be discussed have direct analogies on the home receiver which should help develop a basic understanding.

WIDTH AND HEIGHT—These two adjustments affect the overall size of the image, as well as the aspect ratio. If these controls are not set properly, the camera circuits may not be scanning the entire surface of the tube target. This is similar to blowing up a smaller portion of a film negative in an optical printer. Qualtiy will obviously not be optimum. Inversely, circuits may be overscanning the tube target getting dangerously close to the edge of the tube. Ideally, the diagonal of the scanned area should be about 87% of the actual diameter of the tube target. Moreover, the relationship between these two adjustments must maintain the proper 1.33:1 aspect ratio. We are all familiar with the short-squat or tall-skinny images resulting from improper height or width or a combination of both.

HORIZONTAL LINEARITY AND VERTICAL LINEARITY—These controls are a little more subtle than height and width, but in the same family. Improper vertical linearity could cause an image to be short and squat in the upper portion of the image while elongated and skinny in the lower half of the screen (or vice versa), yet the criteria for overall height and width may be correct. This results in a large circle appearing as an egg, whereas improper height would result in a symmetrical ellipse.

Likewise, improper horizontal linearity would result in the image being compresed on the right side of the screen and elongated on the left or vice versa. Usually the width is adjusted before the horizontal linearity and the height is adjusted before vertical linearity.

SKEW—The skew control is very interesting, as it adjusts the rotational angle of vertical lines only. Turning the skew makes vertical lines appear to turn about the point where they cross a centered horizontal line. Note there is no skew for horizontal lines, as this is redundant. The purpose of skew is to establish a true 90° angle between horizontal and vertical lines. If the horizontal lines are not horizontal relative to camera axis, the entire tube (or deflection yoke) must be mechanically rotated. This rotation and back focus are the only mechanical (nonelectronic) adjustments and should be carried out before any subsequent electronic alignment, but only by a video technician.

HORIZONTAL AND VERTICAL CENTERING—Lastly and most simply, once all the aforementioned criteria are met, the scanned area should be centered within the tube's circumference. If these controls are not adjusted to optimum, the scanned area may be too far to the left/right or up/down on the tube target.

After all the aforementioned adjustments are carried out on the green tube and the *lab engineer* is certain the green channel is precisely calibrated (and the pots painted), the real fun begins. Now the red and blue channels must be perfectly aligned to precisely coincide with the green image.

All the individual adjustments and calibrations that exist for the green channel also are present for the red and blue channels including the previously mentioned registration controls of height, width, vertical and horizontal linearity skew, and vertical and horizontal centering.

Of these, the most simple to adjust are luckily the same ones that most often need adjustment; the vertical and horizontal centering. The procedure for optimizing blue and red is quite easy, thanks to the built-in testing circuits that virtually every professional ENG/EFP camera employs.

The only external device necessary is a registration chart (FIGURE 162) which consists of a pattern dominated by a grid of horizontal and vertical black lines on a white background. In the absence of such a chart, a reasonable facsimile can usually be improvised. The camera is placed on a tripod and the lens aimed at the illuminated chart so that it is centered and just fills the entire picture area. The iris should be

Figure 162

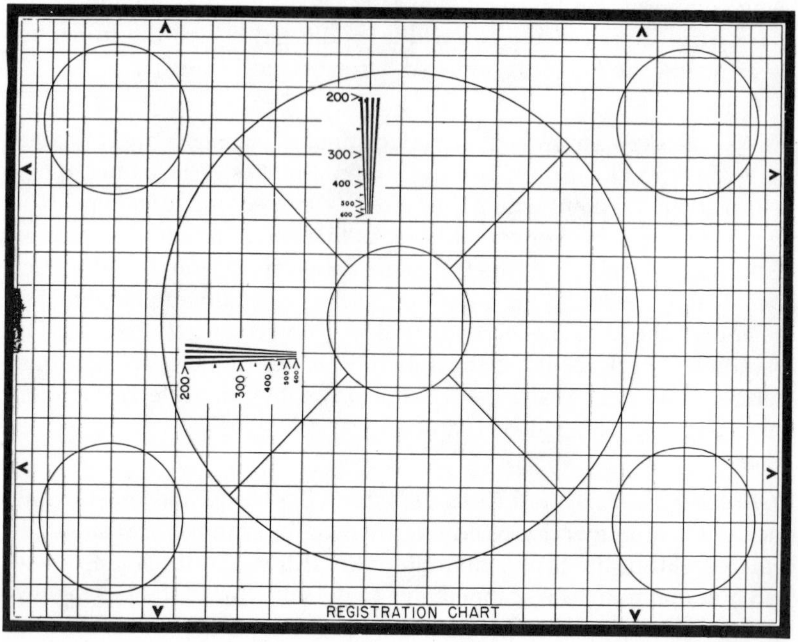

opened to achieve a 70% signal. The camera is then auto white balanced and the detail circuit should be defeated (usually a simple "on/off" switch marked "DTL"). Now the fun begins.

FIGURE 163—These switches are typical of those found on all ENG/EFP cameras. They control the output of both the camera viewfinder and the monitor jack of the camera. Starting from the top, the "R" is the red tube, "G" is the green tube, "B" is the blue tube and "–G" is "minus green" or "negative green" (see text). Any of these switches can be activated singly or in any combination for diagnostic purposes. The bottom switch marked "ENC" provides a normal color encoded picture and defeats the upper four switches when selected.

FIGURE 163 illustrates the set of switches found inside the Ikegami HL-79 camera. Every professional camera has a similar set of switches found either internally or in some cases externally on the camera. These switches control the image to the viewfinder and monitor outputs only and do not usually affect the main video output of the camera. The bottom switch marked "ENC" provides a normal color encoded signal to the viewfinder/monitor and, when activated (right hand position), takes priority over the other switches (i.e. the other switches are literally out of the circuit). However, if the ENC encoder switch is turned off, the other four switches are activated and control the image displayed on the viewfinder/monitor.

The first three switches very simply turn the signals from the red, green and blue channels, respectively, on or off. By turning the green and blue switches off while leaving the red on, only the output of the red tube and its circuits will be displayed, etc. It is the fourth switch, however, that is the most interesting. It is labelled "–G" (minus green) and controls a *negative* image from the green channels only. If the red ("R") channel and minus green channel ("–G") were activated simultaneously with all other switches off, (as in FIGURE 163) the monitor/viewfinder would display the difference between the red and green channels or literally the red image minus the green image.

Now consider the registration chart. The red channel alone will yield a white image with black lines, while the minus green channel will yield a black image with white lines. If both circuits are activated together and the camera were absolutely perfectly registered, (an unattainable feat) the image displayed would be pure white with no lines; the grid pattern would disappear completely.

This is precisely the goal during registration. In the above example, if registration were not perfect, the dark lines of the red channel and the light lines of the minus green would be visible, indicating that they are not perfectly aligned. If such is the case, the red channel *(not the green)* must be manipulated until the grid pattern disappears over the major portion of the frame, indicating that the two sets of lines are perfectly overlapped. In actuality, perfect registration is impossible, especially near the four corners of the frame. However, a good camera and a little patience can yield almost perfect registration for a major portion of the image in the center of the frame, and this is a more realistic goal.

As previously mentioned, it is the horizontal and vertical centering that requires the most frequent adjustment. These controls are usually found externally on most cameras or just behind an access door at the back or side. FIGURE 164 shows these controls on the Ikegami HL-79. With the camera set up as described and the red and minus green

FIGURE 164—The four screws in the upper left control the horizontal and vertical centering.The dots above the screws are colored red and blue to indicated respective color channels. Note that there is no external adjustment for green, as this is the reference channel and should not be altered by the cameraman.

switches only in the "on" position, the red horizontal screw is adjusted until the vertical lines of the grid "disappear" or become least visible. Attention should be focused on the center portion of the screen, not the periphery. As the screw is turned, the dark lines will shift left or right as the light lines remain stationary. The goal is to get the dark lines to overlap perfectly over the light lines, causing both to "disappear." Once this is achieved, the red vertical screw is rocked back and forth to accomplish the same end with the horizontal lines.

Likewise, the red switch is turned off and blue is turned on. With blue and minus green now being displayed, the blue horizontal and blue vertical screws are adjusted in the identical fusion.

This completes the centering portion of the registration. If the resulting patterns of the above two steps (red and blue) yield an almost invisible grid over a major portion of the frame, the camera is probably near optimum calibration and no further registration is necessary. However, the patterns may have resulted in only a small portion of the grid being invisible near the center of the screen, while most of the double line grid is visible over the remaining majority of the area. Under these circumstances, additional registration adjustments are required, which should be carried out only by a qualified technician.

BACK FOCUS

Proper back-focus is essential to sharp pictures, especially at short focal lengths and large apertures. Back-focus on a video camera is easy to check and is, in many cases, easy to adjust.

Most cinematographers are familiar with back-focus, also known as flange-to-focal-plane distance or, simply, lens seating. Basically, the camera lens is a projector lens, focusing a bright image some distance away onto the "screen" which is the film plane or the video tube plane. The back-focus refers to the fact that the image plane must be at the proper position relative to the lens to achieve a sharp, in-focus image.

Just as there is a "depth-of-field" tolerance for the subject, there is a corresponding "depth-of-focus" tolerance for the image plane behind the lens. However, as the aperture increases and the focal length gets *shorter,* this depth-of-focus tolerance becomes extremely narrow. In reality, the back-focus tolerance of a modern wide angle, ultra fast ENG/EFP zoom lens set at 9mm and f/1.6 is non-existent. The back-focus tolerance is so small (less than a thousandth of an inch) that the lens seating has to be "spot on" or the picture will be soft.

Of course, as the aperture gets smaller and the focal length increases, this tolerance is not as critical. An almost sure symptom of improper back-focus is the lens that delivers a sharp image at say 20mm or more, and f/8, and yet looks soft at 10mm and f/1.8. Most important, unlike the fixed focal length lens, the front focusing of a zoom lens *cannot* compensate for or rectify improper back-focus distances.

Most cine lenses do not incorporate back-focus adjustments, nor is it encouraged to "marry" a particular lens to a specific camera. The proper procedure requires the cine lens mount to be shimmed in the shop to precisely the proper flange-to-focal-plane distance by employing a collimator. Likewise, the camera flange-to-focal-plane distance is adjusted with precison micrometers and thus, any lens will fit any camera and maintain proper back-focus.

While this concept of back-focus is identical in a video camera, the practicalities are somewhat different. The video camera employs a complex prism assembly which trisects the image path and directs it to three separate image planes; the red, green and blue pick-up tubes. This fact results in two major differences relative to a film camera. Firstly, this optical complexity makes the marrying of a zoom lens to a particular camera almost a necessity. That is, the back-focus should be adjusted with the lens *on the camera.* Secondly, because there are three image planes, there are actually three back-focus distances and thus three back-focus adjustments.

Actually there are four possible back-focus adjustments on the video camera. Each of the three tubes can be moved in or out relative to the prism assembly and the lens seating can also be adjusted relative to the camera prism. The cameraman should only concern himself with the latter. He should never attempt to adjust the individual tubes in the field.

A cameraman can check overall back-focus of the lens to the camera in the following manner. A focusing target similar to that in FIGURE 165 should be placed as close as possible to the lens, unsually at the lens' minimum focusing distance. Most important, the lens must be wide open at maximum aperture. This can be achieved by controlling the lighting, not the iris. Normal room lighting is usually sufficient to achieve the condition. However, in darker areas a small light can be bounced off the ceiling. If a room is too bright and cannot be dimmed, use an N.D. filter if necessary. However, under all circumstances the lens must be *wide open.* Next, zoom in to the target to full telephoto. Pull a critical focus on the target, white balance, and then zoom out to the extreme minimum focal length. It is imperative that the adjustment be made at maximum aperture and minimum focal length, as this is where the back-focus tolerance is most critical.

Most ENG/EFP lenses have a back-focus adjustment ring at the rearmost part of the lens, just before the lens mount. This ring, usually incorporates a locking screw, as well as an index in the form of a white dot on the ring and a corresponding dot on the lens barrel. According to factory preset nominal lens seating specifications, these two dots should line up for proper lens seating. However, in practice, optimum back-focus adjustment usually results in the dots being slightly displaced relative to one another although in many cases they will actually line up after adjustment. If such dots do not exist, reasonable facsimiles should be created by putting minute marks on the ring and barrel opposite one another before the locking screw is loosened. In all cases, the relative position of the indices should be noted with a pencil or tape mark before the screw is loosened.

With the lens at maximum aperture and shortest focal length, and a record made of the previous alignment, the locking screw can now be loosened. Viewing the target through a high resolution viewfinder or monitor, the ring should be rocked back and forth to achieve the most critical focus of the target. Once this is achieved, the indices should be checked carefully.

If a sharp focus is easily determined and the indices are in the same

FIGURE 165—A focusing target (courtesy of FUJINON)

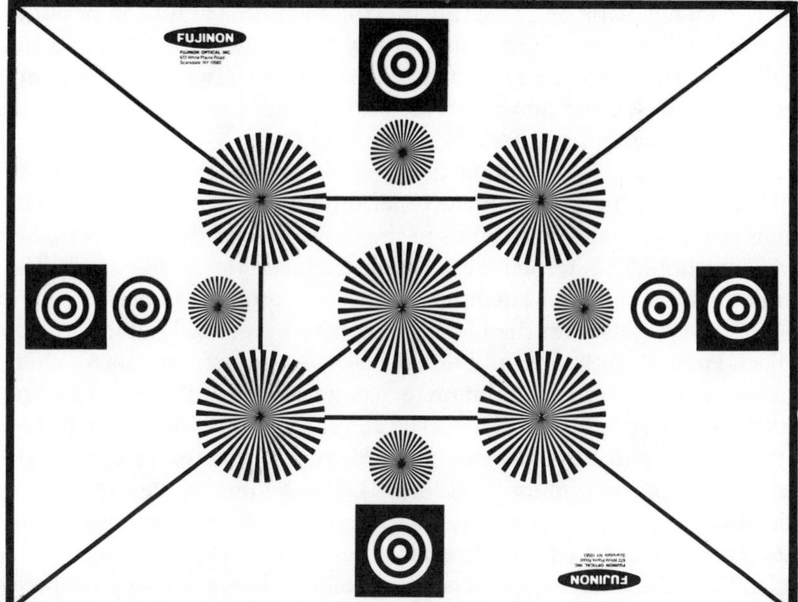

positions relative to one another, retighten the screw and feel secure that the back-focus is probably optimized. However, if the indices have moved, repeat the focusing procedure several times to ensure that the optimum point of focus has been determined properly. If each repeat results in the same point which is different from the original settings or if the point of optimum focus is difficult to determine (a large mushy region of good focus as opposed to a narrow point of critically sharp focus), there is a good chance that the three tubes are not positioned at the same back-focus relative to one another. In either case, determine the point of best focus or choose a point midway between several repeated attempts and tighten the screw locking ring. If, due to the foregoing, the cameraman believes the tubes may not be optimized for a single back-focus distance, he should take actions. Get the camera thoroughly checked by a technician as soon as possible and in the interim refrain from shooting with wide apertures, if possible. If the camera must be used at near or wide open, the extreme short focal lengths should be avoided.

The problem of one tube being out of position relative to the other cannot be rectified by adjusting the lens back-focus, as this will obviously affect all three tubes simultaneously. In the shop, the technican first adjusts the lens back-focus to the green tube *alone*. If the red or blue tubes are not properly aligned at this point, they are brought into the correct image plane by physically moving the problem tube in or out in its mount. This procedure is quite hairy and time-consuming and the entire camera must be realigned and registered after the tube(s) are repositioned. A cameraman should *never* attempt to reposition a tube or loosen a tube mount, especially in the field.

The following is a method designed to enable the cameraman to check the back-focus alignment of all three tubes without any special tools or equipment. If the results of the test indicate a misalignment, the camera should be turned over to an engineer for realignment. The cameraman should *not* attempt to rectify the problem himself.

The test begins with the identical set-up as previously described for "Back-Focus," with one additional step. As before, the focus chart should be placed at the minimum focusing distance of the lens. The lens *must* be *wide open* (maximum aperture). A sharp focus should be pulled at telephoto and then the lens must be zoomed to the extreme wide angle position (minimum focal length). The additional step requires a viewfinder (or monitor) be fed with the output of the green tube only. On most cameras this is quite easy to accomplish.

There are usually a set of switches either internally or externally located that control the signal to the viewfinder and a monitor output.

For example FIGURE 163 illustrates the group of switches found inside the Ikegami HL-79. For the purpose of "step 1" of this test, the encoder must be switched off and the green output *only* switched on ("G switch, second from the top, in the right position—all others in the left position.)

As with the standard back-focus test, note should be made of the back-focus indexes on the lens before the test begins. It would help to put a piece of camera tape along the back-focus ring in the manner of a pull-focus index. The back-focus ring lock is now loosened and the back-focus ring is rocked back and forth to achieve the sharpest focus of the chart target. Repeat this procedure several times noting the resting point for each attempt to determine the optimum focus point. Make a mark on the back-focus ring tape to indicated that best focus. Identify the mark with a "G".

Now turn off the output of the green tube and turn on the red tube ("R" switch) only. Repeat the above procedure. Determine the best focus and make a mark on the tape identified with an "R". Likewise, repeat the entire procedure with only the blue ("B" switch) on. If the camera was properly adjusted, the point of best focus for all three tubes would have been identical. Specifically, the point of best focus for the blue and red test should have resulted in the mark made in step 1 being perfectly aligned with the index. If this is indeed the case, lock up the back-focus ring knowing the back-focus of all three tubes is optimum. If, however, there is more than a very slight shift between the three best focus marks, the camera should be turned over to an engineer with a note describing the results of your test, or better yet, leave the marked tape on the back focus ring.

If the camera must be used in the interim, the best compromise back-focus adjustment should be established. This is done by turning the encoder ("ENC") switch back on and determing the sharpest setting of the back-focus ring. This usually requires averaging repeated attempts to zero in on the best setting. If the three results of the tests are quite different from each other, the largest apertures and shortest focal lengths should be avoided especially in combination, i.e., short focal length at wide aperture.

INSTANT PUSH

The video camera is quite flexible and allows the cameraman to retain control over several techniques that would normally have to be relinquished to the film lab. One of the more simple things that can be done in the video camera is push the EI. The term "EI" is really a misnomer when applied to video. However, it does help to draw an analogy between video and film.

I use my Spectra light meters with video in the identical manner that I do with film. It is very simple to establish the EI of a video camera. Merely illuminate a gray scale step chart and point the camera at it. Adjust the iris for a full video signal, i.e., the white chip just peaking and the medium gray receiving an approximate 50° signal. Note the precise f-stop of the lens at this point. Now place the incident light meter at the chart. With the meter set at 24 fps, rotate the EI scale until the f-stop noted on the lens aligns with the light meter needle. Whatever that EI turns out to be, it can be considered to be the effective EI of the camera for all lighting intents and purposes.

In practice I have found that most current ENG/EFP cameras have an effective EI of approximately 100–150, making them very similar to film cameras loaded with 5247 Eastman Negative. While this sensitivity is quite sufficient for most applications, there are situations when a one- or two-stop push could come in handy. While this is no big deal with film, it can be somewhat of an inconvenience. You cannot push only a portion of a roll; the entire roll must be pushed. In addition, a test must usually be done to determine if the increased grain or loss of contrast will be objectionable. In video, on the other hand, pushing is a snap; literally.

The video term for pushing is "gain." Normal exposure with no extra gain would be called "zero (0) gain," "no gain," or just "normal." All video cameras usually employ an external switch that allows the cameraman to instantly add extra gain, thereby "pushing" his effective EI to a higher value. Six decibels (6dB) of gain is equivalent to a one-stop push. 3dB is a half-stop, 12dB is two stops, etc. Many cameras employ switches providing 0, +6dB, and +12dB of gain representing normal, push-one and push-two stops respectively. Many of the newer cameras provide switches with 0, +9dB, and +18dB of gain, which provides normal, 1½ and 3 stops of push respectively. It is my belief that the next generation of video cameras will have even greater flexibility by employing switches with finer increments of gain, such as 0, +3dB, +6dB, +9dB, etc., thus providing everything from normal to three stops of push in ½ stop increments.

Combining these switches with the instant viewing capability of video, the cameraman can dial in just the precise amount of gain necessary to achieve the desired exposure. Not only can gain be added in the middle of a roll of tape, it can be added in the middle of a shot. On several occasions, while filming a documentary, I found myself following a subject into the proverbial coal bin and have merely added 6dB or 9dB of gain right during the tracking shot, with tape rolling. If the jump in exposure is later found objectionable, it can, of course, be covered with a cutaway.

In production situations the addition of gain can be carefully evaluated on the monitor. As with film there are certain tradeoffs. The video

FIGURE 166—Ikegami HL-83 camera with ML-83 microwave transmitter/control receiver. The cylindrical microwave antenna automatically steers itself to always point back at the base station receiving dish, allowing the cameraman complete freedom to roam at will and turn in any direction. The ML-83 not only sends video and audio back to base station, but also receives control commands and intercom.

equivalent of grain is "noise" and, as with film, the noise level will increase as gain is applied. The increase of visual noise is roughly proportional to the increase in gain and is also expressed in "decibels." Thus, a one-stop push (+6dB gain) will result in an approximately 6dB increase in noise level. The question is obviously when does the noise become objectionable? As with film the answer is subjective and depends upon many factors. Every video camera has a signal-to-noise ratio indicative of the residual noise or "grain" that is inherent in the normal picture. A very good ENG/EFP camera will have a signal-to-noise ratio of 55dB or better. The new diode-gun tube cameras may achieve s/n ratios of 58dB or better. Such cameras are said to be very "quiet" and can obviously withstand copious amounts of gain better than a cheaper, noisier camera that starts out with s/n ratio of only 46dB. Thus a quiet late model camera may give a less grainy picture with +6dB of gain than a cheaper or older camera without any additional gain.

One must also consider the tape format. The ¾″ U-matic format is relatively noisy (46dB s/n), compared with the broadcast quality 1″ type "C" format (48dB s/n). Thus, the ¾″ tape machine can be the limiting factor. In many instances the difference between 0 gain and +6dB gain on the best ENG/EFP cameras will be almost unnoticeable when recorded on a ¾″ U-matic machine. On the other hand, these differences will more likely be discernible when recorded on a 1″ type "C" machine.

Whatever the case may be, the quality of the "push" can be instantly evaluated and a decision be made. The process is certainly fast and convenient and the cameraman is in complete control.

MICROWAVE LINKS

The conventional method for live coverage usually entails prolific use of cables; multiconductor cables, co-ax cables, audio cables, intercom cables, etc. This use of cables to connect the cameras to the base station is quite a headache, to say the least. The problem becomes even more acute when covering large outdoor events, such as golf tournaments or Olympic games where remote cameras can be up to a mile away.

Several means have been developed to cope with these problems. Triax and ecoded co-ax systems multiplex all camera control signals and genlock, as well as video output, audio, and intercom onto a single cable. A more recent development makes use of single tiny fibre-optics cable. While these systems greatly simplify remote camera operation, it is still inconvenient and time consuming to lay several thousand feet of cable, no matter how thin or light it may be.

There is a method which eliminates the cable altogether. By employing a microwave transmitter, a remote camera can easily beam its video signal back to a base station. This method is quite popular with live coverage news teams. The camera is usually linked by cable to a van which then transmits the signal to the station or to a repeater. Most of these systems, however, have several shortcomings. Firstly, the camera is still linked to the van with cable; and secondly, most of these systems do not provide the base station with complete control over the camera which is required for high quality multiple camera production.

These problems have been eliminated in the new Ikegami ML-83 microwave link. The system is designed to be used with the Ikegami HL-83 camera. Pictured in FIGURE 166, the microwave transmitter and control receiver slides onto the special bracket on the side of the HL-83 camera. The camera thus becomes a single one-piece unit weighing about 26 pounds, complete with battery and no wires or cables.

The Ikegami ML-83 has many innovative features. The cylindrical protrusion at the rear of the unit is a special automatic steering microwave transmission antenna. This antenna automatically beams the video signal in the direction of the base station, even when the camera is rotated a complete 360°. This allows the cameraman complete mobility and produces a sharp transmitted image free of multi-path ghosts.

The small antenna at the front of the transmitter receives the control signal from the base station. The base station can control genlock, iris, master black level, R/B gain, R/B H cent, R/B V cent, R/B black level, bars on/off, auto iris on/off, white bal on/off, call, tally, and intercom.

The system has a range of up to 1,500 meters, which is almost one mile. In operation the system is quite flexible. The base station can be separated from its antenna dish by up to 200 meters of co-ax cable. When desired, the transmitter may be separated from the camera. In this mode of operation, the transmitter can be put in a fixed spot, leaving the lightweight camera free to move at the end of a multiconductor cable that can extend up to 100 meters. The base station dish covers an area of 120°, allowing the cameraman to roam almost without restriction.

As mentioned before, within this area the cameraman can move in any direction, even a complete 360°, as the automatic beam antenna always steers itself toward the base station.

As post-production costs rise and the demand for low-cost video in copious quantities continues to increase, the technique of multiple-camera/live switching may prove expedient and economical. The

Ikegami ML-83 facilitates such technique even under the most adverse conditions and with a minimum of set-up time. As cinematographers and film producers learn the language of video, this is one technique with which they should be familiar.

SOLID STATE VIDEO

Virtually all current professional video cameras employ the three tube design. This is quite ironic for several reasons. While the modern video camera makes use of the latest solid state LSI and microprocessor technology for almost every function, the most crucial and primary step of converting the optical image into an electrical signal is relegated to an archaic vacuum tube. Furthermore, it is the inherent delinquencies of these vacuum tubes that account for most of the undesirable anomolies associated with the video image. Much of the advanced solid state circuitry of these cameras is designed to minimize the comet-tailing, lag, and other video vulnerabilities that originate in the tubes. It appears obvious that the next step in the evolution of the video camera is the replacement of the

FIGURE 167—Hitachi SK-1: "The World's First High Resolution Solid-State ENG Camera using MOS Image Sensors." This camera weighs only seven pounds and uses a unitized prism with three MOS (metal oxide semiconductor) image sensors.

FIG 168—RCA Model CCD-1 Solid State CCD Camera—This camera exhibits an unprecedented dynamic range of better than 10,000:1 while maintaining a signal-to-noise ratio of 62dB. Like all CCD designs, burn-in, comet-tailing, and registration problems have been eliminated.

vacuum tubes with solid state devices, thus creating a completely solid state device. That step is already being taken.

Just a few years ago Hitachi announced the SK-1, billed as "The World's First High Resolution Solid-State ENG Camera using MOS image sensors." The MOS (metal oxide semiconductors) image sensors of the SK-1 replaced the conventional tubes and marked the beginning of the all solid state era of video. This first effort definitely demonstrated the advantages of solid state sensors, however with a horizontal resolution of just over 450 lines and a signal-to-noise ratio of 49dB (Y channel), it could not quite measure up to the performance levels established by the best 3 tube cameras.

Soon after the introduction of the SK-1 both NEC and RCA introduced all solid state video cameras using CCDs or charge coupled devices. Both these cameras bring all solid state video closer to reality. These CCD cameras feature virtually perfect registration and geometric fidelity as CCDs do not require conventional scanning circuits with their inherent distortions. The CCD eliminates burn-in, comet-tailing, and lag.

The performance and physical characteristics of these cameras are also noteworthy. The RCA CCD-1 claims an exceptional dynamic range capable of handling highlight ratios of 10,000:1. This camera is designed to pull an image out of the shadows while simultaneously handling direct light, even sun reflections, in the same scene, without burn-in,

FIG 169—NEC Model SP-3A Solid State CCD Camera—A unique twin chip design in the green channel results in over 500 lines of resolution and an exceptional low light sensitivity of almost 4 footcandles at 12dB gain and f1.4. The SP-3A weighs only 5.9 lbs with viewfinder (no lens) and draws a mere 16 watts of power. Shown here mated with a Betacam component recorder, the SP-3A can also dock with 'M' format and ¼″ format recorders as well as operating as a stand alone unit.

blooming, or any other residual effects. Dynamic resolution is exceptional because the CCD captures images in a manner similar to film. Tube type cameras suffer from a partial retention of previous images which tend to blur subsequent frames. The CCD has no image retention and produces a very sharp image much like film where each subsequent frame is an independent entity. The CCD-1 is also rated with an unprecedented signal-to-noise ratio of 62dB. The NEC SP-3A also boasts some exceptional statistics such as a weight of only 5.9 lbs (without lens) and a current draw of a mere 16 watts. A standard 4 AH Snap-On® battery will power the SP-3A for a steady three hours. The NEC SP-3A also features unbelievable low light sensitivity, requiring little more than four footcandles at f1.4 and only 12dB of gain. The SP-3A also uses a unique two chip CCD arrangement in the green channel which results in more than 500 lines resolution. Most important, cinematographers will especially appreciate the overall film-like quality of the CCD image. For complete flexibility, both the RCA and the NEC CCD cameras can be used with separate recorders or they can be used as one piece cam/corders by attaching the appropriate ½″ component recorder.

The full potential of CCD type cameras is awesome and there is little doubt that all professional video cameras will eventually incorporate solid state image sensors.

Index

A
Absorption filters 111
Academy aperture 62, 64, 65
Acetate tape 155
Achromatic lens 94
Ambient noise 199
Anamorphic 61, 63, 67
Anamorphic lens, 65
Anti-halation backing 20, 28, 29
Apertures 57
Auto white balance 274, 275
Automatic iris lens 145
Axial motion 99
Azimuth adjustment 160

B
Butterfly shutter 39
Back focus 115, 287
Barney 49
Batteries—charging 212, 213, 214
Batteries—discharging 209, 212, 213, 214
Batteries 205, 206, 211, 216, 217
Battery capacity 210, 212
Battery cell memory 227
Battery charge retention 207
Battery equalizing 215
Battery failure 220, 221
Battery memory 224
Battery service life 218
Battery storage 208
Bayonet mount 90, 104
Beam-splitters 29
Behind the lens filters 118
Blur 23, 24
Broadcast formats 265

C
C mount 90, 103, 104
Calibration 137, 138, 139
CdS-type cell 136, 137
Center of perspective 100
Chretien, Henri 64
Chromatic aberration 93, 95, 96
CinemaScope 64, 68
Cinerama 75, 76, 77
Claw 36
Cold weather filming 48, 49
Color balance 119
Color fringing 94
Color reversal internegative 71
Color temperature 120, 121, 123, 133, 134
Comet-tailing 245, 247
Compressor/expander 193, 194
Cordless sync 44, 46
Cores 16, 17, 19
Critical flicker frequency 45, 78
Crystal motors 44
Crystal servo 45
Crystal sync 46
Current—DC 232
Current—AC 232

D
DC servo motor 45
Daylight color 121
Depth of focus 88
Dichroic filter 133
Diffraction 91, 92
Diopter lens 90
Distortion 98, 99
Distortion region 201
Dome port 239
Dynamic range 190, 200

E
ENG video camera 90
Edge numbering 20
Electret condenser mike 180, 181
Electric current—foreign 231, 232
Electronic cinematography 245, 246, 252, 254, 255, 258, 259, 355
Emulsion density 8
Ericson, Rune 71
Estar base 20
Exposure degrees 38
Exposure index 116
Exposure times 25

F
F-stops 146, 147, 148
Field curvature 97
Film base 19, 20
Film cameras 23–57
Film data sheets 5
Film formats 57
Film loops 35
Film registration 32, 33
Film static 18
Film storage 12, 13, 34
Filter pack 125
Filters 24, 111, 113, 128, 129
Flange-to-focal plane 288
Flashing 129, 130, 132
Fletcher/Munson effect 169, 170
Flicker 42
Fluorescent filters 126
Fluorescent lighting, 124, 125
Focal length 25, 101, 102
Focal plane shutter 39, 88
Focus calibration 86

Footcandle formula 149
Foote, Paul 92, 101
Frame rates 78
Framing chart 31
Frequency response 161, 162, 167, 168
Fringing 282

G
Gain riding 191, 192
Gamma 9
Gelatin filters 114
Glass laminate filters 114
Grain 10
Ground glass 30
Guillotine shutter 29, 40

H
Hand microphone 182
Hard matte 82
Harmonics 163
Headphones 197, 198
High frequency bias 199, 201, 202, 203
Horizontal linearity 283
Hypergonar anamorphic system 64

I
Image areas 58
Image enhancement 246
Incandescent bulbs 122
Incandescent lighting 125
Incident light 113, 142, 149
Insulation 55

K
Klein, Jordan 236, 240, 241

L
Latitude 7
Lens aberration 93
Lens adapter 105
Lens care 85
Lens damage 91
Lens equivalent 107
Lens mount 89, 102, 103
Lens perspective 99
Lens vibration 86
Lenses 85, 104
Level meters 170, 171
Light meters 135, 138, 140, 141
Light transmittance 6
Light 119
Log exposure scale 8
Loose pin 34
Low frequency filter curves 164
Luminance range 9
Luminance ratio 190, 251

M
Magazines 17
Magnetic sound recording 151, 152
Magnetic sound tape 156
Magnetic track 166
Mercury vapor 125
Microdensitometer 6, 7
Microphone directivity 177, 178
Microphones 175, 176, 177
Microwave transmitter 295
Mirror reflex shutter 29
Mirror shutter 105
Modulation transfer curve 5, 6, 7
Modulometer 171, 173
Mosser, Adrian 71

N
Neutral density filters 116, 117
Nickel cadmium batteries 48, 205, 206, 209, 219
Noise reduction 189
Norwood, Don 140

O
Optical track 166
Optics 92
Oscillating mirror 40, 41

P
Panning 25, 26, 27
Perforations 14, 15, 16
Persistence of vision 23, 78
Perspective 100
Photo-sphere 140
Photo-voltaic cell 135
Photographic daylight 131, 132, 133
Photometric aperture 109, 110
Pilot pins 33
Pilotones 47, 187, 188
Pin registration 35
Pitch 14, 15, 34
Playback head 161
Plumbicon tubes 259, 263
Polar diagram 178
Polarizing filters 111, 112
Polyester tape 155
Power cables 52, 53, 54
Projection 100, 101
Projector pull-down 79
Pull-down claw 33

Q

Quartz lighting 127

R

Raw stock 5
Record head 161
Recording headroom 172
Reflective light meter 142
Reflex system calibration 30
Reflex viewing systems 27, 39
Registration pins 33
Reversal stock 9, 10
Root mean square (RMS) 11, 196

S

Safe action area 60
Sealed cells 206
Selenium cell 136
Sensitometric curve 8
Shipping 50, 51
Short ends 108
Shotgun microphone 195
Shutter blade 79
Shutters 25, 37
Skew control 283
Slaving 46, 47
Solid state shutter 41, 42
Solid state video 296, 297, 298
Sound distortion 175
Sound pressure level 169
Sound recording tape 153, 154
Spectral reflection 113
Splicing 20
Spools 17, 18, 19
Sports filming 24
Spot meters 143
Sprocket holes 36, 37
Standard dynamic mike 181
Step chart 31
Strobing 79
Stroboscoping 24
Super-16 72, 73, 74, 75
Super-8 71
Sync sound 44

T

T-stops 109, 147, 150
TTL meters 143, 144
TV format 59, 60
TV safe action area 81
Tape cinching 158
Tape recorder alignment 159, 160
Tape saturation 163
Tape transport 47
Techniscope 68, 70, 80
Television transmitted area 81
Transmittance curves 127, 128
Transporting equipment 50
Tungsten bulbs 124
Tungsten filament 123
Tungsten halogen 125
Tungsten light 120
Two-track recorder 184, 185, 186

U

Underwater filming 235, 236, 238, 239
Underwater housing 241, 242
Underwater lenses 237

V

VTR power source 229, 230
VTR 264, 265
VU meter 171, 173
Variable shutter 23, 24
Vertical linearity 283
Video cables 294
Video camera maintenance 281
Video cameras 210, 211, 243, 244, 256, 260, 261, 263, 276, 277, 278, 279, 285
Video camera maintenance 280
Video focusing 289, 290
Video gain 293, 294
Video instant push 292
Video lenses 248, 257
Video lighting 251
Video recording 263
Video registration 281, 285
Video signal 270
Video tape recorder 265, 267, 268
Video vs film 252
Viewfinders 27
Visible spectrum 119
Voltage 55, 122, 123
Voltage controlled amplifier 196

W

Wave lengths 119
Waveform monitor 273
Waveform 272
Weld 20
White-clip 247
Wide screen format 61, 67
Winding 16, 17

Notes